Marian Dunn, David Howey and Amanda Ilic

with Nicholas Regan

English for
MECHANICAL ENGINEERING

in Higher Education Studies
Teacher's Book

Series editor: Terry Phillips

English for Specific Academic Purposes

Garnet
EDUCATION

Published by
Garnet Publishing Ltd.
8 Southern Court
South Street
Reading RG1 4QS, UK

First published 2010.
Reprinted 2012.

ISBN 978 1 85964 947 3

British Cataloguing-in-Publication Data
A catalogue record for this book is available from
the British Library.

Production
Series editor: Terry Phillips
Project management: Vale Dominguez, Martin Moore
Editorial team: Louise Elkins, Karen Kinnair-Pugh, Sarah
Mellowes
Academic review: Simon Quinn
Design and layout: Henry Design Associates and Mike Hinks
Photography: Sally Henry and Trevor Cook, shutterstock.com,
clipart.com, gettyimages.com, wellcome images
wellhead gear on page 11: Hartmann Valves

Audio recorded at Motivation Sound Studios produced by EFS
Television Production Ltd

The author and publisher would like to thank Google for
permission to reproduce the results listings on page 70.

Every effort has been made to trace copyright holders and we
apologize in advance for any unintentional omission. We will
be happy to insert the appropriate acknowledgements in any
subsequent editions.

Printed and bound in Lebanon
by International Press: interpress@int-press.com

Contents

Book map 4

Introduction 6

Unit 1   What is engineering? 10

Unit 2   Engineering achievements 28

Unit 3   Forces on materials 44

Unit 4   Computers in engineering 60

Unit 5   MEMS and nanotechnology 76

Unit 6   Friction 102

Unit 7   The future of cars: Battery power 118

Unit 8   Engineering and sustainability 134

Unit 9   Health and safety 154

Unit 10   Accident analysis in construction 176

Unit 11   Wind turbines 196

Unit 12   Water engineering 220

Resource pages 242

Book map

Unit	Topics
1 What is engineering? Listening · Speaking	• definition of engineering • branches of engineering • the history of mechanical engineering
2 Engineering achievements Reading · Writing	• engineering achievements in the 20th century • refrigeration and air conditioning • codes and standards for machines
3 Forces on materials Listening · Speaking	• materials in engineering • forces on materials: stress and strain • five types of forces
4 Computers in engineering Reading · Writing	• computer-assisted manufacturing (CAM) • computer integrated manufacturing (CIM) • using computers for research
5 MEMS and nanotechnology Listening · Speaking	• features of MEMS and nanotechnologies • design and applications • safety and ethical issues concerning nanotechnology
6 Friction Reading · Writing	• characteristics and types of friction • uses of friction in mechanical engineering design • tribology
7 The future of cars: Battery power Listening · Speaking	• battery production • car technologies: internal combustion engine, electric motors and hybrids • research and development
8 Engineering and sustainability Reading · Writing	• concepts in engineering and sustainability • sustainability challenges for engineering
9 Health and safety Listening · Speaking	• health and safety regulations • health and safety in the workplace • case studies: oil rig disasters • case study: rail accident
10 Accident analysis in construction Reading · Writing	• case study: Hyatt Regency Hotel collapse • case studies: 'design and build' contracts
11 Wind turbines Listening · Speaking	• development of wind power • wind turbines: design problems and solutions • horizontal and vertical axis turbines
12 Water engineering Reading · Writing	• types of water and water distribution • desalination technologies • laboratory report: flow in pipes

Vocabulary focus	Skills focus		Unit
• words from general English with a special meaning in engineering • prefixes and suffixes	Listening	• preparing for a lecture • predicting lecture content from the introduction • understanding lecture organization • choosing an appropriate form of notes • making lecture notes	**1**
	Speaking	• speaking from notes	
• English–English dictionaries: headwords · definitions · parts of speech · phonemes · stress markers · countable/uncountable · transitive/intransitive	Reading	• using research questions to focus on relevant information in a text • using topic sentences to get an overview of the text	**2**
	Writing	• writing topic sentences • summarizing a text	
• stress patterns in multi-syllable words • prefixes	Listening	• preparing for a lecture • predicting lecture content • making lecture notes • using different information sources	**3**
	Speaking	• reporting research findings • formulating questions	
• computer jargon • abbreviations and acronyms • discourse and stance markers • verb and noun suffixes	Reading	• identifying topic development within a paragraph • using the Internet effectively • evaluating Internet search results	**4**
	Writing	• reporting research findings	
• word sets: synonyms, antonyms, etc. • the language of trends • common lecture language	Listening	• understanding 'signpost language' in lectures • using symbols and abbreviations in note-taking	**5**
	Speaking	• making effective contributions to a seminar	
• synonyms, replacement subjects, etc., for sentence-level paraphrasing	Reading	• locating key information in complex sentences	**6**
	Writing	• reporting findings from other sources: paraphrasing • writing complex sentences	
• compound nouns • fixed phrases from mechanical engineering • fixed phrases from academic English • common lecture language	Listening	• understanding speaker emphasis	**7**
	Speaking	• asking for clarification • responding to queries and requests for clarification	
• synonyms • nouns from verbs • definitions • common 'direction' verbs in essay titles (discuss, analyze, evaluate, etc.)	Reading	• understanding dependent clauses with passives	**8**
	Writing	• paraphrasing • expanding notes into complex sentences • recognizing different essay/writing assignment types/structures: descriptive · analytical · comparison/evaluation · argument • writing essay plans • writing essays	
• fixed phrases from health and safety • fixed phrases from academic English	Listening	• using the Cornell note-taking system • recognizing digressions in lectures	**9**
	Speaking	• making effective contributions to a seminar • referring to other people's ideas in a seminar	
• 'neutral' and 'marked' words • technical and semi-technical words from engineering • fixed phrases from academic English	Reading	• recognizing the writer's stance and level of confidence or tentativeness • inferring implicit ideas	**10**
	Writing	• writing situation–problem–solution–evaluation essays/writing assignments • using direct quotations • compiling a bibliography/reference list	
• words/phrases used to link ideas (moreover, as a result, etc.) • stress patterns in noun phrases and compounds • fixed phrases from academic English • words/phrases related to wind energy and wind turbines	Listening	• recognizing the speaker's stance • writing up notes in full	**11**
	Speaking	• building an argument in a seminar • agreeing/disagreeing	
• definitions • referring back using pronouns and synonyms • words/phrases to describe mechanical processes in water engineering • common verb + noun phrases used in laboratory reports	Reading	• understanding how ideas in a text are linked • note-making from texts • labelling a diagram	**12**
	Writing	• writing a comparison summary from notes • writing a laboratory report section from notes	

Introduction

The ESAP series

The aim of the titles in the ESAP series is to prepare students for academic study in a particular discipline. In this respect, the series is somewhat different from many ESP (English for Specific Purposes) series, which are aimed at people already working in the field, or about to enter the field. This focus on *study* in the discipline rather than *work* in the field has enabled the authors to focus much more specifically on the skills which a student of engineering studies needs.

It is assumed that prior to using titles in this series students will already have completed a general EAP (English for Academic Purposes) course such as *Skills in English* (Garnet Publishing, up to the end of at least Level 3), and will have achieved an IELTS level of at least 5.

English for Mechanical Engineering

English for Mechanical Engineering is designed for students who plan to take an engineering course entirely or partly in English. The principal aim of *English for Mechanical Engineering* is to teach students to cope with input texts, i.e., listening and reading, in the discipline. However, students will also be expected to produce output texts in speech and writing throughout the course.

The syllabus concentrates on key vocabulary for the discipline and on words and phrases commonly used in academic and technical English. It covers key facts and concepts from the discipline, thereby giving students a flying start for when they meet the same points again in their faculty work. It also focuses on the skills that will enable students to get the most out of lectures and written texts. Finally, it presents the skills required to take part in seminars and tutorials and to produce essay assignments. For a summary of the course content, see the book map on pages 4–5.

Components of the course

The course comprises:
- the student Course Book
- this Teacher's Book, which provides detailed guidance on each lesson, full answer keys, audio transcripts and extra photocopiable resources
- audio CDs with lecture and seminar excerpts

Organization of the course

English for Mechanical Engineering has 12 units, each of which is based on a different aspect of mechanical engineering. Odd-numbered units are based on listening (lecture/seminar extracts). Even-numbered units are based on reading.

Each unit is divided into four lessons:

Lesson 1: vocabulary for the discipline; vocabulary skills such as word-building, use of affixes, use of synonyms for paraphrasing

Lesson 2: reading or listening text and skills development

Lesson 3: reading or listening skills extension. In addition, in later reading units, students are introduced to a writing assignment which is further developed in Lesson 4; in later listening units, students are introduced to a spoken language point (e.g., making an oral presentation at a seminar) which is further developed in Lesson 4

Lesson 4: a parallel listening or reading text to that presented in Lesson 2, which students have to use their new skills (Lesson 3) to decode; in addition, written or spoken work is further practised

The last two pages of each unit, *Vocabulary bank* and *Skills bank*, are a useful summary of the unit content.

Each unit provides between four and six hours of classroom activity with the possibility of a further two to four hours on the suggested extra activities. The course will be suitable, therefore, as the core component of a faculty-specific pre-sessional or foundation course of between 50 and 80 hours.

Vocabulary development

English for Mechanical Engineering attaches great importance to vocabulary. This is why one lesson out of four is devoted to vocabulary and why, in addition, the first exercise at least in many of the other three lessons is a vocabulary exercise. The vocabulary presented can be grouped into two main areas:
- key vocabulary for engineering studies
- key vocabulary for academic English

In addition to presenting specific items of vocabulary, the course concentrates on the vocabulary skills and strategies that will help students to make sense of lectures and texts. Examples include:
- understanding prefixes and suffixes and how these affect the meaning of the base word
- guessing words in context
- using an English–English dictionary effectively
- understanding how certain words/phrases link ideas
- understanding how certain words/phrases show the writer/speaker's point of view

Skills development

Listening and reading in the real world involve extracting communicative value in real time – i.e., as the spoken text is being produced or as you are reading written text. Good listeners and readers do not need to go back to listen or read again most of the time. Indeed, with listening to formal speech such as a lecture, there is no possibility of going back. In many ELT materials second, third, even fourth listenings are common. The approach taken in the ESAP series is very different. We set out to teach and practise 'text-attack' skills – i.e., listening and reading strategies that will enable students to extract communicative value at a single listening or reading.

Students also need to become familiar with the way academic 'outputs' such as reports, essays and oral presentations are structured in English. Conventions may be different in their own language – for example, paragraphing conventions, or introduction–main body–conclusion structure. All students, whatever their background, will benefit from an awareness of the skills and strategies that will help them produce written work of a high standard.

Examples of specific skills practised in the course include:

Listening

- predicting lecture content and organization from the introduction
- following signposts to lecture organization
- choosing an appropriate form of lecture notes
- recognizing the lecturer's stance and level of confidence/tentativeness

Reading

- using research questions to focus on relevant information
- using topic sentences to get an overview of the text
- recognizing the writer's stance and level of confidence/tentativeness
- using the Internet effectively

Speaking

- making effective contributions to a seminar
- asking for clarification – formulating questions
- speaking from notes
- summarizing

Writing

- writing notes
- paraphrasing
- reporting findings from other sources – avoiding plagiarism

- recognizing different essay types and structures
- writing essay plans and essays
- compiling a bibliography/reference list

Specific activities

Certain types of activity are repeated on several occasions throughout the course. This is because these activities are particularly valuable in language learning.

Tasks to activate schemata

It has been known for many years, since the research of Bartlett in the 1930s, that we can only understand incoming information, written or spoken, if we can fit it into a schemata. It is essential that we build these schemata in students before exposing them to new information, so all lessons with listening or reading texts begin with one or more relevant activities.

Prediction activities

Before students are allowed to listen to a section of a lecture or read a text, they are encouraged to make predictions about the contents, in general or even specific terms, based on the context, the introduction to the text or, in the case of reading, the topic sentences in the text. This is based on the theory that active listening and reading involve the receiver in being ahead of the producer.

Working with illustrations, diagrams, figures

Many tasks require students to explain or interpret visual material. This is clearly a key task in a field which makes great use of such material to support written text. Students can be taken back to these visuals later on in the course to ensure that they have not forgotten how to describe and interpret them.

Vocabulary tasks

Many tasks ask students to group key engineering words, to categorize them in some way or to find synonyms or antonyms. These tasks help students to build relationships between words which, research has shown, is a key element in remembering words. In these exercises, the target words are separated into blue boxes so you can quickly return to one of these activities for revision work later.

Gap-fill

Filling in missing words or phrases in a sentence or a text, or labelling a diagram, indicates comprehension both of the missing items and of the context in which they correctly fit. You can vary the activity by, for example, going through the gap-fill text with the whole class first orally, pens down, then setting the same task for individual completion. Gap-fill activities can be photocopied and set as revision at the end of the unit or later, with or without the missing items.

Breaking long sentences into key components

One feature of academic English is the average length of sentences. Traditionally, EFL classes teach students to cope with the complexity of the verb phrase, equating level with more and more arcane verb structures, such as the present perfect modal passive. However, research into academic language, including the corpus research which underlies the *Longman Grammar of Spoken and Written English,* suggests that complexity in academic language does not lie with the verb phrase but rather with the noun phrase and clause joining and embedding. For this reason, students are shown in many exercises later in the course how to break down long sentences into kernel elements, and find the subject, verb and object of each element. This receptive skill is then turned into a productive skill, by encouraging students to think in terms of kernel elements first before building them into complex sentences.

Activities with stance marking

Another key element of academic text is the attitude (or stance) of the writer or speaker to the information which is being imparted. This could be dogmatic, tentative, incredulous, sceptical, and so on. Students must learn the key skill of recognizing words and phrases marked for stance.

Crosswords and other word puzzles

One of the keys to vocabulary learning is repetition. However, the repetition must be active. It is no good if students are simply going through the motions. The course uses crosswords and other kinds of puzzles to bring words back into the students' consciousness through an engaging activity. However, it is understood by the writers that such playful activities are not always seen as serious and academic. The crosswords and other activities are therefore made available as photocopiable resources at the back of the Teacher's Book and can be used at the teacher's discretion, after explaining to the students why they are valuable.

Methodology points

Setting up tasks

The teaching notes for many of the exercises begin with the word *Set ...* . This single word covers a number of vital functions for the teacher, as follows:

- Refer students to the rubric (instructions).
- Check that they understand **what** to do – get one or two students to explain the task in their own words.
- Tell students **how** they are to do the task, if this is not clear in the Course Book instructions – as individual work, pairwork or in groups.
- Go through the example, if there is one. If not, make it clear what the target output is – full sentences, short answers, notes, etc.
- Go through one or two of the items, working with a good student to elicit the required output.

Use of visuals

There is a considerable amount of visual material in the book. This should be exploited in a number of ways:

- before an exercise, to orientate students, to get them thinking about the situation or the task, and to provide an opportunity for a small amount of pre-teaching of vocabulary (be careful not to pre-empt any exercises, though)
- during the exercise, to remind students of important language
- after the activity, to help with related work or to revise the target language

Comparing answers in pairs

This is frequently suggested when students have completed a task individually. It provides all students with a chance to give and explain their answers, which is not possible if the teacher immediately goes through the answers with the whole class.

Self-checking

Learning only takes place after a person has noticed that there is something to learn. This noticing of an individual learning point does not happen at the same time for all students. In many cases, it does not even happen in a useful sense when a teacher has focused on it. So learning occurs to the individual timetable of each student in a group. For this reason, it is important to give students time to notice mistakes in their own work and try to correct them individually. Take every opportunity to get students to self-check to try to force the noticing stage.

Confirmation and correction

Many activities benefit from a learning tension, i.e., a period of time when students are not sure whether something is right or wrong. The advantages of this tension are:

- a chance for all students to become involved in an activity before the correct answers are given

- a higher level of concentration from the students (tension is quite enjoyable!)
- a greater focus on the item as students wait for the correct answer
- a greater involvement in the process – students become committed to their answers and want to know if they are right and, if not, why not

In cases where learning tension of this type is desirable, the teacher's notes say, *Do not confirm or correct (at this point)*.

Feedback

At the end of each task, there should be a feedback stage. During this stage, the correct answers (or a model answer in the case of freer exercises) are given, alternative answers (if any) are accepted, and wrong answers are discussed. Unless students' own answers are required (in the case of very free exercises), answers or model answers are provided in the teacher's notes.

Highlighting grammar

This course is not organized on a grammatical syllabus and does not focus on grammar specifically. It is assumed that students will have covered English grammar to at least upper intermediate level in their general English course. However, at times it will be necessary to focus on the grammar, and indeed occasionally the grammar is a main focus (for example, changing active to passive or vice versa when paraphrasing).

To highlight the grammar:

- focus students' attention on the grammar point, e.g., *Look at the word order in the first sentence.*
- write an example of the grammar point on the board
- ask a student to read out the sentence/phrase
- demonstrate the grammar point in an appropriate way (e.g., numbering to indicate word order; paradigms for verbs; time lines for tenses)
- refer to the board throughout the activity if students are making mistakes

Pronunciation

By itself, the mispronunciation of a single phoneme or a wrong word stress is unlikely to cause a breakdown in communication. However, most L2 users make multiple errors in a single utterance, including errors of word order, tense choice and vocabulary choice. We must therefore try to remove as many sources of error as possible. When you are working with a group of words, make sure that students can pronounce each word with reasonable accuracy in phonemic terms, and with the correct stress for multiple syllable words. Many researchers have found that getting the stress of a word wrong is a bigger cause of miscommunication than getting individual phonemes wrong.

Pair and group activities

Pairwork and group activities are, of course, an opportunity for students to produce spoken language. As mentioned above, this is not the main focus of this course. But the second benefit of these interactional patterns is that they provide an opportunity for the teacher to check three points:

- Are students performing the correct task, in the correct way?
- Do students understand the language of the task they are performing?
- Which elements need to be covered again for the benefit of the class, and which points need to be dealt with on an individual basis with particular students?

Vocabulary and Skills banks

Each unit has clear targets in terms of vocabulary extension and skills development. These are detailed in the checks at the end of the unit (*Vocabulary bank* and *Skills bank*). However, you may wish to refer students to one or both of these pages at the start of work on the unit, so they have a clear idea of the targets. You may also wish to refer to them from time to time during lessons.

1 WHAT IS ENGINEERING?

This introductory unit explores what we mean by the term 'engineering'. Students listen to an extract from a lecture which describes different branches. They also listen to a series of mini-lectures which look at the history of mechanical engineering and a range of issues in engineering. The content of the mini-lectures will be explored in more detail in subsequent units.

Skills focus

🎧 Listening
- preparing for a lecture
- predicting lecture content from the introduction
- understanding lecture organization
- choosing an appropriate form of notes
- making lecture notes

Speaking
- speaking from notes

Vocabulary focus

- words from general English with a special meaning in engineering
- prefixes and suffixes

Key vocabulary

accuracy	jaw	overheat
assemble	kilogram	petrology
assembly	lengthen	powered
centimetre	loosen	pressurize
civil	mechanical	prevention
classify	mechanize	replacement
combustion	megabyte	strengthen
cycle (n)	metal fatigue	supersonic
dynamics	micrometer	tighten
electrical	millilitre	turbine
engineer (n and v)	miscalculate	undercoat
insulator	mount	variable
international	mounting	widen

1.1 Vocabulary

General note

Read the *Vocabulary bank* at the end of the Course Book unit. Decide when, if at all, to refer students to it. The best time is probably at the very end of the lesson or the beginning of the next lesson, as a summary/revision.

Lesson aims

- identify words for the discipline in context, including words which contain affixes
- gain fluency in the target vocabulary

Introduction

Write the phrase *mechanical engineering* on the board. Ask students about the origin of the word *me'chanical*. Elicit *ma'chine* or *me'chanic* and from there get to *me'chanical*. Ask if students know any other related words, e.g.,
'mechanize
ma'chine (as a verb)
ma'chinery
'mechanism

Highlight then drill the shifting stress and the two pronunciations of *ch*.

Ask students where the word *engi'neer* comes from. They will probably say *'engine*. If so, ask them where *engine* comes from. Tell them it is from the same root as *in'genious*, which means very clever.

Language note

Clearly, people in the English-speaking world thought engineers were clever people. Ask students if the word for *engineer* in their language comes from another word.

Exercise A

Set for individual work and pairwork checking. Point out that this is a text which introduces some important basic vocabulary related to engineering – although it may not seem like that at first glance. Do the first one as an example, e.g., *a coat is something you wear on a cold day*. In engineering, it can mean a layer, e.g., a layer of paint – you can mime this or show with a diagram on the board. Ask students the relationship between the meanings in general English and in engineering. (Both mean a layer – a layer of paint or a layer of clothing.) Make sure students understand that they should change the form if necessary, e.g., noun to verb, or past tense to present tense.

11

Feed back, putting the engineering meanings in a table on the board . Tell students to use these structures where possible:

- *a(n) X is (a(n))* ... to define a noun
- *to X is to Y* to define a verb

Make sure students can say the words correctly:

- diphthongs in *coat*, *mount/house*
- /iː/ in *feet* and *teeth*
- no /w/ at the end of *jaw*

Answers

Model answers:
See table below.

Students may not know *mount*, meaning to get on, or *housing*. Explain that, in this case, it is the gerund from *house* – a housing estate not an industrial estate. Some students may not know *estate*, meaning a large number of similar things together.

Exercise B

Set for individual work and pairwork checking. Do the first one as an example. Feed back with the whole class. Ask students for any other words they know which have a special meaning in engineering.

Answers

Model answers:

1 Allow each <u>coat</u> of paint to dry thoroughly before applying the next.
2 Always clean the <u>teeth</u> of the saw after use.
3 Check that the <u>feet</u> of the machine are level.
4 <u>Cap</u> the well immediately and check the pressure on the gauge.
5 <u>Mount</u> the engine on the board using four large bolts.

6 Use the handle to tighten the <u>jaws</u> of the vice.
7 There are four <u>cycles</u> in the operation of an internal combustion engine.
8 Do not raise the <u>arm</u> of the crane above 45 degrees.
9 <u>Couple</u> the two sections together with the pin and secure.
10 Insert the control box in the metal <u>housing</u>.

Other possible words from general English in engineering:
mechanics – how things work rather than people who repair machines
machine (v) – to make something to a high degree of accuracy
engineer (v) – similar meaning to *machine* as a verb
stress – force
load – force
wear – get damaged by use
force – force

Exercise C

Set the first question for pairwork. See which pair can work out the answer first.

Set the remainder for pairwork. Feed back, building up the table in the Answers section on the board.

Answers

Model answers:

1 They all have a base word + extra letters at the beginning/prefixes.
2 See table on next page.
3 Prefix.
4 See table.
5 See table.

	Word	Meaning	Notes
1	coat	a layer	you can talk about *top coat* = final coat of paint and *undercoat* = first coat – see prefixes in Exercise C
2	teeth	the cutting edge	
3	feet	what it stands on	
4	cap	cover and seal from noun to verb	part of speech has changed
5	mount	put one thing, especially an engine, onto another or into its correct place	
6	jaws	the sides of, e.g., a vice or pliers	always plural in this context
7	cycles	the stages of a circular process like the working of an engine	two pronunciations of the letter *c*
8	arm	the part of a machine that extends	
9	couple	join together two things	verb not determiner
10	housing	a box which is designed to hold something	noun not gerund

Prefix	Base word	Meaning of prefix	Another word
centi	metre	a hundredth	centilitre
inter	national	between	intercity
kilo	gram	x 1,000	kilobyte or K
mega	byte	x 1,000,000 or very big	megaton (bomb)
micro	meter	a millionth or very small	microscope
milli	litre	a thousandth	millimetre
mis	calculate	do wrong	misread
over	heat	do more than enough	overtighten
re	do	do again	recycle
semi	circle	half	semiconductor
sub	way	under	subsonic
super	sonic	over or bigger than	supermarket
trans	port*	from one place to another	transplant
under	coat	under or less than should be	undercarriage
un	do	not, opposite	uncouple

*in fact, here *port* comes from *portare* = carry, not from *port* = place for ships

Language note

English is a lexemic language. In other words, the whole meaning of a word is usually contained within the word itself, rather than coming from a root meaning plus prefixes or suffixes (affixes). In most texts, written or spoken, there will only be a tiny number of words with affixes. However, these often add to a base meaning in a predictable way and it is important that students learn to detach affixes from a new word and see if they can find a recognizable base word.

Some words beginning with letters from prefixes are NOT in fact base + prefix, e.g., *refuse*. In other cases, the base word does not exist anymore in English and therefore will not help students, e.g., *transfer*, *transit*, although even in these cases the root meaning of the prefix may be a guide to the meaning of the whole word.

Exercise D

Repeat the procedure from Exercise C.

Answers

Model answers:

1 They all have a base word + extra letters at the end/suffixes.
2 See table.
3 Suffix.
4 See table.
5 See table.

Base word	Suffix	Meaning of suffix	Another word
accura(te)	cy	adjective → noun	fluency
class	ify	make into	rectify
electric	al	noun (electricity) → adjective	mechanical
engine	er	a person who does something or has a qualification in something	mountaineer
insulat(e)	or	thing that does something	conductor
loos(e)	en	make or make more	tighten
petrol	ogy	study of	geology
pressur(e)	ize	make into	oxidize
prevent	ion	verb → noun	invention
replace	ment	verb → noun	improvement
vary → vari	able	can be	replaceable

Language note

Note that with prefixes we rarely change the form of the base word. However, with suffixes, there are often changes to the base word, so students must:

- take off the suffix
- try to reconstruct the base word

Exercise E

Set for pairwork. Try to elicit more than just the words from this lesson. Students should describe the pictures as fully as they can at this stage.

Students may use the following words in their discussion of each picture.

Answers

Possible labels:

1 **coats** of paint (**undercoat**, top coat)
2 circular saw, **teeth**
3 **cap** (of an oil well)
4 **feet** (of a machine)
5 **jaws** (of a table vice)
6 metal **housing**
7 **subway**
8 **mounting** bolts (on an internal combustion engine)
9 **supersonic** plane
10 **electrical** screwdriver
11 **insulator** (on a power line)
12 measuring flask with scale in **millilitres** and centilitres
13 **micrometer** calliper with millimetres and **centimetres**

Closure

If you have not done so already, refer students to the *Vocabulary bank* at the end of Unit 1. Tell students to explain how this lesson can help them deal with new words in context. If you wish, make three groups. Group A looks at the first section, *Using related words*. Group B looks at the second section, *Removing prefixes*. Group C looks at the third section, *Removing suffixes*. Then make sets of three with an ABC in each to explain to each other.

1.2 Listening

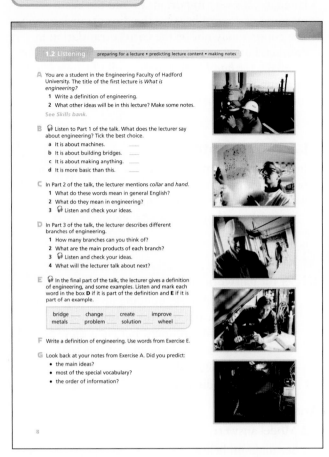

1.2 Listening   preparing for a lecture • predicting lecture content • making notes

A You are a student in the Engineering Faculty of Hadford University. The title of the first lecture is *What is engineering?*
1 Write a definition of engineering.
2 What other ideas will be in this lecture? Make some notes.
See *Skills bank.*

B Listen to Part 1 of the talk. What does the lecturer say about engineering? Tick the best choice.
a It is about machines. ____
b It is about building bridges. ____
c It is about making anything. ____
d It is more basic than this. ____

C In Part 2 of the talk, the lecturer mentions *collar* and *hand*.
1 What do these words mean in general English?
2 What do they mean in engineering?
3 Listen and check your ideas.

D In Part 3 of the talk, the lecturer describes different branches of engineering.
1 How many branches can you think of?
2 What are the main products of each branch?
3 Listen and check your ideas.
4 What will the lecturer talk about next?

E In the final part of the talk, the lecturer gives a definition of engineering, and some examples. Listen and mark each word in the box D if it is part of the definition and E if it is part of an example.

bridge ____   change ____   create ____   improve ____
metals ____   problem ____   solution ____   wheel ____

F Write a definition of engineering. Use words from Exercise E.

G Look back at your notes from Exercise A. Did you predict:
• the main ideas?
• most of the special vocabulary?
• the order of information?

8

General note

The recording should only be played once, since this reflects what happens in a real lecture. Students should be encouraged to listen for the important points, since this is what a native speaker would take from the text. However, students can be referred to the transcript at the end of the lesson to check their detailed understanding, or to try to discover reasons for failing to comprehend.

Read the *Skills bank* at the end of the Course Book unit. Decide when, if at all, to refer students to it. The best time is probably at the very end of the lesson or the beginning of the next lesson, as a summary/revision.

Lesson aims

- prepare for a lecture
- predict lecture content
- make notes

Introduction

1 Show students flashcards of some or all of the words from Lesson 1.1. Tell them to say the words correctly and quickly as you flash each card. Give out each word to one of the students. Say the words again. The student with the word must hold it up. Repeat the process, saying the words in context.

2 Refer students to the photos. Briefly elicit ideas of what they depict. (They will look at the different branches of engineering in more detail in Exercise D.)

Exercise A

1 Set for pair or group work. Feed back, but do not confirm or correct at this time.

2 Set for pairwork. Elicit some ideas but do not confirm or correct.

Methodology note

You may want to refer students to the *Skills bank – Making the most of lectures* at this point. Set the following for individual work and pairwork checking. Tell students to cover the points and try to remember what was under each of the Ps – Plan, Prepare, Predict, Produce. Then tell students to work through the points to make sure they are prepared for the lecture they are about to hear.

Exercise B

Give students time to read the choices. Point out that they are only going to hear the introduction once, as in an authentic lecture situation. Then play Part 1. Feed back. If students' answers differ, discuss which is the best answer and why.

Answers

d It is more basic than this.

Transcript 1.1

Part 1

Welcome to the Engineering Faculty. I want to start by asking a simple question. What is engineering? That's a very simple question, isn't it? We all know the answer – don't we? Let's see.

We know that engineering is about machines. But a bridge isn't a machine and yet engineers build bridges. So let's say it's about making something. OK. If I take some eggs and sugar and flour and make a cake, is that engineering? Not really. It's more fundamental, more basic than any of these things, in my view.

So, what is engineering? What is the intrinsic meaning of this word, a word we use every day and think we understand?

Methodology note

In many course books with listening activities, students are allowed to listen to material again and again. This does not mirror real-life exposure to spoken text. In this course, students are taught to expect only one hearing during the lesson, and are encouraged to develop coping strategies to enable them to extract the key points during this one hearing. Listening texts may be repeated for further analysis but not for initial comprehension.

🎧 Exercise C

Write the two words on the board. Set the two questions for pairwork. Play Part 2. Feed back.

Answers

Model answers:

Word	General English meaning	Engineering meaning
collar	the upper part of a shirt, round the neck	something which goes round the upper part of a machine
hand	a part of the body	person who works, e.g., in a factory

Transcript 🎧 1.2

Part 2

Many words have an intrinsic or basic meaning. We use the words in different situations and they have different surface meanings, but the basic meaning remains the same. Let me give you an example. We use the word *collar* in everyday English. It's part of a shirt. But we also use the word *collar* in engineering. It is part of a machine. Is there any connection between these two words? Yes, there is. A shirt collar goes round the neck and it is on the upper end of the shirt, so a machine collar goes round part of the machine at the upper end.

Somehow, when we are learning our first language, we get a feeling for the basic meaning of words which helps us to understand the same word in a new context. When we are learning another language, it's very important to find the basic meaning of a word because the direct translation in one context may not be the correct translation in another. For example, can you use the word in your language for *hand* in the context of *a factory hand*, meaning someone who works with his or her hands in a factory? Probably not.

Language note

In English, we sometimes name a whole thing from one significant part, e.g., *hand* = a person who works with his/her hands; *motor* = a vehicle with a motor; *jet* = a plane with a jet engine.

🎧 Exercise D

1/2 Set for pairwork. Tell students to make notes.

3 Play Part 3. Feed back, building up a diagram on the board. Point out that the lecturer doesn't mention the main products, but elicit these and add them to the diagram. Explain that this is a *classification* diagram.

4 Set for general discussion.

Answers

1/2 Model answer:

See diagram below.

4 The lecturer will now answer the question: 'What is the basic or intrinsic meaning of engineering?'

Transcript 🎧 1.3

Part 3

So let me go back to my original question. What is engineering? We have mechanical engineering, civil engineering, petroleum engineering and electrical engineering. There are elements of making things, assembling things, working with machines, designing things, in all of these branches of engineering. Ah, *branch*. That's another word where we need to look for the basic meaning … But back to engineering. There is also an element of working with your hands in all the different branches, although now engineers often use

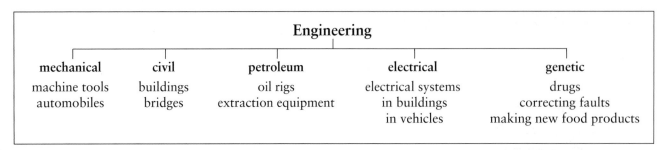

computers as well as their hands. Working with your hands is called *manual* work, and the word *manual* also means a book of instructions in engineering, which shows the origins. Now there is a brand new field – genetic engineering. Genetic engineering is concerned with living things. Can we apply engineering to living things? Then you might hear someone using the word as a verb – *to engineer*. What is the connection? What is the basic or intrinsic meaning?

Methodology note

Up to this point, you have not mentioned how students should record information. Have a look around to see what students are doing. If some are using good methods, make a note and mention that later in the unit.

🎧 Exercise E

Point out that we often define things before or after classifying them. Set for individual work and pairwork checking. Give students plenty of time to look at the words in the box. Play Part 4. Feed back, building up model definitions on the board.

Answers

bridge	E
change	D
create	D
improve	D
metals	E
problem	D
solution	D
wheel	E

Transcript 🎧 1.4

Part 4

Let me suggest that the word *change* is a common factor. In engineering, there are elements of creation and invention, but you must use what is already there. For example, you take some metals and change them into a bridge. But you must follow the natural laws about the behaviour of metals, *and* you must be creative in the design. And of course, there must be a need for the bridge in the first place. You must be providing a better solution than existed before. A new bridge, for example, may make it possible to cross a valley quickly for the first time, or it may be wider or stronger than the previous bridge.

So, engineering requires creative thinking to solve a problem and produce something new or improve something. The first engineer was probably the person who invented the wheel. He … or she … used available resources – probably a large branch – the meaning in general English this time – and realized that the round shape moved across the ground more easily than a square shape.

You should now be able to see why people talk about genetic engineering. It involves changing the genes of living things to make something better, more useful. And what about the verb? When we 'engineer' something, we make it better by using machines.

So, the meaning of 'engineering' is 'change to create something useful'; change for the better, we hope.

Exercise F

Set for individual work and pairwork checking. Feed back, building up a model definition on the board.

Answers

Possible answer:

Engineering means to change, to create something better, to find a solution to a problem.

Exercise G

Refer students back to their notes from Exercise A.

Closure

1 Ask students to give you examples of ways in which mechanical engineers have changed things for the better in recent times – particularly in students' own countries (e.g., new power plants, including renewable energy sources; better/more efficient cars, trains, planes).

2 Refer students to the *Skills bank* if you have not done so already and work through the section *Making the most of lectures*.

1.3 Extending skills

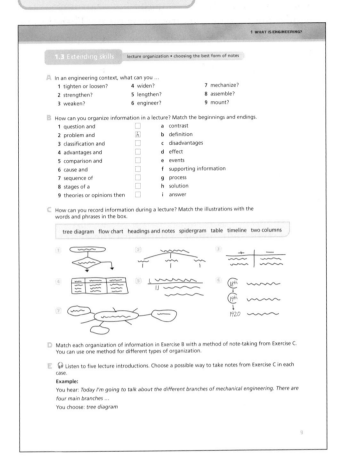

1.3 Extending skills — lecture organization • choosing the best form of notes

A In an engineering context, what can you ...
1 tighten or loosen?   4 widen?   7 mechanize?
2 strengthen?   5 lengthen?   8 assemble?
3 weaken?   6 engineer?   9 mount?

B How can you organize information in a lecture? Match the beginnings and endings.
1 question and   a contrast
2 problem and   [h] b definition
3 classification and   c disadvantages
4 advantages and   d effect
5 comparison and   e events
6 cause and   f supporting information
7 sequence of   g process
8 stages of a   h solution
9 theories or opinions then   i answer

C How can you record information during a lecture? Match the illustrations with the words and phrases in the box.

tree diagram   flow chart   headings and notes   spidergram   table   timeline   two columns

D Match each organization of information in Exercise B with a method of note-taking from Exercise C. You can use one method for different types of organization.

E 🎧 Listen to five lecture introductions. Choose a possible way to take notes from Exercise C in each case.
Example:
You hear: *Today I'm going to talk about the different branches of mechanical engineering. There are four main branches ...*
You choose: *tree diagram*

9

Lesson aims

- identify different types of lecture organization
- use the introduction to a lecture to decide the best form of notes to use

Introduction

Tell students to build up the four Ps of preparing for and attending a lecture: Plan, Prepare, Predict, Produce. You could put students into four groups, each group working on one of the stages, then feeding back to the rest of the class.

Exercise A

Set for pairwork. Feed back orally. The more students can say about these words, the better. Accept anything correct, but let students explain their choice if they choose a combination not given below.

Answers

Possible answers:

1	tighten or loosen	a screw, a bolt, a clamp, vice jaws, a nut, a drill chuck, a spring
2	strengthen	a beam, a spar, a bracket, a plate, a girder, a roof truss, brakes, a mounting, the casing, a cable
3	weaken	a rivet, a joint, a valve, a rail, a mixture, a pin, the casing
4	widen	a bridge, vice jaws, a clamp, an opening, a slot, a groove, the pitch of screw threads
5	lengthen	a beam, a bridge, a slot, a connecting rod, a lever, a girder, a roof truss, a chassis, a crane jib, a cable
6	engineer	any kind of working system or machine so that it is efficient
7	mechanize	any tool, a pulley, transport, an assembly line, a pump
8	assemble	an axle, a component, a valve, a cutting tool, a jack, a wheel, any part of a machine, an assembly
9	mount	a machine, a structure, a drill, a lathe, a wheel

Exercise B

Point out that you can understand a lecture better if you can predict the order of information. Point out also that there are many pairs and patterns in presenting information, e.g., question and answer, or a sequence of events in chronological order.

Set for pairwork. Ask students to write the corresponding letter in each box. Feed back orally. Check pronunciation.

Point out that lecturers may not actually use these words, but if you recognize that what a lecturer is saying is the first of a pair, or the beginning of a sequence, you are ready for the second or next stage later in the lecture.

Answers

1	question and	i	answer
2	problem and	h	solution
3	classification and	b	definition
4	advantages and	c	disadvantages
5	comparison and	a	contrast
6	cause and	d	effect
7	sequence of	e	events
8	stages of a	g	process
9	theories or opinions then	f	supporting information

Exercise C

Identify the first form of notes – a flow chart. Set for individual work and pairwork checking. Feed back, using an OHT or other visual medium if possible.

Answers

1 flow chart
2 tree diagram
3 two columns
4 table
5 headings and notes
6 timeline
7 spidergram

Methodology note

You might like to make larger versions of the illustrations of different note types and pin them up in the classroom for future reference.

Exercise D

Work through the first one as an example. Set for pairwork.

Feed back orally and encourage discussion. Demonstrate how each method of note-taking in Exercise C can be matched with an organizational structure. Point out that:

- a tree diagram is useful for hierarchically arranged information, such as when the information moves from general to specific/examples
- a spidergram is more fluid and flexible, and can be used to show connections between things, such as interactions or causes and effects

Answers

Possible answers:

1 question and answer = headings and notes
2 problem and solution = headings and notes or two-column table
3 classification and definition = tree diagram or spidergram
4 advantages and disadvantages = two-column table
5 comparison and contrast = table
6 cause and effect = spidergram
7 sequence of events = timeline or flow chart
8 stages of a process = flow chart (or circle if it is a cycle)
9 theories or opinions then supporting information = headings and notes or two-column table

🎧 Exercise E

Explain that students are going to hear the introductions to several different lectures. They do not have to take notes, only think about the organization of information and decide what type of notes would be appropriate. Work through the example.

Play each introduction. Pause after each one and allow students to discuss.

Feed back. Students may suggest different answers in some cases. Discuss. Explain that sometimes lecturers move from one information organization to another, e.g., cause and effect then sequence of events.

Answers

Possible answers:

1 tree diagram (classification and definition)
2 spidergram (cause and effect)
3 timeline (sequence of events then flow chart (stages of a process)
4 timeline (sequence of events)
5 tree diagram (classification and definition)
6 table (comparison and contrast) then spidergram (cause and effect)

Transcript 🎧 1.5

Introduction 1

Today I'm going to talk about the different branches of mechanical engineering. There are four main branches. Firstly, there is the development of machines for the production of goods like cars and food. Secondly, there is the development of machines for the production of power – electricity, nuclear. Thirdly, there is the development of military weapons, such as guns, tanks and planes. Finally, there is the branch concerned with environmental control – for example, heating or cooling your environment.

Introduction 2

In this lecture, I'm going to look at metal fatigue. Fatigue means tiredness in general English. Metals can't get tired in the real sense of the word. But, under certain circumstances, they can become weakened. I'm going to look at the causes of metal fatigue, and the effects.

Introduction 3

OK. Are we all ready? Right, I'll begin. For centuries, mechanical engineers have tried to control their environment. In this lecture, we're going to look at one way in which machinery can change a local environment – air conditioning. First, I'm going to talk briefly about the history of air conditioning. Then I'll describe how an air conditioning system works.

Introduction 4

This week I'm going to talk about how it all began. Who were the first true mechanical engineers? When did mechanical engineering begin? We could say it started with the founding of the Institution of Mechanical Engineers in Birmingham, England, in 1847. But really this branch of engineering began some time before, with the Industrial Revolution.

Introduction 5

In this week's lecture, I'm going to consider the functions of a mechanical engineer. There are four main functions which are common to all branches of the profession. Firstly, mechanical engineers must understand and deal with basic principles of mechanical science. Secondly, mechanical engineers are involved in the RDD sequence – that is, research, design and development. Thirdly, there is the question of production – production of goods or production of power. Fourthly, and finally, we have management functions, which include consultancy.

Closure

1 Test students on the pairs from Exercise B. Correct pronunciation again if necessary.
2 Refer students to the *Skills bank – Making perfect lecture notes*.

1.4 Extending skills

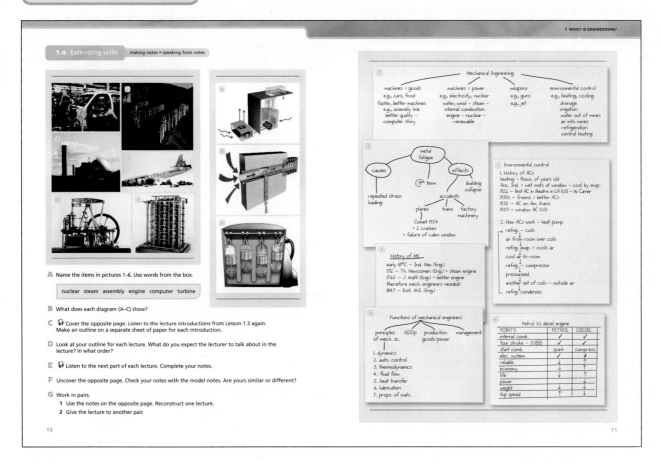

Lesson aims

- make outline notes from lecture introductions
- make notes from a variety of lecture types
- speak from notes

Further practice in:

- predicting lecture content

Introduction

Elicit as much information from the lecture in Lesson 1.2 as possible. If necessary, prompt students by reading parts of the transcript and pausing for students to complete in their own words.

Exercise A

Set for individual work and pairwork checking. Feed back orally, but do not confirm or correct. Point out that they are going to hear about all these things in today's lesson. You will return to these pictures at the end.

For reference, the pictures show:

1 a car assembly line
2 wind power turbines
3 a nuclear power station
4 a plane crash
5 the Newcomen steam engine
6 Charles Babbage's Difference engine

Exercise B

Repeat the procedure from Exercise A – no confirmation or correction.

For reference, the diagrams show:

A a heat pump air-conditioning system
B the Venturi effect
C the four strokes in a petrol engine

Methodology note

It is best that students close the book at this stage, so they are not tempted to look at the model notes. You can give the instructions for the next few stages orally as required.

🎧 Exercise C

Make sure students understand that they are going to hear the introductions from Lesson 1.3 again. Ask them briefly if they can remember any of the content from the introductions. Spend a few moments on this if students are able to contribute.

Elicit suggestions for types of notes (Lesson 1.3, Exercise E).

Explain that this time they must create an outline using an appropriate type of notes. (You can refer them again to the *Skills bank – Making perfect lecture notes*.) Make sure students understand that they don't need to write a lot at this stage – outlines may consist of just a few words, e.g., the start of a spidergram, the first part of a table or diagram. Play each introduction in turn and give students time to choose a note-type, make the outline and check it with other students.

Feed back, getting all the outlines on the board – you may wish to copy them from the first part of the model notes on the right-hand page, or you may prefer to follow your students' suggestions. Clarify the meaning of new words and check pronunciation.

Transcript 🎧 1.5

Introduction 1

Today I'm going to talk about the different branches of mechanical engineering. There are four main branches. Firstly, there is the development of machines for the production of goods like cars and food. Secondly, there is the development of machines for the production of power – electricity, nuclear. Thirdly, there is the development of military weapons, such as guns, tanks and planes. Finally, there is the branch concerned with environmental control – for example, heating or cooling your environment.

Introduction 2

In this lecture, I'm going to look at metal fatigue. Fatigue means tiredness in general English. Metals can't get tired in the real sense of the word. But, under certain circumstances, they can become weakened. I'm going to look at the causes of metal fatigue, and the effects.

Introduction 3

OK. Are we all ready? Right, I'll begin. For centuries, mechanical engineers have tried to control their environment. In this lecture, we're going to look at one way in which machinery can change a local environment – air conditioning. First, I'm going to talk briefly about the history of air conditioning. Then I'll describe how an air conditioning system works.

Introduction 4

This week I'm going to talk about how it all began. Who were the first true mechanical engineers? When did mechanical engineering begin? We could say it started with the founding of the Institution of Mechanical Engineers in Birmingham, England, in 1847. But really this branch of engineering began some time before, with the Industrial Revolution.

Introduction 5

In this week's lecture, I'm going to consider the functions of a mechanical engineer. There are four main functions which are common to all branches of the profession. Firstly, mechanical engineers must understand and deal with basic principles of mechanical science. Secondly, mechanical engineers are involved in the RDD sequence – that is, research, design and development. Thirdly, there is the question of production – production of goods or production of power. Fourthly, and finally, we have management functions, which include consultancy.

Methodology note

Spiral bound or stitched/stapled notebooks are not the best way to keep lecture notes. It is impossible to reorganize or add extra information at a later date, or make a clean copy of notes after a lecture. Encourage students, therefore, to use a loose-leaf file, but make sure that they organize it in a sensible way, with file dividers, and keep it tidy. Tell students to use a separate piece of paper for each outline in this lecture.

Exercise D

Set for pair or group work. Feed back, but do not confirm or correct. Students should be able to predict reasonably well the kind of information which will fit into their outline.

🎧 Exercise E

Before you play the next part of each lecture, refer students to their outline notes again. Tell them to orally reconstruct the introduction from their notes. They don't have to be able to say the exact words, but they should be able to give the gist.

Remind students that they are only going to hear the next part of each lecture once. Play each extract in turn, pausing if necessary to allow students to make notes, but not replaying any section. Tell students to choose an appropriate type of notes for this part of the lecture – it could be a continuation of the type they chose for the introduction, or it could be a different type.

Transcript 🎧 1.6

Lecture 1

Let's look first at the production of goods. Advances in mechanical engineering have led to faster and better machines. This means that machines can produce more things of a higher quality than before. Perhaps the best example of mechanical engineering in the production of goods is the automobile assembly line. At one time, hundreds of people were required to work on the line. Now, there are only a few supervisors controlling machines which do the cutting, welding, assembly and painting. In many cases, the supervisors do not work directly with the machines at all. Instead, they monitor computers which control all the operations. And what about the quality of manufactured goods? Well, one story will illustrate the importance of accuracy in machining. Charles Babbage invented the first computer over 150 years ago, but the machines of his time were not accurate enough to build the machine. With better machining, perhaps the Information Age could have started a hundred years earlier.

Now, what about the production of power? Well, man has used water and the wind for hundreds of years to power mills. But the invention of the steam engine marked the start of the Industrial Revolution. The steam engine was an external combustion engine. In other words, heat was applied externally or outside the main machinery. The invention of the internal combustion engine was the next revolution in the production of power. Then, in the 20th century, we saw the growth of nuclear energy. Interestingly, we are now going back to old sources of power to find renewable energy – wind, water and the sun. Mechanical engineers must make machines to use these renewable sources efficiently.

The third branch of mechanical engineering is the development of military weapons. Many advances in peaceful applications, such as the jet engine, appeared initially for military purposes. So although we may not be happy about it, war has proved a powerful motivation for mechanical engineers.

Finally, let's consider environmental control. Perhaps you think that concern for the environment is a feature of modern life. But in fact, mechanical engineers have always been involved in trying to control or improve the environment. Centuries ago, they were involved in drainage of land in wet countries and irrigation of land in dry countries. Later, they were involved in pumping water out of mines or pumping air in. Now, a lot of mechanical engineers work on refrigeration and central heating systems.

Transcript 🎧 1.7

Lecture 2

Have you ever played with a paper clip? If you try to straighten a paper clip, it's quite difficult. But with enough force you can do it and, with some more force, you can bend it back to the original shape. If you try to straighten the clip again, it's much easier. Finally, you can move the metal backwards and forwards with almost no effort. And it is at this point that if you put a small force on the paper clip, it breaks. We can call the weakening of the paper clip metal fatigue.

So, metal fatigue is caused by repeated stress loading on part of a machine or a vehicle. Stress loading means some kind of force or pressure. Repeated, of course, means again and again. Finally, the metal fails under a very weak stress loading. The effects of metal fatigue can be very serious, including the collapse of buildings, and accidents involving planes, trains and factory machinery.

The term metal fatigue was invented in the 19th century. But it really came to public notice in 1954. On the 10th of January that year, one of the new British passenger jet planes, the Comet, crashed near Italy. Thirty-five people died. Three months later, on the 8th of April 1954, another Comet crashed, again near Italy. All 21 people on board were killed. Scientists examined thousands of fragments of the first crashed plane. They eventually identified the cause as metal fatigue. Apparently, one of the cabin windows failed. In this case, mechanical engineers had the answer. From that day on, all aeroplane windows were made with rounded, instead of square, corners. However, it is still not possible to predict exactly when and where metal fatigue will occur. One solution is to overengineer products so they can bear much greater stress loading than will ever occur in use. But this solution is very expensive.

Transcript 🎧 1.8

Lecture 3

So, let's move on to the history of air conditioning. We could say that cooling the air around us is simply the opposite of heating it. And yet, the second process, space heating, has been known and understood for thousands of years, ever since people discovered how to make and control fires, whereas space cooling is relatively new. Some ancient civilizations had primitive methods. In ancient India, for example, they hung wet mats made of grass over the windows. The hot wind blowing through the wet grass was cooled by evaporation. But the first true air-conditioning machine was built in 1922 and installed in a theatre in Los Angeles, in the United States. It was invented by Willis Carrier. In the 1930s, scientists discovered freons, and these were used to make more efficient air conditioners. By 1935, there was air conditioning on American trains. In 1950, people started to install window ACs to cool single rooms in apartment blocks. Nowadays, economic development in many countries depends on air conditioning because it enables people to work and study in cooled buildings when the ambient or outside temperature exceeds 40 degrees centigrade.

How do air conditioners work? Well, just like the grass mat method in ancient India, the process depends on evaporation. One kind of air conditioner is called a heat pump. The refrigerant – water or some other fluid – is passed through a set of coils. Air from the space to be cooled passes over the coils. The refrigerant evaporates and takes heat from the passing air. We say it *absorbs* the heat – A-B-S-O-R-B-S. The cooled air is then recycled into the space. Meanwhile, the vaporized refrigerant passes into a compressor. It is pressurized and passed through another set of coils. These coils are in contact with the ambient air. Once again, there is a heat transfer – this time from the refrigerant to the outside air. The refrigerant condenses into a liquid and passes back into the evaporator coils again.

Transcript 🎧 1.9

Lecture 4

The Industrial Revolution began in England in the early part of the 18th century. The revolution introduced the use of machines to do work which, until then, had all been done by hand. Some early machines were powered by running water but, in 1712, Thomas Newcomen, an Englishman, used a steam engine to pump water out of a coal mine. The new source of power – steam – revolutionized machinery. In 1765, James Watt, another Englishman, improved Newcomen's engine, and within a hundred years, steam engines were everywhere: on rails, on water and even on the roads. A new kind of engineer was needed for all these machines – the *mechanical* engineer.

Transcript 🎧 1.10

Lecture 5

OK. So let's consider mechanical science first. What are the basic principles of mechanical science? There are seven main areas.

Firstly, dynamics – that's D-Y-N-A-M-I-C-S – which is the relationship between forces and motion. So, for example, in order to make a gate open and close automatically, you need to understand dynamics. Vibration is another important area of dynamics, because vibration can destroy a machine.

Secondly, there's automatic control. Mechanical engineering is often concerned with automating something and controlling it automatically. For example, we can control the gear ratio of a car automatically.

Thirdly, there's thermodynamics – that's T-H-E-R-M-O-dynamics. I expect you all know that *thermo* comes from a Greek word for heat, so thermodynamics is concerned with the relationship between heat, energy and power.

Next, we have fluid flow. When does a mechanical engineer have to worry about fluid flow? Well, there are fluids in most machines – fuel, cooling fluids, lubricants. There are basic principles which tell you how fluid will behave under different circumstances. For example, the Venturi effect dictates that fluid will flow faster through a constricted space. We can see this in a river, for instance, where it narrows.

Fluids are often involved in the next area, too – heat transfer. How do we cool a machine, for example, or heat a room?

I mentioned lubricants just now. Lubrication is the next area. When machines are working, different parts are rubbing together, and these moving surfaces must be lubricated in some way, otherwise the machine will overheat and the part will seize – that means, stick together.

Finally, but perhaps the most important area of all, mechanical engineers must know the properties of different materials. They must know if a particular material is hard or soft, brittle or malleable, a conductor or an insulator.

Exercise F

Allow students to uncover the opposite page or open their books. Give them plenty of time to compare their answers with the model notes. Feed back on the final question.

Exercise G

1 Ask students to work in pairs. Assign pairs a set of notes. They must try to reconstruct the lecture orally – including the introduction – from the notes.

2 Put the pairs together in groups of four, with different topics. Each pair should give their lecture to another pair.

Closure

1 Work on any problems you noticed during the pairwork (Exercise G).

2 Refer back to the pictures at the top of the Course Book page. Students should now be able to name them with confidence.

1 Work through the *Vocabulary bank* and *Skills bank* if you have not already done so, or as a revision of previous study.

2 Use the *Activity bank* (Teacher's Book additional resources section, Resource 1A).

A Set the crossword for individual work (including homework) or pairwork.

Answers

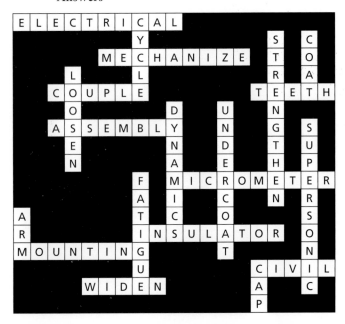

B Play noughts and crosses in pairs. There are two boards. The first contains words with affixes, the second contains names, places, ideas.

Teach students how to play noughts and crosses if they don't know – they take it in turns to try to use the word/phrase in context or explain what the word/phrase means. If they succeed, they can put their symbol – a nought **O** or a cross **X** – in that box. If a person gets three of their own symbols in a line, they win.

First board: Tell students to remove the affixes to find the basic word in each case. Make sure they can tell you the meaning of the basic word (e.g., *pressure* for *pressurize*), but don't elicit the meaning of the affixed word at this stage. Put students in pairs to play the game. Monitor and adjudicate.

Second board: Put students in different pairs to play the second game. Clearly, this time they have to actually remember the facts from the lectures. Don't let them look back at notes.

3 Each of the mini lectures from Lesson 1.4 can lead on to a great deal more work. Tell students to research one of the following, according to which group they ended in. Explain that they must come back and report to the rest of the class in the next lesson/next week.

Lecture	Research
1	Some more advances in mechanical engineering brought about by war
2	A modern case where metal fatigue was blamed for an accident
3	The basic process of heating a room with a central heating system
4	Some key dates in the history of the petrol engine and the diesel engine
5	A key example of each of the RDD stages for a modern invention, e.g., the space rocket
6	One renewable power source with advantages and disadvantages

4 Brainstorm note-taking techniques. For example:

- use spacing between points
- use abbreviations
- use symbols
- underline headings
- use capital letters
- use indenting
- make ordered points
- use different colours
- use key words only

2 ENGINEERING ACHIEVEMENTS

Unit 2 looks at engineering achievements in recent times. The first reading text tells the history of refrigeration and air conditioning. The second reading text looks at the progress towards safety in engineering products, including efforts to develop a code of safety for steam boilers.

Note that students will need dictionaries for some exercises in this unit.

Skills focus

Reading

- using research questions to focus on relevant information in a text
- using topic sentences to get an overview of the text

Writing

- writing topic sentences
- summarizing a text

Vocabulary focus

- English–English dictionaries:
  headwords
  definitions
  parts of speech
  phonemes
  stress markers
  countable/uncountable
  transitive/intransitive

Key vocabulary

air conditioning	energy	operate
apparatus	fluid	operation
code	friction	overheat
condense	inefficient	patent
cool (v)	machine (n and v)	pressure
device	machinery	radiator
efficiency	mechanic	refrigeration
efficient	mechanism	seal (v)
elevator	mechanize	shaft

2.1 Vocabulary

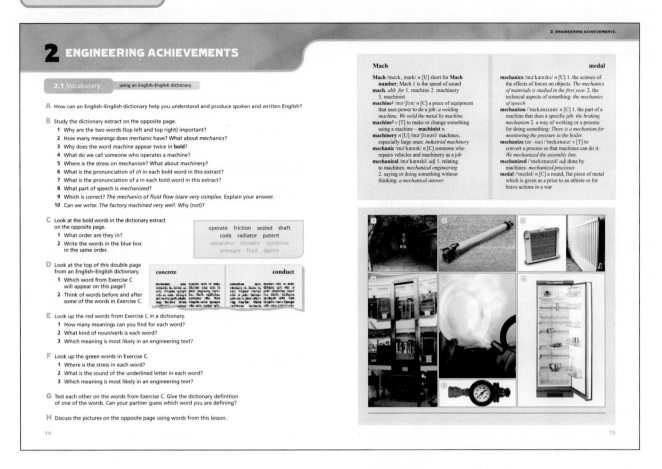

General note

Take in a set of English–English dictionaries.

Read the *Vocabulary bank* at the end of the Course Book unit. Decide when, if at all, to refer students to it. The best time is probably at the very end of the lesson or the beginning of the next lesson, as a summary/revision.

Lesson aims

- learn how to make full use of an English–English dictionary
- gain fluency in the target vocabulary

Introduction

1 Revise the vocabulary from the last unit. Check:
   - meaning
   - pronunciation
   - spelling

2 Ask students whether they use a translation (bilingual) dictionary or an English–English (monolingual) dictionary. Elicit the advantages and disadvantages of a translation dictionary.

Answers

Possible answers:

+	–
good when you know the word in your own language and need a translation into English	not good when there is more than one possible translation of a word – which is the correct one?
when you look up an English word, the translation into your language is easy to understand	English–English dictionaries often have more examples and precise definitions of each word

Methodology note

Recent research has shown that, despite the insistence of generations of language teachers on the use of English–English dictionaries in class, nearly 90 per cent of students use a translation dictionary when studying on their own.

Exercise A

Ask the question as a general discussion. Confirm but do not explain anything. Point out that the next exercise will make the value of this kind of dictionary clear.

Answers

Model answers:

The following information is useful for spoken English:

- stress
- pronunciation of individual phonemes – particularly when a phoneme has multiple pronunciations

The following information is useful for written English:

- information about the type of word – C/U; T/I
- the spelling – although students might make the point that if you don't know the spelling, you can't find the word in the first place, but point out that you can often guess the possible spelling – for example, *mechanize* could be *mek*, but if you don't find it there, you can try *mec* …
- examples of the word in use to memorize
- some synonyms for lexical cohesion – this is a very important point, although you may not want to elaborate on this now

Exercise B

Set for individual work and pairwork checking. Feed back, ideally using an OHT or other visual display of the dictionary extract to highlight points. You might suggest that students annotate the dictionary extract in their books, highlighting symbols, etc., and writing notes on the meaning and value.

Answers

Model answers:

1 They tell you the first and last words on the pages to help you locate the word you want.
2 *Mechanic* – one meaning; *mechanics* – two, plus of course the plural of mechanic because it is a countable noun.
3 Because the same word can be a noun or a verb.
4 A *machinist*.
5 *Mechanism* – on the first syllable; *machinery* – on the second syllable.
6 Sometimes /ʃ/, sometimes /k/ – can students spot the pattern that *ma+ch* = /ʃ/ while *me+ch* = /k/?
7 Two pronunciations – /æ/ or /ə/.
8 Adjective.
9 *Is* – because *mechanics* is uncountable.
10 No – because *machine* is transitive, so it must have an object.

Exercise C

Note: If students are from a Roman alphabet background, you may want to omit this exercise.

1 Students should quickly be able to identify alphabetical order.
2 Set for individual work and pairwork checking. Feed back, getting the words on the board in the correct order. Don't worry about stress and individual phonemes at this point – students will check this later with their dictionaries.

Language note

It may seem self-evident that words in a dictionary are in alphabetical order. But students from certain languages may not automatically recognize this. In the famous Hans Wehr dictionary of written Arabic, for example, you must first convert a given word to its root and look that up, then find the derived form. So *aflaaj* (the plural of *falaj* = irrigation channel) will not be found under A but under F since the root is *f-l-j*.

Exercise D

1 Set for pairwork. Feed back orally, explaining the principle if necessary.
2 Set for pairwork. Ask students to find words connected with engineering if they can. Feed back orally.

Answers

1 *Condense* will appear on the double-page spread.
2 Answers depend on which words students choose.

Exercise E

Give out the dictionaries, if you have not already done so.

Remind students that dictionaries number multiple meanings of the same part of speech and multiple parts of speech. Remind them also of the countable/uncountable and transitive/intransitive markers. (Note that different dictionaries may use different methods for indicating these things. The *Oxford Advanced Learner's Dictionary*, for example, uses [V] for intransitive verbs and [Vn] for transitive verbs.)

Write the headings of the table in the Answers section on the board, and work through the first word as an example.

Set for pairwork. Feed back, building up the table in the Answers section on the board. (Students' answers will vary – accept any appropriate meanings and definitions.)

Answers

Model answers:

Word	Part of speech	Type	Main meaning in engineering	Main meaning(s) in general English
operate	v	T	make a machine work	do a surgical procedure
friction	n	U	the results of surfaces rubbing	bad feeling between people
sealed	adj		made airtight or watertight	agreed
shaft	n	C	1. a hole in the ground for mining; 2. a way of carrying motive power from engine to, e.g., wheels	a long handle on a tool or spear
code	n	C	a set of rules	a secret code
radiator	n	C	1. a cooler; 2. a heater	
patent	n	C	the right to earn money from an invention	adj = obvious

Exercise F

Remind students how stress and the pronunciation of individual phonemes are shown in a dictionary. Refer them to the key to symbols if necessary. Write the headings of the table in the Answers section on the board, and work through the first word as an example.

Set for pairwork. Feed back, building up the table in the Answers section on the board.

Answers

Model answers:

Stress	Sound	Part of speech	Type	Main meaning in engineering	Main meaning in general English
appa'ratus	/ə/	n	U	a piece of equipment	gym equipment
'elevator	/ə/ or /ɪ/*	n	C	a lift	
con'dense	/ə/	v	T/I	change from gas to liquid	abbreviate
'pressure	/ə/	n	C	the result of compressing something	stress
'fluid	/ə/ or /ɪ/*	n	U**	a liquid	adj = changing from day to day
de'vice	/ə/ or /ɪ/*	n	C	a machine	

*depends on personal idiolect

**there is usually a C form of U words – e.g., *the fluids mixed* – when we are talking about different generic items

Exercise G

Demonstrate how to do the exercise by giving a few definitions and getting students to tell you the word (without reading from the board or their books, if possible). Stick to engineering rather than general English definitions and encourage students to do the same.

Exercise H

Work through the pictures. Check that students understand what they show and the relationship to mechanical engineering.

For reference, the pictures show:

1 a mine **shaft**

2 a drive **shaft**

3 two types of **radiator**: cooling an engine and heating a room

4 an **elevator**; people using an elevator **operate** it by pushing buttons; an elevator also has a **shaft**. Some students may be able to explain that many elevators have hydraulic systems containing **fluids**, typically oil

5 the steam from a kettle condensing (liquid → gas → liquid)

6 a refrigerator, which is a **device** for cooling food and drink and which has a **sealed** system. Some students may be able to explain how a modern refrigerator works

7 a **pressure** gauge; pressure gauges can measure the pressure of a fluid (e.g., oil) or a gas (e.g., steam)

Closure

1 Remind students that you can identify the part of speech of an unknown word by looking at the words before or after the word, i.e.,

- nouns often come before and after verbs, so if you know that X is a verb, the next content word before or after is probably a noun
- nouns often come immediately after articles
- verbs often come after names and pronouns
- adjectives often come before nouns or after the verb *be*

Come back to this point when you are feeding back on the reading texts in this unit.

2 Point out that dictionaries often use a small set of words that help to define, e.g., *material, device, tool, equipment, way, kind, theory, principle.* Give definitions using these words and tell students to identify what you are defining, e.g., *It's a tool for tightening and loosening nuts* (spanner); *It's a device for lifting heavy things* (crane or pulley); *It's the principle that explains why heavy things can float* (Archimedes' principle), etc.

2.2 Reading

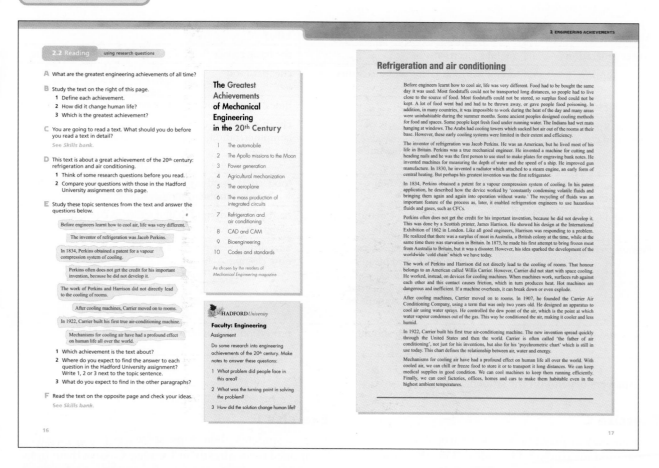

General note

Take in an English–English dictionary.

Read the *Skills bank* section on doing reading research at the end of the Course Book unit. Decide when, if at all, to refer students to it. The best point is probably Exercise C, or at the very end of the lesson or the beginning of the next lesson, as a summary/revision.

Lesson aims

● prepare for reading research
● use research questions to structure reading research

Introduction

1 Hold up an English–English dictionary and say a word from Lesson 2.1. Ask students where approximately they will find it in the dictionary – i.e., beginning, middle, two-thirds of the way through, etc. Follow their advice and read the word at the top left. Ask students if the target word will be before or after. Continue until you get to the right page. Repeat with several more words from Lesson 2.1.

2 Give definitions of some of the engineering words from Lesson 2.1 for students to identify.

Exercise A

Set the question for general discussion.

Answers

Possibly the wheel, or the computer, or the internal combustion engine.

Exercise B

Refer students to the text from *Mechanical Engineering* magazine. Point out that this refers to 20th century achievements.

1/2 Give a couple of examples, e.g.,

The automobile means the car. The automobile made it possible for people to get around quickly, to carry goods.

The Apollo missions involved sending people to the Moon and bringing them back safely. Engineers learnt a lot about a number of areas from the extreme difficulties they had to overcome.

Set for pairwork.

3 Set for general discussion.

Answers

Model answers:

1/2

Achievement	Definition	Effect
Power generation	making electricity	the basic power behind many aspects of modern life
Agricultural mechanization	doing work on farms with machines	cheaper food
The aeroplane	powered flight	quick travel – but of course environmental effects, too
The mass production of integrated circuits	making the important parts of electronic equipment – mass production means making millions quickly and cheaply	cheap electronic equipment leading to mass computerization, home entertainment
Refrigeration and air conditioning	keeping food and other things, including rooms, cold	food safety, food preservation, health, being able to work in hot ambient temperatures
CAD and CAM	computer-aided design or manufacture	better, faster design; manufacture in complex and dangerous situations
Bioengineering	bioengineering often means biomedical engineering, but can also mean food engineering and agricultural engineering. It is the application of engineering principles to biological systems and functions	new drugs, pest-resistant and higher yield crops and now cloning
Codes and standards	deciding how something should be made or operated for safety	protection of workers and the general public

3 Answers depend on the students.

Exercise C

Students may or may not be able to articulate preparation for reading. Elicit ideas. One thing they must identify – reading for a purpose. Point out that they should always be clear about the purpose of their reading. A series of questions to answer, or **research questions**, is one of the best purposes.

Refer students to the *Skills bank* at this stage if you wish.

Exercise D

1 Set for pairwork. Elicit some ideas, but do not confirm or correct.

2 Refer students to the Hadford University research questions at the bottom of the page. Check comprehension, especially of the phrase *turning point*. If students have come up with better research questions, write them on the board for consideration during the actual reading.

Exercise E

Remind students about topic sentences if they haven't mentioned them already in Exercise C. Give them time to read the topic sentences in this exercise. Make sure they have noticed the three names. Point out that the topic sentences are in order, so they give a rough overview of the whole text. Some topic sentences clearly announce what the paragraph will be about. Others may only give a hint of how it will develop.

1 Set for group discussion.

2 Remind students of the research questions. Look at the first research question as an example, then set for pairwork. Point out that they may match a research question to more than one topic sentence, and that some topic sentences may not relate to the research questions (i.e., they don't have to write a number for each topic sentence).

3 Explain that here students look at the topic sentences they *didn't* number in question 2, and try to work out the likely content of each paragraph. Do the first two as examples, then set for pairwork. Feed back, eliciting and checking that they are reasonable possibilities, based on the topic sentence. You can accept multiple ideas for the same paragraph provided they are all possible.

Answers

Possible answers:

1 Refrigeration and air conditioning.

2 The following is a reasonable prediction:

Before engineers learnt how to cool air, life was very different.	1
The inventor of refrigeration was Jacob Perkins.	2
In 1834, Perkins obtained a patent for a vapour compression system of cooling.	
Perkins often does not get the credit for his important invention, because he did not develop it.	
The work of Perkins and Harrison did not directly lead to cooling of rooms.	
After cooling machines, Carrier moved on to rooms.	
In 1922, Carrier built his first true air-conditioning machine.	2
Mechanisms for cooling air have had a profound effect on human life all over the world.	3

3 Answers depend on the students. Discuss.

Exercise F

Point out, if students have not already said this, that the topic sentences are normally the first sentences of each paragraph. Tell students to compare the contents of each paragraph with their predictions. Encourage them to take notes as they read.

If necessary, the reading can be set for homework.

Closure

1 Unless you have set the reading for homework, do some extra work on oral summarizing as a comprehension check after reading (see *Skills bank – Using topic sentences to summarize*). Students work in pairs. One student says a topic sentence and the other student summarizes the paragraph from memory in his/her own words, or if necessary reads the paragraph again and then summarizes it without looking.

2 You may also want to redo the text as a jigsaw – the text is reproduced in the additional resources section at the back of this Teacher's Book (Resource 2B) to facilitate this.

3 As a further activity after reading, remind students of the note-taking skills practised in Unit 1. Discuss appropriate note-taking forms for this text. They can then write notes on the text. Tell them to keep their notes, as they will be useful for the summary exercise in Lesson 2.3.

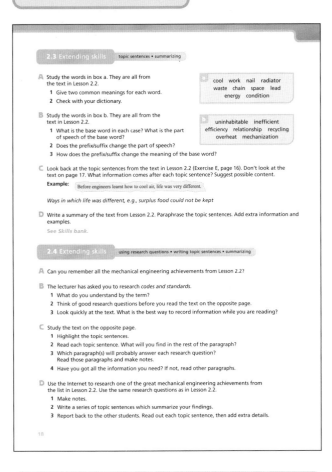

2 Tell students to look up any cases where they didn't get two meanings. Don't let the quick ones shout them out. Feed back orally. (Students' answers will vary – accept any appropriate meanings and definitions.)

Answers

Possible answers:

		Meaning 1		Meaning 2
cool	v or adj	(make) cold	adj	fashionable
work	v	do a job	v	operate or function
nail	n	the hard part of a finger	n	a fixing
radiator	n	a heater	n	a cooler (it's actually doing the same thing, radiating heat, but in one case it heats a room and in the other case it cools a machine)
waste	n	material that is lost or thrown away	v	use too much of something
chain	n	linked metal	n	linked parts of a system
space	n	outer space	n	room, area
lead	v	/liːd/ result in	n	/led/ metal
energy	n	capacity for activity	n	capacity of a body to do work
condition	v	treat, improve	n	state

Methodology note

Don't help students to find words in a text. It's a key reading skill to be able to pattern match, i.e., get a word in your mind's eye and then find it on the page.

Exercise B

Set for individual work and pairwork checking. Students can check these points in a dictionary. Feed back, taking apart the words and showing how the affixes can change the meaning.

General note

Take in a set of English–English dictionaries.

Lesson aims

● produce good topic sentences and a summary text

Further practice in:

● vocabulary from Lesson 2.2

Introduction

Test students on the factual information in the text from the previous lesson, e.g., *Who invented refrigeration? How did Arabs keep rooms cool?*

If a student says, accurately, *I didn't read about that. It wasn't relevant to my research.*, accept it and praise the student.

Exercise A

1 Set for pairwork. Refer students back to the text if necessary. Feed back.

Answers

Model answers:

Word	Base word	Affix and meaning
uninhabitable (adj)	inhabit (v)	*un* = not/*able* = can be
inefficient (adj)	efficient (adj)	*in* = not
efficiency (n)	efficient (adj)	*cy* = adjective ➔ noun
relationship (n)	relation (n)	*ship* = shape or condition (not related to ship = vessel)
recycling (n)	cycle (v)	*re* = *again* *ing* = gerund = the noun made from a verb
overheat (v)	heat (v)	*over* = more than should be
mechanization (n)	mechanize (v) or machine (n)	*ize* = make in this way *ation* = verb ➔ noun

Exercise C

Ideally, display the topic sentences (or give them on a handout) so that students do not have to turn back to pages 16 and 17. The topic sentences are reproduced in the additional resources section to facilitate this (Resource 2C). Work through the example, showing that you can deduce (or in this case to some extent remember) the contents of a paragraph from the topic sentence. Do another example orally. Set for pairwork.

Feed back, eliciting possible paragraph contents and sample information. Only correct ideas which are not based on the topic sentence. Allow students to check back with the text and self-mark.

Discourse note

In academic writing, topic sentences often consist of a general point. The sentences that follow then support the general statement in various ways, such as:

- giving a definition and/or a description
- giving examples
- giving lists of points (e.g., arguments or reasons)
- restating the topic sentence in a different way to help clarify it
- giving more information and detail on the topic sentence to clarify it

Often – but not always – the type of sentence is shown by a 'discourse marker' – e.g., *for example*, *first of all*, etc. This helps to signal to the reader how the writer sees the link between the sentences and is therefore a good clue as to the purpose of the sentences following the topic sentence.

Answers

Possible answers:

Topic sentence	Possible paragraph content	Supporting information/example(s)
Before engineers learnt how to cool air, life was very different.	ways in which life was different	surplus food could not be kept
The inventor of refrigeration was Jacob Perkins.	information about his birth, life, early inventions	a machine for cutting and heading nails
In 1834, Perkins obtained a patent for a vapour compression system of cooling.	information about vapour compression	the device worked by recycling fluids
Perkins often does not get the credit for his important invention, because he did not develop it.	Who did develop it?	James Harrison
The work of Perkins and Harrison did not directly lead to the cooling of rooms.	What led to the cooling of rooms? OR What did it lead to? OR Who invented room cooling?	Willis Carrier invented room cooling
After cooling machines, Carrier moved on to rooms.	more information about his invention	in 1907, he founded the Carrier Air Conditioning Company
In 1922, Carrier built his first true air-conditioning machine.	How did it work? OR Was it successful?	Carrier is often called the father of air conditioning
Mechanisms for cooling air have had a profound effect on human life all over the world.	What effect? condition	can keep medical supplies in good

Exercise D

Refer students to the *Skills bank*. Set for individual work. If students took notes in Lesson 2.2, Exercise F, they should use these notes as the basis for this exercise. Encourage students to add extra information or examples to fill out the summary. Tell students to start in class, while you monitor and assist, and finish for homework.

Methodology note

There are two reasons for students to use their own words in written work (except when quoting and acknowledging sources):

1 The work involved in rewording information and ideas helps us to mentally process them and to retain them in memory.

2 Copying whole sentences from the work of other writers is plagiarism (unless the quotation is acknowledged). Universities disapprove of plagiarism and may mark down students who plagiarize. In the commercial world, an accusation of plagiarism can cause legal problems, and in the academic world, it can severely damage a teacher's reputation and career.

Closure

Tell students to define some of the engineering words from the text on page 17. Alternatively, give definitions of some of the words and tell students to identify the words.

2.4 Extending skills

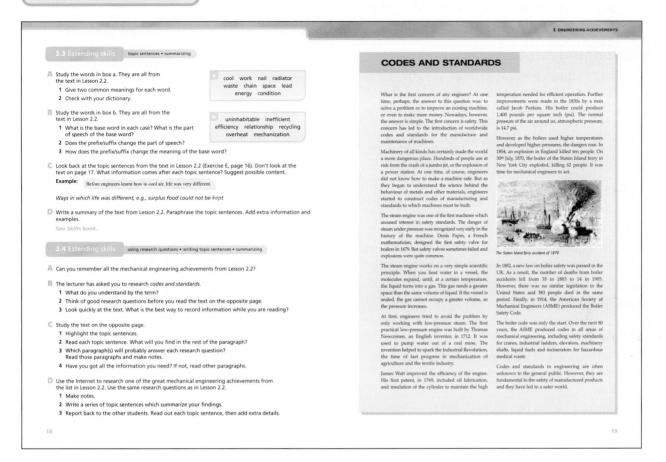

2.3 Extending skills   topic sentences • summarizing

A Study the words in box a. They are all from the text in Lesson 2.2.
  1 Give two common meanings for each word.
  2 Check with your dictionary.

cool work nail radiator
waste chain space lead
energy condition

B Study the words in box b. They are all from the text in Lesson 2.2.
  1 What is the base word in each case? What is the part of speech of the base word?
  2 Does the prefix/suffix change the part of speech?
  3 How does the prefix/suffix change the meaning of the base word?

uninhabitable inefficient
efficiency relationship recycling
overheat mechanization

C Look back at the topic sentences from the text in Lesson 2.2 (Exercise E, page 16). Don't look at the text on page 17. What information comes after each topic sentence? Suggest possible content.

  Example: Before engineers learnt how to cool air, life was very different.

  Ways in which life was different, e.g., surplus food could not be kept

D Write a summary of the text from Lesson 2.2. Paraphrase the topic sentences. Add extra information and examples.
  See Skills bank.

2.4 Extending skills   using research questions • writing topic sentences • summarizing

A Can you remember all the mechanical engineering achievements from Lesson 2.2?

B The lecturer has asked you to research *codes and standards*.
  1 What do you understand by the term?
  2 Think of good research questions before you read the text on the opposite page.
  3 Look quickly at the text. What is the best way to record information while you are reading?

C Study the text on the opposite page.
  1 Highlight the topic sentences.
  2 Read each topic sentence. What will you find in the rest of the paragraph?
  3 Which paragraph(s) will probably answer each research question? Read those paragraphs and make notes.
  4 Have you got all the information you need? If not, read other paragraphs.

D Use the Internet to research one of the great mechanical engineering achievements from the list in Lesson 2.2. Use the same research questions as in Lesson 2.2.
  1 Make notes.
  2 Write a series of topic sentences which summarize your findings.
  3 Report back to the other students. Read out each topic sentence, then add extra details.

18

CODES AND STANDARDS

What is the first concern of any engineer? At one time, perhaps, the answer to this question was: to solve a problem or to improve an existing machine, or even to make more money. Nowadays, however, the answer is simple. The first concern is safety. This concern has led to the introduction of worldwide codes and standards for the manufacture and maintenance of machines.

Machinery of all kinds has certainly made the world a more dangerous place. Hundreds of people are at risk from the crash of a jumbo jet, or the explosion of a power station. At one time, of course, engineers did not know how to make a machine safe. But as they began to understand the science behind the behaviour of metals and other materials, engineers started to construct codes of manufacturing and standards to which machines must be built.

The steam engine was one of the first machines which aroused interest in safety standards. The danger of steam under pressure was recognized very early in the history of the machine. Denis Papin, a French mathematician, designed the first safety valve for boilers in 1679. But safety valves sometimes failed and explosions were quite common.

The steam engine works on a very simple scientific principle. When you heat water in a vessel, the molecules expand, until, at a certain temperature, the liquid turns into a gas. This gas needs a greater space than the same volume of liquid. If the vessel is sealed, the gas cannot occupy a greater volume, so the pressure increases.

At first, engineers tried to avoid the problem by only working with low-pressure steam. The first practical low-pressure engine was built by Thomas Newcomen, an English inventor, in 1712. It was used to pump water out of a coal mine. The invention helped to spark the Industrial Revolution, the time of fast progress in mechanization of agriculture and the textile industry.

James Watt improved the efficiency of the engine. His first patent, in 1769, included oil lubrication, and insulation of the cylinder to maintain the high temperature needed for efficient operation. Further improvements were made in the 1830s by a man called Jacob Perkins. His boiler could produce 1,400 pounds per square inch (psi). The normal pressure of the air around us, atmospheric pressure, is 14.7 psi.

However, as the boilers used higher temperatures and developed higher pressures, the dangers rose. In 1854, an explosion in England killed ten people. On 30th July, 1870, the boiler of the Staten Island ferry in New York City exploded, killing 62 people. It was time for mechanical engineers to act.

The Staten Island ferry accident of 1870

In 1882, a new law on boiler safety was passed in the UK. As a result, the number of deaths from boiler accidents fell from 35 in 1883 to 14 in 1905. However, there was no similar legislation in the United States and 383 people died in the same period. Finally, in 1914, the American Society of Mechanical Engineers (ASME) produced the Boiler Safety Code.

The boiler code was only the start. Over the next 80 years, the ASME produced codes in all areas of mechanical engineering, including safety standards for cranes, industrial ladders, elevators, machinery shafts, liquid fuels and incinerators for hazardous medical waste.

Codes and standards in engineering are often unknown to the general public. However, they are fundamental to the safety of manufactured products and they have led to a safer world.

19

Lesson aims

- use research questions to structure reading research
- write topic sentences for a short research report/summary

Introduction

Give a word from the text in Lesson 2.2 which is part of a phrase. Ask students to try to complete the phrase. It's probably better if you give the first word in the phrase, but you might also try giving the second word at times or at the end of the exercise.

Possible two-word phrases:

steam	engine
central	heating
patent	application
hazardous	fluids/gases
refrigeration	engineers
frozen	meat
cold	chain
water	sprays/vapour
air	conditioning
psychrometric	chart
ambient	temperature

Exercise A

Set for group discussion. Build up the list on the board, with students' books closed.

Answers

the automobile

the Apollo missions to the Moon

power generation

agricultural mechanization

the aeroplane

the mass production of integrated circuits

refrigeration and air conditioning

CAD and CAM

bioengineering

codes and standards

Exercise B

1 Refer students to the title of the text – *Codes and standards*. Set for pairwork. Feed back orally.

2 Remind students of the importance of research questions – reading for a purpose. Set for pairwork. Feed back, writing up suitable questions on the board.

39

3 Elicit the different kinds of notes you can use – see Unit 1 *Skills bank*. Remind students to think about the best kind of notes before and while they are reading.

Methodology note

It is good for students to get into the habit of thinking about the form of their notes before they read a text in detail. If they don't do this, they will tend to be drawn into narrative notes rather than notes which are specifically designed to help them answer their research questions.

Answers

Possible answers:

1 Rules on how to do, make or maintain something.
2 The three questions from Lesson 2.2 would be fine, although students may come up with better ones.
3 See Unit 1 *Skills bank*. A timeline would be an appropriate form of notes.

Exercise C

1 Remind students of the importance of topic sentences. Set for individual work and pairwork checking.
2 Encourage students not to read ahead. Perhaps you should ask students to cover the text and only reveal each topic sentence in turn, then discuss possible contents of the paragraph. Remind them that it is not a good idea to read every part of a text unless you have to. If you have an OHP or other visual display, you can tell students to shut their books and just show the topic sentences from the jigsaw text in the additional resources section (Resource 2D), or you can give them as a handout (Resource 2E).
3 Set the choice of paragraphs for pairwork. Students then read individually, make notes and compare them. Monitor and assist.
4 Give students time to read other paragraphs if they need to.

Discourse note

It is as well to be aware (though you may not feel it is appropriate to discuss with students at this point) that in real academic texts, the topic sentence may not be as obvious as in the texts in this unit. Sometimes there is not an explicit topic sentence, so that the overall topic of the paragraph must be inferred. Or the actual topic sentence for the paragraph can be *near* rather than *at* the beginning of the paragraph. Sometimes, also, the first sentence of a paragraph acts as a topic statement for a succession of paragraphs.

Answers

Possible answers:

2

Topic sentence	Possible paragraph content
What is the first concern of any engineer?	paragraph will answer the question (ideas: design efficient machine, safety, etc.)
Machinery of all kinds has certainly made the world a more dangerous place.	examples of dangers of machinery, e.g., car/plane crashes
The steam engine was one of the first machines which aroused interest in safety standards.	why; dangers of steam engines
The steam engine works on a very simple scientific principle.	description of the principle
At first, engineers tried to avoid the problem by only working with low-pressure steam.	whether this was successful or not
James Watt improved the efficiency of the engine.	how he did this
However, as the boilers used higher temperatures and developed higher pressures, the dangers rose.	what happened – accidents?
In 1882, a new law on boiler safety was passed in the UK.	result of this?
The boiler code was only the start.	other safety laws/standards
Codes and standards in engineering are often unknown to the general public.	conclusion – have improved safety

3 The appropriate paragraphs to read depend on the research questions you and your students decide on.

Exercise D

1 If it is possible to research on the Internet during the lesson, send students to the computers now. They can work in groups. If not, set the task for homework and feed back next lesson.
2 Set for individual work and group work checking.
3 The idea is that students, on the basis of the topic sentences, present their information to fellow students. Make sure students realize that they only have to write the topic sentences. They can add the details in orally. Encourage them to stick to information that is relevant to their research questions.

Closure

1 Focus on some of the vocabulary from the text, including:

manufacture

maintenance

behaviour

safety valve

scientific principle

vessel = container

textile

crane

incinerator

2 You may also want to redo the text as a jigsaw, as before – the text is reproduced in the additional resources section (Resource 2D) to facilitate this.

Extra activities

1 Work through the *Vocabulary bank* and *Skills bank* if you have not already done so, or as a revision of previous study.

2 Use the *Activity bank* (Teacher's Book additional resources section, Resource 2A).

   A Set the wordsearch for individual work (including homework) or pairwork.

   Answers

   B Do the quiz as a whole class, or in teams, or set for homework – students can reread the texts to get the answers if necessary.

   Answers

    1 Jacob Perkins.

    2 1834.

    3 Vapour compression.

    4 James Harrison.

    5 Willis Carrier.

    6 1907–1922.

    7 The first safety valve.

    8 Because the high-pressure steam can burst the boiler casing.

    9 The Industrial Revolution.

    10 Thomas Newcomen.

    11 James Watt.

    12 14.7 psi.

    13 Fatal accidents.

    14 Four of the following: cranes, industrial ladders, elevators, machinery shafts, liquid fuels, incinerators for hazardous medical waste.

3 Ask students to work in small groups to research and feed back to the group on the other mechanical engineering achievements of the 20th century. The three research questions are the same as in Lesson 2.2.

If students are going to do research on the Internet, suggest that they type in *History* then their topic to get some potential texts. Alternatively, you can do this research before the lesson and print off some pages for students to work from.

Remind students that they can't possibly read everything they find, so they must use the topic sentences to decide if a paragraph is worth reading.

4 You can get students to practise their reading aloud – a skill which is not vital but is sometimes useful – by following this approach.

Photocopy and cut up one of the jigsaw texts in the additional resources section (Resources 2B and 2D). Give topic sentences to Student A and the corresponding paragraph to Student B.

Student A reads out a topic sentence.

Student B finds the corresponding paragraph and reads it out.

An alternative is to give Student A the topic sentences and Student B a set of sentences chosen from each paragraph (one sentence per paragraph). Student A reads out the topic sentences one by one. Student B decides which of his/her sentences is likely to appear in the same paragraph as the topic sentence. Both students have to agree that the paragraph sentence matches the topic sentence.

5 Have a competition to practise finding words in a monolingual dictionary. Each student or pair will need an English–English dictionary. Put students in teams with their dictionaries closed. Select a word from the Unit 2 key vocabulary list and instruct students to open their dictionaries and find the word. The first student to find the word is awarded a point for their team. Additional points can be awarded if the student can give the correct pronunciation and meaning.

3 FORCES ON MATERIALS

Unit 3 looks at the properties of materials, such as flexibility and rigidity, and the way that engineers can use these properties to construct the effective machinery. It also looks at the forces which act on components, like tension and compression, and how engineers have to take these forces into account when constructing machines.

Skills focus

🎧 **Listening**

- preparing for a lecture
- predicting lecture content
- making lecture notes
- using different information sources

Speaking

- reporting research findings
- formulating questions

Vocabulary focus

- stress patterns in multi-syllable words
- prefixes

Key vocabulary

alloy	equal (adj)	quality
aluminium	equilibrium	rigid
beam	equivalent	rubber
belt	external	shear
cantilever	flexible	sheet
characteristic	force (n)	spring (n)
component	internal	steel
compression	materials	strain (n)
copper	opposite	stress (n)
deform	overengineer	tension
deformation	parallel	torque
ductile	permanent	underengineer
elastic (adj)	plastic (n and adj)	uniaxial
elasticity	property	wire

3.1 Vocabulary

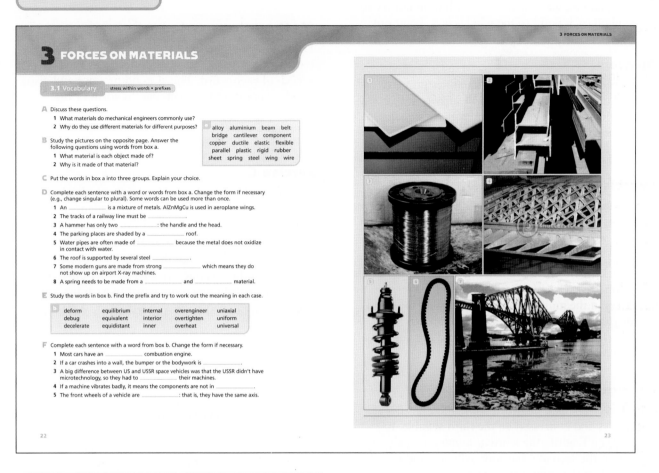

3 FORCES ON MATERIALS

General note

Read the *Vocabulary bank* at the end of the Course Book unit. Decide when, if at all, to refer your students to it. The best time is probably at the very end of the lesson or the beginning of the next lesson, as a summary/revision.

Dictionaries will be useful in this lesson.

Lesson aims

- gain a greater understanding of the importance of stress within words and some of the common patterns
- extend knowledge of words which contain prefixes
- gain fluency in the target vocabulary

Introduction

1 Revise the vocabulary from the first two units. Check:

- meaning
- pronunciation
- spelling

2 Ask students to name all the different materials they can see in the room. Write the names on the board as they identify items. Ask students why that particular material was used for that purpose. Accept any reasonable answer, but force students to think about the question seriously, e.g., *Why is the door made of wood? Because it is light, cheap and easy to work.*

Exercise A

1 Refer students to the first question. Ask *Which of these materials (on the board) are commonly used in mechanical engineering?* You should be able to elicit at least the following engineering materials:

- metals, especially steel, possibly aluminium; perhaps you can get them to deduce that there is copper inside wires in the room
- plastics
- ceramics
- wood
- glass
- rubber (perhaps holding in the glass of the windows?)

Check pronunciation of these words, especially the stress in the multi-syllable words.

2 Put students in pairs to discuss the second question. Feed back orally. If students know particular words for qualities, e.g., *ductile*, accept but do not try to explain each point to the whole class. Point out that you are going to deal with this later.

Answers

Students may tell you about the qualities/properties of particular materials, but the simple answer is that any engineering material has its own properties/qualities/characteristics (teach all three words), which make it suitable for a particular purpose.

Exercise B

Refer students to the pictures on the opposite page. Set questions 1 and 2 for pairwork. Tell students to select relevant words from the box – there are some extra words. They should also identify each item.

Feed back. As students are naming the items, materials and properties, check/correct pronunciation, especially the stress in the multi-syllable words. Elicit the extra words *(parallel, component)* and check/teach the meanings. Point out that the spring and the fan belt are *components*, i.e., parts of something bigger.

Answers

The pictures show:

1 a **plastic sheet** which could be used as a cover for a car port because plastic is light, **flexible** and waterproof

2 a **steel beam** which could be used to support, e.g., a bridge, because it is **rigid** (and, in fact, **flexible** so it can expand and contract with temperature and resonance)

3 a **copper wire** which could be used to carry electricity because copper is **ductile**, i.e., it can be drawn into a wire and is a good conductor

4 an aeroplane **wing**, probably made from an **aluminium** or aluminium **alloy** because it is strong but light (it is probably the alloy AlZnMgCu)

5 a **steel spring** which could be used as a shock absorber in a car because steel made into a spring is **elastic**

6 a **rubber belt** which could be used as a fan belt in a car because rubber is **elastic**

7 a **steel cantilever bridge** which could be used to span a gap because you only need to support it at the ends, not in the middle, which could of course

be difficult to do if you are spanning a river or a deep gorge

Exercise C

1 Set for individual work and pairwork checking. After a few moments, check that students have noticed the three groups and can name them – the headings in the table in the Answers section below.

Feed back, building up the table on the board. Point out there is one extra word – *parallel*. Ask students to add one more word to each list.

2 Set for individual work and pairwork checking. Feed back.

Answers

Model answers:

1/2

Material	Quality of the material (adj)	Object
'alloy alu'minium 'copper 'plastic* 'rubber steel	'ductile e'lastic 'flexible 'plastic* 'rigid	beam belt 'cantilever 'bridge com'ponent sheet spring wing wire
ceramic glass textile	dense heavy light	hundreds of possibilities

*Note that *plastic* can be a noun or an adjective. As an adjective, it means a material which can be forced into a shape and it will remain in that shape. Students could check this with a dictionary.

Exercise D

Set for individual work and pairwork checking. Feed back orally.

Answers

Model answers:

1 An <u>alloy</u> is a mixture of metals. AlZnMgCu is used in aeroplane wings.

2 The tracks of a railway line must be <u>parallel</u>.

3 A hammer has only two <u>components</u>: the handle and the head.

4 The parking places are shaded by a <u>cantilever/plastic</u> roof.

5 Water pipes are often made of <u>copper</u> because the metal does not oxidize in contact with water.

6 The roof is supported by several steel <u>beams</u>.

7 Some modern guns are made from strong <u>plastic(s)</u> which means they do not show up on airport X-ray machines.

8 A spring needs to be made from a <u>flexible</u> and <u>elastic</u> material.

Exercise E

Set for pairwork. Students should look at all three words to find and then deduce the meaning of the prefix. Encourage them to use a phrase as a definition rather than a single-word translation. They need to develop a sense of the broader meaning of the prefix. Feed back, getting the meanings on the board.

Answers

Model answers:

de = remove from, decrease, change

equi = equal to, the same as, even

in = on the inside, going in

over = more than is necessary

uni = one, all the same as

Exercise F

This is further practice in using words with prefixes. Remind students that they must make sure the form of the word fits into the sentence. If students are struggling, point out that all the missing words are from the top row of the box.

Feed back, checking pronunciation and stress patterns.

Answers

Model answers:

1 Most cars have an <u>internal</u> combustion engine.

2 If a car crashes into a wall, the bumper or the bodywork is <u>deformed</u>.

3 A big difference between US and USSR space vehicles was that the USSR didn't have microtechnology, so they had to <u>overengineer</u> their machines.

4 If a machine vibrates badly, it means the components are not in <u>equilibrium</u>.

5 The front wheels of a vehicle are <u>uniaxial</u>: that is, they have the same axis.

Methodology note

With some of these words it is difficult to work out the base word, e.g., *librium*. However, you can point out that you can sometimes understand roughly what a technical word means if you understand the prefix, e.g., *equilibrium* must be something to do with *equal*, so context will help you to guess the rough meaning.

Closure

1 Check meanings of words using the pictures. Ideally, copy onto an OHT or other visual medium and work through the materials and properties again.

2 If you have not already done so, refer students to the *Vocabulary bank* at the end of Unit 3. Work through some or all of the stress patterns.

Language note

The patterns shown in the *Vocabulary bank* in Unit 3 are productive, i.e., they enable you to make more words or apply the rules accurately to other words. The words with unusual patterns tend to be the more common ones, so if students come across a new multi-syllable word at this level, it is likely to conform to the patterns shown. Native speakers recognize the patterns and will naturally apply them to unusual words, e.g., proper nouns. How, for example, would you pronounce these nonsense words?

felacom
bornessity
shimafy
emtonology
scolosphere
nemponium
cagoral
andimakinize
ortepanimation

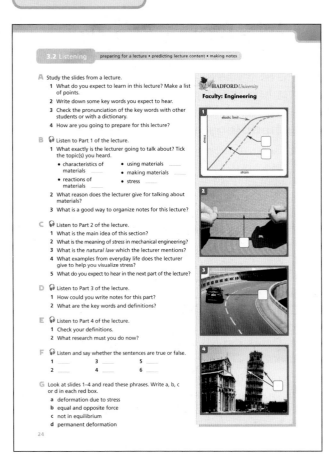

Lesson aims

Further practice in:

- planning and preparing for a lecture
- predicting lecture content
- choosing the best form of notes
- making notes

Introduction

Review key vocabulary by:

- using flashcards
- playing the alphabet game in the extra activities section at the end of this unit

Exercise A

Refer students to the handout with the slides. Write the title *Forces on materials in engineering* on the board.

1 Set for individual work and pairwork checking. Feed back, eliciting some ideas.

2 Brainstorm to elicit key words. Allow the class to decide whether a word should be included.

3 Set for pairwork.

4 Elicit some points – the four Ps (Plan, Prepare, Predict, Produce). If necessary, refer students to Unit 1 *Skills bank* to review the preparation for a lecture. One way to help the students to make provisional notes is to:

- brainstorm what they would include
- organize their topics into a logical sequence

Answers

Answers depend on the students.

🎧 Exercise B

1 Tell students they are only going to hear the introduction to the lecture. Ask what information they expect to get from the introduction (i.e., the outline of the lecture). Give students time to read the choices of topics. Check that they understand the meaning and relevance. Remind them they will only hear the introduction once, as in a lecture. Play Part 1. Allow them to compare answers.

   Feed back. Ask them to justify their choice by saying what they heard related to it. Confirm the correct answer.

2 Elicit ideas. Confirm or correct.

3 Elicit ideas.

Answers

Possible answers:

1 reactions of materials; stress

2 Choosing the correct materials for components is fundamental to good design.

3 Perhaps into a table with materials and their reactions, or headings with bullet points, e.g.,

   Features of stress

   - ...
   - ...
   - ...

   Reactions of materials

   - ...
   - ...
   - ...

Transcript 🎧 1.11

Part 1

OK. Is everybody here? Right, let's start. What I'm going to talk about today is materials in engineering. As you know, when a machine is designed, one of the most critical factors that mechanical engineers have to decide on is the materials to be used. Different materials – steel, aluminium, copper, etc., – have different physical characteristics. For example, aluminium may be the best for the body of a plane, but impossible for the engines. If the wrong material is chosen, the machine will be very expensive due to overengineering, or it could fracture due to underengineering. So we're going to look at the way that different materials react to stress. Every component in a machine undergoes stress of one kind or another. So, choosing the right materials for the components is fundamental to good design. But before we look at the reactions of materials, let's talk about the features of stress.

🎧 Exercise C

Before playing Part 2, refer students to the slides and make sure they recognize what they depict. Ask students what they expect to hear. Give them time to read questions 1–4. Tell them to write only brief notes. The main task is to absorb the meaning. Play Part 2. Give them time to answer questions 1–4. Allow them to compare their answers. Feed back.

When they thoroughly understand *stress*, ask them what they expect to hear in the next part of the lecture (question 5). Elicit ideas but do not confirm or correct.

Answers

Model answers:

1 Main idea = *What is stress? It's the behaviour of materials when a force is applied to them.*

2 Stress is what happens inside a material when a force is applied.

3 Newton's third law of motion – for every action, there is an equal and opposite reaction.

4 Pressing against a wall, driving round a bend, sitting on a beach ball, a rubber band.

5 Answers depend on the students.

Transcript 🎧 1.12

Part 2

When an external force acts on a machine component, internal forces in the component react against it. The rule says that for any force there is an equal and opposite reaction. This is Newton's third law of motion. When you press against a wall, your hand doesn't go through the wall because the wall is pushing it back. Equal and opposite reaction. When the opposite forces are equal, the component is said to be in equilibrium, and this is the ideal state. This internal reaction is called *stress*.

You may have experienced this in driving. If you take a corner fast, although you're turning right, the car feels as if it wants to go left. All is well, however, unless you have misjudged your speed and overstressed your car, then the car does indeed go left.

Similarly, in a machine, as the load increases, the component rearranges itself to support the load. It is deformed – that is, it changes its shape. A simple example: if you sit on a beach ball, it changes its shape. It flattens. When you stand up, it becomes spherical again. If you pull a rubber band, it gets thinner until you release it. This is what happens inside any material under stress – it is deformed. Sometimes we can't see it, but it is happening.

🎧 Exercise D

1 Play the first sentence of Part 3. Ask the first question and elicit ideas.

2 Set the second question for individual work and pairwork checking. Play the rest of the recording. Tell students to take notes. Allow students to compare their definitions. Don't, at this stage, confirm the answers.

Answers

Model answers:

1 A table is good for definitions.

2 See Exercise E.

Transcript 🎧 1.13

Part 3

OK – we need a few definitions now ... The deformation we talked about is known as *strain*. Strain is normal in all materials at work, and, of course, when the load is removed, the stress and strain are reduced, and the component tries to return to its original shape. In the case of a rubber band or the beach ball, there is no problem because of the *elasticity* of rubber. Elasticity is the ability of a material to return to its original shape. Most metals are elastic up to a point. Steel, surprisingly, is very elastic, whereas concrete is definitely not. It's knowing where that point is that is important.

If the load goes beyond the elasticity of the material, the component will never return to its original shape. The graph in slide 1 shows what happens. The solid line indicates that, as the load increases, the component deforms in a linear fashion, i.e., in a straight line, and will return along the same line when the load is removed. However, if the strain goes beyond the elastic limit, the deformation increases significantly, so that the return line is permanently offset – that's the dotted line.

One aspect of elasticity is the *rigidity* of the material. A flexible material can flex – that's where the word comes from, of course – but what does *flex* mean? It means that it can expand and contract – over a long period – without damage. However, if the material is more rigid, fatigue can set in and the result will be similar to the dotted line of the graph, or even total component failure.

Some materials can only withstand a very small amount of stress. This is called *plasticity* – that is, a plastic component under stress will never return to its original shape. Have you ever tried to break a plastic card by bending it repeatedly? A good example of plasticity is a ductile material such as copper, which is so soft it can be drawn out into a wire – and does not return to its original shape. So we have two key words – *stress* and *strain*, and two important qualities of materials – *elasticity* and *plasticity*.

🎧 Exercise E

Part 4 summarizes the definitions of the four key words. Tell students that this is the last part of the lecture. What do they expect to hear? Confirm that it is a summary. Play Part 4.

1 Students should check their definitions as they listen. After the summary has finished, they should correct their definitions and complete their notes.

Guide them to the correct answer: that is, the correct meaning, not necessarily the words given here.

2 Elicit ideas.

Answers

Model answers:

1

Key word	Definition
stress	the behaviour *inside* a material when a force is applied
strain	the deformation caused by the stress
elasticity	the ability to deform and return to its original shape
plasticity	permanent deformation after stress; the inability to return to its original shape

2 The research task is to look at factors which produce stress in a mechanical component.

🎧 Transcript 🎧 1.14

Part 4

So, to summarize, *stress* is the effect of a force on the component, and *strain* is the deformation resulting from it. *Elasticity* means a material can deform and still return to its original shape, whereas *plasticity* means the opposite. The effectiveness of a material used in a machine depends on how it reacts to stress.

OK, that's it for today. Next time we'll look at the factors which produce stress in a mechanical component. Don't forget to do a bit of research on that before you come. Thanks. See you soon.

🎧 Exercise F

These are sentences about the ideas in the lecture. Set for pairwork.

Say or play the sentences. Give time for students to discuss and then respond. Students must justify their answers. Advise them to beware of statements containing absolutes such as *always*, *never*, *all*. These are rarely true.

Answers

1	true	
2	false	Steel is more elastic than concrete.
3	false	Fatigue is more likely in rigid materials.
4	true	
5	false	*Elastic* materials can deform and still return to their original shape.
6	false	Rigid materials are *more likely* to fracture when they deform.

Transcript 🎧 **1.15**

1 When opposite forces are equal, a component is said to be in equilibrium.

2 Concrete is more elastic than steel.

3 Fatigue is more likely in flexible materials.

4 If the load goes beyond the elasticity of the material, the component will not return to its original shape.

5 Once materials are deformed, they can never return to their original shape.

6 Rigid materials always fracture when they deform.

Exercise G

Set for pairwork. Ask students to write a letter in each box corresponding to one of the four phrases. They should justify their choices.

Answers

Slide 1:
The solid line = **deformation due to stress** (a).

The dotted line = **permanent deformation** (d).

Slide 2:
The rubber band is an **equal and opposite force** (b).

Slide 3:
The car going round a bend is an **equal and opposite force** (b). If not, it skids.

Slide 4:
The Leaning Tower of Pisa is **not in equilibrium** (c). That's why it tilts; the tilt increases every year.

Closure

Ask students to explain in their own words:

● what links the four slides
● the phenomena in the slides

Note: Students will need their lecture notes from Lesson 3.2 in the next lesson.

3.3 Extending skills

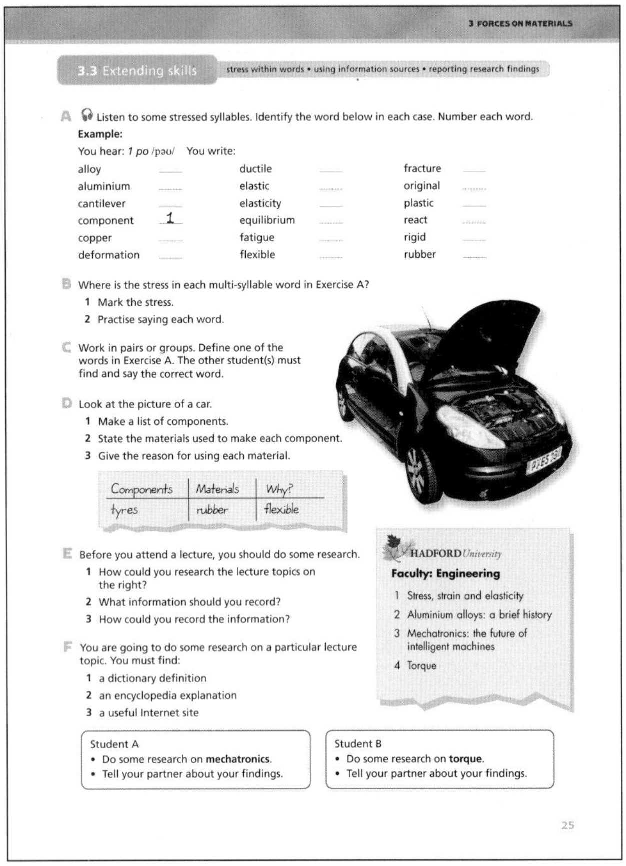

The boxed course book page shows:

3.3 Extending skills — stress within words • using information sources • reporting research findings

A Listen to some stressed syllables. Identify the word below in each case. Number each word.

Example:
You hear: *1 po* /pəʊ/   You write:

alloy	____	ductile	____	fracture	____
aluminium	____	elastic	____	original	____
cantilever	____	elasticity	____	plastic	____
component	_1_	equilibrium	____	react	____
copper	____	fatigue	____	rigid	____
deformation	____	flexible	____	rubber	____

B Where is the stress in each multi-syllable word in Exercise A?
1 Mark the stress.
2 Practise saying each word.

C Work in pairs or groups. Define one of the words in Exercise A. The other student(s) must find and say the correct word.

D Look at the picture of a car.
1 Make a list of components.
2 State the materials used to make each component.
3 Give the reason for using each material.

Components	Materials	Why?
tyres	rubber	flexible

E Before you attend a lecture, you should do some research.
1 How could you research the lecture topics on the right?
2 What information should you record?
3 How could you record the information?

HADFORD *University*
Faculty: Engineering
1 Stress, strain and elasticity
2 Aluminium alloys: a brief history
3 Mechatronics: the future of intelligent machines
4 Torque

F You are going to do some research on a particular lecture topic. You must find:
1 a dictionary definition
2 an encyclopedia explanation
3 a useful Internet site

Student A
• Do some research on **mechatronics**.
• Tell your partner about your findings.

Student B
• Do some research on **torque**.
• Tell your partner about your findings.

25

General note

Read the *Skills bank* at the end of the Course Book unit. Decide when, if at all, to refer students to it. The best time is probably at the very end of the lesson or the beginning of the next lesson, as a summary/revision.

Lesson aim

This lesson is the first in a series about writing an assignment or giving a presentation based on research. The aim of this lesson is to introduce students to sources of information.

Introduction

1 Tell students to ask you questions about the information in the lecture in Lesson 3.2 as if you were the lecturer. Refer them to the *Skills bank* for typical language if you wish.

2 Put students in pairs. Student A must ask Student B about the information in the lecture in Lesson 3.2 to help him/her complete the notes from the lecture. Then they reverse roles. Go round, helping students to identify gaps in their notes and to think of good

questions to get the missing information. Refer them to the *Skills bank* if you wish for language they can use in the pairwork.

Pairs then compare notes and decide what other information would be useful and where they could get it from. For example, technical definitions of the key words might be useful, from a specialist dictionary or an encyclopedia. In the feedback, write a list of research sources on the board, at least including dictionaries, encyclopedias, specialist reference books and the Internet.

Point out that dictionaries are good for definitions, although you may need to go to a specialist dictionary for a technical word. Otherwise, try an encyclopedia, because technical words are often defined in articles when they are first used. You could also try Google's 'define' feature, i.e., type *define: stress*, but remember you will get definitions from all disciplines not just your own, so you need to scan to check the relevant one.

Exercise A

Point out the importance of stressed syllables in words – see *Language note* opposite. In this exercise, students will hear each word with the stressed syllable emphasized, and the rest of the syllables underspoken.

Play the recording, pausing after the first few to check that students understand the task. Feed back, perhaps playing the recording again for each word before checking. Ideally, mark up an OHT or other visual display of the words.

Answers

alloy	8
aluminium	2
cantilever	16
component	1
copper	6
deformation	15
ductile	12
elastic	18
elasticity	3
equilibrium	13
fatigue	9
flexible	4
fracture	10
original	14
plastic	17
react	5
rigid	11
rubber	7

Language note

In English, speakers emphasize the stressed syllable in a multi-syllable word. Sometimes listeners may not even hear the unstressed syllables. Vowels, in any case, often change to schwa or a reduced form in unstressed syllables. Therefore it is essential that students can recognize key words from the stressed syllable alone when they hear them in context.

Transcript 🎧 1.16

1 com'ponent
2 alu'minium
3 ela'sticity
4 'flexible
5 re'act
6 'copper
7 'rubber
8 'alloy
9 fa'tigue
10 'fracture
11 'rigid
12 'ductile
13 equi'librium
14 o'riginal
15 defor'mation
16 'cantilever
17 'plastic
18 e'lastic

Exercise B

Erase the words or turn off the OHT. Ask students to guess or remember where the stressed syllable is on each word. Tell them to mark their idea with a light vertical stroke in pencil. Elicit and drill. Refer students to the *Vocabulary bank* at this stage if you wish.

Answers

See transcript for Exercise A.

Exercise C

Set for pair or group work. Go round and assist/correct.

Exercise D

Refer students to the picture and the table. Put students in groups. Encourage them to use the language from the *Skills bank* to get information from others. Feed back, building up the table in the Answers section on the board. The more components students can name, the better.

Answers

Possible answers:

Components	Materials	Why?
tyres	rubber	flexible
windows	glass	clear, strong
bodywork	steel	strong, plastic (i.e., can be permanently deformed)
bumpers	rubber or chrome	can be deformed and absorbs impact
engine	steel	strong, etc.

Exercise E

Remind students again about the four Ps. Refer students to the lecture topics and the questions. Make sure they understand that all three questions relate to before, rather than during, the lecture. Work through as a whole class if you wish.

Answers

Model answers:

1 Look up key words in a dictionary/encyclopedia/on the Internet. Check pronunciation so you will recognize the words in the lecture, especially *torque*, which, students should discover, has the same pronunciation as *talk*.

2 Lecture 1: meanings of these key words; examples

   Lecture 2: key dates and famous people, if any; key uses of aluminium + metals it is alloyed with commonly

   Lecture 3: predictions on future use of mechatronics

   Lecture 4: key principles for torque

3 Perhaps do a spidergram so that it is easier to brainstorm with fellow students and cover all the possible areas that the lecturer might focus on.

Exercise F

Set for pairwork, giving each member of the pair a different research task. If students have access in class to reference material, allow them to at least start the activity in class. Otherwise, set for homework. Before the feed-back-to-partner stage, refer students to the *Skills bank – Reporting information to other people*.

Closure

Dictate sentences with words from Exercise A in context for students to identify the words again.

3.4 Extending skills

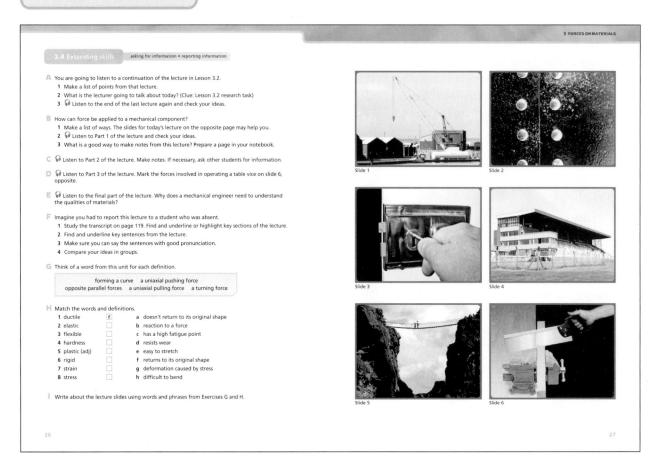

3.4 Extending skills — asking for information • reporting information

A You are going to listen to a continuation of the lecture in Lesson 3.2.
1 Make a list of points from that lecture.
2 What is the lecturer going to talk about today? (Clue: Lesson 3.2 research task)
3 🎧 Listen to the end of the last lecture again and check your ideas.

B How can force be applied to a mechanical component?
1 Make a list of ways. The slides for today's lecture on the opposite page may help you.
2 🎧 Listen to Part 1 of the lecture and check your ideas.
3 What is a good way to make notes from this lecture? Prepare a page in your notebook.

C 🎧 Listen to Part 2 of the lecture. Make notes. If necessary, ask other students for information.

D 🎧 Listen to Part 3 of the lecture. Mark the forces involved in operating a table vice on slide 6, opposite.

E 🎧 Listen to the final part of the lecture. Why does a mechanical engineer need to understand the qualities of materials?

F Imagine you had to report this lecture to a student who was absent.
1 Study the transcript on page 119. Find and underline or highlight key sections of the lecture.
2 Find and underline key sentences from the lecture.
3 Make sure you can say the sentences with good pronunciation.
4 Compare your ideas in groups.

G Think of a word from this unit for each definition.

> forming a curve   a uniaxial pushing force
> opposite parallel forces   a uniaxial pulling force   a turning force

H Match the words and definitions.
1 ductile	e	a	doesn't return to its original shape
2 elastic	☐	b	reaction to a force
3 flexible	☐	c	has a high fatigue point
4 hardness	☐	d	resists wear
5 plastic (adj)	☐	e	easy to stretch
6 rigid	☐	f	returns to its original shape
7 strain	☐	g	deformation caused by stress
8 stress	☐	h	difficult to bend

I Write about the lecture slides using words and phrases from Exercises G and H.

Slide 1 — Slide 2 — Slide 3 — Slide 4 — Slide 5 — Slide 6

26   27

Lesson aims

- ask other people for information

Further practice in:

- choosing the best form of notes
- making notes
- reporting information

Introduction

1 Elicit as much information from the lecture in Lesson 3.2 as possible. If necessary, prompt students by reading parts of the transcript and pausing for students to complete in their own words.

2 Remind students of the language involved in asking for information from other people – see *Skills bank*. Drill some of the sentences if you wish.

🎧 Exercise A

1/2 Set for pairwork. Monitor and assist.

3 Play Part 4 of the lecture from Lesson 3.2 to enable students to check their answers. Feed back.

Elicit information from the students' research (Lesson 3.3). Do not confirm or correct at this stage except pronunciation mistakes on key words. Play the end of the lecture. Feed back.

Transcript 🎧 1.17

Part 4

So, to summarize, *stress* is the effect of a force on the component, and *strain* is the deformation resulting from it. *Elasticity* means a material can deform and still return to its original shape, whereas *plasticity* means the opposite. The effectiveness of a material used in a machine depends on how it reacts to stress.

OK, that's it for today. Next time we'll look at the factors which produce stress in a mechanical component. Don't forget to do a bit of research on that before you come. Thanks. See you soon.

Answers

Model answers:

1 Stress is the effect of a load on the component.
Strain is the deformation resulting from it.
Elasticity means a material can deform and still return to its original shape, whereas plasticity means the opposite.

The effectiveness of a material used in a machine depends on how it reacts to stress.

2/3 The factors which produce stress in a mechanical component.

🎧 Exercise B

Refer students to the lecture slides.

1 Ask students to make the list. Do not confirm or correct.
2 Play Part 1. Feed back orally.
3 Set for pairwork discussion then individual work. Feed back.

Answers

1 Answers depend on the students.
2 We are told there are five ways of applying force. When considering the best way to make notes about this text, these five key words are the key.
3 The best way is probably to write 1–5 then the five key words in the left-hand column. Don't tell them the ones they can't remember. It would be quite normal in a lecture that they can't write all of them down. If they don't remember them all this time, they should at least put the key words they remember in order. They can then listen for the other key words as the text develops.

Transcript 🎧 1.18

Part 1

In the last lecture we talked about the stress in a mechanical component due to the forces applied to it. The amount of stress in a component depends on five factors, including the *way* the force is applied, and, of course, the material itself.

Let's concentrate today on the *way* the force is applied. The directions of forces all break down into five types: *tension, compression, shear, torque* and *bending*.

🎧 Exercise C

Play Part 2 of the lecture. Students should recognize the rhetorical structure – see Answers section – and complete, in effect, a table. When students have done their best individually, put them in pairs or small groups to complete their notes by asking for information from the other student(s).

In the feedback about the direction, allow the correct meaning, not just these words.

Answers

Model answers:

Type of force	Direction	Example
tension	outwards, pulling	the cable of a crane
compression	inwards, pushing	an object in a vice
shear	parallel	two plates riveted together
torque	turning, twisting	a key, a screwdriver, a drive shaft
bending	curving	the jib of a crane, a bridge, a car park

Transcript 🎧 1.19

Part 2

Tension is the pulling force which acts along the length of the component. In other words, the movement is outwards or away from the load. The cable of a crane lifting a load is an example of this. *Compression*, on the other hand, is the opposite. It is a pushing force. The movement is inwards, towards the load. Think of *press*, as in a table vice. Both these forces are uniaxial – that is, the action and reaction act along the same axis, as shown in slides 1 and 6.

When a component is under *shear*, however, although there are still two equal and opposite forces, they are parallel, not uniaxial. Think of a pair of wire cutters. Another good example of a shearing force is a rivet joining two plates, as in slide 2. The rivet is being pulled two ways and, as a result, is the weakest point of the component. Failure at the rivets is common.

Torque is the twisting force. The simplest example of this is a key being turned in a lock. Or a screwdriver turning in the slot of a screw. An example of a large component under torque is the driveshaft of a machine.

Bending occurs when the load action and reaction are further apart. We've already talked about a crane. Look again at the jib – that is, the arm of the crane in slide 1. One end is supported by the structure. A load is suspended from the other end. The natural effect of this is for the jib to bend – to curve down. And it is only the reaction in the structure and the strength of the material which prevents it. This kind of structure – that is, held at one end only – is called a cantilever. Many sports stadiums and car parks are covered by a cantilever roof.

Alternatively, take a beam held at either end, but supporting a load halfway along – for example, a truck parked halfway across a small bridge. The deformation caused by this force would be a downward curve. We can see this more clearly in slide 5. When a component is under a bending force, the outside of the curve is under *tension*, but the inside is under *compression*.

🎧 Exercise D

Set for pairwork. Play Part 3 of the lecture. As before, give students time to do their own work, then set for pair or group completion.

Answers

Model answer:

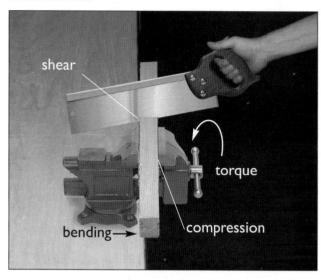

Transcript 🎧 1.20

Part 3

Of course, these different forces don't act alone. A machine will normally have several forces acting in different ways, but as long as it is well designed it will be in equilibrium and will work efficiently. Let's look at one very simple example from the workshop. The table vice. You know how a table vice works – let's have a look at slide 6 now. You turn the handle and the screw thread pulls one set of jaws in to grip the work – a piece of wood, for example. When you turn the handle, you are applying a bending force, but the handle is applying torque to the screw, which in turn applies compression to the work in the vice. If you then saw a piece of the work off, this is a shearing force.

🎧 Exercise E

Set for individual work and pairwork checking. Play Part 4 of the lecture. Feed back orally. Point out that if students do miss information on the way through a lecture, they should wait for the recap which often comes at the end. This recap may enable them to fill in some of the missing information.

Answer

Model answer:

So he/she can choose the right material for the job in hand.

Transcript 🎧 1.21

Part 4

So, to recap, we are looking at stress in components. So far, we have seen the different ways that force can be applied. In industry today, there is much research into methods of processing metals, composite materials and alloys to produce materials which react well to different types of force, so that the mechanical engineer can find the right material for the job in hand.

Exercise F

Refer students to the transcript at the back of the Course Book.

1 Help students to find a key section. Set for individual work to find more.

2 Help students to find a key sentence. Set for individual work to find more.

3 Set for pairwork – students help each other. Monitor and assist.

4 Put students in groups to check whether they have all found the same sections/sentences.

At the end, play the part of the absent student. Act a little stupid – unless a student is absolutely clear in their summary and/or direct quotation, deliberately misunderstand and get another student to try to clarify.

Methodology note

End all listening lessons by referring students to the transcript so they can read the text while the aural memory is still clear. You could set this as standard homework after a listening lesson. You can also get students to highlight key sections and underline key sentences, as in Exercise F above.

Exercise G

Set for individual work and pairwork checking. Feed back, getting the words and definitions on the board.

Answers

forming a curve	bending
a uniaxial pushing force	compression
opposite parallel forces	shear
a uniaxial pulling force	tension
a turning force	torque

Exercise H

Set for pairwork. Monitor and assist. Feed back,
writing the words on the board as students correctly
identify them. Check pronunciation and stress patterns.

Answers

1	ductile	e	easy to stretch
2	elastic	f	returns to its original shapec
3	flexible	c	has a high fatigue point
4	hardness	d	resists wear
5	plastic (adj)	a	doesn't return to its original shape
6	rigid	h	difficult to bend
7	strain	g	deformation caused by stressb
8	stress	b	reaction to a force

Exercise I

Set for individual work and pairwork checking.

Closure

Ask students to think of another example for each type
of force shown in the lecture slides and draw a sketch
of how the force operates.

1 Work through the *Vocabulary bank* and *Skills bank* if you have not already done so, or as a revision of previous study.

2 Use the *Activity bank* (Teacher's Book additional resources section, Resource 3A).

A Set the crossword for individual work (including homework) or pairwork.

Answers

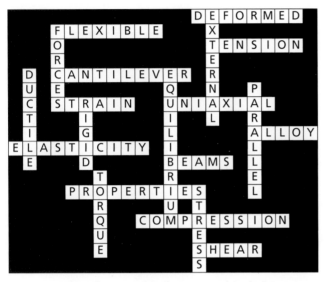

Note: The completed crossword includes one prefix, *uni-*, and one suffix, *-ity*. There are also some non-technical words as follows:

ability
had
lie
notes
or
rate
so
use
you.

B This game practises pronunciation and meaning recognition. It can only be played in groups in class.

Students must think of one word for each of the categories on the bingo card. Allow them to use any of the vocabulary from this unit. They should write their words on card 1, or copy the bingo grid into their notebooks.

Each student says one of their words at random once only, concentrating on the pronunciation. The others must identify the category and cross it out on card 2.

The winner is the first student to identify the correct category for all the words. If the teacher keeps a record of which words have been said, he/she can say when a successful card could have been completed.

3 Students can play this alphabet game by themselves or as a group/class. The aim is to think of a word related to mechanical engineering for each letter of the alphabet. For example:

Student A: aluminium

Student B: aluminium, **b**eam

Student C: aluminium, beam, **c**omponent

Each student adds something from the next letter of the alphabet. They should try to use words from the unit if possible. A student misses a turn if he/she can't remember the items, or add another letter.

4 Get students to research air accidents which have been caused by each kind of stress. They will need to search with key words such as "air accident torque".

Note that a lot of the details will be in very complex English, but students should be able to record the basic details of each accident and report back in the next lesson.

4 COMPUTERS IN ENGINEERING

The theme of this unit is computers. Two aspects of the use of computers relevant to engineering students are addressed: their use in **manufacturing** and their use in **education**. Lessons 4.1, 4.3 and 4.4 guide students to a more efficient use of the Internet and computers in research. Lesson 4.2 looks at the computerization of manufacturing. Note that students will need access to a computer with an Internet connection for some exercises in this unit.

Skills focus

Reading
- identifying topic development within a paragraph
- using the Internet effectively
- evaluating research results

Writing
- reporting research findings

Vocabulary focus
- computer jargon
- abbreviations and acronyms
- discourse and stance markers
- verb and noun suffixes

Key vocabulary

access (n and v)	integral	password
browse	integrate	search (n and v)
compatible	interface (n)	search engine
computerize	interlink (v)	search results
database	keyword	software
document	log in/log on	specification
hardware	log off	username/ID
hyperlink	menu	
input (n and v)	output (n and v)	

Abbreviations and acronyms

The *Jargon Buster* on page 31 of the Course Book lists the meanings of most of these.

CAD	HTML	PDF	URL
CAL	HTTP	PIN	USB
CAM	ISP	PPT	WAN
CIM	LCD	ROM	WWW

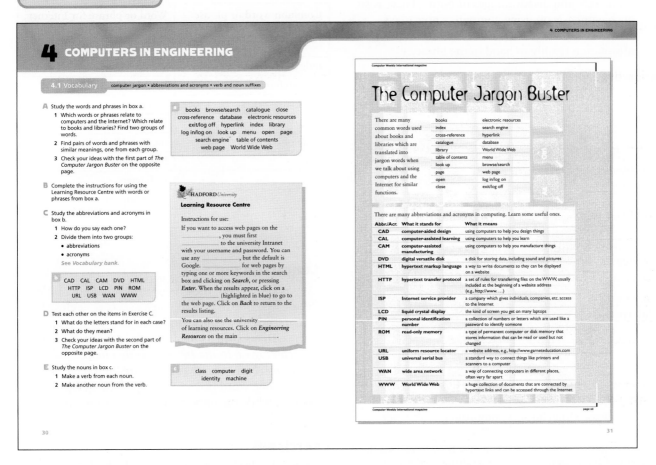

General note

If possible, hold this lesson in a room where there is a computer, or bring in a computer.

Read the *Vocabulary bank* at the end of the Course Book unit. Decide when, if at all, to refer your students to it. The best point is probably Exercise C, or at the very end of the lesson or the beginning of the next lesson, as a summary/revision.

Lesson aim

- gain fluency in the meaning, pronunciation and spelling of key computing terms, acronyms and abbreviations
- understand how verbs can be formed from nouns, and nouns from verbs, through the addition of suffixes

Introduction

Familiarize students with computer terminology using some or all of the following activities.

1   Using a computer or a picture of a computer as a starting point, elicit some or all of the following terms:

PC	CPU (central	USB port
laptop	processing unit)	accessory
monitor	hard disk	printer
screen	floppy disk	scanner
desktop	program	Internet
icon	slot	e-mail
keyboard	CD	database
keys	CD burner	
mouse	DVD	

2   Ask students to suggest verbs used in computing. Elicit some or all of the following. A good way to do this is to open a program such as Word (in English) and look at the words and symbols on the toolbars.

switch on	press	paste
start up	open	enter
shut down	close	delete
log on/log off	exit	insert
click	save	highlight
double-click	select	undo
hold	copy	

3 Ask students whether they normally use the library or the Internet to find information. Elicit the advantages and disadvantages of both. (There is so much emphasis on using computers nowadays, students often forget that there is a lot of information readily to hand in the library.)

Answers

Possible answers:

Library

+	–
easy to look things up in a dictionary or an encyclopedia	books can be out of date
you can find information in your own language	the book may not be in the library when you want it
information is usually correct	most books can't be accessed from home (though this is now starting to change)

Internet

+	–
a lot of information from different sources	difficult to find the right keywords
information is usually more up-to-date than books	difficult to know which results are the best
can be accessed from home	information is often not correct
you can quickly and easily get copies of books or journal articles not in your library	you may have to pay for the books/articles/information

Exercise A

Ask students to study the words in the box and elicit that they all relate to research.

Set for pairwork. If necessary, give an example of a pair: *index*, *search engine*. Tell students to justify the pairs they choose. To help students understand what a database is, refer to ones they are familiar with in your college, e.g., student records, exam results, library catalogues, etc.

Students may argue that some terms are not exact equivalents, e.g., *catalogue/database*. Discuss any objections as they arise.

Answers

Model answers:

Common word or phrase for books and libraries	Word or phrase for Internet and electronic information
books	electronic resources
index	search engine
cross-reference	hyperlink
catalogue	database
library	World Wide Web
table of contents	menu
look up	browse/search
page	web page
open	log in/log on
close	exit/log off

Language note

Log in and *log on*: these two verbs are used a little differently. *Log in* is used when accessing a closed system such as a college Intranet. *Log on* is used for open systems such as the Internet in general, as in *You can log on to the Internet with a hand-held computer*. Note also that the related noun has now become one word (*login*). The opposite of *log in* is *log out*, while the opposite of *log on* is *log off*.

Exercise B

Set for individual work and pairwork checking. Ensure that students read *all* the text and have a general understanding of it before they insert the missing words.

Feed back by reading the paragraph or by using an OHT or other visual display of the text. Discuss alternative ideas and decide whether they are acceptable. Verify whether errors are due to using new words or to misunderstanding the text.

Answers

Model answers:

If you want to access web pages on the <u>World Wide Web</u>, you must first <u>log in</u> to the university Intranet with your username and password. You can use any <u>search engine</u>, but the default is Google. <u>Browse/Search</u> for web pages by typing one or more keywords in the search box and clicking on *Search*, or pressing *Enter*. When the results appear, click on a <u>hyperlink</u> (highlighted in blue) to go to the web page. Click on *Back* to return to the results listing.

You can also use the university <u>database</u> of learning resources. Click on *Engineering Resources* on the main <u>menu</u>.

Exercise C

Set for pairwork. Feed back, eliciting ideas on pronunciation and confirming or correcting. Build up the two lists on the board. Establish that one group are acronyms, i.e., they can be pronounced as words: PIN = /pɪn/. The other group are abbreviations, i.e., they are pronounced as letters: HTTP = H-T-T-P. Drill all the abbreviations and acronyms. Make sure students can say letter names and vowel sounds correctly.

Elicit that words with normal consonant/vowel patterns are *normally* pronounced as a word and those with unusual patterns are *normally* pronounced with single letters. Refer to the *Vocabulary bank* at this stage if you wish.

Methodology note

Don't discuss the meanings at this point. This is covered in the next activity.

Answers

Acronyms: CAD /kæd/, CAL /kæl/, CAM /kæm/, PIN /pɪn/, ROM /rɒm/, WAN /wæn/.

Abbreviations: DVD, HTML, HTTP, ISP, LCD, URL (not pronounced /ɜːl/), USB, WWW.

Exercise D

1 Introduce the verb *stand for*. Elicit examples of common abbreviations and ask what they stand for. Set for pairwork. Tell students to pick out the ones they already know first. Next, they pick out the ones they are familiar with but don't know what they stand for – and guess.

2 Elicit the meanings without reference to the *Jargon Buster* if possible.

3 Refer students to the *Jargon Buster* to verify their answers. As a follow-up, elicit other common abbreviations from IT or engineering.

Language note

If students don't use acronyms or initial abbreviations in their language, a discussion about the reasons for using them is useful. They will then know how to find the meaning of new ones when they meet them. You might point out that abbreviations can sometimes be longer than the thing they abbreviate! For example, World Wide Web is three syllables, whereas WWW is six. It evolved because it is quicker to write, but it is longer, and harder, to say. It is also possible to mix acronyms with abbreviations: for example, JPEG – J /peg/. Point out the field of ICT is developing at an incredible speed and new acronyms and abbreviations are constantly being created.

Exercise E

Set for individual work and pairwork checking. Feed back, highlighting the changes from noun form to verb in the case of *identity/identify* and *machine/mechanize*.

Answers

Model answers:

Noun 1	Verb	Noun 2
class	classify	classification
computer	computerize	computerization
digit	digitize	digitization
identity	identify	identification
machine	mechanize	mechanization

Language note

Both *~ise/~ize* (*~isation/~ization*) forms are acceptable in British English. American English usage is *~ize* (*~ization*).

Closure

Ask students whether they agree with the following statements.

1 Every college student must have a computer.

2 The college library uses a computer to help students find information.

3 College departments use computers to store research data.

4 Students can't do research without a computer.

5 College computers can access research data from other colleges and universities.

6 College computers can access research data from businesses and the media.

7 A personal computer can store information students think is important.

8 Computers can help us to talk with students from other colleges and universities.

9 Computers can help students access data from anywhere in the world.

10 A computer we can carry in our pocket can access worldwide data.

4.2 Reading

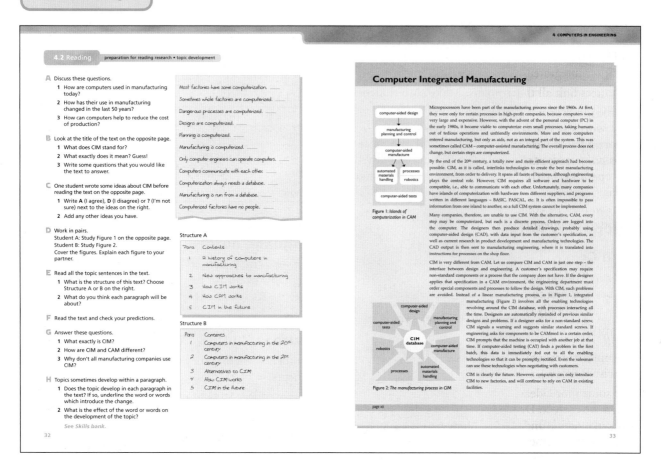

Lesson aim

- prepare to read a text by looking at the title, figures, topic sentences
- understand the purpose of discourse markers and stance markers in the development of a topic

Introduction

Ask students how, where and why they use computers. They should answer in some detail with examples. Encourage them to use the vocabulary, abbreviations and acronyms from Lesson 4.1.

Exercise A

Set for general discussion. Allow students to debate differences of opinion. Encourage them to give examples if they can.

Answers

Possible answers:

1 In all departments, to keep records, control processes, assist in design and planning, monitor quality, store data, inform the workforce, etc.

2 Fifty years ago: a large central computer operated by computer engineers. Now: a network of individual computers around the factory operated by the workforce.

3 Production costs involve labour, time and materials. A computer can reduce the number of workers needed. It can make the production process quicker and more efficient; it can reduce wastage of materials.

Exercise B

1 Write the title of the reading text on the board.

2 Set the question for general discussion. Encourage students to define CIM or speculate on what it might mean.

3 Set for pairwork. Tell students to think of four or five questions with different *Wh~* question words:
What ...?
Where ...?

When ...?
Why ...?
How ...?

Answers

Model answers:

1 Computer-integrated manufacturing.

2 Computers link all the processes of manufacture.

3 Possible questions:
What processes can be computerized?
Where do people use CIM?
When did people start using it?
Who operates the computers?
Why is CIM used?
How can they be computerized?/How can the computers be integrated?

Exercise C

1 Set for individual work and pairwork checking. Feed back, trying to get consensus on each point, but do not actually confirm or correct. Preface your remarks with phrases like: *So most of you think ... You all believe ...* Remind students to look back at these predictions while they are reading the text (Exercise F below).

2 Elicit some more ideas, but once again, do not confirm or correct. Draw students' attention to words like *whole* and *always*. Point out that these words make statements very strong. The truth may actually be better expressed with a limiting word, e.g., *most/some/many*, or with words which express possibility such as *may* or *seem*, or adverbs such as *sometimes, usually, often*.

Exercise D

Set for pairwork. Establish that Figure 1 represents CAM, while Figure 2 represents CIM.

Exercise E

Review paragraph structure – i.e., paragraphs usually begin with a topic sentence which makes a statement that is then expanded in the following sentences. Thus, topic sentences give an indication of the contents of the paragraph. You may wish to refer students to the *Skills bank* at this point.

1 Write the topic sentences from the text on an OHT or other visual medium, or use Resource 4B from the additional resources section. Students should use only the topic sentences for this exercise. Set for individual work and pairwork checking.

2 Set for pairwork. Tell students that close analysis of the topic sentences will help them. Feed back with the whole class. Point out any language features which led them to draw their conclusions.

Answers

1 Text structure B.

2 Possible answers:

	Predicted content
Para 1	the development of computers in manufacturing since the 1960s
Para 2	the latest computerized manufacturing technology
Para 3	why some companies can't use CIM/what companies can use instead of CIM
Para 4	how CIM is different from CAM; more details about CIM
Para 5	how CIM will be widely used in the future

Exercise F

Set the reading. Students should make notes on the differences between their predictions and the text.

Answers

Possible answers:

Note: In every paragraph except paragraph 4, the theme is the same, but two aspects of the theme are addressed.

	Predicted content	Actual content
Para 1	the development of computers in manufacturing since the 1960s	The prediction was correct. It describes the development by using two snapshots of events: 1960s and 1980s.
Para 2	the latest computerized manufacturing technology	It starts by describing CIM, but then explains the problems.
Para 3	why some companies can't use CIM/what companies can use instead of CIM	It explains what is used instead of CIM. The problems of CIM were actually given at the end of paragraph 2. Paragraph 3 is actually about alternatives to CIM.
Para 4	how CIM is different from CAM; more details about CIM	The prediction was correct.
Para 5	how CIM will be widely used in the future	The prediction was correct, but is qualified in the paragraph: this will be a slow process, as CIM can only be introduced in new factories.

Exercise G

1/2 Ask students to write answers to these questions.

3 Set for general discussion and feedback.

Answers

Model answers:

1 CIM is a manufacturing system where every process is interlinked through a central database.

2 With CAM, each step of the process is discrete. Some steps may not be computerized. With CIM, all steps are computerized and centrally controlled through a database.

3 Most factories already have islands of computerization, using incompatible computer products. It is very expensive to replace them with a single integrated system.

Exercise H

The purpose of this exercise is for students to try to identify the information structure of each paragraph and to see how a new step in the progression of ideas may be signalled by a rhetorical marker or phrase.

Refer also to the *Skills bank* at the end of this unit. Elicit more examples of discourse markers and stance markers.

Set for pairwork. Feed back. A good idea is to make an OHT or other visual display of the text and use a highlighter to indicate which are the relevant parts of the text. Students should notice that there is not a discernible topic development in every paragraph.

Answers

Possible answers:

	Discourse marker	Stance marker	Effect
Para 1	At first		to show how something was at an earlier point in time (1960s)
	However		to show contrast (in this case past and present)
Para 2	However		to qualify a statement
		Unfortunately	to show regret
Para 3	With the alternative, CAM		to change from negative statement of what companies can't do to positive statement about what they can do instead
	but		to show contrast
Para 4	–	–	
Para 5	However		to qualify a statement or show the other side – CIM cannot be the future for all factories

Methodology note

It could be argued that words like *but*, *however*, and phrases like *on the other hand* do not fundamentally change the topic of a paragraph. Point this out if you wish. However, (change of topic?) they do bring in a concessive element where the reader of a topic sentence might assume that the whole paragraph would be (for example) positive.

Imagine a school report with the topic sentence: *John is an extremely able student*, which then proceeded with a great deal of praise, but ended with the following: *Despite his many good qualities, however, John will have some difficulty in gaining high marks in his exams unless he concentrates more in class*. We could justifiably claim either that:

1 the whole paragraph is about John and his school work

or

2 the paragraph has two topics – John's positive aspects and his negative aspects.

Closure

1 Divide the class into groups. Write the topic sentences on strips, or photocopy them from the additional resources section (Resource 4B). Make a copy for each group. Students must put them into the correct order.

Alternatively, divide the class into two teams. One team chooses a topic sentence and reads it aloud. The other team must give the information triggered by that topic sentence. Accept a prediction or the actual paragraph content. However, ask students which it is – prediction or actual.

Language note

There is no universal logic to the structuring of information in a text. The order of information is language-specific. For example, oriental languages tend to have a topic sentence or paragraph summary at the end, not the beginning, of the paragraph. Or students whose first language is Arabic might structure a particular type of discourse in a different way from native English speakers. So it is important for students to see what a native speaker writer would use as a 'logical' ordering.

2 Refer students back to the sentences in Exercise C. Students should find it easier to comment on these now that they have read the text.

3 Focus on some of the vocabulary from the text, including:

CAM, CIM
compatible
computerize
data
database
hardware
interface
manufacture
microprocessor
personal computer
software
specification

4.3 Extending skills

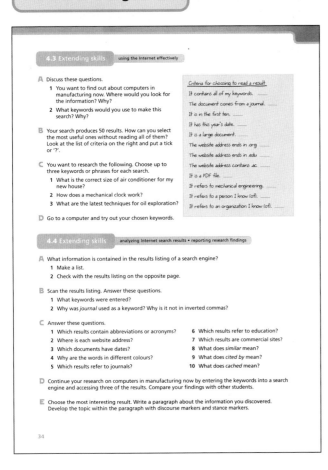

4.3 Extending skills using the Internet effectively

A Discuss these questions.

1. You want to find out about computers in manufacturing now. Where would you look for the information? Why?
2. What keywords would you use to make this search? Why?

B Your search produces 50 results. How can you select the most useful ones without reading all of them? Look at the list of criteria on the right and put a tick or '?'.

C You want to research the following. Choose up to three keywords or phrases for each search.

1. What is the correct size of air conditioner for my new house?
2. How does a mechanical clock work?
3. What are the latest techniques for oil exploration?

D Go to a computer and try out your chosen keywords.

Criteria for choosing to read a result

It contains all of my keywords. ___
The document comes from a journal. ___
It is in the first ten. ___
It has this year's date. ___
It is a large document. ___
The website address ends in .org ___
The website address ends in .edu ___
The website address contains .ac ___
It is a PDF file. ___
It refers to mechanical engineering. ___
It refers to a person I know (of). ___
It refers to an organization I know (of). ___

4.4 Extending skills analyzing Internet search results • reporting research findings

A What information is contained in the results listing of a search engine?

1. Make a list.
2. Check with the results listing on the opposite page.

B Scan the results listing. Answer these questions.

1. What keywords were entered?
2. Why was *journal* used as a keyword? Why is it not in inverted commas?

C Answer these questions.

1. Which results contain abbreviations or acronyms?
2. Where is each website address?
3. Which documents have dates?
4. Why are the words in different colours?
5. Which results refer to journals?
6. Which results refer to education?
7. Which results are commercial sites?
8. What does *similar* mean?
9. What does *cited by* mean?
10. What does *cached* mean?

D Continue your research on computers in manufacturing now by entering the keywords into a search engine and accessing three of the results. Compare your findings with other students.

E Choose the most interesting result. Write a paragraph about the information you discovered. Develop the topic within the paragraph with discourse markers and stance markers.

34

General note

Students will need access to a computer with an Internet connection. If computers are not available during the lesson, this part of the lesson can be set for private study.

Lesson aim

- learn or practise how to use the Internet effectively for research

Introduction

1. Brainstorm the uses of the Internet. Then brainstorm what the important factors are when using the Internet. These should include:
   - the search engines students use and why
   - how to choose *and write* keywords in their preferred search engine
   - how they extract the information they want from the results
2. Put students in groups and ask them to compare how they normally use a computer to find information. Ask each group to produce some advice for using the Internet. Then discuss as a class.

Key words to elicit: *search engine, keyword, website, web page, website address, search result, subject directory*

Note: Where the subject is a new one or a fairly general topic, it is a good idea to start first with a **subject directory** which evaluates sites related to the topic and collects them in one place. Some examples are: Academic Info; BUBL LINK; INFOMINE; The WWW Virtual Library.

Exercise A

Write *computers in manufacturing* on the board.

1. Set for class discussion. Make sure students give reasons for their answers. Accept their answers at this stage.
2. Remind students that words in English often have more than one meaning, so care must be taken to get the desired result.

Answers

Possible answers:

1. In a current technical journal – very useful, as recent articles give the latest information.

   On the Internet – good if the correct keywords are used and a careful selection of results is made. Since it is a general topic, it would benefit from a search with a subject directory such as The World Wide Web Virtual Library on http://vlib.org/.

   In a textbook – useful if there is an up-to-date one, but books take time to publish, so even the latest may be out of date in these technologically fast-moving times.
2. In this list of possible keywords, the first three are obvious starting points; others are also possible.

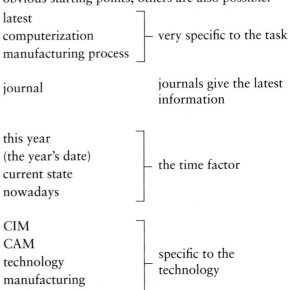

latest computerization manufacturing process	very specific to the task
journal	journals give the latest information
this year (the year's date) current state nowadays	the time factor
CIM CAM technology manufacturing production	specific to the technology

Exercise B

Set for pairwork. Remind students of the research topic.

Feed back, encouraging students to give reasons for their decisions. Emphasize that we only know what *might* be useful at this stage.

Establish that company names often end in .com

Answers

Possible answers:

- ✓ It contains all of my keywords. (*but check that the meaning is the same*)
- ✓ The document comes from a journal. (*current information*)
- ? It is in the first ten. (*a web page can have codes attached to put it high in the list*)
- ✓ It has this year's date. (*current information*)
- ? It is a large document. (*size is no indication of quality*)
- ✓ The website address ends in .org (*because it is a non-profit organization*)
- ✓ The website address ends in .edu (*because it is an educational establishment*)
- ✓ The website address contains .ac (*because it is an educational establishment*)
- ? It is a PDF file. (*file type is no indication of quality*)
- ? It refers to mechanical engineering. (*may not be relevant*)
- ✓ It refers to a person I know (of). (*reliable*)
- ✓ It refers to an organization I know (of). (*reliable*)

> **Language note**
>
> PDF stands for *portable document format*. PDF documents can be viewed and printed on most computers, without the need for each computer to have the same software, fonts, etc. They are created with Adobe Acrobat software.

Exercise C

Set for individual work and pairwork checking. Ask students to compare their choice of keywords with their partner, and justify their choice.

Answers

See Exercise D.

Exercise D

Students should try out different combinations to discover for themselves which gives the best results.

Closure

Tell students to think of their own question for research, as in Exercise C, and find the best web page for the data by entering appropriate keywords.

Ask students to write their question on a piece of paper and sign it. Put all the questions in a box. Students pick out one of the questions at random and go online to find the best page of search results. From those results they can find the most useful web page. They should ask the questioner for verification.

4.4 Extending skills

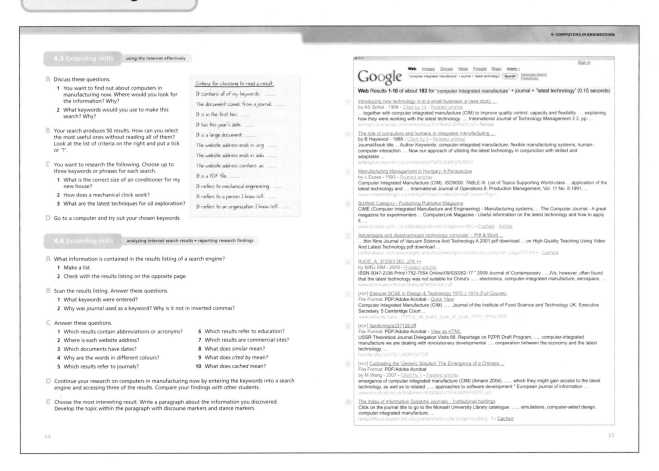

General note

Students will need access to a computer with an Internet connection. If computers are not available during the lesson, this part of the lesson can be set for private study.

Lesson aims

- examine a page of Internet search results critically
- report Internet search findings in a short written summary

Introduction

Ask students what problems they had, what lessons they have learnt and what advice they can give from their Internet search experience in Lesson 4.3. Brainstorm the important factors when searching for information on the Internet and put them in order of importance.

Exercise A

Set for pairwork. Students should first make a list of information they expect to find in search engine results. (They should do this before they look at the search engine results on the right-hand page.) They should then look at the page of results and identify any other information that is there.

Answers

Possible answers:

> number of results
> keywords used
> time taken
> title of document
> type of document
> quotations from the text with keywords highlighted
> date
> web address/URL

70

Exercise B

This is further reinforcement on keywords. Set for pairwork or whole class discussion.

Answers

Model answers:

1 "computer integrated manufacturing", journal, "latest technology"

2 Because journals give the most current information. Inverted commas are put round a phrase to indicate that it is a single meaningful lexical item. In Google, *journal* does not need them, as it is one word.

Exercise C

This detailed examination of the results page should make students aware of the content, so that they can make an educated selection of a web page with useful information. Set for pairwork.

Make sure, in feedback, that students are aware of what the following abbreviations stand for: FTP (file transfer protocol), PDF (portable document format), PPT (PowerPoint), RTF (rich text format).

Answers

Possible answers:

1 Acronyms/abbreviations:

Result 1: Vol.

Result 2: PDF

Result 3: (in website address) www, html, k

Result 4: RTF, HTML

Result 5: PDF, HTML

Result 6: PPT, HTML, p.

Result 7: ORCS, SCI.OP, CFP, OR/MS

Result 8: (in website address) www, html, k

Result 9: (in website address) htm, k

Note: Students may identify further abbreviations in the website addresses.

2 At the end.

3 At the end (if it is given), e.g., 27k.

4 Results 1, (6), 8.

5 Blue = titles and viewing information; green = website address; black = keywords.

6 Results 1, 6, 7.

7 In the heading: 4, 5; in the web address: 1, 3, 4, 5, 7, 8.

8 Results 2, 6.

9 There were other very similar results, so the search engine ignored them. They are available if you click on the words.

10 It is a more efficient way of storing information. (It means that you can go to a copy of the page stored by Google, in case the actual website happens to be down at the time of the search; of course, it could be a little out of date.)

Domain/ organizational code	Type of organization
.ac .edu	educational
.aero	aviation
.biz	business
.co .com	commercial
.gov	government
.org	non-government, non-profit
.net	networks

Country code	Country
.uk	United Kingdom
.hk	Hong Kong
.cn	China
.au	Australia
.de	Germany
.fr	France
.ie	Ireland
.at	Austria

Exercise D

Set the search for individual work. Students should input the keywords again. They will not get exactly the same results page as here, but the results should be comparable. Tell them to take notes.

Feed back, getting students to tell the rest of the class about their most interesting findings. Encourage other students to ask questions.

Exercise E

Set for individual work. Students can complete it in class or for homework.

Closure

1 Focus on some of the vocabulary connected with using the Internet, including:

website
web(site) address/URL
search engine
search results
input
keyword
key in
log in/log on
username
password
access

2 The importance of the care needed when selecting keywords can be demonstrated by a simple classroom activity. Tell the class you are thinking of a particular student who you want to stand up. Say (for example):

It's a man. (all the men stand up and remain standing)

He has dark hair. (only those with dark hair remain standing)

He has a beard.

He has glasses.

He's tall.

His name begins with A.

And so on.

When only one student remains, ask the class to list the minimum number of keywords necessary to identify only that student. Make sure they discard unnecessary ones. For example, if all students have dark hair, that is unnecessary.

3 Finding the keywords for familiar topics is another activity, done in groups. For example, they could:
- find their own college record (name, ID number or date of entry)
- find their last exam results (name, class, subject, date)
- find a book in the library about robots used in manufacturing (robot, manufacture, factory, etc.)

Extra activities

1 Work through the *Vocabulary bank* and *Skills bank* if you have not already done so, or as a revision of previous study.

2 Use the *Activity bank* (Teacher's Book additional resources section, Resource 4A).

A Set the wordsearch for individual work (including homework) or pairwork.

Answers

Verb	Noun
apply	application
classify	classification
computerize	computerization
condense	condensation
deform	deformation
evaporate	evaporation
innovate	innovation
install	installation
insulate	insulation
integrate	integration
interact	interaction
lubricate	lubrication
mechanize	mechanization
modify	modification
operate	operation
pressurize	pressurization
rectify	rectification
refrigerate	refrigeration
replace	replacement
specify	specification

B Set for pairwork. Teach students how to play noughts and crosses if they don't know – they take it in turns to say the abbreviation or acronym, and what it stands for. If they succeed, they can put their symbol – a nought **O** or a cross **X** – in that box. If a person gets three of their own symbols in a line, they win.

3 Write the acronyms and abbreviations from the unit on cards, or photocopy them from the additional resources section (Resource 4C). Divide the class into two teams. A student selects a card and reads it correctly. (Speed is of the essence.) Alternatively, one team picks a card with an acronym or abbreviation; the other team gives the actual words.

4 Elicit other acronyms and abbreviations from the students – in particular, common/useful ones from the field of engineering.

5 Have a class debate: 'CAL is better than face-to-face learning.' Ask two students to prepare an opening argument for and against.

Some points:

For:

- Students are acquiring computer skills that they will need throughout their lives.
- Computers are non-judgemental and students have the opportunity to do and redo exercises as many times as they want/need to.
- Students can work at their own pace.
- Resources aren't confined to the classroom – they can be accessed from other areas, such as the school library or from home.
- CAL can save money – by reducing the number of classrooms/teachers needed.
- CAL gives people who can't attend a face-to-face course (for example, because of distance or mobility problems) the chance to study.
- CAL can be used to extend the range of subjects on offer – for example, if only one student in a school wants to study Greek, it wouldn't be worth employing a teacher. However, the student could study with an online teacher.

Against:

- Not all institutions can afford modern technology.
- It isn't always practical to use a lot of

technology – for example, in areas where there is a poor electricity supply.

- Online resources are only useful if the students who want to use them can access the Internet – this can be difficult and/or expensive in some areas of the world.
- Software and hardware can be expensive – it is not a one-off investment as equipment needs to be kept up-to-date.
- CDs/DVDs can go out of date just as quickly as textbooks.
- Staff training is required – this can be expensive and not all teachers are enthusiastic about CAL.
- Students also need to be trained to use CAL properly, if they are to benefit; this can be time-consuming.
- Students may miss the human contact they have in a face-to-face class.

6 Ask students to work in small groups to research and feed back to the group on other mechanical engineering achievements of the 20th century (see Unit 2, Lesson 2.2). The three research questions could be the same as in Unit 2. If students are going to do research on the Internet, suggest that they type in *History* then their topic to get some potential texts. Alternatively, you can do this research before the lesson and print off some pages for students to work from.

Remind students that they can't possibly read everything they find, so they must use the topic sentences to decide if a paragraph is worth reading.

7 Write *What makes a good website?* on the board. Put students in small groups to make a list of things that they think make a good website – tell them to consider both content and technical details.

Ask students to research how to evaluate websites on the Internet. Useful keywords might be: *website + evaluation + checklist*. Tell students to compare their ideas with the information on the Internet. Do they need to add any more details to their list?

Ask students to design an evaluation checklist and then choose a website that they like/use regularly and evaluate it using their checklist. Give students time to present their website to the class.

Note that for this activity you might like to suggest your students evaluate a website for English language learning. At the end of the activity, you could produce a list of language-learning resources for your students to try out.

5 MEMS AND NANOTECHNOLOGY

The theme of this unit is micro-technologies: MEMS and nanotechnology. The focus is on the design and application of products and materials at very small sizes. The unit also looks at the implications of current and future uses of nanotechnology. The first listening extract, from a lecture, gives a broad introduction to both types of technology. The second listening extract is from a seminar about the safety and ethics of nanotechnology. This leads into seminar practice, followed by a research activity on three further areas of research referred to in the lecture: the history of nanotechnology, current applications and the future of nanotechnology.

Skills focus

 Listening

- understanding 'signpost language' in lectures
- using symbols and abbreviations in note-taking

Speaking

- making effective contributions to a seminar

Vocabulary focus

- word sets: synonyms, antonyms, etc.
- the language of trends
- common lecture language

Key vocabulary

accelerometer	MEMS	rigid
analysis	method	scale (n)
application	micro	sensor
atom	micron (µm)	silicon chip
conductivity	mixture	solid
device	modify	sophisticated
electro-mechanical	molecule	stabilize
element	nanoparticle	strength
ethics	nanotechnology	synthesis
figure	polymer	system
flexible	practical	technique
gyroscope	pressure	three-dimensional
implication	process	tiny
industrial	quantum mechanics	transparent
layer (n)	reaction	use (n)
liquid	repellent	viscosity
manipulate	resistant	volume

5.1 Vocabulary

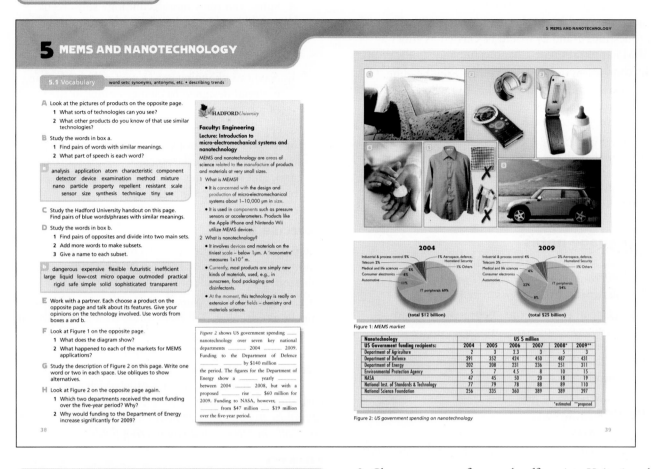

General note

Read the *Vocabulary bank – Vocabulary sets* and *Describing trends* at the end of the Course Book unit. Decide when, if at all, to refer your students to it. The best time is probably at the very end of the lesson or the beginning of the next lesson, as a summary/revision.

Lesson aims

- gain an understanding of lexical cohesion in texts through building word sets, synonyms and opposites/converses
- use appropriate language for describing trends

Introduction

Do some vocabulary revision from the previous units. For example:

1 Choose some words with different meanings in general English and English used in the field of mechanical engineering (see Units 1 and 2). Ask students to say or write two sentences using each word with a different meaning. Some examples are: *couple, cycle, coat, housing, cap,* etc. If necessary, students can work with their dictionaries.

2 Choose some prefixes and suffixes (see Units 1 and 4). Write them on the board. Ask students to give the meaning of the affix and an example of a word.

3 Dictate some of the key vocabulary from Unit 3. Ask students to check their spellings (with a dictionary) and group the words according to their stress patterns.

Exercise A

Set both questions for pairwork discussion and whole class feedback. Do not comment or correct at this point. Students do not need to be able to identify the correct technology, although some may be able to do this. Encourage them to speculate, but do not ask them to give their opinions at this stage (see Exercise E).

Before class feedback, write the headings *MEMS* and *Nanotechnology* on the board.

- Point out that these headings are used instead of more specific words and examples when referring generally to these two technologies.

- Ask if students know what MEMS is an acronym of (micro-electromechanical systems). Elicit prefixes *micro* and *nano* to demonstrate word building.

- Elicit the difference between *micro* and *nano* in terms of measurement. Some students may know. If not, do not give definitions at this point – tell students that they will find the answer as they work through the unit's activities.

Ask students which of their suggestions from Exercise A (questions 1 and 2) would be classed as either a MEMS application or a nanotechnology application.

- Write them on the board under each heading. Correct and inform (very briefly) where appropriate, using information from the model answers below for Exercise A1. Save any discussion for Exercise E.

- Note that all the picture prompts are *nanotechnology applications*, but students should be able to come up with some suggestions for MEMS from Exercise A2.

Language notes

- MEMS is also alternatively written as *micro-electro-mechanical systems* and *MicroElectroMechanical systems*.

- General words/terms such as *MEMS* and *nanotechnology* are called hypernyms or superordinate terms. Words like *sensor* and *accelerometer* are called hyponyms or class members.

Answers

Model answers:

1 1 A wiperless car windshield that is water and dirt repelling.
  2 Mobile phones made with semi-transparent flexible materials.

3 A disinfection light/a hand-held device that disinfects things, e.g., cutlery, baby bottle.

4 Sunscreen (new nanotechnology sunscreens would be clear rather than white).

5 Wrinkle-resistant, stain-repellent clothes/new types of materials for clothes.

6 A colour-changing car (a new polymer/coating material designed to change colour at the touch of a button).

2 Accept all reasonable answers. Some suggestions for MEMS applications are inkjet print heads, sensors, MEMS accelerometers (e.g., for airbags in cars), and similar devices used in many fields (biomedical, for example).

Exercise B

The purpose of this exercise is to build sets of synonyms. This not only helps in understanding textual cohesion, but is useful for paraphrasing.

Set both questions for pairwork. Students should look for pairs of words/items. Tell them to use their dictionaries if necessary to check the grammatical information, and to note if they find other words with similar meanings.

Feed back with the whole class, building up a table on the board, and eliciting other words which can be used with the same meaning. *Note that some synonyms cannot be used as replacement words in some contexts, especially in science and engineering fields.*

Answers

Model answers:

1/2 See table below.

Word 1	Part of speech	Word 2	Part of speech	Words with similar meanings/notes
analysis	n (C)	examination	n (C)	study, investigation, exploration
application	n (C)	use	n (C)	function, purpose, utilization, employment
atom	n (C)	particle	n (C)	molecule, element point out that all these words are similar, but the choice of correct word depends on the context
characteristic	n (C)	property	n (C)	feature, trait, quality, attribute
component	n (C)	device	n (C)	part (esp. for automobiles), mechanism, appliance, application, gadget
detector	n (C)	sensor	n (C)	point out that there is no appropriate replacement word for sensor in a technical sense; detector basically describes what a sensor does
method	n (C)	technique	n (C)	way, approach, procedure
mixture	n (C)	synthesis	n (C)	combination, blend, fusion
nano	adj	tiny	adj	miniscule, microscopic, hardly visible point out that there is no appropriate replacement word for nano in a technical sense
repellent (sp. also repellant)	n and adj	resistant	adj	proof (as a suffix), e.g., waterproof, damp-proof, bullet-proof
scale	n (C)	size	n (C)	range, measure the choice of correct word depends on the context

Exercise C

Set for individual work and pairwork checking. Feed back with the whole class.

Note that some of the pairs are from the blue box in Exercise B. Other pairs are general purpose words frequent in academic contexts.

Check the meaning of any unknown words in the text (e.g., *μm, accelerometer, utilize, nanometre, extension*).

Language note

μm is the symbol for *micrometer* or *micron*. A micron is one millionth of a metre.

Answers

Model answers:

General purpose words	
areas	fields
related to	concerned with
manufacture (n)	production
currently	at the moment

Words from the blue box in Exercise B	
size	scale
components	devices

Exercise D

1 Set for pairwork. Tell students to find all the opposites first and then discuss how the pairs of opposites can first be separated into two **main** sets. Elicit suggestions with reasons. You may need to guide students by telling them how many pairs should be in each of the two sets, and correct where appropriate. Elicit a word or short phrase which describes the two main sets (suggestions are *Physical Properties/Qualities and Evaluative Words/Words that show opinion/judgement*). Feed back on the board (or OHT). Complete the titles of each set and the first column of each table as shown in the Answers section.

2 Do the first pair of words with the whole class as an example. Set the remainder for pairwork. Feed back, completing the second column of each table on the board to create each subset. See also the *Language note* on the next page.

3 Discuss with the whole class. Elicit a word or phrase which describes each subset and add this to the table. See also the *Language note* on the next page.

Answers

Possible answers:

See table below.

SET A: Physical properties/Qualities		
Opposites	Other words	Suggested names for subsets
flexible / rigid	pliable, ductile, malleable, hard, inflexible, unyielding	(degrees of) flexibility
large / micro	sizeable, great, huge, minute, miniscule, tiny	size
liquid / solid	fluid, wet, hard, fixed (as in shape and volume)	states of matter
opaque / transparent	dense, not clear, solid, semi-transparent, clear, see-through	(degrees of) transparency

SET B: Evaluative words/Words that show opinion/judgement		
expensive / low-cost	cheap, inexpensive, economical, cost-effective, costly	cost
dangerous / safe	unsafe, hazardous, risky, harmful, harmless, non-toxic	(degrees of) safety
productive / inefficient	functional, effective, useful, realistic, impractical, unworkable, unfeasible	(degrees of) efficiency/productivity
futuristic / outmoded	advanced, revolutionary, ultramodern, ahead of its time, innovative, old-fashioned, long-established, conventional, traditional	degrees of modernity
simple / sophisticated	basic, primitive, crude, elementary, uncomplicated, advanced, complex, hi-tech	degrees of sophistication

Exercise E

Students can work either in pairs or small groups.
Distribute the table below, which is reproduced on
page 255 (Resource 5B) and contains extra

information and prompts to inform their speaking.
Choose one of the products yourself and invite a
student to work with you to model the task. Talk
about its features and each give your opinions on the
usefulness of the technology involved, using
appropriate vocabulary from boxes a and b and the
tables on the board. Note that this topic and much of
the language will be revisited and extended in Lesson
5.4. Remind students that they must use as much
vocabulary as they can from the lesson, adding other
words or ideas from the table if they need to. Time
should be given for students to look at the notes and
prompts in the table. Feed back as a class discussion.

Answers

Possible answers:
See table below.

Product	Features and language	Evaluation prompts (suggestions only)
1 wiperless car windshield	<ul><li>no windscreen wipers</li><li>transparent nanomaterial constructed in layers</li><li>properties that repel water and dirt</li><li>can screen out harmful rays</li><li>powered by one of the layers that conducts electricity</li></ul>	<ul><li>quite costly to produce? (only prototype manufactured)</li><li>sophisticated process</li><li>safer?</li><li>stronger, lighter, more durable (longer-lasting)</li><li>would it make a difference to driving in bad weather?</li><li>no need to replace wipers</li></ul>
2 mobile phones made with flexible materials	<ul><li>flexible</li><li>bendable, stretchable</li><li>transparent electronics</li><li>can change shape and size</li><li>self-cleaning surfaces</li><li>nanosensors – to monitor health (e.g., blood sugar) and air pollution</li></ul>	<ul><li>futuristic (not available for a good few years)</li><li>how expensive will they initially be?</li><li>sophisticated</li><li>how practical?</li><li>how appealing?</li><li>just a fashion fad?</li></ul>
3 disinfection light	<ul><li>hand-held device; portable; battery-operated</li><li>nano-UV scanner</li><li>compact, collapsible</li><li>for personal use (e.g., toothbrushes, spectacles, mobile phones, kitchen equipment and utensils)</li><li>for office items (e.g., computer keyboards, phones)</li><li>for travellers (airlines, hire cars, restaurants)</li></ul>	<ul><li>commercially available</li><li>quite expensive</li><li>useful</li><li>efficient</li><li>just the latest fad?</li><li>how important is it to disinfect everything we use?</li></ul>
4 sunscreen	<ul><li>use of nanoparticles (zinc oxide or titanium oxide)</li><li>common in many cosmetics</li><li>nanoparticles can make it transparent</li></ul>	<ul><li>could be risky</li><li>could endanger skin cells</li><li>not enough information available regarding risks of nanoparticles</li></ul>
5 wrinkle-resistant, stain-repellent clothes	<ul><li>cotton fibres treated at molecular level</li><li>can be washed less frequently</li><li>size and colour also locked in through chemical treatment</li><li>not permanent (30–50 washes)</li></ul>	<ul><li>appeal of easy-to-care-for clothes? – saves time/money</li><li>more expensive than ordinary clothing, but process not permanent</li><li>wrinkle-resistant does not mean wrinkle-free</li></ul>
6 colour-changing car	<ul><li>colour-changing paints</li><li>special polymer contains paramagnetic nanoparticles</li><li>electric current through paint changes ability to reflect light</li></ul>	<ul><li>what are the benefits?</li><li>useful or just a lifestyle product?</li><li>drawbacks (e.g., getaway cars!)</li></ul>

Exercise F

Introduce the term *market*. Elicit or give a definition for this context, e.g., *Market refers to the group of consumers/manufacturers who are interested in and who purchase a product or service. A product or service may have more than one market.* You may wish to give an example, or elicit suggestions for markets for particular products, e.g., sports cars or golfing holidays.

With the whole class, discuss what Figure 1 shows. Elicit some of the verbs and adverbs which students may need in order to discuss trends in graphs and tables. For example:

Go up	No change	Go down	Adverbs
rise	stay the same	fall	slightly
increase	remain at …	decrease	gradually
grow	doesn't change	decline	steadily
improve	is unchanged	worsen	significantly
double (v)*		drop	sharply
treble (v)*		halve (v)*	dramatically

*Note that these words would not be used in noun form in this context. The verbs are generally used in an intransitive sense when describing trends.

Language note

Other expressions that may also be useful are:

● is (almost) equal to/the same as

● (much) more than/less than

● greater/smaller than

1 Discuss with the whole class. The answer to this question should be one sentence, giving the topic of the graph.

2 Students should write or say a sentence about each MEMS market. Do one as an example together with the class and set the rest for pairwork. Where trends look the same or very similar for any of the application fields, information could be combined in one sentence. Feed back, eliciting sentences from the students. Write correct sentences on the board, or display the model answers on an OHT or other visual medium. Make sure that students notice the prepositions used with the numbers and dates.

Answers

Model answers:

1 The diagram <u>compares</u> MEMS market shares by application fields <u>in</u> 2004 <u>and</u> 2009.

or:

The diagram <u>shows</u> the changes in MEMS market shares, by application field, <u>from</u> 2004 <u>to</u> 2009.

2 *IT peripherals* market share <u>fell</u> <u>significantly</u> from 69% to 54% between 2004 and 2009.

Automotive's market share <u>dropped</u> <u>slightly</u> from 11% to 8% over the period.

Consumer electronics market share <u>increased</u> <u>dramatically</u> from 6% in 2004 to 22% in 2009; in fact, it <u>more than trebled</u> over the period.

Medical & life sciences market share <u>grew</u> by only 1% between 2004 and 2009, from 5% to 6%.

Likewise, *Telecoms'* share <u>increased</u> by only 1%, from 2% to 3%.

This was also the case with *Aerospace, defence, Homeland Security,* whose market share <u>rose</u> from only 1% to 2%.

Industrial & process control share <u>decreased</u> <u>slightly</u> from 5% to 4% between 2004 and 2009.

Underline the verbs and adverbs. Ask students to make nouns from the verbs and adjectives from the adverbs. Alternatively, you could reproduce the table (minus the noun and adjective forms) on the board, on an OHT or on a handout. The incomplete table is reproduced in the additional resources section (Resource 5C) to facilitate this.

Verbs	Nouns	Adverbs	Adjective
rise	a rise	gradually	gradual
increase	an increase	sharply	sharp
grow	growth*	slightly	slight
improve	improvement	markedly	marked
fall	a fall	significantly	significant
decrease	a decrease	rapidly	rapid
drop	a drop	steeply	steep
decline	a decline	steadily	steady

*usually (but not always) uncountable in this sense

Return to the original answer sentences and ask students to make sentences with the same meaning, using the nouns and adjectives in place of the verbs and adverbs. Note that when using the noun + adjective, sentences can be made using *There was …* or *showed*. Do one or two examples orally, then ask students to write the remaining sentences. Feed back.

Answers

Model answers:

IT peripherals market share <u>fell</u> <u>significantly</u> from 69% to 54% between 2004 and 2009.	There was <u>a</u> <u>significant</u> <u>fall</u> in *IT peripherals* market share from 69% to 54% between 2004 and 2009.
Automotive's market share <u>dropped</u> <u>slightly</u> from 11% to 8% over the period.	There was a <u>slight</u> <u>drop</u> in *Automotive's* market share from 11% to 8% over the period.
Consumer electronics market share <u>increased</u> <u>dramatically</u> from 6% in 2004 to 22% in 2009; in fact, it <u>more</u> <u>than</u> <u>trebled</u> over the period.	*Consumer electronics* market share showed a <u>dramatic</u> <u>increase</u> from 6% in 2004 to 22% in 2009…
Medical & life sciences market share <u>grew</u> by only 1% between 2004 and 2009, from 5% to 6%.	There was a <u>growth</u> of only 1% in *Medical & life sciences* market share between 2004 and 2009, from 5% to 6%.
Likewise, *Telecoms'* share <u>increased</u> by only 1%, from 2% to 3%.	Likewise, *Telecoms'* share showed <u>an</u> <u>increase</u> of only 1%, from 2% to 3%.
This was also the case with *Aerospace, defence, Homeland Security*, whose market share <u>rose</u> from only 1% to 2%.	This was also the case with *Aerospace, defence, Homeland Security*, with <u>a</u> <u>rise</u> in market share of only 1% to 2%.
Industrial & process control share <u>decreased</u> <u>slightly</u> from 5% to 4% between 2004 and 2009.	*Industrial & process control* share showed <u>a</u> <u>slight</u> <u>decrease</u> from 5% to 4% between 2004 and 2009.

Exercise G

First ask students to look at Figure 2 and discuss in pairs the information it shows. Feed back. Elicit two types of sentence using a verb/adverb and a noun/adjective to express the changes. For example:

Funding to the Department of Energy <u>increased</u> <u>significantly</u> by $60 million from 2008 to 2009.

Funding to the Department of Energy showed <u>a</u> <u>significant</u> <u>increase</u> of $60 million from 2008 to 2009.

Again, make sure that students notice the prepositions, especially the use of *by* to show the size of the increase.

Set the text completion for individual work and pairwork checking.

Answers

Model answers:

Figure 2 shows US government spending <u>on</u> nanotechnology over seven key national departments <u>from</u>/<u>between</u> 2004 <u>to</u>/<u>and</u> 2009. Funding to the Department of Defence <u>increased</u>/<u>rose</u>/<u>went up</u> <u>dramatically</u> by $140 million <u>over</u>/<u>during</u> the period. The figures for the Department of Energy show a <u>steady</u> yearly <u>increase</u>/<u>rise</u>/<u>growth</u> between 2004 <u>and</u> 2008, but with a proposed <u>significant</u>/<u>marked</u> rise <u>of</u> $60 million for 2009. Funding to NASA, however, <u>decreased</u>/<u>fell</u>/<u>dropped</u> <u>sharply</u>/<u>markedly</u> from $47 million <u>to</u> $19 million over the five-year period.

Exercise H

Set for pairwork The two questions allow students to think critically, using background information, reasoning and speculation. They should be able to see some possible reasons for the trends that could also apply to many other countries. You may wish to teach the difference between the words *imply* and *infer*, for example:

What do the statistics *imply*?

What can we *infer* from the statistics?

Feed back with the whole class.

Answers

Model answers:

1 The Department of Defence (DoD) and the National Science Foundation (NSF) received the most funding. Accept all reasonable answers for the second part of the question. Try to keep the focus of the discussion quite broad, rather than focusing perhaps on US foreign policy. Some suggested reasons are:

- the need to keep ahead with developments in the global 'nanorace' in the face of strong international competition
- heavily funded research and innovations emerging from the NSF would benefit other departments
- a strong focus on national and international security in the 21st century would seem to explain why the DoD is the top funding recipient
- possibilities of chemical and biological warfare could be driving the need for more sophisticated sensors, equipment and clothing, using nanomaterials

- international wars often fought in hostile climates and environments – need for soldiers to cope better (clothing, body armour, lighter equipment, etc.)
- nanomaterials are lighter and stronger – would be ultimately cost effective for the military
- many military innovations were developed for commercial use – effect on economy

2 Funding for new technologies are most probably due to growing political and popular pressure for the government to take action on climate change, soaring energy costs and dependence on oil imports.

Language note

When speculating and offering suggestions, the language of caution should be practised; for example, modal verbs (*can, could, would, might, may*) and other expressions (*it seems that, it appears that, perhaps, would seem to suggest that, probably, possibly,* etc.).

Closure

1 You may want to extend Exercise H to include speculation on the reasons for changes in funding to other departments – for example, the relatively very low, but gradually increasing, funding to the Environmental Protection Agency.

2 Elicit ways in which the statistics in both Figures 1 and 2 could have been presented differently. Which ways would be the most effective?

3 Practise synonyms and opposites for the language of trends, to include verbs, nouns, adverbs and adjectives.

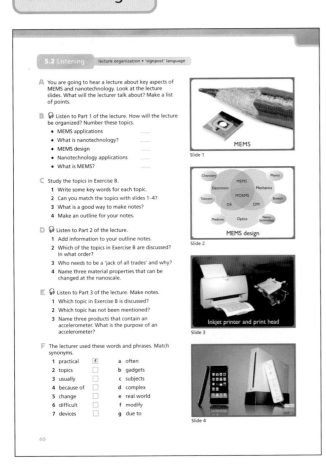

5.2 Listening — lecture organization • 'signpost' language

A You are going to hear a lecture about key aspects of MEMS and nanotechnology. Look at the lecture slides. What will the lecturer talk about? Make a list of points.

B Listen to Part 1 of the lecture. How will the lecture be organized? Number these topics.
• MEMS applications
• What is nanotechnology?
• MEMS design
• Nanotechnology applications
• What is MEMS?

C Study the topics in Exercise B.
1 Write some key words for each topic.
2 Can you match the topics with slides 1–4?
3 What is a good way to make notes?
4 Make an outline for your notes.

D Listen to Part 2 of the lecture.
1 Add information to your outline notes.
2 Which of the topics in Exercise B are discussed? In what order?
3 Who needs to be a 'jack of all trades' and why?
4 Name three material properties that can be changed at the nanoscale.

E Listen to Part 3 of the lecture. Make notes.
1 Which topic in Exercise B is discussed?
2 Which topic has not been mentioned?
3 Name three products that contain an accelerometer. What is the purpose of an accelerometer?

F The lecturer used these words and phrases. Match synonyms.
1 practical   a often
2 topics   b gadgets
3 usually   c subjects
4 because of   d complex
5 change   e real world
6 difficult   f modify
7 devices   g due to

MEMS — Slide 1
MEMS design — Slide 2
Inkjet printer and print head — Slide 3
Slide 4

40

2 Remind students about preparing for a lecture. If you wish, review Unit 1 *Skills bank – Making the most of lectures.*

Exercise A

Remind students that when lecturers begin their talks, they usually provide their listeners with an outline. Remind/tell students about the *signpost language* which speakers use at the beginning to list the areas they will cover. On the board, build the table below, eliciting suggestions from the students. Alternatively (or in addition), you could refer to the *Skills bank* at this point.

Sequencing words		Verbs
To start with, Firstly,		begin/start by …ing
		discuss
		examine
Secondly, Then … After that,	I'll	consider
		mention
		talk about
Finally,		look at
		define
		give a(n)
		outline/overview/ definition/summary of …
		end/finish/conclude by …ing

Refer students to the lecture slides. Set the exercise for pairwork.

Ask students to feed back their possible lecture ideas to the whole class using the signpost language on the board to order their points. Accept any reasonable ideas. One possibility is given below.

Answers

Possible answer:

To start with, the lecturer will talk about the size of MEMS devices. After that, he/she will talk about the different science and engineering subjects involved in MEMS design. Then he/she will discuss inkjet printers and print heads. He/she will finish by looking at products such as Nintendo and iPhones.

General note

Read the *Skills bank – Signpost language in a lecture* at the end of the Course Book unit. Decide when, if at all, to refer students to it. The best time is probably at the very end of the lesson or the beginning of the next lesson, as a summary/revision.

Lesson aims
• improve comprehension through understanding of signposts and lexical cohesion
• deal with disorganization in lectures/fractured text

Further practice in:
• predicting content from own background knowledge and from the lecture introduction
• using the introduction to decide the best form of notes to use

Introduction
1 Review key vocabulary by writing a selection of words from Lesson 5.1 on the board and asking students to put the words in groups, giving reasons for their decisions.

Methodology note

If students are new to the subject of MEMS and nanotechnology, they may only be able to make simple points about the slides, as in the model answer on the previous page. If they already know something about the subject they may realize that the slides illustrate the concepts which the lecturer will discuss, i.e., Slide 1: what MEMS is (including size/scale); Slide 2: MEMS design (including the knowledge of various science and engineering fields that contribute to MEMS design); Slides 3 and 4: MEMS applications.

Note that there are no slides for the two nanotechnology topics, but students do not need to know this yet. This is relevant to Exercises B and C.

🎧 Exercise B

Tell students they are only going to hear the introduction to the lecture. Give students time to read the topics. Check that they understand the meaning. Remind them they will only hear the introduction once, as in a lecture. Tell them to listen out for the signpost language on the board. While they listen, they should number the topics from 1–5 in the order in which the lecturer will talk about them.

Play Part 1. Allow students to compare answers. Feed back. Ask students to say what signpost language they heard related to each topic. Confirm the correct answers.

Answers

- MEMS applications – 3 *(This will lead on to …)*
- What is nanotechnology? – 4 *(After that, I'll talk about …)*
- MEMS design – 2 *(Then I'll look at …)*
- Nanotechnology applications – 5 *(I'll finish by looking at …)*
- What is MEMS? – 1 *(To start with, I'll outline …)*

Transcript 🎧 1.22

Part 1

Good afternoon, everyone. In this series of lectures, we're going to be looking at two topics: micro-electromechanical systems, called MEMS for short, and nanotechnology. MEMS and nanotechnology are popular topics for research at present. In today's lecture, I'll give you a quick overview of both topics. Of course, you'll be going over everything in more detail in your assignments and project exercises.

Now … er, let's see … to start with, I'll outline what MEMS is. Then I'll look at some of the

unique aspects of designing MEMS and why MEMS design requires an interdisciplinary mixture of skills. This will lead on to a discussion of some of the practical applications of MEMS technology in the real world. After that, I'll talk about nanotechnology and why it is an exciting area of research. I'll finish by looking at some of the current and future applications of nanotechnology.

Exercise C

1 Set for pairwork. Divide the topics up among the pairs so that each pair concentrates on one topic. Feed back. Accept any reasonable suggestions. There will probably be overlaps between some of the topics.

2 Refer students to the lecture slides. Students should try to guess which of the topics each slide could refer to. Set for individual work and pairwork checking. Feed back but do not confirm or correct yet.

3 Elicit suggestions from the whole class. If you wish, refer students to Unit 1 *Skills bank*.

4 Set for individual work. Students should prepare an outline on a sheet of paper, preferably using a table (see Answers section and example below). Elicit headings for rows and columns. Tell students that they will need to allocate a whole page for the table so that they have enough space to record information.

Answers

Possible answers:

1 Some key words (from Lesson 5.1) are:

What is MEMS? – *micro, µm (micron), component, device, sensor*

MEMS design – *techniques, electronics, mechanics, device, sensor, sophisticated*

MEMS applications – *markets, sensor, pressure sensor, accelerometer, Nintendo, iPhone*

What is nanotechnology? – *nano, nanometre, tiny, particle, material, properties, sophisticated*

Nanotechnology applications – *any words picked up from Lesson 5.1 concerned with products, materials, functions*

2 Accept any reasonable answers with good justifications.

3 The most useful way to make outline notes for this lecture would be to create a table like the example on the next page. In this way, the two main topics can be easily accommodated and the differences between them clearly recorded. If spidergram notes were used, there would need to be two separate

diagrams: one for MEMS and one for nanotechnology; otherwise it could get very complicated and ultimately may not be very useful.

4 Example of table: students should allocate more space between rows than shown on the table below.

	MEMS	Nanotechnology
Description:	students should allow more space between all rows	
Design:		
Applications:		

Methodology note

The model answers for question 1 consist mainly of vocabulary items from Lesson 5.1. However, if students suggest words that others do not know, it would of course be reasonable to check/clarify meanings of such words at this point.

🎧 Exercise D

Tell students to use their outline from Exercise C to take notes. Which topics do they expect to hear in this section?

Play Part 2. Put students in pairs to compare their notes and discuss the questions.

Feed back. When it becomes clear that the lecturer did not actually stick to the plan in the introduction, say that this happens very often in lectures. Lecturers are human! Although it is a good idea to prepare outline notes, students need to be ready to alter and amend these. Discuss how best to do this. One obvious way is to leave sufficient space in tables for unexpected information. Another way is to use a non-linear approach such as a spidergram (if suitable), where new topics can easily be added.

After checking answers to questions 2 and 3, build a complete set of notes on the board as a table, as in the example in the Answers section.

Answers

Possible answers:

1 See example below.

2 Discussed first: What is MEMS?; second: MEMS design; third: What is nanotechnology?

3 A MEMS engineer, because MEMS design involves knowledge of various science and engineering fields.

	MEMS	NANOTECHNOLOGY
Description:	• 3-D systems • size: 1–10,000 μm range • elect./mech. moving parts	• size: billionth of a metre • quantum mechanics effects (at less than 10 nm) • manipulation of materials on nanoscale • can change material properties, e.g., conductivity, strength, viscosity • change light thro. materials (possible?), e.g., solar cell design
Design:	• similar to silicon chip method • silicon + metals (in layers) • polymers (in future?) • techniques such as finite element method (stress analysis) • factors to consider (e.g., surface tension, electromagnetic forces) • fields involved can include mechanics, materials science, heat transfer, electronics	• difficult to manufacture nanoparticles; processes slow • complex structures • chemical synthesis and self-assembly processes: unproven techniques at nanoscale, but possible?
Applications:		

4 Conductivity, strength and viscosity. This question provides an opportunity to check the meaning and pronunciation of these three words.

Transcript 🎧 1.23
Part 2

So first of all, what is MEMS? You should already have read a description of MEMS in your pre-course notes, but just to remind you: MEMS concerns tiny, three-dimensional systems ranging from about 1–10,000 microns in size, which as we shall see later, are often used in tiny sensors. MEMS are usually a mixture of electronic and mechanical moving parts and, as a result, a MEMS engineer needs to be a 'jack of all trades' – that is, he or she has to know about quite a few different fields, from electronics to mechanics, heat transfer and materials science.

Fundamentally, in terms of design, MEMS devices are made using similar techniques to those used to make silicon chips. In other words, the devices are usually planar and assembled in layers. They are often made of silicon combined with metals, but polymers also hold promise for the future. Well, this might sound like electronics, and it does, obviously, have a lot in common with electronics. But remember that MEMS is also about *micro-mechanical* systems – I mean, things that actually move. What's interesting is that in order to make devices work, engineers need to use techniques such as the finite element method for stress analysis. As a matter of fact, it's the same method that structural engineers use to analyze buildings! Other scientific topics, such as fluid mechanics, heat transfer and electromagnetics, are also important. However, because of the small scale of MEMS, effects such as surface tension and electrostatic forces, which are often disregarded in larger scale designs, become very important and must be taken into account in MEMS analyses.

Now, in nanotechnology – which has even smaller scales, down to a *billionth* of a metre! – the assumptions of classical physics break down further. In fact, at the smallest scales in nanotechnology, you even have to start to consider effects due to quantum mechanics.

The interesting and exciting thing about nanotechnology is that, by manipulating materials on a really, really small scale, we can actually change their properties. For example, conductivity, strength and viscosity can be modified if we can work at scales of less then 100 nanometres. Another possibility is that we can change the way light moves through a material, and this might have exciting applications, for example, in solar cell design.

Manufacturing nanoparticles, however, is difficult. Although we can manipulate individual atoms and molecules using techniques such as atomic force microscopy, the processes are slow and very difficult. Chemical synthesis and self-assembly techniques hold much promise for 'bottom up' molecular manufacturing. However, they are unproven for complex synthetic structural assemblies at the nanoscale.

🎧 Exercise E

Ask students what they expect to hear about in the next part. Refer students to their outline again. Give them time to read the questions. Note that the final part of the lecture will be heard in Lesson 5.3, but there is no need to tell them this at this point. Play Part 3. Set the questions for pairwork. Students should use their notes to help them answer the questions.

Feed back. Note that there is no need to build a set of notes on the board at this point – this will be done in Lesson 5.3. Ask students if they can remember what the lecturer was talking about when she lost her place (nanotechnology) and exactly what she said to indicate that she had lost her place (*Anyway, er … I will talk more about nanotechnology in a moment, but to return to the main point …*).

Answers
Model answers:
1 MEMS applications.
2 Nanotechnology applications.
3 Airbags in cars, Nintendo Wii, Apple iPhones. An accelerometer is a kind of sensor that can be used to measure and control movement and speed.

Transcript 🎧 1.24
Part 3

Anyway, er … I will talk more about nanotechnology in a moment, but to return to the main point … I was going to look at some MEMS applications.

The market for MEMS devices is large, currently about $40 billion per year. But what do these devices actually do? Well, mostly, they are used for sensors. For example, airbags in cars are triggered by an accelerometer and this is often a MEMS device. Electronic pressure sensors, such as those used in car engine control systems, industrial processes and medical devices, also use MEMS technology. Small gyroscopes used to stabilize aircraft, satellites and so on, are often MEMS devices. And, of course, the humble inkjet printer actually includes a sophisticated piece of MEMS –

the inkjet print head. MEMS devices also play a part in the popular Nintendo Wii and the Apple iPhone. Both gadgets include tiny MEMS accelerometers which make them respond as you move or shake them. For example, you can play tennis quite realistically on the Nintendo Wii, which would not be possible without MEMS.

Exercise F

This gives further practice in identifying words and phrases used synonymously in a particular context.

Set for individual work and pairwork checking. Ask students to write the corresponding letter in each box.

Answers

1 e practical / real world
2 c topics / subjects
3 a usually / often
4 g because of / due to
5 f change / modify
6 d difficult / complex
7 b devices / gadgets

Closure

Check that students understand some of the concepts and vocabulary in the unit so far, including words under the following headings. You may wish to write the headings on the board and elicit some of the vocabulary. This encourages students to record and learn words in sets. For more difficult words, you could prompt by writing the beginning of the word or by leaving gaps for some of the letters.

Components and devices:

gadget
accelerometer
sensor
pressure sensor
gyroscope

Methods and processes:

technique
chemical synthesis
self-assembly
assemble
manipulate
modify
combine (with)
complex
stabilize
stress analysis

Fields:

fluid mechanics
quantum mechanics
heat transfer
interdisciplinary
materials science
electromagnetics

Words connected with properties and characteristics:

layer
surface
viscosity
three-dimensional
scale
molecule/molecular
μm
particle
repellent
resistant

Note: Students will need their lecture notes from this lesson in Lesson 5.3.

5.3 Extending skills

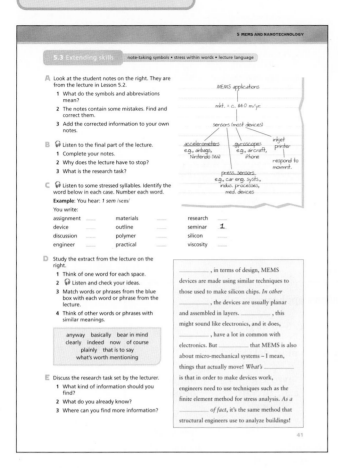

Lesson aims

- use symbols in note-taking
- understand and use lecture language such as stance adverbials (*obviously, indeed*), restatement (*in other words …*) and other commentary-type phrases

Further practice in:

- stress within words
- asking for information
- formulating polite questions

Introduction

As in Unit 3, encourage students to ask you questions about the information in the lecture in Lesson 5.2 as if you were the lecturer. Remind them about asking for information politely. If they can't remember how to do this, you could tell them to revise the *Skills bank* for Unit 3.

Put students in pairs. Student A must ask Student B about the information in the lecture in Lesson 5.2 to help him/her complete the notes from the lecture. Then they reverse roles. Again, they can revise language for this in the *Skills bank* for Unit 3.

Exercise A

With the whole class, discuss the format of the example student notes and elicit the name of this method of note-taking (a tree diagram). If students can't remember, tell them to refer back to Unit 1, Lesson 1.3.

1 Revise/introduce the idea of using symbols and abbreviations when making notes. Ask students to look at the example notes and find the symbols and abbreviated forms. Do they know what these mean? If not, they should try to guess.

   If you wish, expand the table in the Answers section below with more symbols and abbreviations that will be useful for the students. There is also a list at the back of the Course Book for students' reference.

2 Set the question for pairwork. Students will need to agree what the notes are saying and then make the corrections.

3 Set for individual work. Feed back with the whole class and complete the table in the Answers section on the board.

   Ask students which form of notes they think are more effective (the chart or tree diagram) for this section of the lecture. Remind students that they can actually mix note-taking formats within their lecture notes, depending on the content of the lecture. For example, a set of linear notes can feature a small spidergram or tree diagram where appropriate.

   As an additional activity, students can suggest and discuss useful abbreviations for some of the other words in their notes, e.g., *thro. (through); chem. (chemical); synth. (synthesis); incl. (include/s).*

Answers

Model answers:

1

Symbol/ abbreviation	Meaning
mkt.	market
=	equals, the same as, is
c.	approximately, about
$	US dollar
m	million
/yr.	per year; *p.a.* often used instead (*per annum*)
e.g.	(for) example
eng.	engine (in this context)
systs.	systems
indus.	industrial
med.	medical
movmnt.	movement (example of a longer word that can be written without most of its vowels)

Additional useful symbols/ abbreviations	Meaning
bn	billion
bnth.	billionth
&, +	and, plus
>	more than/greater than
<	less than/smaller than
#	number as in #1
μm	micrometre
mm	millimetre
nm	nanometre
cf.	compare
etc.	and all the rest
NB	important

2 Suggested corrections:

- $40 <u>bn</u>/yr
- inkjet <u>print head</u>, not printer
- iPhone should be under <u>accelerometers</u>, *not* <u>gyroscopes</u>; *satellites* missed off under gyroscopes
- '*respond to movmnt.*' should be noted under <u>accelerometers</u>

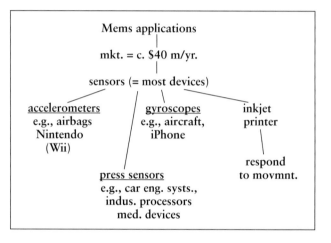

3 Example notes:
See below.

	MEMS	NANOTECHNOLOGY
Description:	• 3-D systems • size: 1–10,000 μm range • elect./mech. moving parts	• size: billionth of a metre • quantum mechanics effects (at less than 10 nm) • manipulation of materials on nanoscale • can change material properties, e.g., conductivity, strength, viscosity • change light thro. materials (possible?), e.g., solar cell design
Design:	• similar to silicon chip method • silicon + metals (in layers) • polymers (in future?) • techniques such as finite element method (stress analysis) • factors to consider (e.g., surface tension, electromagnetic forces) • fields involved can include mechanics, materials science, heat transfer, electronics	• difficult to manufacture nanoparticles; processes slow • complex structures • chemical synthesis and self-assembly processes unproven techniques at nanoscale, but possible?

Applications:	• mkt. = c. $40 bn/yr
	• sensors (most devices):
	   i) accelerometers: car airbags, Nintendo Wii, iPhones – respond to movmnt.
	   ii) pressure sensors: car eng. systs., indus. processes, med. devices
	   iii) gyroscopes: aircraft, satellites
	   iv) inkjet print heads	

Language note

Some abbreviations are universal and some are personal. People often develop their own personal system of symbols and abbreviations. For example, *bn* for *billion* is used by many people, but *eng.* is an example of a longer word *(engine)* abbreviated by the individual who wrote these notes.

Note: Tell students that they need to be careful and consistent when abbreviating certain words in their notes, i.e., if they use *diff.* as an abbreviation for *difficult*, it could be confused with the words *different* or *difference*.

🎧 Exercise B

Tell students they will hear the final part of the lecture. Give them time to read the questions. They should complete their table of notes while listening. Suggest that students practise abbreviations to save time when note-taking.

Play Part 4. Put students in pairs to compare their notes and abbreviations, and to discuss the questions. Feed back. For question 2, ask students if they can remember the exact words used by the lecturer *(oh, dear ... sadly, I see that we've run out of time.).*

Answers

Model answers (last row of chart shown only, with nanotechnology notes shown in right-hand column below):

1

| Applications: | • mkt. = c. $40 bn/yr
• sensors (most devices):
  i) accelerometers: car airbags, Nintendo Wii, iPhones – respond to movmnt.
  ii) pressure sensors: car eng. systs., indus. processes, med. devices
  iii) gyroscopes: aircraft, satellites
  iv) inkjet print heads | • media misconceptions – e.g., v. nr. future
• tiny nanorobots in blood to cure med. probs. (not poss. yet)
• current appls. – use large surface-vol. area (nanoparticles)
• e.g., used in batteries (chem. reaction) – better

End of lecture.
Grp. research areas:
i) history of nanotech.
ii) current appls.
iii) safety & ethical issues
iv) future of nanotech. |

2 Because there is no more time.

3 The research task is to find out about four subjects related to nanotechnology: the history of nanotechnology, current applications, the implications of nanotechnology with regard to safety and ethical issues, and the future of nanotechnology.

Transcript 🎧 1.25

Part 4

To come back to nanotechnology ... there are some really exciting applications for this technology. However, the media has misconceptions about it; for example, suggesting that in the very near future, we might be able to manipulate atoms and molecules using tiny nanorobots, perhaps in our bloodstream, curing all manner of medical problems. This is not currently possible and may take a very long time to develop, if it is actually possible at all. So, let's explore the truth of what nanotechnology is all about.

Many applications make use of the very large surface area-to-volume ratios that are achievable with nanoparticles. This is used successfully in batteries, for example, where the chemical reaction benefits from a good surface area-to-volume ratio at the anode and cathode.

Oh, dear ... sadly, I see that we've run out of time. There is so much more to say about nanotechnology. This means that I'll have to ask you to do some research please. You will be divided into four groups to work on the following subjects. Group one will look at the history of nanotechnology. Group two will look at current applications. Group three will research the implications of nanotechnology in terms of safety and ethical issues. And finally, group four will look at the future of nanotechnology.

🎧 Exercise C

Remind students of the importance of stressed syllables in words. Play the recording, pausing after the first few to check that students understand the task.

Feed back, perhaps playing the recording again for each word before checking. Ideally, mark up an OHT or other visual display of the words.

Answers

assignment	8
device	7
discussion	3
engineer	11
materials	5
outline	10
polymer	9
practical	12
research	2
seminar	1
silicon	4
viscosity	6

Transcript 🎧 1.26

1 'seminar
2 re'search
3 di'scussion
4 'silicon
5 ma'terials
6 vi'scosity
7 de'vice
8 a'ssignment
9 'polymer
10 'outline
11 engi'neer
12 'practical

🎧 Exercise D

This exercise gives students a chance to focus on some typical lecture language.

1 Set for pairwork. Students should try to think of a word for each of the blank spaces.

Note that they should not try to use the words from the box for this. Do not feed back at this point.

2 Tell students they will hear the sentences from the lecture and should fill in the missing words as they listen. There will be pauses at the end of each sentence, but you will play the recording straight through without stopping (as a kind of dictation). Feed back with the whole class, playing the sentences again if necessary. Check the meanings and functions of the words and phrases. Point out the fixed phrases (in italics in the text) and encourage students to learn these. Ask students to repeat the sentences for pronunciation practice, making sure that the stress and intonation are copied from the model.

3 Set for individual work and pairwork checking. Students should check in their dictionaries for meanings or pronunciations of words from the box that they don't know. Feed back, building the first two columns of the table in the Answers section on the board.

4 Elicit suggestions from the whole class for a third column: 'Other similar words/phrases'.

If you wish, students can practise saying the sentences in question 2, but this time with words from questions 3 and 4.

After completing Exercise D, students can be referred to the *Vocabulary bank – Stance* and the *Skills bank – Signpost language in a lecture* for consolidation.

Answers

Model answers:

1/2 <u>Fundamentally</u>, in terms of design, MEMS devices are made using similar techniques to those used to make silicon chips. *In other <u>words</u>*, the devices are usually planar and assembled in layers. <u>Well</u>, this might sound like electronics, and it does, <u>obviously</u>, have a lot in common with electronics. But <u>remember</u> that MEMS is also about micro-mechanical systems – I mean, things that actually move! *What's <u>interesting</u>* is that in order to make devices work, engineers need to use techniques such as the finite element method for stress analysis. *As a <u>matter</u> of fact*, it's the same method that structural engineers use to analyze buildings!

3/4

Word/phrase from the lecture	Words/phrases from the box	Other similar words/phrases
Fundamentally	basically	in essence, really
In other words	that is to say	what I mean is, or, by that I mean
Well	anyway, now	in any case, at any rate
obviously	clearly, plainly	actually, in fact, in effect, to all intents and purposes
remember	bear in mind	don't forget, keep in mind
What's interesting	what's worth mentioning	what's noteworthy, the interesting thing is …, interestingly
As a matter of fact	indeed	actually, in actual fact

Transcript 🎧 1.27

Fundamentally, in terms of design, MEMS devices are made using similar techniques to those used to make silicon chips.

In other words, the devices are usually planar and assembled in layers.

Well, this might sound like electronics, and it does, obviously, have a lot in common with electronics.

But remember that MEMS is also about *micro-mechanical* systems – I mean, things that actually move!

What's interesting is that in order to make devices work, engineers need to use techniques such as the finite element method for stress analysis.

As a matter of fact, it's the same method that structural engineers use to analyze buildings!

Language note

There are three main categories of language here:

1. Stance markers. These are words or phrases that speakers use to show what they feel or think about what they are saying. Adverbs used like this are generally (though not always) positioned at the beginning of the sentence.

2. Phrases used to indicate a restatement or reminders. It is very important for students both to understand and to be able to use these, since speakers frequently need to repeat and explain their points.

3. Other commentary-type phrases that are very common in lectures and discussions.

Exercise E

Remind students of the task set by the lecturer at the end of Part 4. Set the questions for pairwork discussion. Students should first list the sort of information they will need to find, then discuss and make notes on what they already know. Then they should compile a list of possible sources of information.

Feed back on all three questions with the whole class. Do not discuss further at this point, as the topic will be taken up in the next lesson.

If you wish, you can tell students to focus on only one of the research topics in preparation for Lesson 5.4 Exercise G, and to follow up one of their references, not forgetting to record the necessary bibliographical details. Since this will act as preparation for Exercise G, you need to make sure that there are equal numbers of students investigating each topic.

Answers

Possible answers:

1. Answers will depend on the topic. Some suggestions for prompts are:

   The history of nanotechnology: definition/when was the term first coined/by whom?/stages in development

   Current applications: in which fields and industries?/commercial and consumer applications/biomedical applications/environmental applications

   Safety and ethical issues: what aspects or applications of nanotechnology are considered unsafe?/who is concerned?/are there any controls over development and use?

   The future of nanotechnology: positive possible applications (medical and environmental)/possible negative applications (e.g., weaponry)/robotics/how life could change

2. Answers depend on the students.

3. Internet, library, subject textbooks, encyclopedias, etc.

Closure

Play a version of the game 'Just a minute'. Put students in groups of four. Give them an envelope in which they will find topics written on slips of paper. Students take turns to take a slip of paper from the envelope and then talk for one minute on the topic. Encourage them to use as many of the words and phrases from Exercises C and D as they can. Each person should talk for up to a minute without stopping. If they can talk for one minute, they get a point. If they deviate from their topic or can't think of anything more to say, they have to stop. The person who has the most points is the winner.

Some suggestions for topics follow. You may add or substitute other topics broadly related to science, engineering and global issues.

GM food
new biofuels
mobile phones
wind power
solar energy
nuclear energy
robotics
'green' buildings
climate change

You may also want to ask students to use a particular structure for their talk. Or suggest/elicit ways in which short talks can be structured, as follows. This might help students to get started when it is their turn to talk.

from general to particular
for and against
advantages and disadvantages (benefits and drawbacks)
situation/problem/solution
compare and contrast

5.4 Extending skills

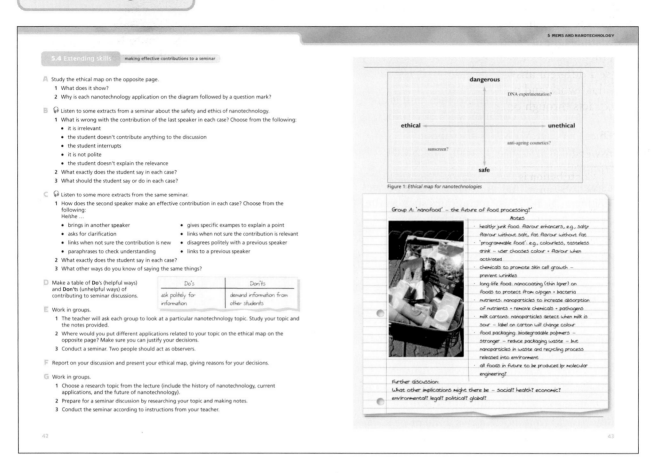

Lesson aims

- make effective and appropriate contributions to a seminar

Further practice in:

- speaking from notes
- reporting information

Introduction

Revise stance words and restatement/deviation phrases from the previous lesson. Give a word or phrase and ask students to give one with a similar meaning. Alternatively, give a sentence or phrase from the lecture in Lessons 5.2 and 5.3 and ask students to tell you the accompanying stance word or restatement phrase, e.g., *... this might sound like electronics, and it does, ... (obviously), have a lot in common with electronics.*

Exercise A

1 Tell students to look at the ethical map on the opposite page. Set for pairwork discussion.

2 Tell students that the ethical map has been created and partially completed by a student researching the safety and ethics of nanotechnology

applications. This should help them to speculate on possible answers. Feed back, accepting any reasonable suggestions.

Answers

Possible answers:

1 It shows how nanotechnologies can be considered according to a scale using a set of four criteria (how safe, dangerous, ethical or unethical). It also shows where example applications can be positioned according to the four criteria.

2 As nanotechnologies are new, the long-term effects and implications are not yet known. The ethical map shows only where the student thinks the applications should be placed, i.e., it is the student's opinion, based on research.

Methodology note

Exercise A prepares students for the listening activities in Exercises B and C which are based on seminar discussions. Exercise A also recycles vocabulary from Lesson 5.1 and extends the discussion around nanotechnology.

94

🎧 Exercise B

In this exercise, students will hear examples of how *not* to contribute to a group discussion.

1/2 Allow students time to read the questions. Tell them they will hear five extracts. They should choose a different answer for each one. Set for individual work and pairwork checking. Play all the extracts through once.

Play the extracts a second time, pausing after each one. Students should write down the actual words, as in a dictation, then check in pairs. When students have completed questions 1 and 2, feed back with the whole class, maybe building up columns 1 and 2 of the table in the Answers section on the board.

3 Set for pairwork discussion. Feed back, adding a third column to the table on the board.

Answers

Model answers:

	Contribution is poor because	Exact words	How to improve
Extract 1	it is irrelevant	Leila: *We watched a great music video on YouTube!*	say something relevant: for example, something about the information they found
Extract 2	it is not polite	Jack: *That's rubbish! She was obviously too busy to talk to us.*	use polite (tentative) language when disagreeing, e.g., *Actually, that's not quite right. I don't think she really had time to talk to us.*
Extract 3	the student doesn't contribute anything to the discussion	Evie: *Well, erm … I don't really know.*	be ready to contribute something when brought into the discussion by the lecturer or other students
Extract 4	the student doesn't explain the relevance	Leila: *Bactericides.*	the comment is relevant to the topic, but she doesn't explain why; she should say, for example, what she said later after the lecturer asked her to explain (i.e., *the silver particles are called 'bactericides'…*)
Extract 5	the student interrupts	Majed: (interrupting) – *actually, that's bacteriostatic. A bactericide, or biocide, actually kills the bacteria.*	he should wait until the speaker has finished

Transcript 🎧 1.28

Extract 1

LECTURER: OK, Jack and Leila, what have you found out about the safety and ethics of nanotechnology?

JACK: Well, first of all, we did an Internet search.

LEILA: We watched a great music video on YouTube!

Extract 2

LECTURER: Stick to the topic, please! Did you try anything else?

LEILA: Well, we went to visit Professor Meyer here at the college who is working on nanotechnology. We had a brief conversation with her and she was interested in our project.

JACK: That's rubbish! She was obviously too busy to talk to us.

Extract 3

LECTURER: Leila, can you give us some examples of the safety concerns with nanotechnology?

LEILA: Yes, we found that there are lots of safety concerns about nanoparticles such as carbon nanotubes. If released into the atmosphere and inhaled, they could be quite dangerous for humans and animals, in a similar way to asbestos dust.

LECTURER: What does everyone else make of this? Evie – what about you?

EVIE: Well, erm … I don't really know …

Extract 4

LECTURER: Jack, did you find any evidence of nanoparticles being harmful?

JACK: Sure. Apparently some companies put silver nanoparticles into socks so that they don't smell. However, when the socks are washed, the silver nanoparticles find their way into the wastewater and destroy useful bacteria in the sewage system.

LEILA: Bactericides.

Extract 5

LECTURER: What do you mean by 'bactericides', Leila?

LEILA: I mean, the silver particles are what are called 'bactericides'. They inhibit the growth of bacteria without …

MAJED: [interrupting] – actually, that's bacteriostatic. A bactericide, or biocide, actually *kills* the bacteria.

🎧 Exercise C

1/2 This time, students will hear good ways of contributing to a discussion. Follow the same procedure as for 1 and 2 in Exercise B above. This time, they need to listen for the second speaker (apart from Extract 7, which is the third 'voice', i.e., the first speaker replying to the second speaker).

Again, when students have completed 1 and 2, feed back with the whole class, maybe building up a table on the board. If you wish, students can look at the transcript at the back of the Course Book.

3 Ask the whole class for other words or phrases that can be used for the strategy and add a third column to the table as below.

Answers

Model answers:

	Helpful strategy	Exact words	Other ways to say it
Extract 6	brings in another speaker	Leila: *What do you think, Majed?*	What do you make of this, Majed?
Extract 7	asks for clarification	Evie: *Sorry, I don't follow. Could you possibly explain why that's relevant?*	I don't quite understand. Could you say a bit more about …?
Extract 8	gives specific examples to explain a point	Jack: *… Let's take the example of rotaxane.*	In the case of rotaxane, for instance …
Extract 9	paraphrases to check understanding	Jack: *If I understand you correctly, you mean …*	So what you're saying is …
Extract 10	disagrees politely with a previous speaker	Majed: *I'm not sure this is likely to happen.*	I don't think I agree with that. In my opinion …
Extract 11	links to a previous speaker	Leila: *As Jack said earlier …*	Going back to what Jack said a while ago …
Extract 12	links when not sure the contribution is new	Evie: *Has anybody made the point that …?*	I don't know if this has been said already, but …
Extract 13	links when not sure the contribution is relevant	Majed: *I don't know if this is relevant, but …*	I'm not sure if this is a little off the point, but …

Transcript 🎧 1.29

Extract 6

LECTURER: Let's go back to the wider questions. What are the implications of advances in nanotechnology?

LEILA: At the moment, nanotechnology is at the 'first generation' stage – things like the passive nanoparticles we've been talking about. However, in the future we might see more advanced, active nanotechnology. What do you think, Majed?

MAJED: Absolutely. Some people have been talking about molecular self-assembly and self-replicating machines. These might have serious safety implications.

Extract 7

EVIE: Isn't that a long way in the future?

LEILA: Well, I was surprised that actually, synthetic chemistry is able to synthesize just about any molecular structure, today.

EVIE: Sorry, I don't follow. Could you possibly explain why that's relevant?

LEILA: Well, the techniques could be extended to produce nanotechnology machines.

Extract 8

MAJED: This just sounds like science fiction, though.

JACK: Actually, this is already happening. Let's take the example of rotaxane. This is a complex molecule which is almost like a very simple molecular machine, a bit like an axle in a bearing. It can be used as a molecular switch amongst other things.

Extract 9

EVIE: Imagine if you could build a machine like a robot, clever enough to synthesize chemicals. It could be very dangerous.

JACK: If I understand you correctly, you mean some kind of self-replicating machine that builds copies of itself from the materials around it.

EVIE: Yes, something like that. It would self-replicate and grow exponentially in number and could consume the whole world!

Extract 10

JACK: But surely that's a concern? I mean, imagine how frightening it would be if someone actually invented a self-replicating nanorobot 50 years from now.

MAJED: I'm not sure this is likely to happen. It's very difficult to assemble things on a molecular and atomic level because the only tools that are available are a similar size to the atoms and molecules themselves. I think this kind of machine is impossible.

Extract 11

LECTURER: So, do you think governments should regulate the safety of nanotechnology?

LEILA: As Jack said earlier, some nanoparticles can be bad for the environment. So, yes, I think governments should carefully regulate nanotechnology.

Extract 12

LECTURER: Any other ideas?

EVIE: Has anybody made the point that overregulation of a new and innovative area might just stifle invention?

LECTURER: No, that's a good point, Evie, and it hasn't been mentioned yet.

Extract 13

LECTURER: So, what regulation could be imposed?

MAJED: I don't know if this is relevant, but occupational health and safety regulations that are routinely applied, say, in chemical manufacture, could be extended to cover new kinds of nanomaterials. I think it's in everyone's interest, including the innovators, to make sure there are no safety disasters.

LECTURER: An excellent point, thanks.

Exercise D

Set for group work. Tell students to brainstorm suggestions for more good and bad seminar strategies. They should think about what helps a seminar discussion to be successful. It may help to think about having seminar discussions in their own language, but they should also think about what is involved in having a seminar discussion in English. Aspects to consider include language, how to contribute to discussions and how to behave.

Feed back, making a list on the board.

Answers

Possible answers:

Do's	Don'ts
prepare the topic beforehand	
ask politely for information	demand information from other students
try to use correct language	
speak clearly	mumble, whisper or shout
say when you agree with someone	get angry if someone disagrees with you
link correctly with previous speakers	
build on points made by other speakers	
make a contribution, even if you are not sure if it is new or relevant	stay silent, waiting for 'the perfect moment'
be constructive	be negative
give specific examples to help explain a point	be vague
listen carefully to what others say	start a side conversation
allow others to speak	dominate the discussion
paraphrase to check understanding	

Exercise E

Set students to work in groups of five or six. Give the groups a letter: A, B or C. If you have more than three groups, you will have to allocate one of the topics to two groups. If you have two groups only, you could allow the students a choice of topic from the three available.

Group As should look at the task card notes on nanofood on the opposite page. The task cards for Group B (medical applications) and Group C (military applications) are on page 103.

In each group, there should be two observers and three or four discussing. The observers should make sure that the group completes all aspects of the task, ensuring that all group members have opportunities to contribute. They may also need to move the group along when a suitable amount of time has been spent on individual points. The observers are also group members and can contribute to the discussion, but should not dominate the proceedings.

Groups should also appoint one person to take notes on the discussion, since they will have to present their findings to another group or to the whole class. Provide each group with either a large sheet of paper on which to draw their own ethical map or, preferably, an OHT and pens.

Procedure:

- Individually, students in each group should study the task card for their topic, underline key words, and make additional notes in response to the 'Further discussion' on a separate sheet or in a notebook.

- Seminar preparation could be a homework task if you arrange for the seminar to take place in the following day's class. If this is the case, you could ask students to do additional Internet or library research before the class, and study the seminar language and transcript from Exercise C.

- Students can use a dictionary to look up unfamiliar words in the notes. Alternatively, they could make a note of anything they are not sure about to raise in the seminar. This would be an authentic way of clarifying uncertainties, and would allow others to contribute their own understanding.

- Before the discussion, revise some of the seminar language from Exercise C; for example, *what would you say if/when you want to disagree/ask for clarification/link to a previous speaker*, etc. ...?

- During the discussion, groups will first need to decide where to position the various nanotechnology applications from their task card on their ethical map. Some applications may be straightforward; others may be controversial, but they need to be able to justify their decisions. Where there is disagreement, the note-taker in the group should make a note of it. (Such a disagreement can be discussed later with the whole class when the group presents its findings.)

- Each group should address the 'Further discussion' question at the bottom of the task card. Monitor the groups and help with suggestions if necessary. For example, the last bullet point on Group A's card asks whether all foods in the future will be produced by molecular engineering. From an economic point of view, ask the group how this would affect world trade or food shortages in certain world regions. Groups do not have to come up with implications for all the suggested areas – only those they think are most relevant to their topic.

- The students acting as observers for the discussion should use a checklist of things to watch for. Sample checklists are provided in the additional resources section (Resource 5D) – students simply mark in each cell whenever the behaviour occurs.

Exercise F

Before the groups report on their discussion, remind them about speaking from notes (see Unit 1 *Skills bank*).

First, the observers should give an overview of how the seminar discussion went and should highlight especially good practice. They can also report on poor contributions, but this needs to be done carefully and constructively (possibly without mentioning names), so that individuals are not embarrassed or upset.

Then the person who took notes should present the findings of their group to the other groups. This task could be shared. For example, one person could present and explain their ethical map, while the note-taker could present the group's thoughts on further implications. Any points for discussion could be passed to the other groups. Set a time limit for the presentations.

Finally, feed back to the whole class on what you heard as you listened to the groups. Suggest improvements for words and phrases, and highlight good practice.

Exercise G

Students work in new groups to research, make notes and conduct seminars on the other three areas of research referred to in the lecture, as below. Students should do their research outside class time, and bring their notes to the class. Remind them to practise using symbols and abbreviations when note-taking, and refer them to the list at the back of the Course Book. Students should try to keep their notes as concise as possible, only noting down key points from their reading, with a few examples where relevant. Students must also note bibliographical details of their sources of information.

Group A: the history of nanotechnology (key dates, key people, early developments)

Group B: current applications

Group C: the future of nanotechnology

- For Groups B and C, you should specify particular fields in order to narrow down the topic, and also to prevent repetition of information covered in Exercise E.

  Other fields are: Transportation, Agriculture & the Environment, Energy, Computing & IT.

- As with Exercise E, in each group there should be two observers and three or four discussing. Provide each group with either a large sheet of paper or, preferably, an OHT and pens, on which to note key points related to their topic.

- During the discussion, group members should share their research information and decide on a list of key points (say, a maximum of four). They should then discuss what they want to say about each of the key points and make brief notes. Each group member should be responsible for taking notes on one of the key points.

- At the end of the discussion, the observers should feed back – only to the group this time – on how the seminar discussion went and should highlight especially good practice. They can also report on poor contributions, but sensitively as per previous seminar. Monitor groups at this point, and make suggestions where appropriate.

- Each group should then give a short presentation to another group or to the whole class. Again, this task should be shared. For example, one person could introduce the topic and key points. Each member should then present the group's discussion of that point, using their notes from the seminar. At the end (or at the end of each key point), the audience could be invited to ask questions or make comments. In this way, a further 'mini-seminar' can be generated in an authentic context. You may wish to set a time limit for the presentations and questions.

- Finally, feed back to the whole class on what you heard as you listened to the seminar presentations. Suggest improvements for words and phrases, and highlight good practice.

Closure

1 If you wish, refer students to the *Skills bank – Seminar language* for consolidation.

2 Focus on the meaning and pronunciation of some useful content words from the seminar extract in Lesson 5.4. For example:

asbestos

atmosphere

bacteria

implication

inhale

innovative/innovator

invention

nanorobot

regulate/regulation

passive

relevant

self-replicating

1 Work through the *Vocabulary bank* and *Skills bank* if you have not already done so, or as a revision of previous study.

2 Use the *Activity bank* (Teacher's Book additional resources section, Resource 5A).

   A Set the crossword for individual work (including homework) or pairwork.

   Answers

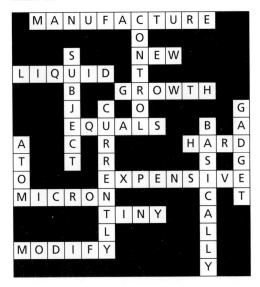

   B Students should select any six words from the box (listed in *Students' words* column above). Call out words at random from the *Teacher's words* column, not forgetting to note which words you have called. Students cross out the antonym, if they have it on their card. When someone has managed to cross out all the words on his/her bingo card, he/she should call out *Bingo!* Check to see if all the words are correctly crossed out. If the student has made a mistake, they are out of the game. The first person to correctly cross out all the words on his/her bingo card is the winner.

An alternative is to put students in groups to play the game, with one student acting as the teacher. In this case, you will need to prepare a list of teacher's words for each group.

Students' words	Teacher's words
dangerous	harmless
complex	simple
expensive	economical
fall	rise
flexible	rigid
futuristic	old-fashioned
less	wore
liquid	solid
micro	large
passive	active
productive	inefficient
relevant	unimportant
sharply	gradually
slightly	significantly
transparent	opaque

6 FRICTION

Unit 6 deals with the theme of friction. It focuses on the useful and detrimental characteristics of friction, which are central to the design process in mechanical engineering. Lesson 6.1 looks at the basic types of friction, and the calculation of the coefficient of friction for various materials in contact. The reading text in Lesson 6.2 discusses considerations of friction in mechanical engineering design, and how it can be utilized and minimized as appropriate to different machines. The unit finishes with a study of tribology, the science and technology of interaction between surfaces in relative motion.

Skills focus

Reading
- locating key information in complex sentences

Writing
- reporting findings from other sources: paraphrasing
- writing complex sentences

Vocabulary focus
- synonyms, replacement subjects, etc., for sentence-level paraphrasing

Key vocabulary

abrasive (adj)	force (n)	pitting (n)
acoustic	friction	ratio
adhesive (adj)	gear (n)	resist(ance)
bearing (n)	generate	ridge (n)
coefficient	initiate	seize (v)
constant (adj)	kinetic	static (adj)
corollary (adj)	lubrication	stationary
detrimental	machining (n)	tribology
effect	magnitude	value (n)
efficiency	maximum	wear (n and v)
erosive (adj)	motion	weld (v)

6.1 Vocabulary

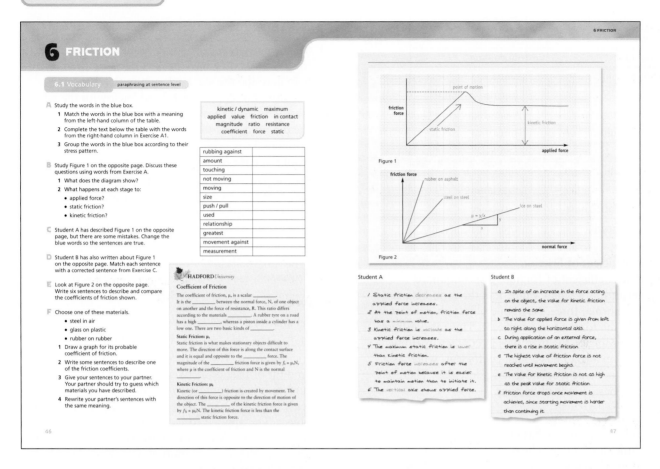

General note

Read the *Vocabulary bank* at the end of the Course Book unit. Decide when, if at all, to refer students to it. The best time is probably at the very end of the lesson or the beginning of the next lesson, as a summary/revision.

Lesson aims

- paraphrase at sentence level using passives, synonyms, negatives, replacement subjects

Further practice in:

- affixes
- stress within words
- word sets – synonyms, antonyms

Introduction

Revise words describing graphs. Draw a line graph on the board. The line should rise and fall, sharply and gradually, have a peak and a point where it levels off. Point to each part of the line and ask students to give you the appropriate verb and adverb. Alternatively, draw your own line graph and describe it. Students should try to draw an identical line graph from your description while you are talking.

Exercise A

1 Refer students to the table. Point out that they are looking for similar meanings, not synonyms. Do the first one with the group, then set the exercise for individual work and pairwork checking. Tell students to use their dictionaries if they need to check meanings, grammatical category, etc. Feed back with the whole class, building the table in the Answers section on the board.

2 Give students a few minutes to read through the text *Coefficient of Friction* without filling any of the gaps. Do the first one or two with the class, then set the exercise for pairwork. Feed back with the whole class, checking pronunciation of the key vocabulary. Focus particularly on correct word stress.

3 Ask students to group the words according to their stress pattern. Feed back with the whole class, checking pronunciation.

Answers

1

rubbing against	friction
amount	value
touching	in contact
not moving	static
moving	kinetic / dynamic
size	magnitude
push / pull	force
used	applied
relationship	ratio
greatest	maximum
movement against	resistance
measurement	coefficient

2 **Coefficient of Friction**

The coefficient of friction, μ (pronounced /mjuː/), is a scalar <u>value</u>. It is the <u>ratio</u> between the normal force, N, of one object on another and the force of resistance, R. This ratio differs according to the materials <u>in contact</u>. A rubber tyre on a road has a high <u>coefficient</u>, whereas a piston inside a cylinder has a low one. There are two basic kinds of <u>friction</u>.

Static Friction: μ_s
Static friction is what makes stationary objects difficult to move. The direction of this force is along the contact surface and it is equal and opposite to the <u>applied</u> force. The magnitude of the <u>static</u> friction force is given by $f_s = \mu_s N$, where μ is the coefficient of friction and N is the normal <u>force</u>.

Kinetic Friction: μ_k
Kinetic (or <u>dynamic</u>) friction is created by movement. The direction of this force is opposite to the direction of motion of the object. The <u>magnitude</u> of the kinetic friction force is given by $f_k = \mu_k N$. The kinetic friction force is less than the <u>maximum</u> static friction force.

3 The correct word stress for the words in the right-hand column is:
   'friction
   'value
   in 'contact
   'static
   ki'netic
   dy'namic
   'magnitude
   'force
   a'pplied
   'ratio
   'maximum

   re'sistance
   coe'fficient

Exercise B

1 Set for pairwork discussion. Students should refer to the words they have looked at in Exercise A to help describe the stages shown in the diagram. Monitor, but don't assist. Feed back with the whole class, checking that students can give the topic of the diagram, and the meanings of the vertical and horizontal axes. Elicit words which can be used from Exercise A.

2 Set for pairwork discussion. Remind students about words they have already studied for describing trends in graphs. Feed back with the whole class, asking one or two students to describe the stages of friction. Make sure that students use the present simple tense to talk about the stages as this is a *process*.

Answers

Model answers:

1 Figure 1 shows a graph of <u>applied force</u> against <u>friction force</u>. The vertical axis represents the <u>amount</u> of <u>friction</u> between the object and the surface it is <u>in contact</u> with, and the horizontal axis represents the <u>magnitude</u> of the <u>force</u> applied to the object. The <u>applied force</u> and the <u>friction force</u> both begin at zero. Two main phases are shown: before and after the point of motion, which is when the object begins to move.

  <u>Static friction</u> is the <u>force</u> which <u>resists</u> the initiation of motion. At the point of motion, <u>friction force</u> has its <u>maximum value</u>.

  After the point of motion, <u>kinetic friction resists</u> the continued movement of the object.

  As can be seen, the <u>magnitude</u> of the <u>applied force</u> and <u>friction force</u>, and the type of <u>friction</u> operating, vary with each stage.

2 **Applied force:** in the beginning there is no applied force, which means there is no friction. The magnitude of the force applied to the object increases through both the static friction and kinetic friction phases.

  Static friction: as force is applied, static friction starts to increase. It takes some time before sufficient force is applied to reach the point of motion. This happens when the applied force overcomes static friction, and the object begins to move.

  Kinetic friction: once the point of motion is passed, the type of friction operating becomes kinetic friction. During the phase immediately after the point of motion is achieved, the magnitude of friction force falls and then levels off. Although applied force continues to increase, the value for kinetic friction remains constant from this point onward.

Exercise C

As well as requiring the use of antonyms, this exercise checks that students have understood the diagram in Exercise B. Set for individual work and pairwork checking. Feed back with the whole class. A good way to do this is to use an OHT or other visual medium with blanks for the blue words (see additional resources section, Resource 6B).

Answers

Model answers:

1 Static friction <u>increases</u> as the applied force increases.

2 At the point of motion, friction force has a <u>maximum</u> value.

3 Kinetic friction is <u>constant</u> as the applied force increases.

4 The maximum static friction is <u>higher</u> than kinetic friction.

5 Friction force <u>decreases</u> after the point of motion because it is easier to maintain motion than to initiate it.

6 The <u>horizontal</u> axis shows applied force.

Exercise D

Introduce the idea of paraphrasing – or restating. Elicit from the students the main ways to do this at sentence level, namely:

- using different grammar
- using different words
- reordering the information

Write these points on the board. Also make the point very strongly that a paraphrase is not a paraphrase unless 90% of the language is different. There are some words which must remain the same, but these are very few, and are likely to be words specific to the subject, such as *kinetic friction*. It is best to try to use all three of the above strategies, if possible.

Students should look carefully at the corrected sentences from Exercise C and then compare them with the paraphrases. The first step is to identify which sentences match. Set for individual work and pairwork checking. It may be helpful for the students if you reproduce the corrected sentences from Exercise C and the sentences in Exercise D on strips of paper so that they can move them around. Both sets of sentences are reproduced in the additional resources section (Resource 6C) to facilitate this.

Feed back with the whole class. A good way to do this

is to reproduce the sentences on an OHT or other visual display, with each sentence cut into a separate strip. Lay the sentences on the OHP one at a time, as you agree what is the correct match.

Once the sentences are correctly paired, ask students to locate the parts of each sentence which seem to match. They will need to look at the overall meaning of each phrase, using what they know about the subject, to make sure that the phrases are similar. Set for pairwork. Feed back with the whole group, using the OHT strips and highlighting the matching parts with coloured pens.

Answers

Model answers:

1 Static friction increases as the applied force increases.	c During application of an external force, there is a rise in static friction.
2 At the point of motion, friction force has a maximum value.	d The highest value of friction force is not reached until movement begins.
3 Kinetic friction is constant as the applied force increases.	a In spite of an increase in the force acting on the object, the value for kinetic friction remains the same.
4 The maximum static friction is higher than kinetic friction.	e The value for kinetic friction is not as high as the peak value for static friction.
5 Friction force decreases after the point of motion because it is easier to maintain motion than to initiate it.	f Friction force drops once movement is achieved, since starting movement is harder than continuing it.
6 The horizontal axis shows applied force.	b The value for applied force is given from left to right along the horizontal axis.

A final step is to discuss the changes that have been made in detail. Students should refer to the list of types of changes you have written on the board. Look at each paraphrase with the class and ask students what changes have been made. Be specific about the types of vocabulary or grammar changes. For example, in the first answer above, the paraphrase reorders the information, uses replacement subject *there*, uses a time clause and changes some of the vocabulary.

Exercise E

Put students in pairs to discuss Figure 2 and write their sentences. Feed back with the whole group. Write some sentences on the board.

Answers

Possible answers:

1 The gradient of a graph, which is given by y divided by x, represents here the coefficient of friction for each situation shown.

2 Rubber on asphalt has a higher coefficient of friction than steel on steel.

3 The coefficient of friction for each situation is constant.

4 Ice on steel has a lower coefficient of friction than steel on steel.

5 The normal force is shown on the x axis.

6 The resulting friction force is shown on the vertical axis.

Exercise F

1/2 Set for individual work.

3 Set for pairwork. Go round and check what students have written, giving advice if necessary.

4 Set for individual work or for homework. Tell students to try to follow the advice for paraphrasing in Exercise D, i.e., to reorder the information and to change vocabulary and grammar as far as possible. You may wish to refer students to the *Vocabulary bank* at this point to provide a reminder for grammar structures to use.

Closure

Discussion:

1 Can students think of other materials with coefficients of friction similar to those shown in Figures 1 and 2?

2 What can designers do to change the coefficient of friction of a given material or combination of materials?

6.2 Reading

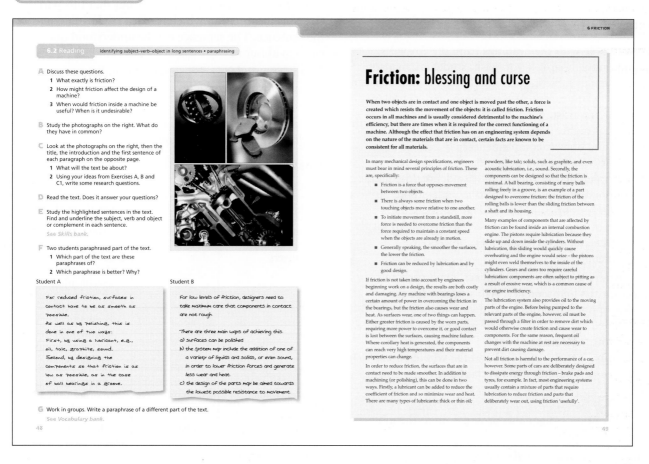

Lesson aims

- identify the kernel SVC/O of a long sentence

Further practice in:

- research questions
- topic sentences
- paraphrasing

Introduction

Remind the class about techniques when using written texts for research. Ask:

What is it a good idea to do:

- *before reading?* (think of research questions)
- *while you are reading?* (look for topic sentences)
- *after reading?* (check answers to the research questions)

What words in a text signal the development of a topic in a new direction? (markers showing contrast such as *but*, *however*, *at the same time*, *on the other hand*, etc.).

If you wish, refer students to Unit 4 *Skills bank*.

Exercise A

Set for general discussion. Allow students to debate differences of opinion. Encourage them to give examples if they can. Do not correct or give information at this point, as these topics will be dealt with in the text.

Exercise B

Set for individual work. Feed back with the whole class.

Answers

Friction – they show things which reduce friction (e.g., bearings, oil) – or use friction (e.g., brake pads).

Exercise C

Set for individual work. Elicit ideas, but do not confirm or correct.

Exercise D

Set for individual work. Feed back with the whole class.

Exercise E

Draw a table with the headings from the Answers section on the board. If you wish, students can also draw a similar table in their notebooks. Explain that in academic writing, sentences can seem very complex. This is often not so much because the sentence structure is highly complex in itself, but that the subjects and objects/complements may consist of clauses or complex noun phrases. Often the verb is quite simple. But in order to fully understand a text, the grammar of a sentence must be understood. Subject + verb + object or complement is the basic sentence structure of English. Students need to be able to locate the subjects, main verbs and their objects or complements.

Elicit from the students the subject, main verb and object for the first sentence. Ask students for the *headword* of each subject, main verb and object (underlined in the table in the Answers section). Write them in the table on the board. Using high-speed questioning, get students to build the whole phrase that constitutes the subject/main verb/object/complement.

Example 1:

The lubrication <u>system</u> also <u>provides</u> <u>oil</u> to the moving parts of the engine.

> *What is this sentence about?* = a system
> *What does the system do?* = it provides
> *What does it provide?* = oil
> *Which oil?* = oil in general (zero article)

Write these headwords in the table on the board. Then elicit the remaining words and add to the table:

> *Which system exactly?* = the lubrication system
> *Give me more information about how it provides oil* = (it provides it) to the moving parts of the engine

Example 2:

This example shows how to deal with relative clauses.

Many <u>examples</u> of components that are affected by friction can <u>be found</u> inside an internal combustion engine.

> *What is this sentence about in general?* = examples
> *More particularly?* = <u>examples</u> of components that are affected by friction
> *What's the main verb in this sentence?* = find (found)
> *Where are they found?* = inside an internal combustion engine

The idea is that students should be able to extract something which contains the kernel even if it does not make complete sense without the full phrase.

Ask students to identify the leading prepositional/adverbial phrase in the third sentence (*In order to reduce friction …*). Point out that this part contains information which is extra to the main part of the sentence. The sentence can be understood quite easily without it.

Set the remainder of the exercise for individual work followed by pairwork checking. Finally, feed back with the whole class.

You may wish to refer students to the *Skills bank – Finding the main information*.

Answers

Model answers:

Subject	Verb	Object/complement
In many design specification engineers	must <u>bear</u> in mind	1 several principles of friction 2 in any mechanical design specification
1 if friction 2 the results	1 is not <u>taken</u> into account 2 <u>are</u>	1 by <u>engineers</u> beginning work on a design 2 both costly and damaging
the surfaces that are in contact	need to be <u>made</u>	1 smoother 2 in order to reduce friction*
Many <u>examples</u> of components that are affected by friction	can be <u>found</u>	inside an <u>internal combustion engine</u>.
The lubrication <u>system</u>	<u>provides</u>	<u>oil</u> to the moving parts of <u>the engine</u>
Not all <u>friction</u>	<u>is</u>	harmful to the <u>performance</u> of a car

*see explanation after Example 2 above

Exercise F

Set for individual work and pairwork checking. Make sure that students identify the original phrases in the text first (the first four sentences of paragraph 4) before looking at the paraphrases.

Feed back with the whole class. A good way to demonstrate how Student A's text contains too many words from the original is to use an OHT or other visual medium and highlight the common words in colour. (A table giving the sentences plus commentary is included in the additional resources section – Resources 6D and 6E.) Check that students are able to say which parts of the paraphrase match with the original, and which structures have been used.

Answers

1 The first part of paragraph 4.
2 Student B's paraphrase is better, because it uses fewer words from the original text and uses different sentence structures.

Language note

It is important that students understand that when paraphrasing, it is not sufficient to change a word here and there and leave most of the words and the basic sentence structure unchanged. This approach is known as 'patch-writing' and is considered to be plagiarism. It is also important when paraphrasing not to change the meaning of the original – also quite hard to do.

Exercise G

Refer students to the *Vocabulary bank* at this stage. Review paraphrasing skills with the whole class before starting this exercise.

Divide the text into parts. For example, each paragraph can be divided into two so that there are eight different sections (though, of course, you should not use the first part of paragraph 4). Give each section to different students to work on. Alternatively, you could choose one part of the text for all students to work on, for example the second part of paragraph 4. This can be done in class or, if you prefer, as individual work/homework.

If students are doing the work in class in groups or pairs, a good way to provide feedback is to get them to write their paraphrase on an OHT or other visual medium. Show each paraphrase (or a selection) to the class and ask for comments. Say what is good about the work. Point out where there are errors and ask for suggestions on how to improve it. Make any corrections on the OHT with a different coloured pen.

Closure

1 Divide the class into two teams. Write the five topic sentences from the reading text on strips, or photocopy them from the additional resources section (Resource 6F). One team chooses a topic sentence and reads it aloud. The other team must give the information triggered by that topic sentence. Accept only the actual paragraph content.

2 Dictate the following to the class:

Think of an engineering system, other than an internal combustion engine, which …

… *uses oil as lubricant*
… *contains polished surfaces in contact*
… *has components that are expected to wear*
… *contains ball bearings rolling in a groove*
… *requires movement from a standstill*
… *generates a lot of heat*
… *takes advantage of friction*
… *contains a piston moving in a cylinder*

Students work in pairs to think of systems which fit the descriptions. The first pair to find a system for each category are the winners. Feed back with the whole class.

6.3 Extending skills

6.3 Extending skills · understanding complex sentences

A Study the words in box a from the text in Lesson 6.2.
1 What part of speech are they in the text?
2 Find one or more words in the text with a similar meaning to each word.

> occur   machine   consider
> effect   movement   need   damaging
> cause   component   reduce

B Complete the summary with words from Exercise A.

C Study the words in box b.
1 What is each base word and its meaning?
2 How does the affix change the part of speech?
3 What is the meaning in the text in Lesson 6.2?

D Study sentences A–E on the opposite page.
1 Copy and complete Table 1. Put the parts of each sentence in the correct box.
2 Rewrite the main part of each sentence, changing the verb from active to passive or vice versa.

E Look at the 'Other verbs' column in Table 1.
1 How are the clauses linked to the main part of the sentence?
2 In sentences A–C, what does each relative pronoun refer to?
3 Make the clauses into complete sentences.

> Friction is a force which _____ when two _____ which are in contact move relative to each other. In a _____, friction is generally considered to be _____ to the system as it _____ heat and wear, and extra power is _____ to overcome it. Lubrication and careful polishing are used by designers to help _____ the _____ of friction.

> costly   bearing   failure
> lubricant   minimize   freely
> pitting   harmful   performance

6.4 Extending skills · writing complex sentences

A Make one sentence for each box on the right, using the method given in red. Include the words in blue. Write all the sentences as one paragraph.

> They reduce wear.
> They use lubrication to reduce friction.
> relative, passive, participle   The main way

B Study the notes on the opposite page which a student made about tribology. Write up the notes. Include the sentences from Exercise A.
1 Divide the notes into sections to make suitable paragraphs. Where should the paragraph in Exercise A go?
2 Decide which ideas are suitable topic sentences for the paragraphs. Which idea can you use as a topic sentence for the paragraph in Exercise A?
3 Make full sentences from the notes, joining ideas where possible, to make one continuous text.

> Designers place a layer of oil between two surfaces. This forms a barrier.
> The barrier prevents the surfaces from coming into contact with one another.
> passive, participle, relative   To achieve this

> Designers commonly use mineral oils.
> Designers use other very low shear strength materials.
> Examples include talc, graphite, lead, gold.
> passive, ellipsis   ... such as

(A) Without lubrication, this sliding would quickly cause overheating.

(B) Oil is passed through a filter in which all dust and dirt which might cause friction is removed.

(C) Corrosive wear, which is a common cause of car engine inefficiency, often damages the cylinder head itself.

(D) In addition to polishing key components, designers reduce friction in two ways.

(E) Having cleaned the oil, the lubrication system pumps it to the relevant parts of the engine.

Table 1: Breaking a complex sentence into constituent parts

	Main S	Main V	Main O/C	Other V + S/O/C	Adv. phrases
A	this sliding	would (quickly) cause	overheating	and the engine would seize	without lubrication
B					

Friction & wear: A study – tribology
- tribology = science and technology of interaction between surfaces in rel. motion
- surfaces appear smooth BUT under microscope, still uneven
- when 2 surfaces brought together → actual contact only at ridges
- contact force spread over rel. v. small area
- intense pressure @ contact points → wear
- Tribology concerned w. 3 types of wear:
  - adhesive = surface worn away, e.g., sole of shoe → can seize, i.e., lock together
  - abrasive = 1 material harder → scratches other, softer one
  - erosive = hard particles between surfaces → pitting
- How reduce wear?
- Lubrication
  e.g., mineral oils, other very low shear strength materials
- Some situations, friction necessary:
  e.g., skis → friction = help & hindrance:
  one hand, reduce friction (shops apply wax to bottom of skis) → skiers travel v. quickly
  other hand, skier turns & digs edges of skis into snow → friction must be sufficient to turn w. control

50 / 51

Lesson aims

- study sentence structure in more detail
- identify the main information in:
  an active sentence
  a passive sentence
  a complex sentence with participles
  a complex sentence with embedded clauses

Further practice in:

- vocabulary from Lesson 6.2

Introduction

Ask students to see how many phrases or compound nouns they can make with the word *force*. Tell students to brainstorm a list in pairs. Feed back with the whole class.

Possible answers: *gravitational force/force of gravity, friction force, magnetic force, applied force, normal force, braking force, maximum/minimum force, increased/decreased force, constant force, vector force, rotational force, net force, resultant force,* etc.

Exercise A

Ask students to study the words in the box and to find the words in the text. Set for individual work and

pairwork checking. Tell students not to use their dictionaries to begin with but to use what they know to guess meanings and parts of speech. If necessary, they should use dictionaries when checking in pairs. Deal with any common problems with the whole class.

Answers

Model answers (paragraph numbers in brackets):

Word	Part of speech	Similar meaning
occur (1)	v (I)	happen (3)
machine (1, 3, 6)	n (C)	engineering system (1, 7)
consider (1)	v (T)	bear in mind (1) taken into account (3)
effect (1)	n (C)	result (3, 5)
movement (1, 2)	n (U)	motion (2)
need (2, 4)	v (T)	require (1, 2, 5)
damaging (3)	adj	harmful (7) detrimental (1)
cause (3, 5, 6)	v (T)	generate (3) create (1, 6)
component (3, 4, 5, 6)	n (C)	part (3, 4, 6, 7)
reduce (2, 4, 7)	v (T)	minimize (4)

Exercise B

Set for individual work and pairwork checking. Students should make use of all the words they have discussed in Exercise A (i.e., the synonyms as well as the words in the box). Feed back with the whole class.

Answers

Model answers:

Friction is a force which <u>occurs</u>/<u>happens</u> when two <u>parts</u>/<u>components</u> which are in contact move relative to each other. In a <u>machine</u>/<u>engineering system</u>, friction is generally considered to be <u>harmful</u>/<u>damaging</u>/<u>detrimental</u> to the system as it <u>causes</u>/<u>generates</u>/<u>creates</u> heat and wear, and extra power is <u>needed</u>/<u>required</u> to overcome it. Lubrication and careful polishing are used by designers to help <u>reduce</u>/<u>minimize</u> the <u>effects</u>/<u>results</u> of friction.

> ### Language note
>
> The use of words as synonyms often depends on the context. For example, there is a verb in the second sentence of the summary, *consider*, which is often synonymous with *bear in mind*. However, in this second sentence, *considered* is more synonymous with *thought to be*.

Exercise C

Set for pairwork. Feed back with the whole class. Note that not all the base words have specifically mechanical engineering meanings. Tell students to explain the meaning in mechanical engineering terms as far as possible.

Answers

Model answers:
See table below.

> ### Language note
>
> Rules in language are made to be broken. The suffix ~*ly* normally makes an adjective into an adverb, e.g., *free – freely*, but there are common cases where this is not what happens. Here, the noun *cost* is made into an adjective *costly* by the addition of ~*ly*. Other anomalies are:
>
> *friend – friendly*
> *kind – kindly*
>
> Note that *cost* is neutral, whereas *costly* is a stance adjective – it suggests that the writer or speaker thinks the price is so high that it will cause a loss or disadvantage to the company. In this regard, *expensive* is not a true synonym since it does not have this same negative connotation. *Pricey*, however, does.

Word	Base and meaning	Effect of affix	Meaning in text
costly (3)	cost (n, C) – the price	~*ly* = adjective ending	causing a loss of money
bearing (3)	bear (v, T) – to carry/support a weight	~*ing* = noun ending	a joint in a machine which contains balls to help it move easily
failure (3)	fail (v, I) – to be unsuccessful in an attempt to do something	~*ure* = noun ending	a mechanical breakdown
lubricant (4)	lubricate (v, T) – to add a substance such as oil to allow machinery to move more easily	~*ant* = noun ending	a substance added to surfaces in contact to reduce friction
minimize (4)	minimum (adj) – the smallest possible; can only be used before the noun, i.e., *The minimum amount* not *The amount is minimum*; sometimes a noun followed by *of*: *a minimum of …*	~*ize* = verb ending	to reduce to the smallest amount/lowest level possible
freely (4)	free 1. (adj) not restricted in movement or action 2. (adj) given without a requirement to pay 3. (v) to release; to make free (1)	~*ly* = adverb ending	without restriction of movement
pitting (5)	pit (n, C) – a deep hole in the ground	~*ing* = noun ending	damage to a smooth surface consisting of many shallow holes or indentations
harmful (7)	harm 1. (v) to hurt; to injure physically 2. (n, U) physical damage or injury	~*ful* = adjective ending	causing a system to be less effective
performance (7)	perform 1. (v, T) to do a task, often a difficult one 2. (v, T) to play music, etc., for an audience 3. (n, I) *well/badly*: to achieve results in difficult conditions	~*ance* = noun ending	the correct functioning of an engineering system

Exercise D

1 Copy the table headings from the Answers section onto the board and complete the example with the students. Tell them that when they look at the 'Other verbs' column, they may well find several, and should number each verb and subject/object/complement section separately. Point out that the order of each part of the sentence is not reflected in the table: the table is just a way to analyze the sentences.

Set the rest of the sentences for individual work and pairwork checking. Feed back with the whole class. Draw their attention to the 'main' parts of the sentence: it is very important in reading that they should be able to identify these. Notice also that the main parts can stand on their own and make complete sentences.

2 Set for individual work. If the clause is active it should be changed to passive, and vice versa.

Answers

1 Model answers:
See table below.

2 Possible answers:

A Overheating would quickly be caused.

B (The system) passes oil through a filter.

C The cylinder head itself is often damaged by corrosive wear.

D Friction is reduced (in two ways) by designers.

E The oil is pumped (by the lubrication system) to the relevant parts of the engine.

Exercise E

This exercise involves looking carefully at the dependent clauses in sentences A–E.

1 Say that these clauses have special ways to link them to the main part of the sentence. Do this exercise with the whole class, using an OHT or other visual medium of the table in Exercise D, and a highlighter pen to mark the relevant words. (A version of the table without underlining is included in the additional resources section – Resource 6G.) Go through the clauses asking students what words or other ways are used to link the clauses to the main part of the sentence.

2 Set for individual work and pairwork checking. Students should look at each sentence and identify the antecedents of the relative pronouns. You could ask them to use a highlighter pen or to draw circles and arrows linking the words.

3 Students must be able to get the basic or kernel meaning of the clause. Take sentence A as an example and write it on the board. Point out that the relative pronouns and other ways of linking these clauses to the main clause will need to be changed or got rid of. Students should aim to write something that makes good sense as a complete sentence. They can break a sentence into shorter sentences if necessary.

Set the remaining clauses for individual work. Feed back with the whole class. Accept anything that makes good sense.

	Main subject	Main verb	Main object/complement	Other verbs + their subjects + objects/complements	Adverbial phrases
A	this sliding	would (quickly) cause	overheating	and the engine would seize	without lubrication
B	Oil	is passed	(through) a filter	<u>in which</u> all dust and dirt <u>which</u> might cause friction is removed	
C	Corrosive wear	damages	the cylinder head itself	<u>which</u> is a common cause of car engine inefficiency	often
D	designers	reduce	friction	<u>In addition to</u> polishing key components, …	in two ways
E	the lubrication system	pumps	it	<u>Having cleaned</u> the oil, …	to the relevant parts of the engine

*underlined text = means by which dependent clause is joined to main clause

Answers

1 See table in Exercise D on the previous page. Sentences A–C use relative clauses. D and E use participle clauses (*In addition to; Having cleaned*).

2 A *which* = a force

   B *which* = 1 a filter

   2 dust and dirt

   C *which* = corrosive wear

3 Possible answers:

   A A force resists the movement of one relative to the other.

   B 1 All dust and dirt is removed through a filter.
   2 The dust and dirt might cause friction.

   C Corrosive wear is a common cause of car engine inefficiency.

   D Designers (also) polish key components.

   E The lubrication system cleans the oil.

> **Language note**
>
> A dependent clause contains a verb and a subject and is a secondary part of a sentence. It is dependent because it 'depends' on the main clause. A main clause can stand by itself as a complete sentence in its own right (usually). A dependent clause always goes with a main clause and cannot stand by itself as a sentence in its own right.
>
> Dependent clauses are typically joined to main clauses with certain types of words: for example, relative pronouns (e.g., *who, which*, etc.), linking adverbials (e.g., *if, when, before, although, whereas*, etc.); words associated with reporting speech (e.g., *that*, a Wh~ word such as *what* or *why*), and so on.
>
> Some dependent clauses are non-finite, that is, they don't have a 'full verb' but a participle form (e.g., *having finished, opening*) and the subject may not be stated.
>
> For more on this, see a good grammar reference book.

Closure

Write the following underlined beginnings and endings of words on the board or dictate them. Ask students to give the (or a) complete word. Accept alternatives and other parts of speech.

<u>co</u>(efficient)

<u>initi</u>(ate)

<u>res</u>(ist)(ance)

<u>mach</u>(ine)

<u>stat</u>(ionary)

<u>fric</u>(tion)

(maxi)<u>mum</u>

(bear)<u>ing</u>

(effect)<u>ive</u>

(kinet)<u>ic</u>

6.4 Extending skills

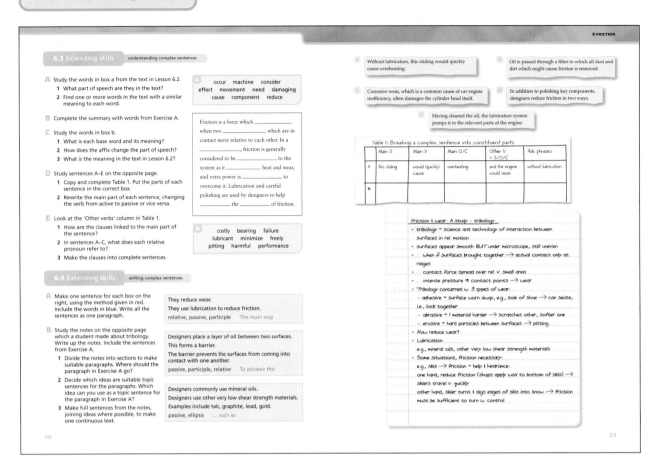

Lesson aims

- write complex sentences:

  with passives

  joining with participles

  embedding clauses

  adding prepositional phrases

Further practice in:

- writing topic sentences
- expanding a topic sentence into a paragraph

Introduction

Ask students to think about and discuss the following questions:

1 What does wear mean in engineering systems?

2 What might be meant by the terms *adhesive*, *abrasive* and *erosive* wear?

3 What kind of systems might suffer from them?

4 How might designers avoid or overcome them?

Exercise A

Set for individual work and pairwork checking. If necessary, do the first box with the whole class. Make sure students understand that they should write the three sentences as a continuous paragraph.

Feed back with the whole class. Accept any answers that make good sense. Point out where the phrases in blue act as linkers between the sentences to make a continuous paragraph.

Answer

Possible answer:

The main way in which wear is reduced is by using lubrication to reduce friction. To achieve this, a layer of oil is placed between two surfaces, forming a barrier that prevents the surfaces from coming into contact with one another. Mineral oils and other very low shear strength materials are commonly used, such as talc, graphite, lead or even gold.

114

Exercise B

In this exercise, students are required to use all they have practised about sentence structure as well as revise what they know about topic sentences and paragraphing.

Set for pairwork. Do not feed back after each question, but allow students to work through the questions, proceeding to write up the whole text. They will need to decide where is the best place for the paragraph in Exercise A, and should also add this to their text. Students can change the wording and add extra phrases to help the flow of the text, as long as the sense remains the same.

If possible, pairs should write their text on an OHT or other visual medium. Select two or three OHTs for display and comments by the whole class. Make any corrections on the text yourself with a coloured pen. Alternatively, circulate the transparencies to other pairs to correct and comment on. These pairs then display the corrected work and explain why they have made the corrections.

Answers

Possible answers:

1/2 Paragraph divisions are given below, with the possible topic sentences underlined. Note that other answers may be possible.

Friction & wear: A study – tribology

Tribology = science and technology of interaction between surfaces in rel. motion

- surfaces appear smooth BUT under microscope, still uneven
  - ∴ when 2 surfaces brought together → actual contact only at ridges
  - ∴ contact force spread over rel. v. small area
  - ∴ intense pressure @ contact points → wear

Tribology concerned w. 3 types of wear:

- adhesive = surface worn away, e.g., sole of shoe → can seize, i.e., lock together
- abrasive = 1 material harder → scratches other, softer one
- erosive = hard particles between surfaces → pitting.

How reduce wear?

- Lubrication
  e.g., mineral oils, other very low shear strength materials

---

Some situations, friction necessary:

e.g., skis → friction = help & hindrance:

one hand, reduce friction (shops apply wax to bottom of skis) → skiers travel v. quickly

other hand, skier turns & digs edges of skis into snow → friction must be sufficient to turn w. control.

---

3 <u>The science and technology of the interaction between surfaces in relative motion is called tribology.</u> Regardless of how smooth a surface appears, it is clearly still uneven when viewed under a microscope. As a result of unevenness, when two surfaces are brought together, the actual surface contact is only at the ridges. The contact force is spread over a relatively very small surface area, which creates intense pressure at the points of contact and causes wear.

<u>Tribology is concerned with three kinds of wear.</u> The first, when the surfaces are worn away, is called *adhesive* wear. This can result in scuffing (like the soles of shoes), and in extreme cases the surfaces will seize; that is, they will lock together. The second kind, called *abrasive wear*, occurs where one surface is harder than the other and causes scratches in the softer material. The third is *erosive* wear and occurs when hard particles find their way between the surfaces and result in pitting.

<u>How can wear be reduced?</u> The main way in which wear is reduced is by using lubrication to reduce friction. To achieve this, a layer of oil is placed between two surfaces, forming a barrier that prevents the surfaces from coming into contact with one another. Mineral oils and other very low shear strength materials are commonly used, such as talc, graphite, lead or even gold.

<u>In some situations, however, friction is necessary.</u> In the case of skis, friction is both a help and a hindrance. On the one hand, in order to reduce friction and help skiers travel very quickly, ski shops apply wax to the bottom of the skis. However, when a skier turns the skis so that the edges dig into the snow, it is at this point that then friction must enable him to maintain sufficient contact with the snow to turn with control.

Closure

Give students some very simple three- or four-word SVO/C sentences from the unit (or make some yourself) and ask them to add as many phrases and clauses as they can to make a long complex sentence. Who can make the longest sentence?

For example:

Friction can cause wear

→ *In engineering systems, when components or surfaces move in relation to each other but are not lubricated, the resulting **friction can cause wear** of different types, as well as generating a lot of heat, which needs to be dissipated from the system …*

(42 words)

Extra activities

1 Work through the *Vocabulary bank* and *Skills bank* if you have not already done so, or as a revision of previous study.

2 Use the *Activity bank* (Teacher's Book additional resources section, Resource 6A).

A Set the wordsearch for individual work (including homework) or pairwork.

Answers

Verb	Noun
apply	application
brake	brake
erode	erosion
fail	failure
force	force
function	functioning
generate	generation
initiate	initiation
lubricate	lubrication
machine	machine
maintain	maintenance
move	motion
oil	oil
oppose	opposition
peak	peak
perform	performance
reduce	reduction
resist	resistance
specify	specification
wear	wear

B Students work in pairs or small groups and try to think of word pairs. They should be able to explain the meaning.

Alternatively, photocopy (enlarged) the words from the additional resources section (Resource 6H) and cut up into cards. Put the A and B words into separate envelopes. Put students into groups of four. Make one set of A and one set of B words for each group. Give one pair in each group the A words and the other pair the B words. Each pair takes it in turns to pick a word from their envelope. The other pair must try to find a word from their own envelope which can go with it.

Accept all reasonable word pairs. Possible pairs are:

Answers

A	B
acoustic	lubrication
ball	bearing
brake	pads
constant	speed
contact	surface
corollary	heat
correct	functioning
design	specification
detrimental	effect
engine	inefficiency
engineering	system
erosive/abrasive/adhesive	wear
friction/normal/applied	force
horizontal/vertical	axis
machine	failure
material	properties
mineral	oils
scalar/peak	value
shear	strength
static/kinetic	friction
stationary	object

7 THE FUTURE OF CARS: BATTERY POWER

In this unit, the focus is on research and development and associated issues. The first listening extract, from a lecture, looks at the need for a review of conventional technology, particularly with regard to its effect on the environment. It also describes the three main types of alternative power supply for cars: the internal combustion engine (ICE), electric motors and hybrids. Finally, the importance of scheduling in planning the widespread introduction of new technology is emphasized. The second listening extract is from a seminar in which criteria for assessing the applicability of technologies to car manufacture are discussed.

Skills focus

🎧 Listening

- understanding speaker emphasis

Speaking

- asking for clarification
- responding to queries and requests for clarification

Vocabulary focus

- compound nouns
- fixed phrases from mechanical engineering
- fixed phrases from academic English
- common lecture language

Key vocabulary

See also the list of fixed phrases from academic English in the *Vocabulary bank* (Course Book page 60).

biofuels	drag	hydrogen	research (n and v)
braking	efficiency	laminating process	sheer (n)
capacity	electric motor	manufacturing	solar cells
carbon dioxide	electrochemical	performance	stick (v)
catalyst	electrode	polypropylene	stress
characteristics	flexible	power supply	technology
chemical reaction	fossil fuels	press (n)	temperature
coefficient	fuel cell	prototype	voltage
compressed air	generate	range	
conventional	greenhouse gas	regenerative braking	
development	hybrid (n)	reliability target	

7.1 Vocabulary

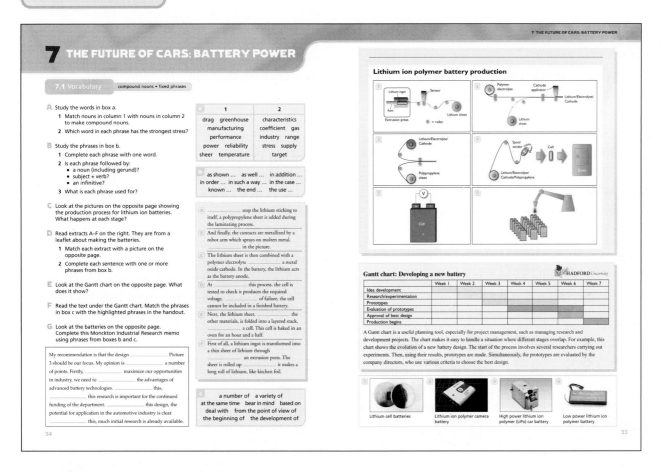

General note

Read the *Vocabulary bank* at the end of the Course Book unit. Decide when, if at all, to refer your students to it. The best time is probably at the very end of the lesson or the beginning of the next lesson, as a summary/revision.

Lesson aims

- understand and use some general academic fixed phrases
- understand and use fixed phrases and compound nouns from the discipline

Introduction

1 Revise some noun phrases (noun + noun, adjective + noun) from previous units. Give students two or three minutes to make word stars with a base word, trying to find as many possible combinations as they can (preferably without having to look at dictionaries).

For example:

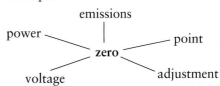

Other base words which could be used are *electric/maximum/ambient/thermal/carbon/fuel*. If they are stuck for ideas, tell them to look back at previous units.

2 Introduce the topic of the lesson by looking at the pictures of lithium ion batteries. How are they made?

Exercise A

Set for individual work and pairwork checking. Feed back with the whole class, making sure that the stress pattern is correct. Ask students to suggest other fixed phrases which could be made using the words in column 2.

Answers

Model answers:

'drag coefficient

greenhouse 'gas

manu'facturing industry

per'formance characteristics

'power supply

relia'bility target

'sheer stress

'temperature range

Exercise B

1/2 Set for individual work and pairwork checking. Feed back with the whole class, building the first three columns of the table in the Answers section on the board.

3 Add the fourth column with the heading 'Use to …'. Give an example of the kind of thing you are looking for, i.e., a phrase which can describe why you would choose to use this fixed phrase. Elicit suggestions from the students to complete the table, supplying the information yourself if students don't know the answer. If students are not sure about the meaning of some of the phrases, give them some example sentences and tell them that you will look further at how they are used shortly. Leave the table on the board as you will return to it.

Answers

Model answers:

Phrase		Followed by …	Use to …
as shown	in/by	noun/ gerund	indicate a diagram or table
as well	as	noun/ gerund	add information
in addition	to	noun/ gerund	add information
in order	to	infinitive	give the purpose for doing something
in such a way	that*	subject + verb	give the result of doing something
in the case	of	noun/ gerund	mention something
known	as	noun	give the special name for something
the end	of	noun	refer to the end of something
the use	of	noun	refer to the use of something

as to is also possible after *in such a way*, although in this exercise, one word is required

Exercise C

Set for pairwork. Students should try to identify what each picture represents. One pair can describe each picture to the whole class. On the board, build up as many key words to describe the process as students can come up with. If students don't know some important words, tell them they will meet them shortly.

Answers

Answers depend on the students.

Exercise D

Explain that the information from the leaflet goes with the pictures they have just discussed. Each extract (A–F) goes with one picture. Students should first read the extracts, checking words they can't guess in the dictionary. They should not pay attention to the spaces at this point.

1 Set for pairwork. Feed back with the whole class. Add any key words which might have been useful in Exercise C to the board.

2 Set for individual work. Refer back to the table in Exercise B, which will help students to choose the correct phrase. Feed back with the whole class.

Answers

Model answers:

Picture	Extract
1	F First of all, a lithium ingot is transformed into a thin sheet of lithium through <u>the use of</u> an extrusion press. The sheet is rolled up <u>in such a way that</u> it makes a long roll of lithium, like kitchen foil.
2	C The lithium sheet is then combined with a polymer electrolyte <u>as well as</u> a metal oxide cathode. In the battery, the lithium acts as the battery anode.
3	A <u>In order to</u> stop the lithium sticking to itself, a polypropylene sheet is added during the laminating process.
4	E Next, the lithium sheet, <u>in addition to</u> the other materials, is folded into a layered stack, <u>known as</u> a cell. This cell is baked in an oven for an hour and a half.
5	D At <u>the end of</u> this process, the cell is tested to check it produces the required voltage. In <u>the case of</u> failure, the cell cannot be included in a finished battery.
6	B And finally, the contacts are metallized by a robot arm which sprays on molten metal, <u>as shown</u> in the picture.

If you wish, ask students to return to the table in Exercise B and write one sentence for each of the fixed phrases to show their meaning. If you can put this into the context of a production process which students are very familiar with, so much the better.

Exercise E

Introduce the Gantt chart – if students have not seen one before – by saying that it is a highly important tool in project management, which is useful for scheduling research and development projects. It shows how different stages in a process follow each other and/or overlap.

Set for pairwork discussion. Feed back with the whole group, making sure that students understand the concept behind the chart. Do not correct or confirm students' views of the content at this point.

Subject note

The Gantt chart was the invention of Henry Laurence Gantt (1861–1919), who was a mechanical engineer. Gantt developed his charts in the early 20th century. His invention was hugely important in management then as well as now. It can be used for large-scale construction projects as well as for small pieces of work that an individual person may have to do.

Exercise F

Set for individual work and pairwork checking. Students should use their dictionaries if they are not sure of the meaning of the phrases. Note that some phrases can be used for the same thing – it is a good idea to use a different word to avoid repetition. Ask students to say which sentence goes with which part of the chart. Which part of the diagram is not mentioned?

Answers

Model answers:

A Gantt chart is a useful planning tool, especially *(for)* from the point of view of project management, such as managing research and development projects. The chart makes it easy to *(handle)* deal with a situation where *(different)* a number of stages overlap. For example, this chart shows *(the evolution of)* the development of a new battery design. *(The start of)* The beginning of the process involves *(several)* a number of researchers carrying out experiments. Then, *(using)* based on their results, prototypes are made. *(Simultaneously)* At the same time, the prototypes are evaluated by the company directors, who *(use)* bear in mind *(various)* a number of/a variety of criteria to choose the best design.

Language note

The fixed phrases here are used in a situation which describes a series of chronological stages. However, the same words can be used when writing or talking in more general abstract academic terms, for example when introducing an essay or lecture or piece of research. This use of these words will be covered later in the unit.

Exercise G

Set for pairwork. Feed back with the whole class.

Answers

Model answers:

My recommendation is that the design (as) shown in Picture 3 should be our focus. My opinion is based on a number of points. Firstly, in order to maximize our opportunities in industry, we need to bear in mind the advantages of advanced battery technologies. In addition to/as well as this, the development of this research is important for the continued funding of the department. In the case of this design, the potential for application in the automotive industry is clear. In addition to/as well as this, much initial research is already available.

Closure

Tell students to cover the text and then describe:

- the typical main stages of a design process, e.g., battery manufacture
- what a typical Gantt chart looks like and what it includes

7.2 Listening

7.2 Listening fixed phrases • sequencing information in sentences

A You are going to hear this lecture. Write four questions you would like answered.

B 🎧 Listen to Part 1 of the lecture.
1 What is the lecturer going to talk about today? Write *yes, no* or *not mentioned*.
   • hybrid engines
   • biofuels
   • other options
   • compressed air
   • electric cars
   • manufacturing
2 What is biofuel?

C 🎧 Listen to Part 2 of the lecture.
1 Make notes in an appropriate form.
2 What is another word for *mineral fuels*?
3 What minerals are currently used as fuel? Give some examples.
4 Were your questions in Exercise A answered?

D Match each phrase in the first column of the table on the right with the type of information that can follow.

E 🎧 Listen to Part 3 of the lecture.
1 Make notes on the information that comes after the phrases in Exercise D.
2 Were your questions in Exercise A answered?

F 🎧 Listen for sentences 1–4 in Part 4 of the lecture. Which sentence (a or b) follows in each case? Why? *See Skills bank.*
1 The internal combustion engine is the conventional technology.
   a In this type of technology, a fairly large engine capacity is required.
   b A fairly large engine capacity is required in this type of technology.
2 This works against forces that cause drag.
   a Examples of these forces are weight and friction.
   b Weight and friction are examples of these forces.
3 A second possibility is to make a much lighter engine.
   a With a lighter engine, the important thing is that a much more efficient car can be produced.
   b What's important with a lighter engine is that a much more efficient car can be produced.
4 So lastly, we come to the hybrid engine.
   a In a hybrid, a different feature is that there is a combination petrol and electric engine.
   b What's different is that in a hybrid, there is a combination petrol and electric engine.

G This lecturer is not very well organized. What problems are there in the lecture?

56

HADFORD *University*

Faculty: Mechanical Engineering

Car technology (Lecture 1)

Lecture overview
   • greenhouse gases
   • electric cars
   • 'hybrids'
   • manufacturing

Fixed phrase	Followed by ...
1 An important concept (is) ...	a different way to think about the topic
2 What do I mean by ...?	an imaginary example
3 Looking at it another way, ...	a concluding comment giving a result of something
4 Say ...	a comment about a diagram or picture
5 In efficiency terms, ...	a new idea or topic that the lecturer wants to discuss
6 As you can see, ...	a key statement or idea
7 In this way ...	a general idea put into an engineering context
8 The point is ...	an explanation of a word or phrase

Lesson aims

- improve comprehension through recognition of fixed phrases and what follows them in terms of words/type of information
- understand how information can be sequenced in different ways within a sentence, e.g., for emphasis (see *Skills bank*)

Further practice in:
- understanding fractured text

General note

Read the *Skills bank – 'Given' and 'new' information in sentences* at the end of the Course Book unit. Decide when, if at all, to refer students to it. The best time, as before, is probably at the very end of the lesson or the beginning of the next lesson, as a summary/revision. Alternatively, use the *Skills bank* in conjunction with Exercise F.

Introduction

Review key vocabulary by writing a selection of words from Lesson 7.1 on the board and asking students to put them into phrases of two or more words.

Exercise A

Remind students about preparing for a lecture. If you wish, review Unit 1 *Skills bank – Making the most of lectures*. Remind students that, when they begin their talks, lecturers usually provide their listeners with an outline in order to aid comprehension. Elicit from the students the kinds of signpost words lecturers might use (e.g., *To start with, ... , Firstly, ... , I'll begin/start by ...ing*, etc.). If necessary, refer students to Unit 5.

Refer students to the lecture slide. Tell them to look at the title and bullet points and to list ideas/make questions for each bullet point. At this stage do not explain any words from the slide, or allow students to check in their dictionaries, as the meanings will be dealt with in the lecture. Set the exercise for pairwork.

Feed back with the whole class: ask several students to read out their questions. Write some of the questions on the board.

🎧 Exercise B

Tell students they are going to hear the introduction to the lecture – not the whole thing. Give students time to read questions 1 and 2. Remind them they will only hear the recording once. Play Part 1. Allow students to compare their answers.

Feed back. Confirm the correct answers. Note that 'manufacturing' is mentioned on the slide, but not in the introduction, so we have no idea if this will be covered or not.

Note: Clarify the difference with the students between *no* and *not mentioned* here: *no* means that the lecturer states that he will not deal with the topic today; *not mentioned* means that he does not say whether he will include it or not today – he says nothing about it.

Answers

Model answers:

1

hybrid engines	yes
biofuels	no
other options	no
compressed air	no
electric cars	yes
manufacturing	not mentioned

2 Biofuel is fuel made from agricultural crops. It is also known as agrofuel.

122

Transcript 🎧 2.1

Part 1

Good afternoon, everyone. What I'm going to talk about today is at the core of design for the road transport industry: specifically, whether a combination of old and new car engine technologies can produce an ideal power supply. In other words, are hybrid engines the car technology of the future?

We have begun to research more efficient power sources, bearing in mind that many current cars are based on technology that is over a hundred years old. Plus, it is very dirty. Newer alternatives include fuels made from agricultural crops. But this agrofuel, which is also known as 'biofuel', is also problematic. What I mean is, there are always mechanical and economic pros and cons in new technologies. Anyway, we'll look at biofuels later – I mean another day.

So, er … in later lectures, we'll also go on to consider other options being researched by engineers, including even compressed air. Today, however, we will deal with the features of electric cars and hybrid cars.

🎧 Exercise C

Refer students to the first point on the lecture slide ('greenhouse gases'). Ask students to suggest an appropriate type of notes. The key word here is *gases*, which should instantly trigger the idea of a flow chart (see Unit 1) or cycle diagram.

Give students time to read the questions. Can they suggest the other key words which accompany *fuels*? (i.e., *renewable*, *unleaded*). Write these on the board. Play Part 2.

Put students in pairs to compare their notes and discuss the questions. With the whole class, ask students how many answers to their questions in Exercise A they heard.

Build the flow chart from the Answers section on the board, at the same time checking the answers to questions 2 and 3, and eliciting synonyms for the words in the chart.

Answers

Model answers:

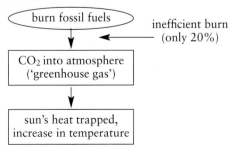

2 Fossil fuels

3 Oil, natural gas, coal, wood

4 Answers depend on students' questions.

Transcript 🎧 2.2

Part 2

As we have seen in earlier sessions, fossil fuel engines are currently quite inefficient. As we know, only about 20% of the energy in your fuel actually gets converted, or is used in moving the vehicle. But that is not the only concern.

Now, another term for fossil fuels is *mineral* fuels. And as well as being inefficient, burning them releases carbon dioxide into the atmosphere, as we saw previously. Now, CO_2 is a greenhouse gas. 'Greenhouse' in this case can be thought of as trapping the sun's heat around the earth, causing the average temperature to rise. In other words, as we continue to burn oil, natural gas and coal – and wood – the global temperature increases. And then, finally, we might see catastrophic results.

Exercise D

Explain that these are common phrases in an academic context such as a lecture. Knowing the meaning of the phrases will help a lot with comprehension. Make sure students understand that the items in the second column are not in the correct order.

Set for individual work and pairwork checking. Tell students to check the meaning of any words they don't know in a dictionary. They should be able to guess the meanings of the phrases, even if they don't actually know the phrases.

Feed back with the whole class, completing the first two columns of the chart in the Answers section for Exercise E on the board. (Alternatively, make an OHT or other visual display from Resource 7B in the additional resources section.) Once the 'Followed by …' column is completed, this will act as a predictive support for Part 3 of the lecture.

Methodology note

Two-column activities are good for pair checking and practice. Once students have got the correct answers they can test each other in pairs. Student A covers the first column and tries to remember the phrases, then B covers the second column and tries to remember the purpose of each phrase.

You can then check memory by getting students to close their books and giving a phrase; students (as a group or individually) must give its purpose. Then change roles.

🎧 Exercise E

1 Tell students that in the next part of the lecture they will hear the phrases in Exercise D. They know now what *type* of information is likely to follow. Now they must try to hear what *actual* information is given. If you wish, photocopy the table in the additional resources section (Resource 7B) for students to write their answers on.

Do the first one as an example. Play the first sentence of the recording and stop after *'regenerative braking'*. Ask students: *What is the important concept?* (Answer: *'regenerative braking'*.)

Play the rest of the recording, pausing briefly at the points indicated by a // to allow students to make notes. Put students in pairs to check their answers.

Feed back with the whole class, asking questions based on the words in the 'Followed by …' column. For example:

After phrase number 2, what is the word or phrase that is explained?

After phrase number 6, what is the diagram that is commented on?

2 Refer back to students' questions in Exercise A. Discuss with the whole class whether they heard any answers to their questions.

Answers

Model answers:

1

	Fixed phrase	Followed by …	Actual information (suggested answers)
1	An important concept (is) …	a new idea or topic that the lecturer wants to discuss	regenerative braking
2	What do I mean by …?	an explanation of a word or phrase	explanation of regenerative braking
3	Looking at it another way, …	a different way to think about the topic	electric cars have serious drawbacks
4	Say …	an imaginary example	a situation in which braking is central
5	In efficiency terms, …	a general idea put into an engineering context	added value can be calculated in terms of efficiency
6	As you can see, …	a comment about a diagram or picture	the storage of kinetic energy from braking
7	In this way …	a concluding comment giving a result of something	every time we brake, energy can be stored
8	The point is …	a key statement or idea	efficiency is increased by using the car to create the power source

2 Answers depend on students' questions.

Transcript 🎧 2.3

Part 3

Now, an important concept in new car technology is regenerative braking. What do I mean by regenerative braking? I'll explain.

Electric cars have huge advantages: no fuel tank, oil pump or filter; no valves, cams, fan belts or clutch, like in an internal combustion engine. All this means is that an electric car is fairly simple under the hood; all it needs is a battery.

However, looking at it another way, there are serious drawbacks. First of all, batteries are currently not as good a method of energy storage as petrol fuel itself – they are quite heavy for the amount of energy they store. The idea of regenerative braking goes some way to solving this.

Let's look at an example. Say you're driving for a long time on a road with a lot of bends. When the brakes are applied, there's a lot of kinetic energy going to waste as the vehicle slows down. The friction in the brakes generates energy in the form of heat that just dissipates into the air. In efficiency terms, this is a huge waste. To help you understand this idea clearly, you can look for a moment at the Monckton Industrial Research leaflet I have given you. As you can see, in a hybrid or electric car, that energy is converted into electricity by the motor (running as a generator) and stored in a battery. In this way, every time we decelerate, energy is stored for use later in the electric motor. The point is that by using the operation of the car to produce the power source, efficiency increases significantly.

🎧 Exercise F

The purpose of this exercise is to look at how information tends to be structured in sentences. It also requires very close attention to the listening text.

Before listening, allow students time to read through the sentences. In pairs, set them to discuss which sentence (**a** or **b**) they think will follow the numbered sentences.

Play Part 4 all the way through. Students should choose sentence **a** or **b**. Put them in pairs to check and discuss why **a** or **b** was the sentence they heard.

Feed back with the whole class. Deal with sentences 1 and 2 first. Tell students that all the sentences are correct, but sentence **a** 'sounds better' when it comes after the first sentence. This is because of the way that sentences go together and the way in which information is organized in a sentence. Draw the table on the next page on the board. Show how the underlined words in the second sentence have been mentioned in the first sentence. In the second sentence, the underlined words are 'old' or 'given' information. When sentences follow each other in a conversation (or a piece of writing), usually the 'given' information comes in the first part of a sentence.

Now look at sentences 3 and 4. These are different. The normal choice would be the **a** sentences. However, here the speaker wanted to emphasize the idea of 'important' and 'different'. So a *Wh~* cleft sentence structure was used, which changes the usual order of

information. Show this on the table as below. This 'fronting' of information has the effect of special focus for emphasis.

Further examples of different ways to 'front' information and more practice will be given in Lesson 7.3.

First sentence		Second sentence	
		Given information	New information
1 The internal combustion engine is the <u>conventional technology</u>.		**a** In <u>this type of technology</u>, ... is required.	... a fairly large engine capacity
2 This works against <u>forces that cause drag</u>.		**a** <u>Examples of these forces</u> ...	... are weight and friction.
3 A second possibility is <u>to make a much lighter engine.</u>	normal order	**a** With a <u>lighter engine</u>, ...	... <u>the important thing</u> is that a much more efficient car can be produced.
	special focus	**b** What's <u>important</u> with a lighter engine is ...	... that a much more efficient car can be produced.
4 So lastly, we come to <u>the hybrid engine</u>.	normal order	**a** In <u>a hybrid</u>, ...	... a <u>different</u> feature is that there is a combination petrol and electric engine.
special focus		**b** What's <u>different</u> is ...	... that in a hybrid, there is a combination petrol and electric engine.

Language note

In English, important information can be placed at the beginning or at the end of a sentence. There are two types of important information. The first part of the sentence contains the topic and the second part contains some kind of information or comment about the topic. Usually the comment is the more syntactically complicated part of the sentence.

Once a piece of text or a piece of conversation (i.e., a piece of discourse) has gone beyond the first sentence, a 'given'/'new' principle operates. Information which is 'given', in other words that has already been mentioned, goes at the beginning of the sentence. Normally speaking, information which is new goes at the end of the sentence. So in the second sentence of a piece of discourse, an aspect of the comment from the previous sentence may become the topic. Thus the topic of the second sentence, if it has already been mentioned in the previous sentence, is also 'given'. Of course, the given information may not be referred to with exactly the same words in the second sentence. Other ways to refer to the given information include reference words (*it, he, she, this, that, these, those*, etc.) or vocabulary items with similar meanings.

Information structure is covered in the *Skills bank* in the Course Book unit.

Transcript 🎧 2.4

Part 4

Now ... er ... let's see ... oh dear, I see we're running short of time ... so let's move on to the second new technology.

You've probably seen hybrid cars on the roads. So how are they different? Of course, the internal combustion engine is the conventional technology. In this type of technology, a fairly large engine capacity is required. The bigger engine allows a large and constant amount of power to be generated. This works against forces that cause drag. Examples of these forces are weight and friction. You can get from zero to high power very quickly. It also allows quick acceleration. But in fact, only a small amount of the engine power – perhaps about a tenth of the maximum capacity – is needed to drive at a steady pace. The additional power is there only for acceleration. And a big engine creates problems: it is heavy and inefficient at part load, and as a result requires the use of extra fuel.

A second possibility is to make a much lighter engine. What's important with a lighter engine is that a much more efficient car can be produced. When we use small engines, we use smaller cylinders, holding less fuel and using lighter pistons, and we can control how we load it, and so save more fuel.

However, we would need to introduce some other way of giving us that extra boost power for acceleration. So lastly, we come to the hybrid engine. What's different is that in a hybrid, there is a combination petrol and electric engine. As well as a small petrol engine for cruising, we introduce a light electric motor with a bigger battery to give us the extra power for acceleration. And just like the electric car, the hybrid can store energy through the process of regenerative braking.

Now ... oh dear, I was going to mention advantages and disadvantages of this technology, but ... ah ... I see that time is moving on. So instead, I'm going to ...

Exercise G

Set for pairwork discussion. Feed back with the whole class. Note that the lecture has not yet finished. The last part will be heard in Lesson 7.3.

Answers

Model answers:

Manufacturing was not mentioned in the introduction, but is on the lecture slide.

The lecturer is running out of time.

The lecturer has not had time to talk about advantages and disadvantages of hybrid technology.

Closure

Ask students to group these products according to whether they think they are most likely to be made with petrol, electric or hybrid engines, and why.

bicycle

bus

construction equipment

golf buggy

large family saloon car

military vehicle

moon exploration vehicle

motorbike

racing car

small town car

taxi

train

7.3 Extending skills

7.3 Extending skills · stress within words · fixed phrases · giving sentences a special focus

A Listen to some stressed syllables. Identify the word below in each case. Number each word.
Example:
You hear: 1 bus /bʌs/ You write:

acceleration ___	conventional ___	generate ___
biofuel ___	efficiency ___	greenhouse ___
capacity ___	electric ___	maximum ___
combustion 1	engine ___	technology ___

B Listen to the final part of the lecture from Lesson 7.2.
1 Complete the notes on the right by adding a symbol in each space.
2 What research task(s) are students asked to do?

C Study the phrases from the lecture in the blue box (below right). For which of the following purposes did the lecturer use each phrase?
- to introduce a new topic
- to finish a list
- to emphasize a major point
- to give an example
- to add points
- to restate

D Rewrite these sentences to give a special focus. Begin with the words in brackets.
1 Henry Gantt came up with an idea to help with scheduling. (It)
2 Gantt invented his charts in the early 1900s. (It)
3 Research and development is very important for this whole area. (What)
4 Making hybrid and electric cars more widespread is highly complex because the industry has to consider a wide variety of factors. (Two sentences. First = It; second = The reason)
5 Gantt charts show what processes are happening at any one time. (The advantage)
See Skills bank.

E Choose one section of the lecture. Refer to your notes and give a spoken summary. Use the fixed phrases and ways of giving special focus that you have looked at.

F Work with a partner.
1 Make a Gantt chart for an activity, project or process.
2 Present your chart to another pair. Practise using fixed phrases and ways of giving special focus.
See Vocabulary bank and Skills bank.

Make new tech. widespread complex.
1. some factors ___ key problems in the tech., drivers want long trips ___ resolve limited range of elec. cars
2. v. little maintenance infrastructure ___ not attractive to public
Manufacturing challenges design?
How to introduce machinery maintenance networks?
Henry Gantt ___ Gantt charts (early 1900s)
Hybrid ___ elec. cars rely on new tech. ___ untested ___ public not confident ___ Gantt charts used for planning

et cetera
In other words, …
Let's take …
Let me put it another way.
Not to mention the fact that …
Plus there's the fact that …
The fact of the matter is, …
You've probably heard of …

57

Lesson aims

- extend knowledge of fixed phrases commonly used in lectures
- give sentences a special focus (see *Skills bank*)

Further practice in:

- stress within words

Introduction

As in Units 3 and 5, tell students to ask you questions about the information in the lecture in Lesson 7.2 as if you were the lecturer. Remind them about asking for information politely. If they need to revise how to do this, tell them to look back at the *Skills bank* for Unit 3.

Exercise A

Remind students of the importance of stressed syllables in words (see the teaching notes for Unit 3, Lesson 3.3, Exercise A). Play the recording, pausing after the first few to check that students understand the task.

Feed back, perhaps playing the recording again for each word before checking. Ideally, mark up an OHT or other projection of the words. Finally, check students' pronunciation of the words.

Answers

acceleration	3
biofuel	4
capacity	5
combustion	1
conventional	9
efficiency	10
electric	12
engine	7
generate	2
greenhouse	11
maximum	6
technology	8

Transcript 2.5

1 com'bustion
2 'generate
3 accele'ration
4 'biofuel
5 ca'pacity
6 'maximum
7 'engine
8 tech'nology
9 con'ventional
10 ef'ficiency
11 'greenhouse
12 e'lectric

Exercise B

Write these words on the board and ask students to say what symbols you can use for them when taking notes. Put the symbols on the board.

because	∵
for example	e.g.
is, means	=
invented, leads to*	→
therefore, so	∴
and	& +
a list	numbers or bullet points
or	/

*the arrow has a wide range of possible meanings, including *made, produced, did, causes, results in*, etc.

Tell students they will hear the final part of the lecture. Ask them to read the notes through. Remind them also to listen for their research task. Play Part 5.

Put students in pairs to compare their symbols. Feed back with the whole class, if possible using an OHT or other visual display of the notes. Discuss acceptable alternatives, e.g., *machinery & maintenance networks instead of machinery/maintenance networks.*

Answers

Model answers:

1 Make new tech. widespread = complex ∵

    1 some factors = key problems in the tech., e.g., drivers want long trips → resolve limited range of elec. cars

    2 v. little maintenance infrastructure → not attractive to public

       Manufacturing challenges = design?

       How to introduce machinery / maintenance networks?

       Henry Gantt → Gantt charts (early 1900s)

       Hybrid & elec. cars rely on new tech. = untested / public not confident ∴ Gantt charts used for planning

2 They must research the main areas of research for the development of new engine technologies.

Transcript 🎧 2.6

Part 5

I'm going to finish with some comments on the challenges of production – in other words, manufacturing.

Now, the fact of the matter is, it's a highly complex task to make hybrid and electric cars more widespread. The reason for this is that the car industry has to consider a variety of different factors – not to mention the fact that some of these factors are key problems in the technology itself. Let's take mileage: drivers want to make long trips, so the limited independent range of electric cars has to be resolved. Plus, there's the fact that there is very little infrastructure for maintenance; that makes the cars unattractive to the public.

OK. Where was I? Oh yes … So, manufacturing challenges include not only product design, but planning of how the products, and the new production machinery, maintenance networks, et cetera, can be introduced in a staged way. You've probably heard about Gantt charts? It was Henry Gantt who came up with a very simple idea to help with scheduling, to enable these sorts of changes to be implemented – the Gantt chart. Gantt charts help with organizing and planning changes. The advantage of Gantt charts is that they show what

processes are happening at any one time. So, although it was in the early 1900s that Gantt invented his charts, they are still very much used today. This carefully staged development is important because hybrid and electric cars rely on new technologies which are untested in industry, and don't enjoy public confidence.

To sum up, then, new engine technologies are relatively immature. Let me put it another way … alternatives to fossil fuels aren't ready to be introduced into mainstream, mass-market manufacturing at a competitive price.

Oh, I almost forgot to mention your research topics. OK, well, what's important for this whole area is research and development. So I'd like you to find out about the main areas of research at the moment for the development of these technologies.

Exercise C

Set for pairwork. Feed back with the whole class. If necessary, play the relevant sections again. Ask for other phrases which have similar meanings, particularly from Lesson 7.3, and also from Unit 5. Build the table in the Answers section on the board. Accept any suitable words or phrases for the third column.

Answers

Model answers:

Use	Fixed phrase	Other phrases
to introduce a new topic	You've probably heard of/about …	Now, an important concept is …
to make a major point	The fact of the matter is, …	Actually, … In fact, … The point is that …
to add points	I almost forgot to mention … Not to mention the fact that … Plus there's the fact that …	also, and, too
to finish a list	et cetera	and so on
to give an example	Let's take …	For example, … e.g., … Let's look at an example of this. For instance, …
to restate	Let me put it another way. In other words, …	What I mean is … That is to say, … By that I mean … To put it another way, …

Language note

The phrases above are appropriate in speaking. Many are not suitable for written language, for which different phrases should be used.

Exercise D

Students need to decide which word(s) should receive the particular focus and then try to rewrite the sentences. Depending on the class, they can work in pairs or individually first.

Feed back with the whole class. Take each sentence in turn. Ask for suggestions as to which aspect could receive special emphasis (actual words are underlined below). Accept any reasonable answers. If you wish, replay Part 5 of the lecture for students to check their answers. Note that:

● sentences 1, 2 and the first part of 4 use an *It* construction to give the special focus

● sentence 3 uses a *Wh~* cleft sentence already seen in Lesson 7.2

● sentences 4 and 5 introduce new, general words (often found in academic contexts) followed by *is* plus a *that* clause

Answers

Model answers:

1 <u>Henry Gantt</u> came up with an idea to help with scheduling. (*It*)

It was Henry Gantt who came up with an idea to help with scheduling.

2 Gantt invented his charts <u>in the early 1900s</u>. (*It*)
It was in the early 1900s that Gantt invented his charts.

3 Research and development is very <u>important</u> for this whole area. (*What*)

What's very important for this whole area is research and development.

4 Making hybrid and electric cars more widespread is <u>highly complex because</u> the industry has to consider a wide variety of factors. (*Two sentences. First = 'It'; Second = 'The reason'*)

It's a highly complex task to make hybrid and electric cars more widespread. The reason for this is that the industry has to consider a wide variety of factors.

5 <u>Gantt charts</u> show what processes are happening at any one time. (*The advantage*)

The advantage of Gantt charts is that they show what processes are happening at any one time.

After completing Exercises C and D, students can be referred to the *Vocabulary bank* and the *Skills bank* for consolidation and preparation for Exercise E.

Exercise E

Set the initial preparation for individual work. Students can refer to their notes in Lesson 7.2 (Exercises C and E) or the notes for completion in Lesson 7.3 (Exercise B). They should think about how they can use the phrases they have looked at, and ways of giving special focus/emphasis. (Note: They should not write out exactly what they are going to say in complete sentences and then read!)

Put students in pairs to give their oral summaries to each other, preferably pairing students who have chosen different sections to summarize.

Go around the class noting any problems or especially good examples of language use. You may wish to choose one or two individuals to give their summary to the whole class.

With the whole class, feed back any language or other difficulties which you noticed.

Exercise F

1 Set for pairwork. Suggest simple activities like making a cup of tea or a sandwich or writing an essay. Students should first list all the different processes and then decide how to order them and which processes overlap. They should make a Gantt chart and put the activities in it. They should decide what time units to use.

2 Put the pairs in groups of four to present their charts to each other.

Closure

Dictate some words for which students have learnt note-taking symbols or abbreviations, such as *and, minus, approximately, less than, results in, therefore, because,* etc., *as, since, for example, approximately.* Students should write the symbol or abbreviation.

Remind them of the list of symbols and abbreviations at the back of the Course Book.

7.4 Extending skills

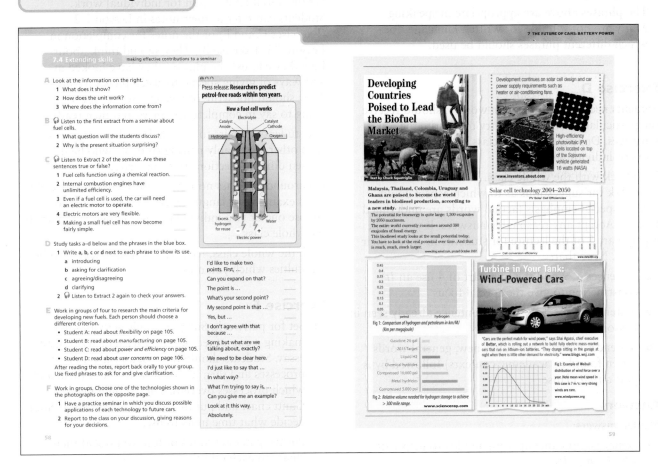

7.4 Extending skills · making effective contributions to a seminar

A Look at the information on the right.
  1 What does it show?
  2 How does the unit work?
  3 Where does the information come from?

B 🎧 Listen to the first extract from a seminar about fuel cells.
  1 What question will the students discuss?
  2 Why is the present situation surprising?

C 🎧 Listen to Extract 2 of the seminar. Are these sentences true or false?
  1 Fuel cells function using a chemical reaction.
  2 Internal combustion engines have unlimited efficiency.
  3 Even if a fuel cell is used, the car will need an electric motor to operate.
  4 Electric motors are very flexible.
  5 Making a small fuel cell has now become fairly simple.

D Study tasks a–d below and the phrases in the blue box.
  1 Write a, b, c or d next to each phrase to show its use.
    a introducing
    b asking for clarification
    c agreeing/disagreeing
    d clarifying
  2 🎧 Listen to Extract 2 again to check your answers.

E Work in groups of four to research the main criteria for developing new fuels. Each person should choose a different criterion.
  • Student A: read about *flexibility* on page 105.
  • Student B: read about *manufacturing* on page 105.
  • Student C: read about *power and efficiency* on page 105.
  • Student D: read about *user concerns* on page 106.
  After reading the notes, report back orally to your group. Use fixed phrases to ask for and give clarification.

F Work in groups. Choose one of the technologies shown in the photographs on the opposite page.
  1 Have a practice seminar in which you discuss possible applications of each technology to future cars.
  2 Report to the class on your discussion, giving reasons for your decisions.

Lesson aims

● make effective contributions to a seminar:
  using pre-organizers – *I'd like to make two points; I don't agree with that because …*
  responding to queries by clarifying – *What I'm trying to say is … ; What I meant was …*

Introduction

Revise phrases from the previous lessons. Give a word or phrase and ask students to give one with a similar meaning. Ask for phrases from the previous lesson which can be used to:

● introduce a new topic
● emphasize a major point
● add a point
● finish a list
● give an example

Exercise A

Set for pairwork discussion. Feed back.

Answers

Possible answers:

1 It shows a diagram of a simple fuel cell, showing how it works.

2 Hydrogen and oxygen are passed into a system containing an electrolyte. A chemical reaction happens between them in which electricity is produced. The exhaust products are water (H_2O) and excess hydrogen (H_2).

3 The headline comes from a press release.

🎧 Exercise B

Allow students time to read the two questions. Play Part 1 once only. Check answers in pairs. Feed back with the whole class.

Answers

Model answers:

1 Why are fuel cells not more commonly used commercially?

2 Fuel cells function in a way that is fully understood, and produce a large amount of energy efficiently. The market is looking for an environmentally friendly alternative to petrol.

Transcript 🎧 2.7

Extract 1

Now, as we know, power supply is one of the most important issues in the design of more environmentally friendly cars. I asked you to look at the case of fuel cells, which have become the focus of a lot of investment. Fuel cells function in a way we fully understand, and produce a large amount of energy efficiently. The market, we are told, is looking for a new, environmentally friendly, alternative to petrol. So, why are fuel cells not more commonly used commercially? Let's have some ideas. Firstly, can someone explain how a fuel cell works, please?

🎧 Exercise C

Allow students time to read the questions. Play Extract 2 straight through once while they mark the answers true or false. Check in pairs and/or with the whole class. Check any unknown vocabulary, such as *expand on*, *potential applications*.

Answers

1 true	
2 false	They have a maximum efficiency (defined by the Carnot law of thermodynamics).
3 true	
4 true	
5 false	The idea seems simple, but fuel cells still need large amounts of surrounding equipment to function.

Transcript 🎧 2.8

Extract 2

Note: The underlining relates to Exercise D.

LEILA: A fuel cell is an electrochemical cell, but instead of having all the fuel contained within it, as a battery does, the fuel and oxidant pass *through* it.

EVIE: Can you expand on that, Leila?

LEILA: Sure. The cell has a positive and a negative electrode in an electrolyte. Ions flow between them as part of the chemical reaction.

LECTURER: Thanks, Leila. OK, can anyone tell me what advantages fuel cells might have for vehicles?

MAJED: I'd like to make two points. First, traditional internal combustion engines have a maximum efficiency called the Carnot efficiency. This limit is governed by fundamental thermodynamics.

EVIE: So?

MAJED: Well, the point is, fuel cells are not limited by the Carnot efficiency, so they might be able to achieve higher efficiencies than heat engines.

LECTURER: What's your second point, Majed?

MAJED: My second point is that fuel cells produce electricity direct. Electricity is a very versatile form of energy, and that means that fuel cells have a wide variety of potential applications.

EVIE: Yes, but it's a disadvantage in a car application. The cell can't drive the wheels direct, so you have to put in an electric motor!

MAJED: I don't agree with that, Evie, because electric motors are a great way of producing shaft power.

JACK: Sorry, but what are we talking about exactly?

MAJED: OK, look at it this way. Electric motors have a very high power and high torque at a wide range of speeds. Plus, they give the designer a lot of flexibility.

JACK: Can you give me an example?

MAJED: Sure. You may not need to include a gearbox with an electric car, because of the excellent torque-speed characteristics of the motor.

LECTURER: You're all making good points about motors. But let's focus on fuel cells. We need to be clear here that fuel cells are only just beginning to be commercially available.

LEILA: Yes. One big issue is that the fuel cell stack requires a lot of additional equipment around it, just to make it work and keep it going.

EVIE: In what way?

LEILA: I mean pumps, control systems, management systems ... What I'm trying to say is, although a fuel cell appears in essence to be a beautifully simple device, making a small practical one is difficult.

JACK: I'd just like to say that they are also quite expensive for certain applications.

LECTURER: Why is this?

JACK: Because the catalyst used in the chemical reaction is usually platinum, which is a rare and expensive element.

LECTURER: Absolutely. There's still work to be done. But durability and reliability targets have begun to be met, so the possibility for mass production may soon become a reality.

🎧 Exercise D

Check the meaning of 'introducing' phrases. This means a phrase to use before your main statement to announce that you are going to say something. It may also signal how much you are going to say, or how important you think what you are going to say is.

1 Set for individual work and pairwork checking. Feed back.

2 Play Extract 2 from Exercise C. Ask students to tell you to stop when they hear each phrase (underlined in the transcript on the previous page). Check what kind of phrase they think it is. Get students to repeat the phrase to copy the intonation. If you wish, ask students to suggest other phrases that could be used in the same way.

Answers

Model answers:

Can you expand on that?	b
I'd like to make two points. First, …	a
The point is …	d
What's your second point?	b
My second point is that …	a
Yes, but …	c
I don't agree with that because …	c
Sorry, but what are we talking about, exactly?	b
Look at it this way.	d
Can you give me an example?	b
We need to be clear here.	d
In what way?	b
What I'm trying to say is, …	d
I'd just like to say that …	a
Absolutely.	c

Exercise E

With the whole class, revise asking for information. Remind students of the questions used by the lecturer in Unit 5, Lesson 5.3 (see Unit 5 *Skills bank*). Remind students also about reporting information to people (see Unit 3 *Skills bank*).

Set students to work in groups of four. Each student should choose one criterion for developing new fuels and turn to the relevant page to make notes on the information. When everyone is ready they should feed back to their group, giving an oral report on the information. It's important that they do not simply read aloud the information, but use it to inform their speaking.

Alternatively, the research activity can be done as a 'wall dictation' as follows. Use Resource 7C in the additional resources section. Make large A3 (or A4) size copies of the fuel sources information (one type of research per page) and pin the sheets on the classroom walls. Each student should leave his/her seat and go to the wall to find the information he/she needs. Students should not write anything down: instead they should read and try to remember the information. Then they return to their group and tell them the information. If they forget something, they can go back to the wall to have another look.

Circulate, encouraging students to ask for clarification and to use the appropriate phrases when giving clarification. Note where students are having difficulty with language and where things are going well. When everyone has finished, feed back to the class on points you have noticed while listening in to the discussions.

Exercise F

Move on from Exercise E to this simulation. Encourage students to make this as realistic as possible by choosing a technology that they know or can identify with.

Alternatively, you could have a 'pyramid discussion'. Choose one technology for the whole class to debate and put students in pairs to discuss its potential applications. After a short while, the pair should join together with another pair. This group of four should then come to an agreement on the most important applications. The group of four should then join another group of four. One or two people from each group of eight should then present the decision and the reasons for the decision to the class. It will help their presentation if they use visual aids such as diagrams. Finally, the whole class should try to reach agreement on the most potentially useful technology, taking a vote if necessary.

Remind students about agreeing and disagreeing, and about good and bad ways to contribute to seminar discussions (refer to Unit 5 if necessary).

While the representatives are presenting their group decisions, you should occasionally interrupt with a wrong interpretation so that students are forced to clarify their statements. Or you could ask for clarification.

Closure

Choose three technologies from the following list. Ask students to first discuss and then *describe* and *evaluate* the usefulness of each technology for cars in their own country:

- wind power
- wave power
- agrofuels
- electric motors
- ICEs
- solar power
- hybrid engines

Extra activities

1 Work through the *Vocabulary bank* and *Skills bank* if you have not already done so, or as a revision of previous study.

2 Use the *Activity bank* (Teacher's Book additional resources section, Resources 7A).

   A Set the crossword for individual work (including homework) or pairwork.

   Answers

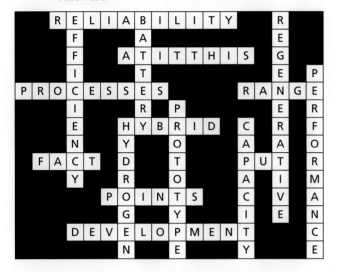

3 Make some statements about what you're going to do after the class and ask students to transform them into *Wh~* cleft sentences. For example:

I'm going to have a coffee after the class.

→ *What you're going to do after the class is have a coffee.*

I might go to a film tonight.

→ *What you might do tonight is go to a film.*

Put students in pairs to practise.

8 ENGINEERING AND SUSTAINABILITY

This unit looks at the concept of sustainability and the extent to which engineering holds the key to future sustainable development. The reading text focuses on the challenges to engineering, with particular regard to energy, materials and waste.

Skills focus

Reading
- understanding dependent clauses with passives

Writing
- paraphrasing
- expanding notes into complex sentences
- recognizing different essay/writing assignment types/structures:
  descriptive
  analytical
  comparison/evaluation
  problem/solution
- writing essay plans
- writing essays

Vocabulary focus
- synonyms
- nouns from verbs
- definitions
- common 'direction' verbs in essay titles (*discuss, analyze, evaluate*, etc.)

Key vocabulary

carbon emissions	emission	pollution
climate change	environment	recycling
combustion	exploit	renewable(s)
consumption	finite	replenishable
cradle to cradle	fossil fuel	resource
cradle to grave	greenhouse gas	sustainability
depletion	hydrocarbon	sustainable development
development	imply	triple bottom line
disposal	manufacture	utilize
ecosystem	material	waste (n)
efficiency	planet	

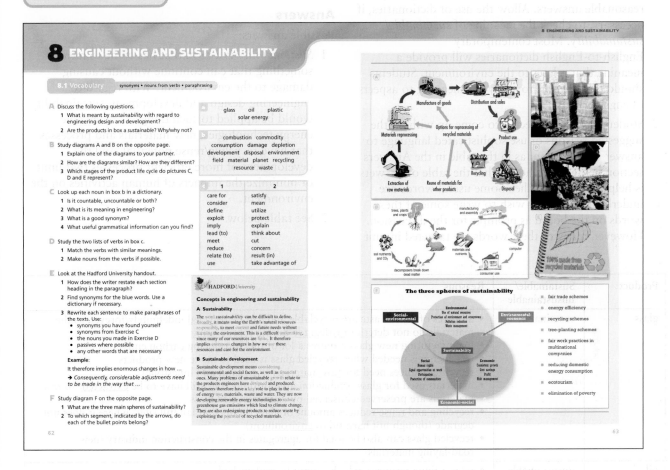

Lesson aims

- extend knowledge of synonyms and word sets (enables paraphrasing at word level)
- make nouns and noun phrases from verbs (enables paraphrasing at sentence level)

Further practice in paraphrasing at sentence level with:

- passives
- synonymous phrases
- negatives
- replacement subjects

Introduction

Revise ways of paraphrasing sentences. Write the following sentences from Unit 6 on the board and ask students to say what changes have been made to the paraphrased sentences.

Original sentence: *The horizontal axis shows applied force.*

Paraphrase: *Applied force is shown in the horizontal axis.*

(answer: change active to passive)

Original sentence: *In spite of an increase in the force acting on the object, the value for kinetic friction remains the same.*

Paraphrase: *The kinetic friction's value remains the same even though the force acting on the object has increased.*

(answer: change in word order, replacement subject)

Exercise A

1 Set for pairwork or class discussion. Accept any reasonable answers. Allow the use of dictionaries, if necessary, to check the meaning of *sustainable/sustainability*. Most contemporary English-to-English dictionaries will provide a meaning that relates to the environment. Students should then be able to apply the meaning to aspects of engineering.

2 Students are not expected to come up with all the suggested reasons or use sophisticated language to answer the question (as in the table in the Answers section below). It is hoped that the table of answers is helpful for the teacher. Some useful words are underlined. You may wish to write some of these words on the board as prompts for the discussion. However, many of these words are targeted in unit activities, so there is no need to pre-teach too many at this point.

Answers

Possible answers:

1 *Sustainability* is a term that has come to mean something that can continue without causing damage to the environment. With regard to engineering design and development, sustainability would be applied to such things as renewable energy technologies, new materials and processes that have recycling/reuse potential, and the development of more efficient processes that limit or minimize the impacts of human activities on the environment.

2 See table below.

Product	Sustainable/ unsustainable	Reasons
glass	sustainable	• all types of glass waste are recyclable and can be <u>recycled</u> indefinitely/forever, as the materials do not <u>deteriorate/degrade</u> during <u>reprocessing</u> • manufacturing new glass requires a lot of <u>fuel</u>, producing <u>carbon emissions</u> • less <u>energy</u> is needed when recycled glass is used to make new products • recycling reduces need for <u>raw materials</u> (e.g., sand and limestone) • materials used for glass production are not <u>finite</u>, but still have to be <u>extracted</u>, so raw materials are preserved/conserved by using recycled glass • recycling and <u>reuse</u> reduces amount of glass dumped in landfill sites, where it does not degrade (though not harmful to <u>environment</u>) • recycled glass can also be used for aggregates in the construction industry (new road-laying materials)
oil	unsustainable	• oil is a finite resource, which cannot be <u>replenished</u> • commodities produced from oil are sources of <u>pollution</u> • provides economic and social benefits (jobs, fuel for transportation, industry, domestic use, etc.) but causes harm to the environment • '<u>sustainable</u>' development in oil industry focuses on improving technologies to manage finite resources, and recycling possibilities for products and materials • industry claims to abide by environmental controls to <u>limit/minimize</u> environmental impacts (legal requirements) • oil <u>biodegrades/breaks down</u> in natural environment, but takes a long time • additional problem of dismantling disused <u>offshore</u> oil/gas installations (platforms); more than 6,500 installations worldwide, many built more than 30 years ago; dismantling could be <u>hazardous</u>
plastic	both	• all types of plastic are <u>capable</u> of being recycled • *but* production and use of plastics has environmental impacts: large quantities of finite resources (<u>fossil fuels</u>) are needed as raw material (oil) and as energy for manufacturing • manufacturing needs quantities of other resources (e.g., water) and produces waste and <u>emissions</u> • involves hazardous chemicals (used as stabilizers and colourants) • most plastic products are <u>non-degradable</u>; when disposed of in landfill sites, they will stay around forever • current problems with recycling <u>domestic</u> plastic waste: collection and manual sorting due to numerous types of plastic • some development of degradable plastics (e.g., carrier bags) which degrade under certain conditions (e.g., in sunlight); but may lead to increase in <u>methane</u> emissions • development in <u>bio-plastics</u> (e.g., polymers made from plant sugars)
solar energy	sustainable	• <u>renewable</u> • a clean fuel technology; no carbon emissions from solar-to-fuel technologies • one of few major options as an alternative to fossil fuels • can be <u>generated</u> domestically (roof-mounted cells); also relevant is design of homes to maximize solar heat • benefits to economy, environment and society

Exercise B

1/2 Set for pairwork discussion. Teach the expression *life cycle* in relation to product manufacture and use. Students take it in turns to describe and explain diagram A or B and then discuss similarities and differences. Tell students to bear in mind the points they have just discussed. Feed back with the whole class. Check understanding and pronunciation of technical/sub-technical vocabulary shown in diagram A (e.g., *extraction, disposal, reuse, recycling*).

3 Set for pairwork discussion. Feed back with the whole class.

Answers

Possible answers:

1 A The diagram shows the life cycle of a product (in this case, a washing machine) from raw material extraction to end of life. The two options shown at end of life are disposal or recycling. The recycling option shows how materials can be reused for other products through reprocessing and manufacture. This is a simple demonstration of sustainability.

   B The diagram shows how the life cycle of a product should try to mimic the life cycle of the natural world. In nature, the ecosystem could not survive without this process; it has only positive effects. The life cycle of a product is shown in the same positive light (as a simple, natural process), but even such attempts at sustainability will produce negative impacts on the environment (e.g., through the use of energy during manufacture and reprocessing).

2 The diagrams are similar in the way they show sustainable processes at work, although diagram A is more detailed. They are different in that diagram B compares the life cycle of a product with nature, whilst diagram A focuses only on the industrial process.

3 Picture C shows waste materials packaged and ready for <u>recycling</u>.

   Picture D shows waste being dumped in a landfill site (<u>disposal</u>).

   Picture E shows a recycled paper product (<u>reuse of materials</u>).

Exercise C

Set for pairwork. You may wish to divide the work up between different pairs. For question 4 (useful grammatical information), tell students to look out for words that can have the same form when used as a noun or verb, nouns that can be only singular or only plural, nouns that change their meaning when used as U or C, etc.

Feed back, building up the table in the Answers section on the board.

Answers

Model answers:
See table below.

Word	C/U	Meaning in engineering	Synonym	Useful grammatical information
combustion	U	related to the burning of fossil fuels	burning	
commodity	C	1. product of engineering 2. manufactured goods	product	can be used in some contexts as a synonym for a product, but also refers to something that can be reprocessed and resold (a benefit)
consumption	U	1. the amount of something used or consumed (e.g., *fuel consumption* in a car or worldwide *oil consumption*) 2. the using up of a (natural) resource faster than it is replenished	1. use (n) 2. using up, depletion	v = consume
damage	U/C (in law only)	a bad effect/negative impact on something (e.g., environment); harm done to something	harm	often + *to* = damage to something plural = only in law: damages (compensation) v = damage
depletion	U	reduction in/of the amount of something that is available	reduction, decrease, fall (but depends on context)	collocation = depletion of natural resources
development	C/U	1. improving an existing product or process, or developing new ones 2. growth	1. improvement 2. advancement	1. C 2. U (as in *sustainable development*)
disposal	U	… of products and materials at end of life (e.g., in landfill sites) as opposed to recycling	dumping (informal), discarding	common uses = • *the* disposal of something • *waste* disposal

Word	C/U	Meaning in engineering	Synonym	Useful grammatical information
environment	C/U	1. the *natural* environment 2. the *built* environment	1. the natural world 2. urban surroundings	1. commonly referred to as *the* environment (def. art.), although the plural form is also used, e.g., *all sorts of living things can survive in extreme <u>environments</u>* adj = environmental
field	C	particular area or subject concerned	area, matter (but depends on context)	
material	C/U	general term for substances or components used in production or manufacturing (e.g., *raw* materials)	substance, stuff (informal)	hypernym
planet	C	the world	*the* earth, *the* world	*the planet* is often used as a synonym when referring to environmental issues; note the def. art. is used single/plural form used when referring to space/the solar system
recycling	U	the process of dealing with used products, items or materials so that they can be reused	reprocessing, reusing, salvaging (depending on context)	v = recycle adj = recyclable
resource	C	finite and renewable (natural) materials/minerals or sources, e.g., fossil fuels, solar energy	material/s, source or supply (depending on context)	adj (*resourceful*) <u>not</u> used in this context = applies to people/personality
waste	U	1. by-products of industrial processes to be discarded 2. unwanted materials or resources (used and/or discarded)	no suitable synonym	almost always uncountable in this context, or single form as in *sewage should be regarded not as <u>waste</u> but as a resource* v = waste adj = waste (as in *waste materials*)

Exercise D

Set for individual work and pairwork checking. Make sure students understand that they should find a verb in column 2 with a similar meaning to one of the verbs in column 1.

Feed back with the whole class, discussing the extent to which the verbs are exact synonyms, and if not, identifying any differences in meaning. Point out that the meaning of words can change in subtle ways according to context.

Answers

Model answers:

Verb	Noun	Verb	Noun
care for	care	protect	protection
consider	consideration	think about	–
define	definition	explain	explanation
exploit	exploitation	take advantage of	–
imply	implication	mean	meaning
lead (to)	–	result (in)	result
meet	–	satisfy	satisfaction
reduce	reduction	cut	cut (a cut *in* …)
relate (to)	(in) relation (to)	concern	no noun in this meaning
use	use	utilize	utilization

Exercise E

This is an exercise in paraphrasing based on word and sentence level techniques. As well as finding their own synonyms from memory and using the synonyms already discussed in Exercises C and D, students will use noun phrases in place of verb phrases as a technique in paraphrasing. Students should also make passive sentences wherever they can. See Language note on the next page.

1 Set for individual work. Feed back with the whole class.

2 Set for individual work and pairwork checking.

3 Set for pairwork; pairs then check with other pairs. Alternatively, tell some students to write their answers on an OHT or other visual medium for discussion by the whole class.

Language note

In the hard sciences, many subject/content words and phrases often cannot or should not be paraphrased. Trying to find a synonym for a term such as *sustainable development* would be pointless and probably inappropriate. Even replacing the word *materials,* as in raw materials and in other engineering contexts, would not be appropriate. The following is a list of words that students should be very careful about when paraphrasing.

climate change	recycle/recycling
develop/development	renewable
energy	resources
environment	sustainability
greenhouse gas	sustainable
emissions	development
materials	technology
product	waste

Answers

Model answers:

1 A Sustainability = using the Earth's natural resources responsibly, to meet current and future needs without harming the environment

  B Sustainable development = considering environmental and social factors, as well as financial ones

2 Possible synonyms (including synonyms from Exercises C and D):

  A Sustainability

  The (*word*) term/concept *sustainability* can be difficult to define. (Broadly) Generally/Largely/Roughly, it means using the Earth's natural resources (*responsibly*) wisely/sensibly/carefully, to meet (*current*) present and future needs without (*harming*) damaging/destroying the environment. This is a difficult (*undertaking*) task, since many of our resources are (*finite*) limited. It therefore implies (*enormous*) huge/major/considerable changes in how we (*use*) utilize these resources and care for the environment.

  B Sustainable development

  Sustainable development means (*considering*) thinking about environmental and social factors, as well as (*financial*) economic ones. Many problems of unsustainable (*growth*) development relate to the products engineers have (*designed*) planned/created and produced. Engineers therefore have a (*key*) major/significant role to play in the (*areas*) fields of energy (*use*) consumption, materials, waste and water. They are now developing renewable energy technologies to (*reduce*) cut greenhouse gas emissions which lead to climate change. They are also redesigning products to reduce waste by exploiting the (*potential*) possibilities of recycled materials.

3 Possible paraphrases:

  A Sustainability

  Sustainability is a complex concept to explain.

  It largely implies the sensible use of the planet's resources, so that present and future requirements can be satisfied, without damage being caused to the environment.

  However, because a lot of our natural resources are limited, this is a complex task.

  Consequently, considerable adjustments need to be made in the way resources are utilized and the environment protected.

  B Sustainable development

  For sustainable development to take place, environmental and social concerns, in addition to economic issues, need to be addressed.

  The creation and manufacture of products by engineers has led to numerous problems associated with unsustainable development.

  Thus, engineers can make a significant contribution in the fields of energy consumption, materials, waste and water conservation.

  Renewable energy technologies are currently being developed to cut emissions of greenhouse gases which result in climate change.

  In addition, products are being redesigned to cut waste by taking advantage of the possibilities of recycled materials.

Exercise F

1 Set for pair or small group discussion. Make sure students know what *sphere* means. Elicit the meaning of each of the three categories. This question is basically to make sure that students understand the diagram before approaching question 2. You may wish to extend the activity by eliciting other points that could be added to the three main spheres. Feed back with the whole class.

2 Set for pair or small group discussion. Make sure students know what *segment* means.

  Feed back with the whole class. Accept any reasonable suggestions, as some of the points are debatable. Students should be able to justify their decisions.

Answers

Possible answers:

1 Environmental, social and economic. Another way of naming the spheres is 'Planet, people and profit'.

2 ● fair trade schemes: *economic-social*

- energy efficiency: *environmental-economic*
- recycling schemes: *environmental-economic and/or social-environmental*
- tree-planting schemes: *social-environmental*
- fair work practices in multinational companies: *economic-social*
- reducing domestic energy consumption: *social-environmental and/or economic-social*
- ecotourism: *environmental-economic (business related) and/or social-environmental (individual action)*
- elimination of poverty: *economic-social*

Closure

Either:

1 Ask students to work in small groups to think of ways of redesigning an everyday product or process for sustainability and/or of ways that an existing product can be recycled/reprocessed and used. A good way to start would be to think of an item that we would normally throw away, or a world environmental problem that needs resolving (e.g., water shortages). Encourage students to use vocabulary from the lesson in their discussion. Feed back to the class.

Or:

2 If culturally appropriate, ask students to work in small groups and make a list of processes/products specific to their own country or countries that are unsustainable. Their discussion should include ways to improve sustainability. Feed back to the class.

8.2 Reading

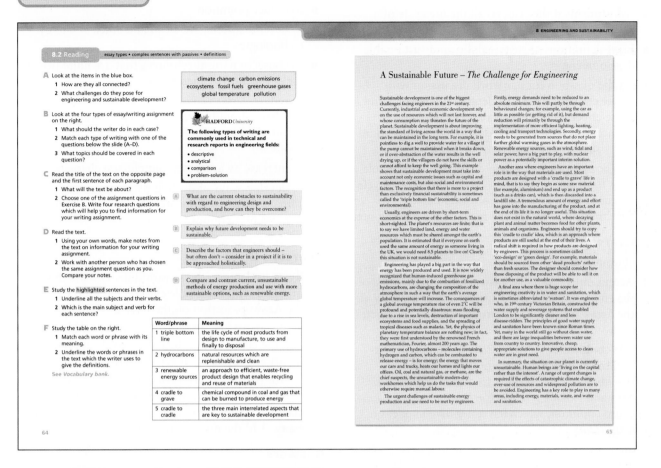

Lesson aims

- understand types of writing assignment
- interpret writing task questions
- find the main information in a passive clause
- understand internal definitions (see *Vocabulary bank*)

Further practice in:

- reading research
- finding the kernel of a long sentence

Introduction

With the whole class, discuss how to use written texts as sources of information when completing a writing task. Ask students:

1 *How can you choose useful sources?* (to get an idea of whether a text might be useful, survey the text, i.e., look at the title, look at the beginning and the end and the first line of each paragraph; in other words, skim-read to get an approximate idea of the text contents)

2 *If you decide that a text is going to be useful, what is it a good idea to do …*

- *… before reading?* (think of questions related to the writing task to which you would like to find some answers)

- *… while reading?* (identify useful parts of the text; make notes **in your own words**)

- *… after reading?* (check answers to the questions)

Exercise A

Revise concepts from Lesson 8.1 with books closed:

- Ask students if they can recall the life cycle of a product.
- Elicit definitions of sustainability and sustainable development.

1 Set the question for pairwork discussion with whole class feedback. Students could either write cause/effect sentences, make notes showing connections with arrows, or show the connections in a visual way (a flow chart or mind map).

2 Set for pair or small group discussion with whole class feedback. The question is intended to recycle language from Lesson 8.1 on sustainable development, which is the focus of the reading text.

Answers

Possible answers:

1 Accept any reasonable answers that show some of the connections. A good answer will show how all the items are connected through cause and effect, e.g.,

The combustion of *fossil fuels* produces *carbon emissions*, which contribute to the increase in *greenhouse gases*, leading to *global temperature* rises and *climate change*. *Carbon emissions* also cause *pollution*, which has a negative impact on *ecosystems*.

2 Accept any reasonable answers. Some of the challenges are:

- to reduce pollution
- to develop alternative clean and efficient energy technologies
- to conserve natural resources that are finite (fossil fuels) for future generations
- to reduce carbon emissions and greenhouse gases (students should have some background knowledge about global emissions agreements, i.e., the Kyoto Protocol)
- to increase awareness about climate change
- to develop ways of dealing with current impacts of climate change (e.g., water shortages, flooding, etc., in particular regions of the world)

Exercise B

1 Refer students to the lecture slide. Discuss this question with the whole class. Build up the table in the Answers section on the board.

2 Set for pairwork. Feed back with the whole class. Ask the class to say which key words in each question tell you what type of writing it is.

3 Set for pairwork. Feed back using the second table in the Answers section, discussing with the whole class what topics will need to be included in each essay. Add the notes in the third column.

Answers

See the following tables.

Possible answers:

1

	What the writer should do
Descriptive writing	describe or summarize key ideas/key events/key points. Give the plain facts. Could involve writing about: a narrative description (a history of something/an invention); a process (how something happens); key ideas in a theory; main points of an article (answers the question *What is/are …?*)
Analytical writing	try to analyze (= go behind the plain facts) or explain something or give reasons for a situation; may also question accepted ideas and assumptions (answers the question *Why/how …?*)
Comparison	compare two or more aspects/ideas/concepts/things, etc.; usually also evaluate, i.e., say which is better/of more worth, etc.
Problem-solution	describe the current situation, state what the problem(s) is/are as consequences of the situation, i.e., why they are problems (cause and effect); propose solutions, evaluate solutions (answers the question *What/how …?*)

2/3

Key words are underlined:

Type of writing	Question	Topics
Descriptive writing	C <u>Describe the factors</u> that engineers should – but often don't – consider in a project if it is to be approached holistically.	• holistic: what is it? Why important? • environmental factors + examples • social factors + examples • reasons why engineers often don't consider them: economic factors • reasons why they should/consequences of non-holistic approach
Analytical writing	B <u>Explain why</u> future development needs to be sustainable.	• sustainable development: what is it? • examples of current unsustainable processes: energy, materials, waste, water • impacts: environmental, social, economic • what needs to be done to achieve sustainability • new developments: renewable energy, recycled materials
Comparison	D <u>Compare and contrast</u> current, unsustainable methods of energy production and use with more sustainable options, such as renewable energy.	• unsustainable energy production and use: what is it? • advantages/disadvantages of fossil fuels • renewable options: solar, wind, hydro • advantages/disadvantages
Problem-solution	A <u>What are the current obstacles</u> to sustainability with regard to engineering design and production, and <u>how can they be overcome</u>? See the *Language note* below.	• sustainability: what is it? • obstacles: energy production and use, materials and waste • solutions: new clean energy technologies, recycling, reuse of materials, legislation, global agreements • how good are solutions?

Language note

Problem-solution questions often do not contain the words *problem* or *solution*. Other common frames are:

What are the *challenges*? How can the *challenges* be met?

What are the *issues/concerns*? How can the *issues/concerns* be addressed?

What are the *difficulties*? How can they be *resolved*?

Exercise C

1 Set for individual work. Feed back with the whole class. Accept all reasonable answers. This is a *prediction* exercise, so make sure that students only look at the topic sentences. You may wish to write the topic sentences on the board and ask students to close their books.

2 If necessary, remind students of the purpose of research questions and do one or two examples as a class. Set for individual work and pairwork checking. Feed back, getting good research questions for each writing assignment topic on the board.

Answers

Possible answers:

1 The title of the text implies that the current situation is unsustainable. It suggests that a

sustainable future will be in the hands of engineers. The word *challenge* suggests that i) it will not be an easy task and ii) engineers may be put to the test.

Paragraph 1 will introduce and explain the concept of sustainable development.

Paragraph 2 will explain why engineers are driven by short-term economics.

Paragraph 3 will outline the current situation regarding energy production and use and explain why it is now a problem. The topic sentence seems to suggests that the writer largely blames engineering for the situation we are in.

Paragraph 4 will explain what the urgent issues are for energy production and use, and why engineers are responsible for addressing them. The paragraph will probably discuss energy conservation and new energy technologies.

Paragraph 5 will explain why engineering innovations are also needed in materials use; recycling will probably be one of the key points.

Paragraph 6 will describe current problems concerning water and sanitation and suggest areas for improvement and innovation.

Paragraph 7 will summarize the main points and perhaps reiterate the need for urgent action.

2 Answers depend on the students.

Exercise D

Set for individual work then pairwork comparison/checking.

Allow students time to read the questions. Before starting the exercise, remind students about abbreviations and symbols, and ask them to look back at note-taking methods in Unit 1. Tell them to choose the best method for the writing assignment they have chosen. Feed back to the class.

Suggested methods are:

A (problem-solution) = flow chart, tree diagram, headings and notes or spidergram

B (analytical) = headings and notes or spidergram

C (descriptive) = headings and notes or spidergram

D (comparison) = two columns or headings and notes

If you wish, students can make notes under the headings in the 'Topics' column of the table in Exercise B on the previous page. Encourage students to make notes in their own words. Monitor the activity.

Exercise E

Set for individual work and pairwork checking. Students could copy out the sentences in their notebooks and then underline all the verbs and subjects.

Feed back with the whole class, building up the table in the Answers section on the board. Point out that each sentence has two verbs, which means that each sentence has two *clauses*. This means that the sentences are complex. (A simple sentence has only one main verb and subject.) To enable students to identify which is the 'main' part of the sentence (in bold in the table below), ask how the two clauses are 'joined' and add the joining words (here: *in the way that, that and in how*). The main part of the sentence is linked to the dependent part with these words.

Check understanding of the passives in each case by asking how each clause and sentence could be rephrased with an active verb, e.g.,

1 Engineering has played a big part in the way that we produce and use energy.

2 Secondly, we need to generate energy from sources that do not place further global warming gases in the atmosphere.

3 It requires a radical shift in how engineers design products.

Answers

Possible answers:

	Joining word	Subject	Verb	Object/complement
1		**Engineering**	**has played**	**a big part**
	(in the way) that	energy	has been produced and used.	
2		**energy**	**needs to be generated**	from sources
	that		do not place	further <u>global warming gases</u>* in the atmosphere.
3		**A radical shift**	**is required**	
	(in) how	products	are designed	by engineers.

*the underlined noun is the headword of the noun phrase

Language note

The choice of whether to use an active or a passive construction often depends on how the writer wants to structure the information. Refer to Unit 7 *Skills bank* for a note on information structure.

Exercise F

Set for individual work and pairwork checking. In question 2, tell students to look for the actual words used and the punctuation, grammatical and vocabulary devices which are used to indicate meanings.

Feed back with the whole class, pointing out the structures given in the third column of the table for question 2 in the Answers section. If you wish, refer students to the *Vocabulary bank – Understanding new words: using definitions*.

Answers

1

Word/phrase	Meaning
1 triple bottom line	the three main interrelated aspects that are key to sustainable development
2 hydrocarbons	chemical compound in coal and gas that can be burned to produce energy
3 renewable energy sources	natural resources which are replenishable and clean
4 cradle to grave	the life cycle of most products from design to manufacture, to use and finally to disposal
5 cradle to cradle	an approach to efficient, waste-free product design that enables recycling and reuse of materials

2 Model answers:

Word/phrase	Actual words giving the meaning	Punctuation/vocab/structure
triple bottom line	… (economic, social and environmental).	word/phrase followed by definition in brackets
hydrocarbons	… – molecules containing hydrogen and carbon …	word immediately followed by a dash (–)
renewable energy sources	…, such as wind, tidal and solar power, …	word/phrase followed by a comma, + *such as* + definitive examples of the word/phrase, followed by another comma
cradle to grave	…, that is to say they begin as some raw material …	word/phrase followed by a comma, + *that is to say* + example process
cradle to cradle	… which is an approach where products are still useful at the end of their lives.	word/phrase followed by comma + *which is a/an*

Closure

1 For paraphrasing practice, write the following sentence (from paragraph 6 of the reading text) on the board or on an OHT:

The principles of good water supply and sanitation have been known since Roman times.

Elicit words and phrases that can be paraphrased, e.g., *the principles of* = the concept of

since Roman times = since the Roman era

Now elicit ways to change the structure of the sentence (using an active instead of the passive verb, inserting a subject) and any other changes, e.g., *People have been aware of the concept of good water supply and sanitation since the Roman era.*

You may wish to take this example further by suggesting a different beginning to the sentence, and inviting students to finish it, e.g.,

It was the Romans who … (first introduced the concept of good water supply and sanitation).

2 Set for pairwork. Write the following two further consecutive sentences on the board or on an OHT and ask students to write the sentences in their notebooks. Tell them to work on the sentences together and follow the same paraphrasing procedure. Monitor the activity and help with suggestions where necessary. Feed back to the class. You may wish to invite individual students to the board to present their paraphrases.

Yet, many in the world still go without clean water, and there are large inequalities between water use from country to country.

Innovative, cheap, appropriate solutions to give people access to clean water are in great need.

Possible paraphrases:

Even now, however, there are large numbers of people worldwide who do not have access to clean water, with huge gaps in water provision between different countries.

What are urgently required are new, inexpensive and suitable solutions to enable access to uncontaminated water.

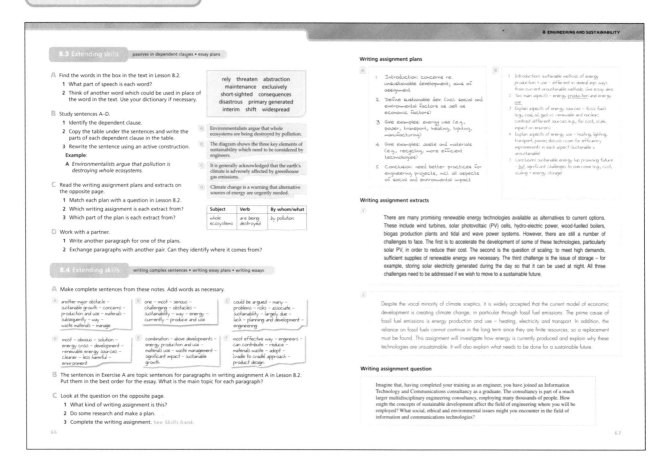

Lesson aims

- find the main information in a passive dependent clause
- recognize appropriate writing plans for essay types

Further practice in:

- vocabulary from Lesson 8.2

Introduction

Choose about 10–15 words from the previous unit which you think that students should revise. Write them in a random arrangement and at different angles (i.e., not in a vertical list) on an OHT or on the board. Allow students two minutes to look at and remember the words, and then take them away. Students should write down all the words they can remember.

Exercise A

Set for individual work and pairwork checking. Tell students that they must first find the word in the text so that they can work out the meaning and part of speech in context and choose an *appropriate* synonym. See the *Language note* on the opposite page. Feed back with the whole class.

Answers

Model answers (paragraph numbers are given in brackets):

Word	Part of speech	Another word
rely (1)	v	depend
threaten (1)	v	endanger, jeopardize
abstraction (1)	n (U)	withdrawal, extraction, mining
maintenance* (1)	adj	running, upkeep
exclusively (1)	adv	only, solely
short-sighted (2)	adj	thoughtless, unthinking (about the future)
consequences (3)	n (C)	results, effects, impact
disastrous (3)	adj	devastating, catastrophic
primary (3)	adj	main, chief, prime, foremost, principal
generated (4)	v	produced, created
interim* (4)	adj	temporary, provisional, short-term, intermediate
shift (5)	n (C)	change, transformation
widespread (7)	adj	extensive

*in either contexts, *maintenance* and *interim* can be nouns (see Language note, opposite)

Exercise B

Set for individual work and pairwork checking. Make sure that students can correctly identify the main clause, the dependent clause and the linking word. Do the first transformation with the class to check that they know what to do. Note that they do not need to rewrite the main clauses. Also, if no agent is given they will need to supply one themselves.

Language note

The adjectives *maintenance* and *interim* in the reading text can also be used as nouns. It is important, therefore, for students to check part of speech <u>in context</u>; otherwise, dictionary use could produce inappropriate synonyms.

Answers

Model answers:

1/2

Main clause	Linking word	Dependent clause		
		Subject	Verb	By whom/what
A Environmentalists argue	that	whole ecosystems	are being destroyed	by pollution.
B The diagram shows the three key elements of sustainability	which	(key elements) which*	need to be considered	by engineers.
C It is generally acknowledged	that	the earth's climate	is (adversely) affected	by greenhouse gas emissions.
D Climate change is a warning	that	alternative sources of energy	are (urgently) needed.	

*note that in B the relative pronoun is the subject of the dependent clause

3 A Environmentalists argue that pollution is destroying whole ecosystems.

B The diagram shows the three key elements of sustainability which engineers need to consider.

C It is generally acknowledged that greenhouse gas emissions are adversely affecting the earth's climate.

D Climate change is a warning that we urgently need alternative sources of energy.

Exercise C

Tell students to look back at the writing assignment questions in Lesson 8.2. You may also need to remind them of the topics which you decided are suitable for the writing assignment.

Set all three questions for individual work and pairwork checking. Feed back with the whole class. Ask students to say what aspects of the plans and the extracts enabled them to be identified. Check that students can match the parts of the extracts with the corresponding parts of the writing assignment plan.

Answers

Model answers:

1 Plan A = writing assignment question B: *'Explain why future development needs to be sustainable.'*

Plan B = writing assignment question D: *'Compare and contrast current, unsustainable methods of energy production and use with more sustainable options, such as renewable energy.'*

2 Extract 1 = plan B
Extract 2 = plan A

3 Extract 1 = Plan B, point 5: *Conclusion: sustainable energy has a **promising future** – but significant **challenges to overcome** in terms of cost, scaling and energy storage.*

Extract 2 = Plan A, point 1: Introduction: ***concerns related to unsustainable development**; aims of assignment*

Note: This extract is only <u>part</u> of the introduction to the assignment: it deals with one of the concerns (energy production and use).

Exercise D

Remind students about writing topic sentences. Set for pairwork. Even students who chose one of these two essay questions in Lesson 8.2 should refer to the model writing assignment plans/notes in the Course Book. In all cases, students should write using their own words, i.e., paraphrase the ideas in the text.

If you wish, you could ask some students – perhaps those who finish early – to write their paragraphs on an OHT or other visual display for all the class to look at. Comment on the extent to which students have managed to paraphrase, whether they have successfully covered the point in the plan, and whether their topic sentence is well supported by the sentences that follow.

Closure

Ask students to finish the following sentences as quickly as possible.

'Cradle to grave' means …

'Cradle to cradle' is …

Greenhouse gases are …

'Triple bottom line' means …

Hydrocarbons are chemical compounds that …

A good example of sustainable development is …

8.4 Extending skills

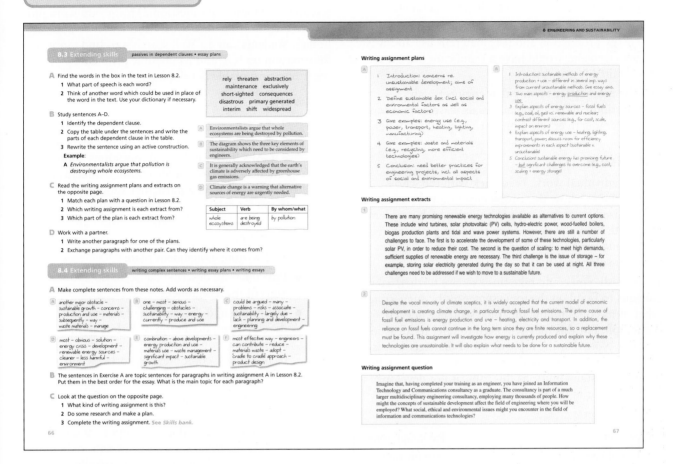

Lesson aims

- expand notes into complex sentences
- make a writing assignment plan
- write an essay/assignment

Further practice in:

- writing topic sentences
- expanding a topic sentence into a paragraph
- writing complex sentences with passives
- identifying required essay/writing assignment type

Introduction

Remind students about complex and compound sentences – that is, sentences with more than one clause. Remind students that academic texts typically consist of sentences with several clauses. Give the following simple sentences (or make your own) and ask students to add some more clauses to them:

Solar energy is a renewable energy technology.

Engineers should try to copy the 'cradle to cradle' idea.

The planet's resources are finite.

Current energy production relies mainly on fossil fuels.

Nuclear energy is a fairly new technology.

Exercise A

Set for individual work and pairwork checking. Remind students that they should try to make sentences in a good 'academic' style. Also remind them to use passives where necessary/possible, and to look out for ways of making dependent clauses, such as relative pronouns, linking words, etc. They will also need to pay attention to making correct verb tenses.

Feed back with the whole class.

Answers

Possible answers:

A Another major obstacle to sustainable growth concerns the production and use of materials, and subsequently, the way waste materials are managed.

B One of the most serious and challenging obstacles to sustainability is the way energy is currently produced and used.

C It could be argued that many of the problems and risks associated with sustainability are largely due to the lack of planning and development in engineering.

D The most obvious solution to the energy crisis is the development of renewable energy sources that are cleaner and less harmful to the environment.

E A combination of the above developments in energy production and use, materials use and waste management, would have a significant impact on sustainable growth.

F The most effective way that engineers can contribute to reducing materials waste is to adopt the 'cradle to cradle' approach to product design.

Exercise B

Set for individual work. Feed back with the whole class. Point out how this problem-solution assignment is organized by proposing a solution to each problem discussed, before moving on to the next problem. (See *Skills bank* for an alternative approach to problem-solution.)

If you wish, you could take this exercise further, asking students to build on the topic sentences by suggesting what ideas could follow the topic sentence in each paragraph. For this they will need to refer to ideas in the text. Note that the topic of water management is not referred to in the assignment topic sentences with regard to sustainability, as this topic is not developed to a great extent in the reading text.

Model answers:

Topic sentences	Paragraph topic
C It could be argued that many of the problems and risks associated with sustainability are largely due to the lack of planning and development in engineering.	introduction
B One of the most serious and challenging obstacles to sustainability is the way energy is currently produced and used.	problem 1
D The most obvious solution to the energy crisis is the development of renewable energy sources that are cleaner and less harmful to the environment.	solution to problem 1
A Another major obstacle to sustainable growth concerns the production and use of materials, and subsequently, in the way waste materials are managed.	problem 2
F The most effective way that engineers can contribute to reducing materials waste is to adopt the 'cradle to cradle' approach to product design.	solution to problem 2
E A combination of the above developments in energy production and use, materials use and waste management, would have a significant impact on sustainable growth.	conclusion

Exercise C

Discuss question 1 with the whole class. Set the research and planning (question 2) for group work, and the writing for individual work (this could be done at home). Students can do Web searches to find more information on ICT and its possible problems regarding sustainable development.

Answers

Model answer:

1 This writing assignment is descriptive/analytical since it asks 'how' and 'what' questions about a hypothetical scenario. It also pushes students to do detailed research on a particular subject (service provision models) and to think creatively and laterally about their response to sustainable development.

2 Possible writing assignment plan:

- Introduction: describe the scenario and the aims of the assignment
- Definition and description of sustainable development; definition of ICT (a term covering various data and voice network technologies, computer networks, security networks and broadcasting systems)
- Environmental considerations in the design of ICT products:
  - Material use (reducing component count, reducing toxic substances, weight reduction, use of new environmentally friendly materials)
  - Energy use (low power circuitry, standby and switch off modes, etc.)
  - Modular design – leasing and service provision schemes, take-back schemes, design for disassembly and recycling
  - End of life considerations, 'cradle to cradle' ideas
- Social and ethical considerations in ICT:
  - Impact of ICTs on office work, gender (in)equality, job design
  - The 'digital divide'
  - New patterns of working, working from home
- Conclusion: ICT has great potential to empower and connect people, but there is huge potential to improve the design of ICT products to make them less environmentally damaging and more socially relevant, meeting real (rather than perceived) needs.

Closure

Ask students if they can remember a word from the unit ...

	Example(s)
beginning with c	consumption, climate, carbon
beginning with i	interim, industrial, implementation
ending with y	energy, imply, commodity, supply, urgently
ending with s (but not a plural form)	process, gas, mass, enormous, address, pointless
with two syllables	solar, triple, planet, reduce
with three syllables	combustion, disposal, depletion
with four syllables	environment, development, sustainable, manufacture
which is a verb	define, exploit, explain, utilize, relate (to)
which is an uncountable noun	consumption, combustion, energy
which is an adverb*	responsibly, environmentally, exclusively, potentially
which has a prefix	recycle, reuse, unsustainable, redesign, ecosystem, ecotourism, renewable
which goes together with another word	climate change, greenhouse gas, fossil fuels, carbon emissions, sustainable development
which goes together with two other words	cradle to grave, cradle to cradle, triple bottom line, greenhouse gas emissions
which is difficult to pronounce*	environmentalists, acknowledged, sphere (students' answers will vary; will also be influenced by their first language)

*if they have problems with these categories, allow them to skim through the reading text

Accept all reasonable answers.

Extra activities

1 Work through the *Vocabulary bank* and *Skills bank* if you have not already done so, or as a revision of previous study.

2 Use the *Activity bank* (Teacher's Book additional resources section, Resource 8A).

  A Set the wordsearch for individual work (including homework) or pairwork. Establish that the words are uncountable in the context in which they are used in the unit, although some can be countable in other contexts.

  Answers

```
E S U S T A I N A B I L I T Y
C N R G R O W T H M W L E A S
A O E R G S T R R I C U N A G
S U N R R E C Y C L I N G N N
A C A S G O A T N U C O I P M
N P O N U Y U T I E A R N R A
I S P M T M A L R G U H E O I
T S E E B T P E S T A C E D N
A G A P U U H T C S T R R U T
T U I T N P S A I H I E I C E
I G L A S S F T N O T N N T N
O R T O T U A N I S N I G I A
N T M E N P C M A O T U L O N
P T O A I E N W N S N M I N C
A C M P O L L U T I O N R T E
```

  B Set the spelling exercise for individual work and pairwork checking. If students are having difficulty, give them the first letter of the word. If they still have difficulty, give them the second letter and/or tell them what part of speech the word is.

  Answers

Jumbled word	Correct spelling
corueser	resource
wothrg	growth
tamicle	climate
clercey	recycle
moscuptinon	consumption
sycometes	ecosystem
wablereen	renewable
teenager	generate
untilloop	pollution
metpoldeven	development

3 Check word stress by writing the following words on the board *without* stress markings. Students have to mark the stress and pronounce the words correctly.

  'concept
  en'vironment
  environ'mental
  'damage
  sus'tainable
  sustaina'bility
  manu'facturing
  'interim

4 Remind students of how to give definitions (see Lesson 8.2). Then select five or six familiar items (e.g., iPod, laptop, sunglasses, pen, mobile phone) and ask students to think of definitions (e.g., it's something that you use to listen to music; you need these when it is sunny; etc.).

This can also be done the other way round by giving the definitions and asking students to guess the word; once they get the idea students can come up with items, questions and definitions themselves. Other forms for definitions can include:

  This is a place where …
  This is a company which …
  This is used for …
  This is made from/of …

Other categories which can be used to practise both the language of definition and engineering include:

● types of materials from Unit 3, e.g., plastic, rubber, steel, alloy, etc.

● types of devices and components from Unit 5, e.g., accelerometer, gyroscope, sensor, etc.

An alternative is the Weakest Link TV quiz show format, e.g., *What 'S' is a type of renewable energy technology?* (solar energy.)

9 HEALTH AND SAFETY

This is the first of two units on health and safety (H&S). This unit's lecture focuses on the key principles of workplace health and safety in an engineering context. The lecture also illustrates these principles through two authentic case studies involving an oil rig disaster and a train derailment.

Skills focus

🎧 **Listening**

- using the Cornell note-taking system
- recognizing digressions in lectures

Speaking

- making effective contributions to a seminar
- referring to other people's ideas in a seminar

Vocabulary focus

- fixed phrases from health and safety
- fixed phrases from academic English

Key vocabulary

See also the list of fixed phrases from academic English in the *Vocabulary bank* (Course Book page 76).

breathing apparatus	fatigue	maintenance	reactor
chemical plant	first aid	measure (n)	regulation
confined space	flammable	negligence	responsibility
disaster	hazard	non-compliance	risk
duty	health and safety	oil rig/platform	risk assessment
emergency	incident	offshore	speed restriction
explosion	inspection	personal protective equipment (PPE)	supervision
explosive	investigation		training
facility	legal	plant (n)	
fail safe (v)	machinery	prevention	

9.1 Vocabulary

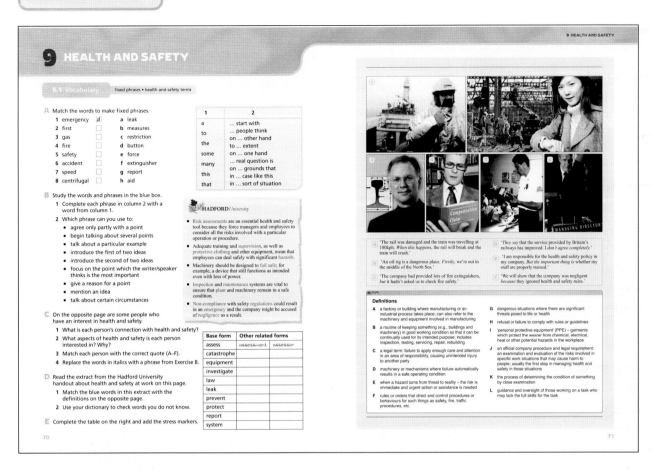

General note

Read the *Vocabulary bank* at the end of the Course Book unit. Decide when, if at all, to refer your students to it. The best time is probably at the very end of the lesson or the beginning of the next lesson, as a summary/revision.

Lesson aims

- understand and use some fixed phrases/compound nouns from engineering
- understand and use some fixed phrases from academic English

Introduction

Introduce the topic for the unit. Ask students what they think health and safety in the workplace means and write suggestions on the board. Some suggestions are:

a safe working environment

safe working practices and processes

identifying hazards and risks to health in the workplace and taking action to reduce or remove them

training for employers and employees on health and safety issues

legal obligations by management and employees to comply with health and safety regulations

With course books closed, brainstorm any vocabulary students can think of connected with workplace health and safety in engineering contexts. Answers will depend on the students and their existing knowledge. Some suggestions are:

accident

machinery/equipment

protective clothing/footwear/hard hat/helmet/face mask

maintenance/repair/inspections

dangerous chemicals/substances/gas/oil

explosion/fire

etc.

Accept any reasonable suggestions and write any useful words on the board.

Exercise A

This gives practice in compound noun phrases (noun + noun, adjective + noun) connected with accidents and incidents in the workplace in engineering contexts. (These phrases will also occur in the listening text.)

Set for individual work or pairwork. Ask students to write the corresponding letter in each box. Check that students know the meanings and that they can pronounce the compounds with the main stress on the correct word. Accept any reasonable alternatives (e.g., possibly *emergency measures* and *safety report*). Ask students to make sentences with the compounds.

Answers

Model answers:

1 e'mergency	button	n + n
2 first	'aid	adj + n
3 'gas	leak	n + n
4 'fire	extinguisher	n + n
5 'safety	measures	n + n
6 'accident	report	n + n
7 'speed	restriction	n + n
8 centrifugal	'force	adj + n

Language note

Normally n + n compounds = stress on first noun; adj + noun compounds = stress on noun.

Exercise B

Set for individual work and pairwork checking. Point out that some of the words in the first column of the blue box must be used more than once. Feed back with the whole class.

Answers

Model answers:

to start with	to begin talking about several points
many/some people think	to mention an idea
on the other hand	to introduce the second of two ideas
to some extent	to agree only partly with a point
on the one hand	to introduce the first of two ideas
the real question is	to focus on the point which the writer/speaker thinks is the most important
on the grounds that	to give a reason for a point
in a case like this	to talk about a particular example
in this/that sort of situation	to talk about certain circumstances

Exercise C

1/2 Set for pairwork discussion. Accept all reasonable answers.

3 Set for individual work and pairwork checking.

4 Set for individual work. Check with the whole class, asking students to read out the quotation with the alternative phrase inserted in place of the original words in italics.

Answers

Suggested answers:

1/2 1 is an oil rig worker – would be interested in the safety of the rig in terms of fire/explosions/severe weather conditions.

2 is a train passenger – would be interested in the safety of both trains and tracks; also the experience/competence of the train driver.

3 is a design engineer for a rail company or rail maintenance company – would be interested in the design and condition of the tracks, how they are laid and maintained, etc.

4 is a lawyer – would be interested in the legal requirements of health and safety in the workplace, e.g., negligence and non-compliance.

5 is a Fire Safety Officer – would be interested in hazards and fire prevention procedures, particularly in high-risk situations.

6 is a managing director – would be interested in all aspects of health and safety in the company due to legal requirements to protect the workforce; would also be interested in the cost of implementing health and safety requirements, including training and supervision.

3 1 (oil rig worker): quote B

2 (train passenger): quote D

3 (design engineer): quote A

4 (lawyer): quote F

5 (Fire Safety Officer): quote C

6 (managing director): quote E

4

A	*When this happens*	*In this sort of situation*, the rail will break and the train will crash.
B	*Firstly*	*To start with*, we're out in the middle of the North Sea.
C	*but*	… *on the other hand* it hadn't asked us to check fire safety.
D	*They say*	*Many/Some people think* that the service provided by Britain's railways has improved.
D	*don't agree completely*	*I agree to some extent*.
E	*But the important thing is*	But *the real question is* whether my staff are properly trained.
F	*because*	We will show that the company was negligent *on the grounds that* they ignored health and safety rules.

Exercise D

This exercise gives some key terms relating to health and safety.

Set students to read the handout extract first and ask them to discuss in pairs which of the blue words they know and which are new for them. Feed back with the whole class, to establish how much is known. Where students give correct explanations tell them they are right, and where they are wrong also tell them, but do not give the right answer at this point.

Set questions 1 and 2 for individual work and pairwork checking. Feed back with the whole class, checking the meaning of other possibly unknown words. Make sure students know the difference between a *risk* and a *hazard* and between *maintenance* and *inspection*.

The words will be used throughout this unit, and many will be used in the following unit, so don't worry too much about practice at this point. However, for extra practice at this point if you wish, set students to work in pairs. One student should shut the book. The other student should say one of the words for the first student to explain. Then change over.

Answers

Model answers:

See table below.

risk assessment	J	an official company procedure and legal requirement: an examination and evaluation of the risks involved in specific work situations that may cause harm to people; usually the first step in managing health and safety in those situations
supervision	L	guidance and oversight of those working on a task who may lack the full skills for the task
protective clothing	I	'personal protective equipment' (PPE) – garments which protect the wearer from chemical, electrical, heat or other potential hazards in the workplace
hazards	G	dangerous situations where there are significant threats posed to life or health
fail safe	D	machinery or mechanisms where failure automatically results in a safe operating condition
inspection	K	the process of determining the condition of something by close examination
maintenance	B	a routine of keeping something (e.g., buildings and machinery) in good working condition so that it can be continually used for its intended purpose; includes inspection, testing, servicing, repair, rebuilding
plant	A	a factory or building where manufacturing or an industrial process takes place; can also refer to the machinery and equipment involved in manufacturing
non-compliance	H	refusal or failure to comply with rules or guidelines
regulations	F	rules or orders that direct and control procedures or behaviours for such things as safety, fire, traffic procedures, etc.
emergency	E	when a hazard turns from threat to reality – the risk is immediate and urgent action or assistance is needed
negligence	C	a legal term: failure to apply enough care and attention in an area of responsibility, causing unintended injury to another party

Exercise E

Set for individual work. Tell students to use their dictionaries to check on the meanings and grammatical categories of the words if they are not sure. Ask them to mark the stress on each word. Feed back with the whole class. Check students can pronounce all the words correctly, particularly those where the word stress shifts.

Answers

Model answers:

Base form	Other related forms	
a'ssess (v)	a'ssessment n (C/U)	a'ssessor n (C)
ca'tastrophe n (C/U)	cata'strophic (adj)	cata'strophically (adv)
e'quipment n (U)	e'quip (v)	
in'vestigate (v)	investi'gation n (C/U)	in'vestigator n (C)
'law n (C/U)	'lawful (adj)	'lawless (adj) 'lawyer n (C)
'leak n (C), v	'leakage n (C/U)	'leaky (adj)
pre'vent (v)	pre'vention n (U)	pre'ventative (adj)
pro'tect (v)	pro'tection n (C/U)	pro'tective (adj)
re'port n (C), v	re'porter n (C)	re'portedly (adv), re'portage n (U) (or repor'tage – less common)
'system n (C/U)	system'atic (adj)	system'atically (adv) sys'temic (adj)

Language note

With a good class, you can spend plenty of time on the issue of whether each noun is used as countable or uncountable or both, i.e., can the word be made plural, and if so, does that change the meaning?

Closure

It is important that students are familiar with the health and safety terminology from this lesson. On the board, write some terms from the lesson and ask students to give a definition; choose items from Exercises A and D. Or read out a definition and ask students to tell you the appropriate word or phrase. Check the pronunciation. This exercise can also be done as a dictation.

Alternatively, write the words and definitions on different cards and give a card to each student. The student then reads out the word or the definition and the rest of the class must produce the correct answer.

9.2 Listening

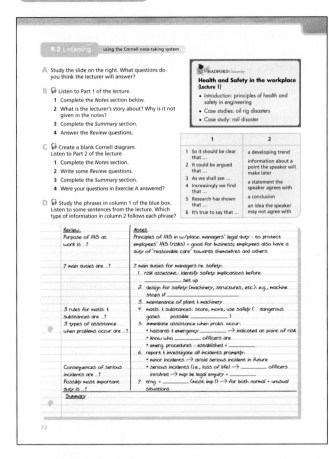

General note

Read the *Skills bank – Using the Cornell note-taking system* at the end of the Course Book unit. Decide when, if at all, to refer students to it. The best time is probably at the very end of the lesson or the beginning of the next lesson, as a summary/revision.

Lesson aims

- use the Cornell note-taking system

Further practice in:

- listening for an established purpose
- understanding fractured text
- recognition of fixed phrases and what type of information comes next
- using abbreviations and symbols in note-taking

Introduction

1 Review key vocabulary from this unit by writing a selection of words from Lesson 9.1 on the board and asking students to put the words in groups, giving reasons for their decisions.

2 Revise note-taking symbols and abbreviations by using extra activity 3 at the end of this unit.

3 Introduce the elements of the Cornell note-taking system. Try to elicit some of the R words. Ask students to try to think of five words beginning with *re~* with six or seven letters that are good strategies to use when studying and taking notes. Write the words as follows on the board:

RE _ _ _ _	= record
RE _ _ _ _	= reduce
RE _ _ _ _	= recite
RE _ _ _ _ _	= reflect
RE _ _ _ _	= review

Discuss with the class what each word might mean when taking notes. Try to elicit the following, helping where needed.

record   Take notes during the lecture.

reduce   After the lecture, turn the notes into one- or two-word questions or 'cues' which help you remember the key information.

recite   Say the questions and answers aloud.

reflect   Decide on the best way to summarize the key information in the lecture.

review   Look again at the key words and the summary (and do this regularly).

Tell students that in this lesson they will be introduced to this system of note-taking – which can be used both for lectures, and also for reading and for revision for exams later. Do not say much more at this point; they will see how the system works as the lesson progresses.

Subject note

The Cornell system was developed by Walter Pauk at Cornell University, USA. (Pauk, W. and Owens, R. (2007). *How to Study in College* (9th edition). (Boston: Houghton Mifflin.) Pauk advised students to use a large, loose-leaf notebook, with holes punched for filing. This is better than a bound notebook, because you can organize the notes in a file binder. You can also take out notes and rewrite them. Pauk's method, which is now called the Cornell system, is based on a specific page layout.

Pauk told students to divide up the page into three areas. The first area is a column 5 cm wide on the left side of the page. This is the cue area. The main part of the page is the note-taking area. At the bottom of the page is a row 8 cm high, which is the summary area. The basic grid with information on what each section should contain is reproduced in the additional resources section (Resource 9B).

The note-taking and learning process involves the *Five Rs* in the order listed in the introduction to this lesson (and in the *Skills bank*). There are many references on the Internet for this system. Two useful ones at the time of writing are:

www.yorku.ca/cdc/lsp/skillbuilding/notetaking.html

http://lsc.sas.cornell.edu/Sidebars/Study_Skills_Resources/cornellsystem.pdf

Exercise A

Set for pairwork discussion. Refer students to the lecture slide. Tell them to look at the title and bullet points and for each bullet point to make questions which they expect the lecturer to answer. Do not explain any words from the slide, or allow students to check in their dictionaries at this point, as the meanings of these words will be dealt with in the lecture.

Feed back with the whole class, asking several students to read out their questions. Write some of the questions on the board if you wish.

🎧 Exercise B

1/2/3 Refer students to the notes at the bottom of the page. Tell them that this student has used the Cornell system to take notes but has not managed to complete everything and so has left some gaps. (Note that this is quite a normal occurrence in note-taking – details may need to be filled in later, for example by checking with other people.)

Allow students time to read the gapped notes and work out what the abbreviations are likely to mean. Also make sure they read question 2 and are ready to listen out for a short digression.

Play Part 1, pausing after each major point if you wish.

Tell students to work in pairs to compare their answers to questions 1 and 2, and to complete the summary in 3. Feed back with the whole class, using an OHT or other visual display of the answers if you wish. The completed notes are reproduced in Resource 9C, in the additional resources section, to facilitate this.

4 Now focus on the *recite* element of the Cornell system. Point out that here the student has completed the *Review* section. Tell students to cover up the *Notes* section of the answer and ask them if they can say anything about the first and second questions in the *Review*. Then put students in pairs to test each other on the remaining notes.

Answers

Model answers:

1/3/4 See table on opposite page and Resource 9C.

2 The lecturer gives an example of health and safety in food labelling that illustrates a lack of common sense. It is not in the notes because it is a digression – that is, a simple everyday illustration to communicate an important point, but one that is not concerned with health and safety in engineering contexts.

Transcript 🎧 2.9

Part 1

Good morning, everyone. This is the first of a series of lectures on health and safety in the workplace. So, first of all, we're going to look at some of the most important principles of health and safety in an engineering context.

All managers have a duty under the law to protect their employees' health and safety. But what does that entail? Well, manufacturing is a business and its legitimate purpose is to make a profit. But there will always be some risk associated with manufacturing. So it should be clear that it also makes good business sense, in the end, for managers to assess and manage risk in a responsible way. Not everyone is aware of this, but employees also have a duty of 'reasonable care' – towards themselves and others.

Now, it could be argued that health and safety principles are sometimes applied without common sense. So, for example – for people who are allergic to nuts – food manufacturers put statements such as 'may contain nuts' not only on the side of any products that may contain *traces* of nuts, but even on packets of peanuts themselves! But extreme examples like this can hide the real importance of health and safety.

Anyway, to get back to the main topic, there are seven primary duties for managers responsible for workplace safety.

Firstly, there should be a clear risk assessment policy that is applied consistently. The purpose of this is to identify all the safety implications of a particular procedure *before* the procedure is put into operation. Many accidents in the workplace are the result of inadequate risk assessment.

Secondly, all facilities – I mean machinery, structures, procedures, etc. – should be designed for safety. For example, a machine that automatically stops if the control box is opened. Then there's maintenance of the plant and machinery. An example we can all understand is car brake pads – they wear down with use and need to be checked periodically to make sure they're safe. Maintenance means repairing or replacing things when they are too worn.

Next, management has to ensure that all materials and substances are stored, moved and used safely. We could think of explosive or flammable gases, such as oxygen, hydrogen or methane. These gases are often stored in pressurized cylinders, which must be kept in ventilated cages outside buildings, so that in the case of a leak, there's no dangerous build-up of gas.

Fifthly, there has to be immediate and adequate assistance when problems arise. Hazards and emergency buttons should be clearly indicated at the point of risk and everyone should know who the first aid officers are. And emergency procedures should be well established and practised, so that everyone knows what to do.

The next duty is that all incidents should be reported promptly, investigated thoroughly and systems put in place to prevent a repetition. Reporting quite a minor incident and working out what went wrong can often prevent a more serious incident in the future. With very serious incidents involving loss of life, government safety officers will become involved and there may be a legal investigation and even changes to the law.

Lastly, and perhaps most importantly, is essential training and supervision. Employees need to know what to do, not only when things are going 'normally', but also when unusual situations occur.

In the next two parts of the lecture, we'll look firstly at two incidents in the oil industry and then at a railway incident where one or more of these principles were overlooked. As we shall see, the results can be disastrous if risk assessments aren't undertaken or reviewed, if there's inadequate training of employees, or if cost-cutting reduces safety.

Review	Notes
Purpose of H&S at work is …? others.	Principles of H&S in w/place: managers' <u>legal</u> duty – to protect employees' H&S (risks) + good for business; employees also have a duty of 'reasonable care' towards themselves and
7 main duties are …?	7 main duties for managers re. safety: 1. risk assessmt.: identify safety implications before *procedures* set up 2. design for safety (machinery, structures, etc.): e.g., machine stops if *control box opened* 3. maintenance of plant & machinery
3 rules for matls. & substances are …? 3 types of assistance when problems occur are …?	4. matls. & substances: store, move, use safely (∵ dangerous gases ➔ possible *leaks*) 5. immediate assistance when probs. occur: • hazards & emergency *buttons* ➔ indicated at point of risk • know who *first aid* officers are • emerg. procedures – established + *practised* 6. report & investigate all incidents promptly: • minor incidents ➔ avoid serious incident in future
Consequences of serious incidents are …? Possibly most important duty is …?	• serious incidents (i.e., loss of life) ➔ *government safety* officers involved ➔ may be legal enquiry + *changes to law* 7. trng. + *supervision* (most imp.?) ➔ for both normal + unusual situations

Summary

There are seven key health and safety principles in engineering workplace contexts that cover risk assessment, safety and maintenance of plant and machinery, hazardous materials, accidents and emergency procedures, and training and supervision. These are all legal requirements and the responsibility of management. However, employees also have a duty of 'reasonable care'.

🎧 Exercise C

1 Tell students to divide up a page of their notebooks into the three sections of the Cornell system. They should try to take notes in the *Notes* section as they listen. Warn them that they may not be able to complete their notes while writing so they should leave spaces which they can fill in later.

Play Part 2 straight through. Then put students in pairs to complete any gaps in their notes. Feed back with the whole class. Build up a set of notes on the board. The notes below are quite detailed because it's a case study where certain details are key to the outcome and findings.

2/3 Set students to work in pairs to complete the *Review* questions and the *Summary*. Feed back with the whole class.

4 Discuss with the class the extent to which their pre-questions in Exercise A have been answered.

Answers

Possible answers:

Review	Notes
	Oil rig disasters:
GRACE system: what is it for …?	<u>GRACE system:</u> • trng. tool ➜ learn from past incidents & mistakes • designed by BP + used by many industries
Glomar accident: what happened? Cause …?	<u>Case 1: Glomar Arctic IV mobile rig: Scotland 1998</u> • 2 welders killed in leg of rig – propane gas leak – ignited ➜ explosion + fire • cause = molten metal particles on hose during repair work
Investigation findings included …?	<u>Investigation by Scottish courts:</u> co. ignored H&S regs., incl.: 1. no proper risk assess. – risks in confined space with poss. gas leaks 2. workers not properly trained/supervised 3. safety checks not followed 4. no fire extinguishers or other equipt. at scene; no communication with deck; no emergency plan 5. no fire inspection: co. refused local Fire Brigade insp. – had own firefighting team – <u>but</u> couldn't deal with emergency ∴ Fire Brig. couldn't reach workers: i) didn't know layout of rig, ii) access to accident area v. difficult + unsafe
Lessons and conclusions are …?	<u>Lessons learnt:</u> – risk assessments must be made + reviewed – all situations – job in confined space + open flame ➜ risk of fire – fire hazard – should have fire inspection – co. guilty of non-compliance with own & nat. safety regs., ➜ negligence – lessons of Piper Alpha 1988 (world's worst offshore disaster) ignored
Summary	
Glomar oil rig disaster 1998: the deaths of two welders in an explosion and fire was caused by the rig company's negligence, through non-compliance with national health and safety regulations. The accident investigation found that there was no risk assessment done, a lack of training and supervision, a lack of essential equipment for working in a confined space with an open flame, and no fire inspection.	

Transcript 🎧 2.10

Part 2

Let's move on now to examine the first of two oil rig disasters to find out what went wrong, using the GRACE system (that's G-R-A-C-E). GRACE is a training tool to improve safety, by learning from previous incidents where mistakes were made.

BP designed the GRACE system for the petroleum industry, but increasingly we find that it's been taken up by many other industries.

This first case concerns the Glomar Arctic IV mobile exploration oil rig which was docked in Dundee harbour in Scotland for repairs in 1998.

Two welders were working inside one of the legs of the rig when a propane gas leak, from a damaged hose, ignited as they attempted to light a cutting torch. There was an explosion and a fire in which both men were killed. Molten metal particles had previously fallen on the hose during their repair work and this had caused a hole from which the gas leaked.

Now, this may sound like a simple accident, but the investigation by the Scottish courts revealed that the company had ignored a whole range of health and safety regulations.

- For a start, no proper risk assessment had been carried out by either the rig operators or the contractors. Nor was there even an adequate understanding of the risks involved in working in confined spaces with the possibility of a gas leak.
- Secondly, it was found that the workers were not properly trained or supervised.
- Thirdly, a system of safety checks hadn't been followed.
- And fourthly, it was found that there were no fire extinguishers or gas detectors at the scene; nor were the workers provided with breathing apparatus or a means of communication with deck personnel. In fact, there was no clear plan for dealing with an emergency.
- Just two days before the accident, the company had refused to let the local fire brigade make an inspection, saying that they had their own firefighting team. But this firefighting team was unable to deal with the emergency as it had had no training for such an event. As a result, the fire brigade couldn't reach the workers in time because, firstly, they didn't know the layout of the rig, and secondly, access to the accident area was extremely difficult and unsafe.

So, what lessons can we learn from this case? Well, firstly and most importantly, risk assessments *must* be made in all situations, however simple they may seem. And these assessments *must* be reviewed. What would a risk assessment of this case have concluded? First, the job was in a confined space, and welding uses an open flame. So, there was the risk of fire. Second, with a fire hazard, the company should have asked for a fire inspection themselves. Instead, they prevented one from taking place.

Research has shown that the preventative measures in this case would not have added much to the cost. The company was guilty of non-compliance with their own *and* national safety regulations – in other words, it was negligent. It's true to say that the lessons here should have been obvious, but the accident report observed that the lessons of Piper Alpha in 1988, the world's worst-ever offshore disaster, were ignored. That's two words – P-I-P-E-R – Piper, and A-L-P-H-A – Alpha.

Now … I wanted to go on to talk about the Piper Alpha disaster, but it's quite a lengthy case, so I think I'll come back to it if we have time. Alternatively, I may let you do some research yourself …

🎧 Exercise D

Allow students time to read the phrases and the types of information, making sure that they understand any difficult words. Note that they are being asked not for the words that the speaker uses, but what *type* of information the words represent. Note also that the information types may be needed more than once.

Play the sentences one at a time, allowing time for students to identify the type of information which follows. Check answers after each sentence, making sure that students understand the actual information that follows.

Answers

Model answers:

See table below.

	Fixed phrase	Type of information that follows	Actual words/information
1	So it should be clear that …	a conclusion	it also makes good business sense in the end for managers to assess and manage risk in a responsible way
2	It could be argued that …	an idea the speaker may not agree with	health and safety principles are sometimes applied without common sense
3	As we shall see, …	information about a point the speaker will make later	the results can be disastrous if risk assessments aren't undertaken or reviewed, if there's inadequate training of employees, or if cost cutting reduces safety
4	Increasingly we find that …	a developing trend	it's been taken up by many other industries
5	Research has shown that …	a statement the speaker agrees with	the preventative measures in this case would not have added much to the cost
6	It's true to say that …	a statement the speaker agrees with	the lessons here should have been obvious, but the accident report observed that the lessons of Piper Alpha in 1988, the world's worst-ever offshore disaster, were ignored

Transcript 🎧 **2.11**

1 So it should be clear that it also makes good business sense, in the end, for managers to assess and manage risk in a responsible way.

2 Now, it could be argued that health and safety principles are sometimes applied without common sense.

3 As we shall see, the results can be disastrous if risk assessments aren't undertaken or reviewed, if there's inadequate training of employees, or if cost-cutting reduces safety.

4 BP designed the GRACE system for the petroleum industry, but increasingly we find that it's been taken up by many other industries.

5 Research has shown that the preventative measures in this case would not have added much to the cost.

6 It's true to say that the lessons here should have been obvious, but the accident report observed that the lessons of Piper Alpha in 1988, the world's worst-ever offshore disaster, were ignored.

Closure

Predicting information: play short sections from the lecture again. Stop the recording just before a word or phrase you want students to produce and ask them what comes next in the lecture. For example:

All managers have a duty under the law to [STOP] ... *protect their employees' health and safety.*

The next duty is that all incidents should be [STOP] ... *reported promptly, investigated thoroughly and systems put in place to prevent a repetition.*

GRACE is a training tool to [STOP] ... *improve safety, by learning from previous incidents where mistakes were made.*

Alternatively, do this exercise by reading out parts of the transcript.

9.3 Extending skills

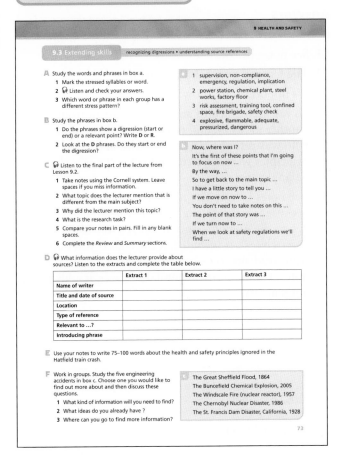

stress in a phrase. Feed back with the whole class, checking students' pronunciation, especially of the compound words, and eliciting the odd ones out.

Answers

Model answers:

1/3 1 super'vision, non-com'pliance, *e'mergency* (stress is on second syllable), regu'lation, impli'cation

2 'power station, 'chemical plant, 'steel works, *factory 'floor* (stress on second word)

3 'risk assessment, 'training tool, *con'fined 'space* (stress on second word), 'fire brigade, 'safety check

4 *ex'plosive* (stress is on second syllable), 'flammable, 'adequate, 'pressurized, 'dangerous

Transcript 🎧 2.12

1 super'vision, non-com'pliance, e'mergency, regu'lation, impli'cation

2 'power station, 'chemical plant, 'steel works, factory 'floor

3 'risk assessment, 'training tool, con'fined 'space, 'fire brigade, 'safety check

4 ex'plosive, 'flammable, 'adequate, 'pressurized, 'dangerous

Exercise B

Point out that the phrases in the box are likely to introduce either a digression or a relevant point. The students' task is to identify which is more probable.

Set for individual work and pairwork checking. Feed back with the whole class. Note that most of these phrases occurred in the lecture in Lesson 9.2. Some have occurred in previous units and one or two are new. Note also that the end of a digression is actually a transition back to the main point.

Answers

Model answers:

Now, where was I? **D** (end)
It's the first of these points that I'm going to focus on now … **R**
By the way, … **D** (start)
So to get back to the main topic … **D** (end)
I have a little story to tell you … **D** (start)
If we move on now to … **R**
You don't need to take notes on this … **D** (start)
The point of that story was … **D** (end)
If we turn now to … **R**
When we look at safety regulations we'll find … **R**

Lesson aims

- recognize digressions: start and end
- understand reference to other people's ideas: source, quotes, relevance

Further practice in:

- stress within words and phrases
- leaving space in notes for missing information

Introduction

Revise the lecture in Lesson 9.2 by asking students to use their Cornell notes. They should cover up the *Notes* section and use the *Review* and *Summary* sections to help recall the contents of the lecture. They could work in pairs to do this.

Exercise A

1 Set for individual work and pairwork checking. Students can underline the stressed syllables.

2 Play the recording and get students to check their answers.

3 Set for individual work and pairwork checking. Tell students they need to identify the odd one out in terms of stress (not the meanings of the words). In groups 2 and 3, make sure that they focus on word

🎧 Exercise C

Refer students to the lecture slide in Lesson 9.2. Ask them what sort of things can cause a rail disaster (train crash). What aspects of health and safety do they think the lecturer will mention?

Tell them to prepare a page to take notes using the Cornell system. Remind them that they may not get all the information. If they miss something, they should leave a space. They can fill it in after the lecture.

Let them read the questions through and tell them to listen out for the answers to questions 2, 3 and 4.

1 Play Part 3 straight through. Students should complete the *Notes* section.

2–4 Set for pairwork. Feed back with the whole class. Ask for suggestions for phrases to use to find out about the importance of digressions, e.g., *Why did the lecturer start talking about …? I didn't understand the bit about … Is it important?* and so on (see *Skills bank*). Set question 3 for pairwork.

5/6 Set for pairwork. Students compare their notes, complete any blank spaces and then write the *Review* and *Summary* sections.

Feed back with the whole class, building a set of notes on the board.

Answers

Possible answers:

1 See notes below.

2 The Cornell note-taking system.

3 It's important to know how to take good notes.

4 To research a health and safety incident from another industry, and to consider what happened, who was responsible, what health and safety principles were ignored, and what changes should be implemented.

5/6 See notes below. The notes are quite detailed because it is a case study where certain details are key to the outcome and findings. Note also that the research task is included at the end. If you don't want students to record the research task in their notes, tell them beforehand. However, it adds to the authenticity.

Review	Notes
	Rail disaster: Hatfield train crash – UK Oct. 2000
What was the accident …?	Accident details: • train travelling 190 kph left rails on r/hand bend • 4 passengers killed, 70 injured
Cause was …?	• cause = massive fatigue in a rail – broke into > 300 pieces ('gauge corner cracking')
What circumstances contributed to accident? Who was involved?	Circumstances prior to accident: • maintenance co. – told R/track of prob. rail 2 yrs. b4 • Nov. (one yr. b4 accident) – site mgr. reported cracking + urgent repair needed – arranged for next Apr.
What safety measures were taken?	• interim: no safety measures (no speed restr.; no diversions) • Apr. – track closed for repair – but new rails not arrived • arrived May – left by track – trains not stopped – busy period • to be repaired end Oct. • 2 mths. b4 crash, R/track warned again – big risk of derailment
What health & safety measures were ignored?	Conclusions/Findings: 'accident waiting to happen': • syst. of safety and maint. inspections inadequate • when damage found – no proper risk assess. • no speed restr.
Who was responsible?	• respons. for safety ÷ betw. rail co. & maint. co. – neither took full respons. • see Report 2006: website – Office of Rail Regulation
What is the research task?	Research task: tutorials next wk. • groups of four • H&S incident from other industry, e.g., chem. processing, biotech., construction, etc. (1974 Flixborough disaster?) To find out: • what happened • who responsible • what H&S principles ignored • what changes to avoid repetition

Summary

The Hatfield train crash in the UK in October 2000, in which 4 people died and 70 were injured, was caused by a damaged rail detected two years before the accident. The system of safety and maintenance inspections prior to the accident were found to be inadequate, and there were no safety measures when the damage was first detected. Repairs were long overdue and the situation deteriorated, resulting in the crash. Both Railtrack and the maintenance company were negligent, but neither took full responsibility.

Transcript 🎧 2.13

Part 3

If we turn now to another incident, this time in the rail industry, we can see how failures in safety systems again had fatal consequences. The post-incident inquiry stated that it was 'one of the worst examples of sustained industrial negligence'. I'm referring to the Hatfield train crash in the UK in October 2000, when an express train travelling at 190 kph left the rails as it took a right-hand bend. Centrifugal force threw it across the track. Four passengers were killed and 70 injured. The cause of the accident was massive fatigue in a rail, which shattered into over 300 pieces.

The maintenance company had told Railtrack (who ran the railways) that there was a problem in this rail *two years* before. In November, one year before the accident, the site manager reported severe cracking and said that the track needed repairing. This repair, although critical, was arranged for the following April.

Now, bearing in mind that rail failure would cause a disaster, what measures would *you* have recommended between November and April to ensure the safety of the trains? … What about a speed restriction? A damaged rail would be safe at under 30 kph. Or some of the trains on that line could have been diverted, to reduce stress.

In fact, nothing was done. Then, in April, the track was closed for repair – but the new rails hadn't arrived. When they finally arrived in May, they were left beside the track, because Railtrack was reluctant to stop trains during the busy summer period. The repair was then scheduled for the end of October, but tragically, the accident happened two weeks before this.

Ah … I see some of you are using the Cornell note-taking system. That's good. If you want to know more about this system, I suggest you look at *How to Study in College* by Walter Pauk, 9th edition, published 2007. It should be in the university library. I'm sure you all know the importance of taking good notes – and this system is particularly useful.

Now, I'm going to talk about the engineering problem in this incident. You don't need to take notes on this, but you may find it interesting.

When a train travels along the rail, the contact area between wheel and rail is about 2 cm long if train and track are in perfect equilibrium. The 100-ton load of vehicle and machinery on eight wheels would be shared by eight of these contact spots. So the rails are designed to support a weight of 12.5 tons.

But when we look at a *curve*, we find that the load is different. Look at the diagram on the board. You can see that the centrifugal force pushes the wheel against the outside rail of a curve. Instead of a downward compression load, the load is against the corner of the rail. To restore the equilibrium at high speed, the track is tilted like a cycle racing track, resulting in an extra stress on the inner corner of the higher rail – which is called the gauge corner. Under lateral pressure, the rails crack on the corner, which is known as 'gauge corner cracking'.

So where was I? Oh yes. The Hatfield accident was caused by gauge corner cracking. Two months before the crash, Railtrack was warned again that there was a significant risk of derailment from a broken rail. In the crash, the rail cracked along 135 metres – 35 metres of which shattered into 300 pieces. Naturally, the train derailed.

By the way, according to a 2004 article entitled 'Rolling contact fatigue on the British railway system', this was a widespread and serious problem in the late 1990s. You can find the article online via the Science Direct database. I'll write all the details on the board at the end of the lecture.

The point of this case is that it was an accident waiting to happen, but it could have been prevented. The system of safety and maintenance inspections was inadequate. When the damaged rail had been identified, no proper risk assessment was done and trains were allowed to continue travelling at dangerous speeds. Also, as responsibility for safety was divided between the rail company and the maintenance company, neither took full responsibility. You can read the official report of the incident on the Internet, if you want to note this down … go to the Office of Rail Regulation website and search for the Hatfield train derailment final report by the Independent Investigation Board, July 2006. I also have a hard copy, if anyone wants to borrow it.

Right, I'd like you to do some research please, to present in tutorials next week. I'd like you to work in groups of four on health and safety incidents from other industries – for example, chemical processing, biotechnology, construction and so on. For example, you could look at the 1974 Flixborough disaster. Each group should consider what happened, who was responsible, what health and safety principles were ignored, and what changes should be implemented to avoid repetition.

🎧 Exercise D

Tell students that lecturers will often give references while they talk and it is important to note down any references. The kinds of information may differ – they may just be names of books or articles, they may be an exact quotation (a 'direct quote') or they may be a paraphrase (sometimes called an 'indirect quotation').

Refer students to the table and check that they know what each row represents.

Play each extract and allow students time to complete the sections of the table. Check with the whole class.

Answers

Model answers:

	Extract 1	Extract 2	Extract 3
Name of writer	Walter Pauk	Not given – to be written on board at end of lecture	Independent Investigation Board
Title and date of source	*How to Study in College*, 9th edition, 2007	'Rolling contact fatigue on the British railway system', 2004	Hatfield train derailment final report, July 2006
Location	university library	Science Direct database	Web and hard copy available to borrow from lecturer
Type of reference	name of book	indirect quotation/paraphrase	name of report
Relevant to ...?	Cornell note-taking	rail fatigue and gauge corner cracking	summing-up of the incident re. health and safety principles ignored
Introducing phrase	I suggest you look at ...	according to ...	You can read the ... go to ... and search for ...

Transcript 🎧 2.14

Extract 1

Ah ... I see some of you are using the Cornell note-taking system. That's good. If you want to know more about this system, I suggest you look at *How to Study in College* by Walter Pauk, 9th edition, published 2007. It should be in the university library.

Extract 2

By the way, according to a 2004 article entitled 'Rolling contact fatigue on the British railway system', this was a widespread and serious problem in the late 1990s. You can find the article online via the Science Direct database. I'll write all the details on the board at the end of the lecture.

Extract 3

You can read the official report of the incident on the Internet, if you want to note this down ... go to the Office of Rail Regulation website and search for the Hatfield train derailment final report by the Independent Investigation Board, July 2006. I also have a hard copy, if anyone wants to borrow it.

Exercise E

Set for individual work – possibly homework – or else a pair/small group writing task. If the latter, tell students to put their writing on an OHT or other visual medium so that the whole class can see and comment on what has been written. You can correct language errors on the OHT.

Exercise F

Tell students to work in groups of three or four. Either give each group one of the topics or allow them to choose. Make sure that each topic is covered by at least one, and preferably two groups.

Feed back on questions 1–3 with the whole class. Tell them that each student should now carry out research into the group's topic (i.e., one of the engineering accidents), and they should decide how to divide up the work. They should each try to find at least two different sources, if possible. You will also need to arrange the date for the feedback and discussion of the information – this is the focus of Exercise D in Lesson 9.4. Tell students that in Lesson 9.4 they will take part in a seminar on this topic.

Answers

Possible answers:

1 Information to find: You may need to prompt/remind students about the research questions at the end of the lecture, i.e., '*Each group should consider what happened, who was responsible, what health and safety principles were ignored, and what changes should be implemented to avoid repetition.*' The last aspect may be quite difficult in some cases, so another aspect could be

researched, such as the aftermath of the accident. With a large topic, such as the Chernobyl disaster, one of the aspects could be split between two students.

3 Use the library and the Internet to find out the necessary information. Information on all topics below can be found through the search facility on this website

- http://en.wikipedia.org

St. Francis Dam

- http://www.scvtv.com/html/legacy frankrock.html (video with historical photos and film footage – good listening resource)

Chernobyl Nuclear Disaster

- http://ngm.nationalgeographic.com/ 2006/04/inside-chernobyl/stone-text

Windscale Fire

- http://news.bbc.co.uk/onthisday/hi/dates/ stories/november/8/newsid_ 3181000/3181342.stm:

- http://www.nucleartourist.com/events/ windscal.htm

Great Sheffield Flood

- http://freepages.genealogy.rootsweb.ancestry. com/~mossvalley/mv2/sheffield-flood.html (newspaper article from 1864)

Buncefield Chemical Explosion

- http://news.bbc.co.uk/1/shared/bsp/hi/pdfs/ 09_05_06_buncefield_report.pdf (official report via the bbc)

- http://news.bbc.co.uk/1/hi/uk/4752819.stm

Alternatively (or in addition), depending on your teaching situation and access to sources of information – you can make photocopies of the notes provided in Resource 9D in this book.

Closure

Collocations: write the following words on the board and tell students to work in pairs to think of phrases or a phrase connected with health and safety from the unit or from their own knowledge that start(s) with each word. Feed back with the whole class.

fire

gas

safety

health and safety

accident

legal

Answers

Possible answers:

fire safety officer, fire brigade, fire service, fire extinguisher, fire hazard, fire regulations, fire inspection

gas leak, gas detector, gas monitor

safety check, safety inspection, safety measures

health and safety regulations/policy/requirements/principles/risk

accident report, accident prevention

legal requirement, legal responsibility, legal investigation, legal duty

9.4 Extending skills

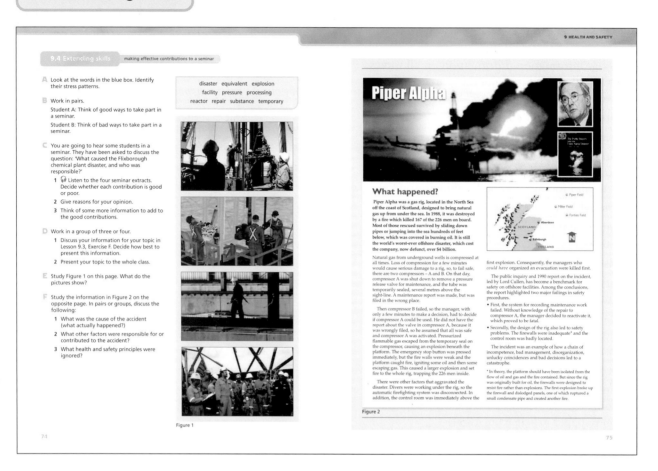

9.4 Extending skills — making effective contributions to a seminar

A Look at the words in the blue box. Identify their stress patterns.

disaster equivalent explosion
facility pressure processing
reactor repair substance temporary

B Work in pairs.
Student A: Think of good ways to take part in a seminar.
Student B: Think of bad ways to take part in a seminar.

C You are going to hear some students in a seminar. They have been asked to discuss the question: 'What caused the Flixborough chemical plant disaster, and who was responsible?'
1 Listen to the four seminar extracts. Decide whether each contribution is good or poor.
2 Give reasons for your opinion.
3 Think of some more information to add to the good contributions.

D Work in a group of three or four.
1 Discuss your information for your topic in Lesson 9.3, Exercise F. Decide how best to present this information.
2 Present your topic to the whole class.

E Study Figure 1 on this page. What do the pictures show?

F Study the information in Figure 2 on the opposite page. In pairs or groups, discuss the following:
1 What was the cause of the accident (what actually happened?)
2 What other factors were responsible for or contributed to the accident?
3 What health and safety principles were ignored?

Figure 1

Piper Alpha

What happened?

Piper Alpha was a gas rig, located in the North Sea off the coast of Scotland, designed to bring natural gas up from under the sea. In 1988, it was destroyed by a fire which killed 167 of the 226 men on board. Most of those rescued survived by sliding down pipes or jumping into the sea hundreds of feet below, which was covered in burning oil. It is still the world's worst-ever offshore disaster, which cost the company, now defunct, over $4 billion.

Natural gas from underground wells is compressed at all times. Loss of compression for a few minutes would cause serious damage to a rig, so, to fail safe, there are two compressors – A and B. On that day, compressor A was shut down to remove a pressure release valve for maintenance, and the tube was temporarily sealed, several metres above the sight-line. A maintenance report was made, but was filed in the wrong place.

Then compressor B failed, so the manager, with only a few minutes to make a decision, had to decide if compressor A could be used. He did not have the report about the valve in compressor A, because it was wrongly filed, so he assumed that all was safe and compressor A was activated. Pressurized flammable gas escaped from the temporary seal on the compressor, causing an explosion beneath the platform. The emergency stop button was pressed immediately, but the fire walls were weak and the platform caught fire, igniting some oil and then some escaping gas. This caused a larger explosion and set fire to the whole rig, trapping the 226 men inside.

There were other factors that aggravated the disaster. Divers were working under the rig, so the automatic firefighting system was disconnected. In addition, the control room was immediately above the first explosion. Consequently, the managers who *could have* organized an evacuation were killed first.

The public inquiry and 1990 report on the incident, led by Lord Cullen, has become a benchmark for safety on offshore facilities. Among the conclusions, the report highlighted two major failings in safety procedures.

• First, the system for recording maintenance work failed. Without knowledge of the repair to compressor A, the manager decided to reactivate it, which proved to be fatal.

• Secondly, the design of the rig also led to safety problems. The firewalls were inadequate* and the control room was badly located.

The incident was an example of how a chain of incompetence, bad management, disorganization, unlucky coincidences and bad decisions led to a catastrophe.

* In theory, the platform should have been isolated from the flow of oil and gas and the fire contained. But since the rig was originally built for oil, the firewalls were designed to resist fire rather than explosions. The first explosion broke up the firewall and dislodged panels, one of which ruptured a small condensate pipe and created another fire.

Figure 2

General note

Students will need the information they researched for Lesson 9.3, Exercise F.

Decide how you want students to present their information, e.g.,

• short talk with/without PowerPoint, OHT or other visual medium
• to the whole class or to another group

Make sure that students understand the options for the presentation types.

Lesson aims

• make effective contributions to a seminar

Further practice in:

• stress within words

Introduction

Use a few of the review cues from the Cornell notes in Lesson 9.3 for students to try to recall information from (and structure of) the account of the Hatfield train derailment.

If students appear to be having difficulty remembering, ask them to look again at their own notes from Exercise C in Lesson 9.3.

Exercise A

Set for individual work and pairwork checking.

Answers

Model answers:

Oo	pressure, substance
oO	repair
Ooo	processing
oOo	disaster, explosion, reactor
oOoo	equivalent, facility
Oooo	temporary

Exercise B

This is revision from Unit 5. Set for individual work and pairwork checking. Feed back with the whole class. Give a time limit and see which pair can think of the most Do's and Don'ts in the time. Refer to Unit 5 Lesson 5.4 for suggestions if you need to.

170

Answers

Possible answers:

Do's	Don'ts
prepare the topic beforehand	
ask politely for information	demand information from other students
try to use correct language	
speak clearly	mumble, whisper or shout
say when you agree with someone	get angry if someone disagrees with you
link correctly with previous speakers	
build on points made by other speakers	
make a contribution, even if you are not sure if it is new or relevant	stay silent, waiting for 'the perfect moment'
be constructive	be negative
give specific examples to help explain a point	be vague
listen carefully to what others say	start a side conversation
allow others to speak	dominate the discussion
paraphrase to check understanding	
use clear visuals	

🎧 Exercise C

Check that students understand the topic for the seminar discussion. Ask them what they might expect to hear. Work through these extracts one at a time. Complete questions 1–3 for each extract before moving on to the next.

1 Set for individual work.

2 First check that students have understood the extract as well as possible. Then ask for opinions from the whole class on the contribution.

3 Once everyone has a clear notion of whether the contribution is a good one, ask for suggestions for additional points. Alternatively, set this part for pairwork after you have completed questions 1 and 2.

Answers

Model answers:

See table below.

	✔	✗	Reasons	Possible additional information
Extract 1	✔		speaks clearly explains the points clearly answers correctly uses good fixed phrases	a brief explanation of the purpose of the pipe, i.e., what was the leaked substance and what ignited it? some reference to the official inquiry
Extract 2		✗	doesn't speak clearly only partly addresses the question, but in a confused way unprepared and poor use of visuals	
Extract 3		✗	speaks clearly, but doesn't answer the question the points are not relevant to the question – focuses on what the chemical plant produced rather than the disaster	
Extract 4	✔		speaks clearly explains the points clearly answers correctly uses good fixed phrases; has prepared well	some information about who conducted the later research referred to, and why additional information about the series of problems referred to, and how they contributed to the accident

Transcript 🎧 2.15

Extract 1

The Flixborough disaster was an explosion at a chemical plant. Twenty-eight people were killed and thirty-six seriously injured. It seems quite clearly to have been an engineering error. While a reactor was being repaired, engineers designed a temporary pipe between two other reactors, which ruptured. By the way, these engineers apparently had no experience in designing high-pressure pipework, and the pipe was not properly tested either.

Extract 2

Erm, I think one of the problems at Flixborough was poor management of the, uh, repair work. Um, this is very important. We can see why this is very important. I have a slide here – oh, sorry, that's the wrong slide. How do you go backwards on PowerPoint? Right. Um, so you can see I think the issue, err, was a problem, um, with the repairs made to the reactor, uh …

Extract 3

Flixborough was a chemical processing facility. We could ask the question 'what did they produce'? Well, the plant produced a chemical called caprolactam, which was used to manufacture nylon. The process involved another substance, cyclohexane, a flammable and dangerous chemical. Cyclohexane is actually a combination of hydrogen and carbon and has the chemical formula C_6H_{12}. It is used as a solvent and …

Extract 4

By the way, the explosion that occurred as a result of this disaster was equivalent to 15 tons of TNT, and the resulting fires burned for ten days. So, who was responsible? The official inquiry at the time concluded that the pipe had failed due to unforeseen stresses, and that inexperienced engineers were at fault. However, later research has shown that it was more than just a simple mechanical fault, and that ignorance and a series of problems, including the presence of water in the reactors, contributed to the accident.

Exercise D

Students should work in the same groups as their research groups from Lesson 9.3, Exercise F. They will need to have with them the research they have done individually on the group's chosen topic.

1 Tell each group to discuss the information that they have found and agree on how to structure their information based on the research questions. This will form the outline of their presentation. Students will need to decide who is going to speak when and say what. Encourage them to practise presenting to each other before talking to the whole class.

2 Allow each group a maximum of ten minutes for the presentation. Then allow some time for questions. If more than one group have done the same topic, encourage disagreement and critical analysis. Remind the groups when discussing to use all the good techniques and phrases they have learnt.

Exercise E

This is a prediction exercise that leads into a case study of the Piper Alpha oil rig disaster referred to at the end of the second part of the lecture in Lesson 9.2. This activity will give more practice in discussion.

1 To set the context and to revise the vocabulary of health and safety, first refer students to the pictures in Figure 1:

● With the whole class, elicit first what types of jobs are shown (working on an oil rig).

● Then elicit what is possibly happening in each picture. Suggestions are:

Pictures 1/2: these look like drilling operations

Picture 3: this appears to be a worker performing a dangerous task or inspection at height

Picture 4: this looks like a training or safety session before an operation: note the man on the right who appears to be addressing the group, and the man on the left with the clipboard, who could be either making notes or checking a list

● Then elicit words from the pictures in connection with health and safety (e.g., words that refer to equipment, clothing, machinery, possible risks/accidents, etc.).

● Tell students that in the next exercise, they will be finding out about Piper Alpha, the world's worst-ever offshore disaster. As a prediction activity, ask for suggestions about what might have caused the disaster. Write some of the suggestions on the board, but don't give any information at this stage.

Exercise F

Put students in pairs or groups. Give them time to read all the questions. In their groups, students should divide the questions between them in order to find the information. Individuals should make brief notes relevant to their question from the texts and then share their findings orally with their partners. Each group can then join another group for a seminar to discuss and agree on their findings. Note that this is not a close reading task – students should use their reading skills to find information quickly. The focus of the exercise is speaking.

Ensure that students understand what each question is asking. For clarification, refer to the notes below:

1 *What was the cause of the accident (what actually happened?)*: this seems fairly straightforward, but the group member concerned should be careful not to include contributory factors which form the answer for question 2.

2 *What other factors were responsible for or contributed to the accident?*: this questions goes beyond the actual accident itself, and looks at other factors that came into play (i.e., the unfortunate coincidences referred to in the text).

3 *What health and safety principles were ignored?*: this question is perhaps the hardest, as it encompasses questions 1 and 2. The answer is partly provided in the text, but the group member also needs to evaluate the information about the various causes and make judgements about what went wrong and why. When sharing this information, other group members can help by contributing their opinions.

Closure

Use the *Vocabulary bank* at the end of the Course Book unit to check that the group can remember the meaning, spelling and pronunciation of the health and safety vocabulary used in an engineering context.

Extra activities

This unit contains a lot of technical and semi-technical vocabulary. Students will need lots of practice with the vocabulary.

1 Work through the *Vocabulary bank* and *Skills bank* if you have not already done so, or as revision of previous study.

2 Use the *Activity bank* (Teacher's Book additional resources section, Resource 9A).

A Set the crossword for individual work (including homework) or pairwork.

Answers

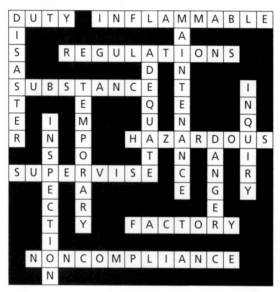

B Ask students to look at the nouns in the table: are plural forms of the nouns possible? Tell students to use an English–English dictionary or online definitions to help them find out the answers to the following questions.

1 Which forms are countable and which are uncountable?

2 Do the countable and uncountable forms have different meanings?

Answers

Noun	Countable or uncountable?	Notes
accident	C	often referred to as an *incident* in a public inquiry
clothing	U	as in protective clothing
emergency	C	
equipment	U	
gas	C/U	pl. gases
machinery	U	as in *plant and machinery*, although plant can also refer to machinery
maintenance	U	
negligence	U	used as a legal term in official inquiries
oil	C/U	almost always uncountable when referring to petroleum
pressure	C/U	uncountable in an engineering context, e.g., as in *pressure valve, gas pressure*

3 Revise note-taking symbols – see the list at the back of the Course Book. Check back to Unit 5 if necessary. Give the meanings and ask students to write down the symbol (or do it the other way round). Then ask students to think about and discuss which ones they actually use. Are there any other ones that they have come across that they think are useful?

Alternatively, write the meanings on a set of cards. Put students in groups of about six with two teams in each group. Give each group a pile of cards. A student from each team picks a card and, without showing the members of his/her team, draws the appropriate symbol. The members of his/her team must say what the symbol stands for. If the student writes the correct symbol and the team gets the meaning right, the team gets a point. If the student writes the wrong symbol and/or the team gets it wrong, the team loses a point. The teams take it in turns to pick a card.

4 Identify engineering acronyms which will be useful for your students. Use the same procedure as in Activity 3. Note that acronyms will often differ between fields of engineering and new ones come into operation regularly. If your students are studying in a UK or European-based context, the following may be useful:

Acronym	Meaning
BERR	The UK's Department for Business, Enterprise & Regulatory Reform; previously the Department of Trade and Industry (DTI)
BSI	British Standards Institute
BTU	British Thermal Unit
HSE	Health and Safety Executive: UK authority responsible for regulating the risks to health and safety arising from work activities
CCS	Carbon Capture and Storage (storage of captured CO_2)
COSHH	Control of Substances Hazardous to Health: UK regulations
EA	Environment Agency: the leading public organization for protecting and improving the environment in England & Wales
ESD	Emergency Shutdown System: an automatic system for shutting down plant to prevent escalation of a potentially hazardous situation
GHG	greenhouse gases
Hazid	Hazard Identification: the process of identifying probable hazards for a Quantified Risk Assessment (QRA)
IAEA	International Atomic Energy Agency: works for the safe, secure and peaceful uses of nuclear science and technology
IEA	International Energy Agency
OPEC	Organization of the Petroleum Exporting Countries – its aim is to co-ordinate the petroleum policies of the Member Countries to safeguard individual and collective interests
PTW	Permit-to-work: a formal written authority that allows potentially hazardous work to start only after safe procedures have been defined; provides a clear record that all potential hazards have been considered
QRA	Quantitative Risk Assessment: a method for quantifying major accident hazards (estimation of frequencies) and potential effects
RBI	Risk Based Inspection
STOP	Safety Training and Observation Programme: scheme designed to create a culture of noticing potential hazards before they cause an accident

Some useful glossaries can be found at:

http://www.contractorsunlimited.co.uk/glossary.shtml

http://www.interfacebus.com/Engineering_Acronyms.html

http://www.draftsperson.net/index.php?title=Acronyms_and_Abbreviations_in_Engineering

10 ACCIDENT ANALYSIS IN CONSTRUCTION

This is the second of two units on aspects of health and safety (H&S). The key focus of the unit, and the subject of the reading text, is an authentic case study of a construction accident: the collapse of the Hyatt Regency Hotel in Kansas City in 1981. The study describes the accident in technical detail and discusses several interrelated causes.

Skills focus

Reading

- recognizing the writer's stance and level of confidence or tentativeness
- inferring implicit ideas

Writing

- writing situation–problem–solution–evaluation essays/writing assignments
- using direct quotations
- compiling a bibliography/reference list

Vocabulary focus

- 'neutral' and 'marked' words
- technical and semi-technical words from engineering
- fixed phrases from academic English

Key vocabulary

bearing	design specification	rod
box beam	diameter	schematic
butt-welding	elevation	screw (n and v)
cause (n and v)	fabricate	span (n and v)
claim (n and v)	fabricator	specify
client	flange	stress
collapse (n and v)	flaw	structural
continuous	load (n and v)	suspend
contractor	modification	tender (n)
corrugated steel	nut	threaded rod
deck	phase	truss
design and build (D/B)	resonance	weld (v)

10.1 Vocabulary

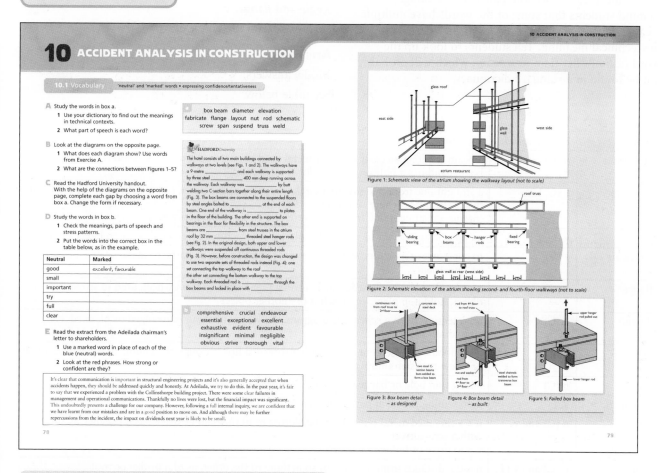

10 ACCIDENT ANALYSIS IN CONSTRUCTION

10.1 Vocabulary · 'neutral' and 'marked' words · expressing confidence/tentativeness

A Study the words in box a.
1 Use your dictionary to find out the meanings in technical contexts.
2 What part of speech is each word?

B Look at the diagrams on the opposite page.
1 What does each diagram show? Use words from Exercise A.
2 What are the connections between Figures 1–5?

C Read the Hadford University handout. With the help of the diagrams on the opposite page, complete each gap by choosing a word from box a. Change the form if necessary.

D Study the words in box b.
1 Check the meanings, parts of speech and stress patterns.
2 Put the words into the correct box in the table below, as in the example.

Neutral	Marked
good	excellent, favourable
small	
important	
try	
full	
clear	

E Read the extract from the Adeilada chairman's letter to shareholders.
1 Use a marked word in place of each of the blue (neutral) words.
2 Look at the red phrases. How strong or confident are they?

> box beam diameter elevation
> fabricate flange layout nut rod schematic
> screw span suspend truss weld

HADFORD *University*

The hotel consists of two main buildings connected by walkways at two levels (see Figs. 1 and 2). The walkways have a 9-metre _____ and each walkway is supported by three steel _____ 400 mm deep running across the walkway. Each walkway was _____ by butt welding two C-section bars together along their entire length (Fig. 3). The box beams are connected to the suspended floors by steel angles bolted to _____ at the end of each beam. One end of the walkway is _____ to plates in the floor of the building. The other end is supported on bearings in the floor for flexibility in the structure. The box beams are _____ from steel trusses in the atrium roof by 32 mm _____ threaded steel hanger rods (see Fig. 2). In the original design, both upper and lower walkways were suspended off continuous threaded rods (Fig. 3). However, before construction, the design was changed to use two separate sets of threaded rods instead (Fig. 4): one set connecting the top walkway to the roof _____, the other set connecting the bottom walkway to the top walkway. Each threaded rod is _____ through the box beams and locked in place with _____.

> comprehensive crucial endeavour
> essential exceptional excellent
> exhaustive evident favourable
> insignificant minimal negligible
> obvious strive thorough vital

It's clear that communication is important in structural engineering projects and it's also generally accepted that when accidents happen, they should be addressed quickly and honestly. At Adeilada, we try to do this. In the past year, it's fair to say that we experienced a problem with the Collinsthorpe building project. There were some clear failures in management and operational communications. Thankfully no lives were lost, but the financial impact was significant. This undoubtedly presents a challenge for our company. However, following a full internal inquiry, we are confident that we have learnt from our mistakes and are in a good position to move on. And although there may be further repercussions from the incident, the impact on dividends next year is likely to be small.

Figure 1: Schematic view of the atrium showing the walkway layout (not to scale)

Figure 2: Schematic elevation of the atrium showing second- and fourth-floor walkways (not to scale)

Figure 3: Box beam detail – as designed

Figure 4: Box beam detail – as built

Figure 5: Failed box beam

78   79

General note

Read the *Vocabulary bank* at the end of the Course Book unit. Decide when, if at all, to refer your students to it. The best time is probably at the very end of the lesson or the beginning of the next lesson, as a summary/revision.

Lesson aims

- understand when words are 'neutral' and when they are 'marked' (see *Vocabulary bank*)
- understand and use phrases expressing confidence/tentativeness (see *Vocabulary bank*)

Further practice in:
- vocabulary from the discipline
- fixed phrases from academic English
- stress within words and phrases
- synonyms

Introduction

1 Brainstorm vocabulary from the previous unit related to health and safety. Tell students to work in pairs and to write down sentences using the following words to show that they have understood their meanings. Feed back with the whole class. Check pronunciation and sentence structures where appropriate. For example:

- Risk assessments give managers and employees a health and safety tool to consider all the risks involved with a particular operation or procedure.
- Protective clothing and other equipment helps employees to deal with significant hazards.

2 Revise the following phrases used in academic writing. Ask students what sort of information will follow these phrases.

On the other hand …
In conclusion …
To put it another way …
As Smith (2002) pointed out …
Research has shown that …
Part of the difficulty is …
To start with …
This can be defined as …
As a result …
Finally …
Given what has been shown above …

Exercise A

Set for individual work and pairwork checking. Remind students that some of the words have multiple meanings in other contexts and that they need to select the technical meaning. Tell students to look up the word *beam* rather than *box beam*, which will probably not be found in a standard dictionary.

As a related activity, elicit the difference in meaning between *beam* and *rod*; *elevation* and *layout*; *nut*, *screw* and *flange*.

Feed back with the whole class.

Answers

Model answers:

See table below.

Word	Part of speech	Meaning
box beam	n (C)	a beam is a long piece of wood or metal used in construction; a *box* beam is built from boards and has a hollow, rectangular cross section
di'ameter	n (C, U)	a straight line from one side of a circle or sphere to the other, passing through the centre of the circle, or the length of this line (*radius* = a straight line from the centre of a circle to the perimeter)
ele'vation	n (C, U)	an upright side, front or rear of a building or structure represented in an architect's drawing
'fabricate	v (T)	to construct or assemble something out of components or parts; to make or produce goods or equipment
flange*	n (C)	a protruding rim or flat edge such as on a pipe, beam or train wheel, used to strengthen an object, hold it in place, or attach it to another object
'layout	n (C)	representing, as in a schematic diagram, the way something is arranged or planned, e.g., a building
nut	n (C)	a small block of metal or wood with a threaded hole through the middle to fit around a bolt or screw to fasten things together
rod	n (C)	a long thin pole or bar made from metal or wood
sche'matic	adj	representing the main parts of something in a simple way
screw	n (C) and v	n = a threaded metal pin with a flat slotted head that can be driven as a fastener by turning with a screwdriver v = to drive or tighten (a screw)
span	n (C) and v (T)	n = the distance from one side of something to the other, as of a bridge or roof e.g., *the Akashi-Kaikyo Bridge in Japan has the largest span in the world* v = to stretch or extend across, over or around e.g., *thirty four bridges span the River Thames in London*
su'spend	v (T)	to hang (something) from a high place e.g., *a chandelier was suspended from the ceiling of the ballroom*
truss	n (C)	a rigid framework of wood or metal used to support a structure such as a roof or a bridge
weld	v (T)	to join two pieces of metal together by applying heat, sometimes with pressure

*inform students that pictures of flanges can be found at http://en.wikipedia.org/wiki/Flange, or via a simple Google Images search.

Exercise B

1/2 Set for pairwork. Tell students to cover page 78 so that they are not tempted to look at the Hadford University handout. Students should work together to describe the diagrams to each other as best they can. Encourage them to use words from Exercise A as well as words in the diagrams. Give them plenty of time to work through Figures 3–5. Weaker students may need some prompting, especially with Figures 3–5. For question 2, encourage students to speculate on what happened to the structure.

Feed back with the whole class. Accept anything reasonable.

Answers

Possible answers:

1 *Figure 1* shows the **schematic layout** of a public building with a glass roof and a restaurant on the ground floor. There are walkways on two of the floors above the restaurant on the west side, with one walkway on the east side. The walkways are **suspended** by long rods from the roof and don't appear to be connected to the walls.

Figure 2 shows the same building from the side **elevation** of the west side. We can see more clearly now that the walkways are on the 2nd and 4th floors. There is a lot more technical detail, showing how the **hanger rods** are fixed from the **roof truss** down through the two walkways which are supported by **box beams**.

Figures 3–5 show very detailed diagrams of how **box beams** are **fabricated** and connected to the **rods** and walkways (decks). *Figure 3* shows an original design with a continuous rod from the roof to the 2nd floor; *Figure 4* shows how the **box beam** and **rods** were *actually* fabricated, i.e., discontinuous rods; *Figure 5* shows how such a **fabrication** can fail, where one of the rods becomes disconnected from the **box beam**.

2 Overall, the diagrams show, in increasing detail, how part of a building was designed and constructed. It appears that the structure failed in some way because of how the hanger rods were connected to the box beams. It looks like one of the hanger rods from the roof to the 4th floor failed, but it's not clear whether this happened to all the rods. If all the hanger rods failed for some reason, then the walkway would collapse.

Exercise C

Set for individual work and pairwork checking. Tell students to read through the whole passage first for sense, and then go through each sentence again to work out whether each gap represents a noun or a verb. When completing the gaps, students then need to decide, with the help of the diagrams, whether the nouns are single or plural, and what form the verbs take. Advise students to complete the gaps they find easiest first. Note that they may have problems with *span* and *screw*, which can be either nouns or verbs.

Feed back with the whole class. Ask students how the description in the handout compares with their own descriptions of the diagrams in Exercise B.

Answers

Model answers:

The hotel consists of two main buildings connected by walkways at two levels (see Figs. 1 and 2). The walkways have a 9-metre span and each walkway is supported by three steel box beams 400 mm deep running across the walkway. Each walkway was fabricated by butt welding two C-section bars together along their entire length (Fig. 3). The box beams are connected to the suspended floors by steel angles bolted to flanges at the end of each beam. One end of the walkway is welded to plates in the floor of the building. The other end is supported on bearings in the floor for flexibility in the structure. The box beams are suspended from steel trusses in the atrium roof by 32 mm diameter threaded steel hanger rods (see Fig. 2). In the original design, both upper and lower walkways were suspended off continuous threaded rods (Fig. 3). However, before construction, the design was changed to use two separate sets of threaded rods instead (Fig. 4): one set connecting the top walkway to the roof truss; the other set

connecting the bottom walkway to the top walkway. Each threaded rod is screwed through the box beams and locked in place with nuts.

Exercise D

Introduce the idea of 'neutral' and 'marked' vocabulary (see *Language note* below and *Vocabulary bank*). Set for individual work and pairwork checking.

Feed back, discussing any differences of opinion about whether the words are marked, and in what sense they are marked. (Some students may argue that *minimal* and *insignificant* are not marked, for example. Others may argue that they are marked, because they suggest not just that something is small, but that it is important/unimportant. Compare *There is a small problem with the design* and *There is an insignificant problem with the design*.)

Answers

Model answers:

Neutral	Marked
good	'excellent, 'favourable, ex'ceptional (adj)
small	insig'nificant*, 'minimal, 'negligible (adj)
important	'vital, 'crucial, e'ssential (adj)
try	en'deavour (v and n), strive (v)
full	compre'hensive, ex'haustive, 'thorough (adj)
clear	'obvious, 'evident (adj)

*insignificant can also mean unimportant, depending on context

Language note

One way of looking at vocabulary is to think about 'neutral' and 'marked' items. Many words in English are neutral, i.e., they are very common and they do not imply any particular view on the part of the writer or speaker. However, there are often apparent synonyms which are 'marked' for stance or opinion. Neutral words are usually thought of as basic vocabulary (the adjectives often have opposites, e.g., *big/small; good/bad*). Marked words tend to be less frequent and are therefore learnt later.

The marked words in Exercise D are not totally synonymous. Their appropriate use and interpretation will be dependent on the context and also on collocation constraints. For example, one can say that a building is 'massive', but not (in the same sense) 'significant'.

Exercise E

1 Set for individual work and pairwork checking. Make sure that students understand any words they are not sure of. Feed back with the whole class by asking individual students to read out a sentence. Make sure that the pronunciation and stress patterns of the marked words are correct.

2 Put the table from the Answers section on the board. Make sure that students understand *confident* and *tentative*. Elicit answers from the whole class and complete the table. Point out that these phrases are usually found in conversation or in informal writing such as this. Academic writing also requires writers to show degrees of confidence and tentativeness. The mechanisms for this will be covered in the next lesson.

Answers

Model answers:

1 It's clear that communication is *(important)* <u>vital/crucial/essential</u> in structural engineering projects and it's also generally accepted that when accidents happen, they should be addressed quickly and honestly. At Adeilada, we *(try)* <u>endeavour/strive</u> to do this. In the past year, it's fair to say that we experienced a problem with the Collinsthorpe building project. There were some *(clear)* <u>obvious/evident</u> failures in management and operational communications. Thankfully no lives were lost, but the financial impact was significant. This undoubtedly presents a challenge for our company. However, following a/an *(full)* <u>comprehensive/ exhaustive/thorough</u> internal inquiry, we are confident that we have learnt from our mistakes and are in a/an *(good)* <u>excellent/favourable/exceptional</u> position to move on. And although there may be further repercussions from the incident, the impact on dividends next year is likely to be *(small)* <u>insignificant/minimal/negligible</u>.

2

	Very confident	Fairly confident	Tentative (= not confident)
It's clear that	✔		
it's also generally accepted that		✔	
they should be		✔	
it's fair to say that		✔	
This undoubtedly presents	✔		
we are confident that	✔		
there may be			✔
is likely to be		✔	

Closure

1 For further practice of neutral and marked vocabulary, ask students to write down some basic words, e.g., four verbs, four nouns and four adjectives. Put a list of these on the board and ask students if they are neutral or marked. See if you can find any opposites. Ask students to find some synonyms for neutral words – they can use a dictionary. A synonyms dictionary or Microsoft Word thesaurus can be useful here as well.

2 Ask pairs to take turns in defining as accurately as they can some of the words from Exercise A (box a) without mentioning the word itself. Partners should try to guess the word.

10.2 Reading

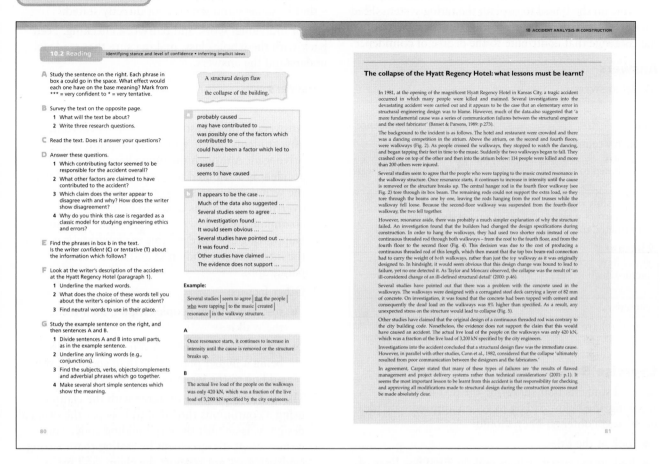

10.2 Reading   identifying stance and level of confidence • inferring implicit ideas

A Study the sentence on the right. Each phrase in box c could go in the space. What effect would each one have on the base meaning? Mark from *** = very confident to * = very tentative.

B Survey the text on the opposite page.
1 What will the text be about?
2 Write three research questions.

C Read the text. Does it answer your questions?

D Answer these questions.
1 Which contributing factor seemed to be responsible for the accident overall?
2 What other factors are claimed to have contributed to the accident?
3 Which claim does the writer appear to disagree with and why? How does the writer show disagreement?
4 Why do you think this case is regarded as a classic model for studying engineering ethics and errors?

E Find the phrases in box b in the text. Is the writer confident (C) or tentative (T) about the information which follows?

F Look at the writer's description of the accident at the Hyatt Regency Hotel (paragraph 1).
1 Underline the marked words.
2 What does the choice of these words tell you about the writer's opinion of the accident?
3 Find neutral words to use in their place.

G Study the example sentence on the right, and then sentences A and B.
1 Divide sentences A and B into small parts, as in the example sentence.
2 Underline any linking words (e.g., conjunctions).
3 Find the subjects, verbs, objects/complements and adverbial phrases which go together.
4 Make several short simple sentences which show the meaning.

General note

Read the *Skills bank – Identifying the parts in a long sentence* at the end of the Course Book unit. Decide when, if at all, to refer students to it. The best time is probably at the very end of the lesson or the beginning of the next lesson, as a summary/revision.

Lesson aims

- identify the writer's stance on information from the use of marked words
- identify the writer's level of confidence in the research or information
- infer implicit ideas

Further practice in:

- finding the main information in a sentence

Introduction

Introduce the idea of degree of confidence in information, which is usually shown in academic writing. More often than not, writers will avoid very categorical statements, such as 'X was the cause of Y', and will demonstrate the extent to which they are sure about something through various different linguistic devices, such as modals and hedging words and phrases.

Put this table on the board or on an OHT to help explain the idea:

100% *** definitely true. The writer is very confident	X caused Y
75% ** probably true. The writer is a little tentative	X probably/is likely to have caused Y
50% * possibly true. The writer is very tentative	X may/might/could have/possibly caused Y

Exercise A

Set the exercise for pairwork. Students should refer to the table on the board to explain the rating system. Feed back with the whole class, pointing out the aspects of the language that contribute to the degree of confidence.

Answers

Model answers:

Word/ phrase	Rating	Words which show less than 100% confidence
probably caused may have contributed to	**	probably may contributed (i.e., there were other reasons)
was possibly one of the factors which contributed to	*	possibly one of the factors (i.e., there were several factors) contributed
could have been a factor which led to	*	could a factor (i.e., there were other factors)
caused	***	–
seems to have caused	**	seems

Exercise B

Remind students that surveying the text means scanning and skim-reading to get an approximate idea of the text contents. They should:

- look at the title
- look at the first few lines and the final few lines of the text
- look at the first sentence of each paragraph

Note that this is in order to get a very approximate idea of the contents of the text. This will enable students to formulate questions about the text for which they might try to find answers. Students should be discouraged from reading deeply at this point, as they will be able to do this later.

Set for individual work and pairwork discussion. Each pair should agree three questions. Feed back with the whole class. Write some research questions on the board.

Exercise C

Set for individual work followed by pairwork discussion. Feed back with the whole class. Ask whether the questions you have put on the board have been answered in the text.

Exercise D

These questions require students to 'infer' information – that is, understand what is not directly stated.

Set for individual work and pairwork checking. Feed back with the whole class, making sure that students understand the answers.

Answers

Model answers:

1 Answers to this question may differ, according to how students decide which explanation seems to be privileged. Although the immediate cause of the accident is attributed to a structural design flaw, the writer seems to support the view that the overriding cause was down to failure in communication between designer and fabricator (supporting evidence for this explanation is used in the introduction, body text and concluding paragraph).

2 Other factors:
- resonance from people tapping their feet on the walkway
- a problem with the concrete on the walkways being a higher percentage than specified, thus adding to the weight on the walkways

3 The writer appears to disagree with the claim that using a continuous threaded rod, as per the original design, was against the city building code. The writer shows disagreement by stating that existing evidence does not support the claim, and by providing facts and figures regarding the acceptable live load on the walkways specified by city engineers themselves.

4 For several reasons: the fundamental errors that were made in a modern era; the problem of communication inherent in D/B projects if not carried out properly; the ongoing debate about causes; and the seriousness of the accident in terms of lives lost.

Exercise E

Set for individual work and pairwork checking. Feed back with the whole class. Point out that these phrases are very important in academic writing and will help to determine whether something is a fact or an opinion – an important aspect of reading comprehension. They are also used by writers in developing their arguments for or against a particular point of view.

Answers

Model answers:

… it appears to be the case that an elementary error in structural engineering design was to blame.	T
… much of the data also suggested that 'a more fundamental cause was a series of communication failures between the structural engineer and the steel fabricator' (Banset & Parsons, 1989: p.273).	T
Several studies seem to agree that the people who were tapping to the music created resonance in the walkway structure.	T
An investigation found that the builders had changed the design specifications during construction.	C
In hindsight, it would seem obvious that this design change was bound to lead to failure, yet no one detected it.	C
Several studies have pointed out that there was a problem with the concrete used in the walkways.	T
… it was found that the concrete had been topped with cement and consequently the dead load on the walkways was 8% higher than specified.	C
Other studies have claimed that the original design of a continuous threaded rod was contrary to the city building code.	T
Nonetheless, the evidence does not support the claim that this would have caused an accident.	C

Exercise F

Set for pairwork. Feed back with whole class. Discuss any differences in students' answers, and whether neutral equivalents are hard to find for some of the words. Note that marked words in the quotation in this paragraph are not underlined – words in a quotation should never be changed.

Answers

Possible answers:

1 In 1981, at the opening of the magnificent Hyatt Regency Hotel in Kansas City, a tragic accident occurred in which many people were killed and maimed. Several investigations into the devastating accident were carried out and it appears to be the case that an elementary error in structural engineering design was to blame. However, much of the data also suggested that 'a more fundamental cause was a series of communication failures between the structural engineer and the steel fabricator' (Banset & Parsons, 1989: p.273).

2 The choice of words emphasizes the writer's opinion of the shocking nature of such a needless accident in a new, state-of-the-art building. The phrase 'elementary error' implies that such a basic error was inexcusable and avoidable.

3

Marked word	Neutral alternative
magnificent	impressive*
tragic	unfortunate
maimed	permanently injured
devastating	upsetting, worrying, distressing
elementary	simple
to blame	responsible, the cause

*impressive is probably the most neutral alternative in this context

Exercise G

Draw the table from the Answers section (see next page) on the board. Ask students to look at the example sentence and say which box each part of the sentence should go in. Complete the table for the example sentence as shown. Point out that noun phrases are so called because they are made up of several words. In each case, elicit which words are the core of the noun phrases (shown in bold in the table in the Answers section). Do the same with the verbs. Ask students to suggest how the sentence can be rewritten in several short, very simple sentences in which noun phrases and verb phrases are reduced to the core meaning as far as possible. Demonstrate with these examples if necessary:

The people created resonance in the walkway structure.

The people were tapping to the music.

Several studies seem to agree about this.

Tell students to have a look at the example sentence again and elicit how the units of meaning above have been combined into one longer sentence.

Set questions 1–4 (relating to sentences A and B) for individual work and pairwork checking. Feed back with the whole class.

Answers

Model answers:

1/2 A Once resonance | starts, | it | continues to increase | in intensity | until the cause | is removed | or the structure | breaks up.

B The actual live load of the people on the walkways | was | only 420 kN, | which was | a fraction of the live load of 3,200 kN | specified | by the city engineers.

	Subject noun phrases	Verb phrases	Object/complement noun phrases	Adverbial phrases	Notes
Example	Several **studies**	seem to **agree**			
	the **people**	were **tapping**	who (= the people)	to the music	
		created	**resonance** in the walkway structure.		
A	**resonance**	**starts**			
	it	**continues** to increase		in intensity	*it* refers to the subject *resonance*
	the **cause**	**is removed** (or)			*or* is a linking word or conjunction. It can join two noun phrases as here, or two clauses
	the **structure**	**breaks up.**			
B	The actual **live load** of the people on the walkways	**was**	only 420 kN		
		was			
	a fraction of the **live load** of 3,200 kN	**specified by**		the city engineers	

4 **Possible sentences:**

A Once resonance starts, it continues to increase.

Resonance increases in intensity.

Resonance stops when the cause is removed.

Resonance stops when the structure breaks up.

Resonance stops when the caused is removed or when the structure breaks up.

B The actual live load of the people on the walkways was only 420 kN.

A live load of 3,200 kN was specified by city engineers.

The actual live load was a fraction of the live load of 3,200 kN.

The actual live load of the people on the walkways was a fraction of the maximum specified.

Language note

1 Subjects and objects will always be nouns, with or without modifying adjectives.

Complements can be

- nouns: *He is a doctor.*
- adjectives: *He is French.*
- adverbs: *He is ready.*

2 There are several types of conjunction in English.

Coordinating conjunctions such as *and, or, but* link elements of equal grammatical status.

Correlative conjunctions have two items: *either ... or ... ; both ... and ... .*

Subordinating conjunctions relate clauses to each other using single words (e.g., *that* with verbs of saying, thinking, etc., *after, as, before, if, although, while*) or phrases (e.g., *as soon as, in order to, provided that ...*).

See a good grammar reference book for full explanations.

3 Adverbial phrases add information about the actions or processes described by the verb phrase.

Closure

Here are some sentences about construction accidents and health and safety issues. Ask students to identify any *neutral* or *unmarked* vocabulary items in each sentence and to suggest more marked words to add stance so as to make the sentence sound more interesting, exciting or dramatic, as if they were writing a news item. Use the example below, with possible words already underlined, for whole class discussion. Set the further two sentences for pairwork. Feed back, comparing answers and discussing any differences of opinion.

Example with *unmarked* words underlined:

There was a <u>call</u> for <u>big</u> improvements in safety at construction sites after a recent series of <u>unfortunate</u> accidents.

Possible changes:

There was a *(call)* <u>demand/(an) appeal/petition</u>* for *(big)* <u>huge/vast/substantial/extensive/major</u> improvements in safety at construction sites after a recent series of *(unfortunate)* <u>devastating/horrendous/shocking/appalling/terrible</u>* accidents.

*note that these words are not exactly synonymous – the choice of word would depend on the situation and writer's stance; it could be interesting to elicit how meaning can be subtly changed by word choice.

1 City authorities have <u>requested</u> <u>broad</u> changes to the way tower cranes are inspected and monitored, following a <u>dangerous</u> crane collapse that left eight people <u>badly</u> injured.

2 The accident inquiry concluded that the cost-cutting on materials by the building contractors was <u>unwise</u> and had <u>harmed</u> the <u>good</u> reputation of the structural design company.

Possible changes:

1 City authorities have *(requested)* <u>ordered/demanded/called for/insisted on</u> *(broad)* <u>extensive/sweeping/thorough/comprehensive</u> changes to the way tower cranes are inspected and monitored, following a *(dangerous)* <u>life-threatening/terrifying/perilous</u> crane collapse that left eight people *(badly)* <u>seriously/severely/critically/gravely/horribly</u> injured.

2 The accident inquiry concluded that the cost-cutting on materials by the building contractors was *(unwise)* <u>irresponsible/reckless/negligent</u> and had *(harmed)* <u>damaged/ruined/destroyed</u> the *(good)* <u>excellent/outstanding/first-rate</u> reputation of the structural design company.

---

10 ACCIDENT ANALYSIS IN CONSTRUCTION

10.3 Extending skills essay types • situation–problem–solution–evaluation essays

A Read the three essay questions. What types of writing assignment are they?

B Look at text A on the opposite page. Copy and complete Table 1.

C Look at text B on the opposite page. Copy and complete Table 2.

D Read the title of essay 3 again.
1 Make a plan for this essay.
2 Write a topic sentence for each paragraph in the body of the essay.
3 Write a concluding paragraph.

1 Compare the different explanations of what caused the accident at the Hyatt Regency Hotel in 1981.

2 Explain how failure to communicate effectively between designer and fabricator could lead to a serious accident.

3 Describe the problems that can occur in 'design and build' projects and consider how these problems can be resolved.

Table 1

Situation	
Problem(s)	
Solution	

Table 2

Solution	
Arguments for	
Argument against	

10.4 Extending skills writing complex sentences • references • quotations

A Expand these simple sentences. Add extra information. Use the ideas in Lesson 10.3.
1 Problems can occur in D/B projects.
2 D/B contractors may cut costs on materials.
3 There can be confusion over project management.
4 Overall responsibility by one organization is necessary.
5 The solution may not satisfy the client.

B Look at text C on the opposite page. Copy and complete Tables 1–3.

C Look at text D on the opposite page.
1 Complete a further row of Table 1.
2 How could you write this as a reference?

D What do the symbols and abbreviations in the blue box mean?

E Look back at the text on page 81 (Lesson 10.2) and at text B on the opposite page.
1 Find all the research sources (e.g., Banset & Parsons, 1989: p.273).
2 Mark the page numbers for books and journals next to the correct reference in the list (C) on the opposite page.
3 What punctuation and formatting is used before and within each direct quotation? Why?
4 What words are used to introduce each direct quotation? Why does the writer choose each word?

Table 1: *Referencing books*

Author(s)	Place	Date	Publisher

Table 2: *Referencing journals*

Name of journal	Volume	Pages

Table 3: *Referencing websites*

Retrieval date	URL

&	©	edn.	ed(s).	et al.
n.d.	p.	pp.	vol.	

Case Study 1

For any property developer, time is money, and there is usually financial pressure for buildings to be built as quickly as possible. As a result of this, developers sometimes choose to overlap the design and construction phases of a project. In other words, the construction actually begins before the entire building is completely designed! This is different to the traditional approach where the building is designed first, then a call for tenders is made in order to employ a contractor who then constructs the building. The overlapping approach is called 'design and build' (D/B). It has advantages, but can lead to confusion and safety problems, as the Hyatt Regency Hotel disaster shows. In a D/B project, one organization (usually the main contractor) would become responsible for everything. This would require very careful management of responsibilities and clear internal communication. The contractor must also be ready to adjust or correct work because of unforeseen problems. *Source: Butler, 2007*

Case Study 2

One potential solution to the problem of constructing safe, good quality buildings properly is to overlap the design and build phases of a project in a design and build contract. Despite the potential problems of design and build, there are many advantages to using the approach. One advantage is that it may actually save the client money, both in speeding up the program but also in curtailing overbudget spend. The risk to the client may be smaller in D/B because of the shorter timescale. Also, from the client's perspective, there is only one organization to deal with (usually the main contractor), and there is less chance of 'the buck being passed' when things go wrong. However, many of the apparent advantages of D/B may equally be disadvantages. For example, as Carper (2001) points out, a D/B contractor could take reckless short cuts with materials choices and structural design without consultation, which could result in failures and accidents.

References

Banset, E. A., & Parsons, G. M. (1989). Communications failure in Hyatt Regency disaster. *Journal of Professional Issues in Engineering, 115(3)*, 273–288.

Carper, K. L. (2001). Forensic engineering - the perspective from N. America. In: Campbell, P. (ed.) *Learning from Construction Failures*. Caithness: Whittles Publishing.

Cons, R., Jacobitz, T, Olsen, P, & Rains, M. (1982). *The Hyatt Regency walkway collapse*. Retrieved December 8, 2008, from http://www.rosehulman.edu/Class/ce/HTML/publications/momentold/winter96-97/hyatt.html

Taylor, R. K., & Moncarz, P. D. (2000). Engineering process failure – Hyatt walkway collapse. *Journal of Performance of Constructed Facilities, 14(2)*, 46–56.

Case studies in engineering ethics

Marion Butler

Norton & Stamp

First published in 2007
by Norton & Stamp Ltd.
11 Vine Lane, London EC4P 5EI
© 2007 Marion Butler
Reprinted 2009

All rights reserved. No part of this publication may be reproduced, stored in a retrieval system, or transmitted in any form or by any means, electronic, mechanical, photocopying, recording or otherwise without the prior written permission of the Publishers.

British Library Cataloguing-in-Publication Data
A catalogue record for this book is available from the British Library.

Typeset by Ace Graphics, Barnstaple, Devon, UK
Printed and bound by PW Enterprises, Bude, Cornwall, UK

ISBN 0-321-09488-5

82   83

General note

The closure activity for this lesson (ethics case studies) will need some preparation if it is used in class. Alternatively, students could do their own preparation for homework.

Lesson aims

- understand situation–problem–solution–evaluation structure in essays/writing assignments
- understand the use of information in this type of assignment structure to:

   describe

   give cause and effect

   compare

   evaluate

   argue for

Further practice in:

- identifying required writing assignment types
- producing an outline
- writing key sentences – which can be expanded in the next lesson into longer sentences

Introduction

Revise the different types of essay that were examined in Unit 8. Say or write on the board some key words or phrases from essay titles such as the following:

State …

Outline …

Describe …

Compare …

Evaluate …

Discuss …

Account for …

Why …?

How …?

To what extent …?

How far …?

Ask students to say

- what type of essay is required
- what type of organizational structure should be used

If students find this difficult, refer them to the *Skills bank* for Unit 8.

Exercise A

Set for individual work and pairwork checking.

Feed back with the whole class. Point out that in real life, writing assignments given by lecturers often involve several types of writing in one essay. This is the case with essay 3. Tell students that, in fact, a possible structure for essay 3 would be the following, which is commonly found in many types of writing (including newspapers and academic writing).

Situation: description of a state of affairs, often giving some reasons and background information	description
Problem(s): the problems which are caused by the state of affairs; plus the effects of these problems	description (cause and effect)
Solution(s): ways of dealing with the problems (i) which may have been tried in the past or are being tried now (ii) which will, may or could be tried in the future; suggestions for further solutions	description (+ possibly suggestion)
Evaluation of solution(s): comparison of solutions; opinion on how successful the solutions are or could be + justification; an opinion on which is the best option + justification	comparison and argument

Tell students they will plan (and possibly write) this assignment.

Answers

Model answers:

1 Comparison, plus some evaluation.

2 Analysis.

3 Problem (including description, cause and effect) and solution(s) (including description, evaluation/argument/opinion) – see table above.

Exercise B

Tell students that there are two possible ways of viewing the situation/problem/solution in text A, and therefore two different ways of completing Table 1. Do not give any more prompts at this point, as the two versions can be elicited during feedback.

Set for individual work and pairwork checking. Feed back with the whole class.

Answers

The first version in Table 1 identifies 'design and build' as the existing *situation*; the second version identifies 'design and build' as the *solution* to the situation/problem of financial pressures.

Model answers:

Version 1

Situation	because of time/money constraints, developers sometimes overlap design and construction phases of a project before design is completed ('design and build' or D/B)
Problem(s)	D/B can lead to safety problems and confusion about who is in charge, who makes decisions, and how decisions are communicated
Solution	one of the organizations involved (usually the main contractor) would become responsible for everything

Version 2

Situation/ problem	financial pressure for/from developers to build quickly
Solution	overlap design and construction phases of a project before design is completed ('design and build' or D/B) to save time and money

Exercise C

Set for individual work and pairwork checking. Feed back with the whole class.

Answers

Model answers:

Solution	overlap design and build phases
Arguments for	• could save client money – speed up project and prevent overspending on budget • only one organization to deal with (usually the main building contractor)
Argument against	• contractor could make careless cost-cutting decisions re. materials + structural design (no obligation to consult) → failures, accidents

Exercise D

1 Set for pairwork discussion. Remind students to refer back to the text in Lesson 10.2 for ideas and information, as well as the texts they have discussed in this lesson. Remind students about the basic structure of an essay (introduction – main body – conclusion).

If you wish, you can give students the first two columns of the table in the Answers section, with the third column empty for them to complete. The table is reproduced in the additional resources section (Resource 10B) for this purpose.

Feed back with the whole class. Build the plan on the board, using the ideas in the Answers section to help.

2 Ask students to write some topic sentences for the four body paragraphs, using the information in the plan. Remind students that topic sentences need to be very general. Set for individual work.

Feed back with the whole class, writing some examples on the board.

3 Set for pairwork, then discussion with the whole class. Or if you prefer, set for individual homework. The ideas should be those of the students. Remind them to introduce their ideas with suitable phrases.

Note: Students will need their essay plans again in Lesson 10.4.

Answers

1 Possible essay plan below:

Introduction		Examples of ideas
introduce the topic area and define any key terms give the outline of the essay		define what 'design and build' (D/B) is, and why it has become an alternative to traditional approach *In this essay, I will discuss a D/B approach …* *I will illustrate/describe … (examples)* *I will consider … (solutions)* *I will conclude … (evaluation/comment on solution(s))*

Body
 	
solutions
	Para 1:
	situation/problems
	(general)
		many advantages of D/B, but problems can occur → impact on safety:
		  1. poor internal communication → problems/decision-making → serious errors → safety issues
		  2. D/B contractors: cost-cutting on materials → safety issues
		  3. confusion re. who is in control of project: who takes responsibility for decision-making?

	Para 2: problems (specific example)	example case: Hyatt Regency walkway collapse: • brief outline of event (structural collapse) • cause of accident: design flaw – fabricator's change to design of walkway supports • overall responsibility for accident – relate to general problems above re. failures in communication
	Para 3:	1. from outset – one organization to take overall responsibility for project delivery + safety 2. clear, internal communication to avoid confusion 3. communication/consultation with clients & other parties when potential probs. arise
	Para 4: evaluations of solutions	positives and negatives: • overall responsibility for project delivery – key to ensuring safety: cannot 'pass the buck' • competent management + communication → key to safety *but:* • cannot eliminate human error • may not satisfy client re. time/money – but if structure is dangerous → bigger problem for client
Conclusion		*In my view/As I see it, the solution is … because …* *Firstly …* *Secondly …* *Thirdly …*

2 Possible topic sentences:

Para 1	Although there are many advantages to adopting a D/B approach to property development, there are also many drawbacks that can affect safety.
Para 2	The case of the Hyatt Regency Hotel walkway collapse illustrates the devastating consequences of a poorly managed D/B project.
Para 3	The most obvious solution to the potential dangers of a D/B approach, as the Hyatt Regency case demonstrates, is to ensure from the outset that one organization has complete responsibility for project delivery and safety.
Para 4	Solutions to this problem need to strike a balance between ethical, competent management and client satisfaction.

3 Students' own concluding paragraphs.

Language note

Although 'situation–problem–solution–evaluation of solution' is often said to be an organizing principle in writing, in practice it is sometimes difficult to distinguish between the situation and the problem: they may sometimes seem to be the same thing. The important thing is to be clear about the main *focus* of the essay – that is, the answer to the question *What am I writing about?* – and to structure the essay around this.

Closure

Find some case studies on engineering accidents/safety issues/ethics that would be useful either for role play scenarios or group discussion. Students could be presented with situations (background information, chronology of events, etc.) and asked to decide on the most likely causes of the accident or problem/who was responsible/what should be done.

Two good resources at the time of writing are:

1 **Teaching Engineering Ethics: A Case Study Approach**

   available at:

   http://ethics.tamu.edu/pritchar/an-intro.htm

   This resource contains more than 30 cases addressing a range of problems and dilemmas that can occur in engineering contexts.

2 **The Online Ethics Center at the National Academy of Engineering**

   available at:

   http://www.onlineethics.org/Resources/Cases.aspx

   This resource contains numerous professional practice cases, based loosely on authentic incidents.

---

10 ACCIDENT ANALYSIS IN CONSTRUCTION

10.3 Extending skills · essay types • situation–problem–solution–evaluation essays

A Read the three essay questions. What types of writing assignment are they?

B Look at text A on the opposite page. Copy and complete Table 1.

C Look at text B on the opposite page. Copy and complete Table 2.

D Read the title of essay 3 again.
1 Make a plan for this essay.
2 Write a topic sentence for each paragraph in the body of the essay.
3 Write a concluding paragraph.

1 Compare the different explanations of what caused the accident at the Hyatt Regency Hotel in 1981.

2 Explain how failure to communicate effectively between designer and fabricator could lead to a serious accident.

3 Describe the problems that can occur in 'design and build' projects and consider how these problems can be resolved.

Table 1

Situation	
Problem(s)	
Solution	

Table 2

Solution	
Arguments for	
Argument against	

10.4 Extending skills · writing complex sentences • references • quotations

A Expand these simple sentences. Add extra information. Use the ideas in Lesson 10.3.
1 Problems can occur in D/B projects.
2 D/B contractors may cut costs on materials.
3 There can be confusion over project management.
4 Overall responsibility by one organization is necessary.
5 The solution may not satisfy the client.

B Look at text C on the opposite page. Copy and complete Tables 1–3.

C Look at text D on the opposite page.
1 Complete a further row of Table 1.
2 How could you write this as a reference?

D What do the symbols and abbreviations in the blue box mean?

E Look back at the text on page 81 (Lesson 10.2) and at text B on the opposite page.
1 Find all the research sources (e.g., Banset & Parsons, 1989: p.273).
2 Mark the page numbers for books and journals next to the correct reference in the list (C) on the opposite page.
3 What punctuation and formatting is used before and within each direct quotation? Why?
4 What words are used to introduce each direct quotation? Why does the writer choose each word?

Table 1: Referencing books

Author(s)	Place	Date	Publisher

Table 2: Referencing journals

Name of journal	Volume	Pages

Table 3: Referencing websites

Retrieval date	URL

| & | © | edn. | ed(s). | et al. |
| | n.d. | p. | pp. | vol. |

82

Case Study 1

For any property developer, time is money, and there is usually financial pressure for buildings to be built as quickly as possible. As a result of this, developers sometimes choose to overlap the design and construction phases of a project. In other words, the construction actually begins before the entire building is completely designed! This is different to the traditional approach where the building is designed first, then a call for tenders is made in order to employ a contractor who then constructs the building. The overlapping approach is called 'design and build' (D/B). It has advantages, but can lead to confusion and safety problems, as the Hyatt Regency Hotel disaster shows. In a D/B project, one organization (usually the main contractor) would become responsible for everything. This would require very careful management of responsibilities and clear internal communication. The contractor must also be able to adjust or correct work because of unforeseen problems.

Source: Butler, 2007

Case Study 2

One potential solution to the problem of constructing safe, good quality buildings properly is to overlap the design and build phases of a project in a design and build contract. Despite the potential problems of design and build, there are many advantages to using the approach. One advantage is that it may actually save the client money, both in speeding up the program but also in curtailing overbudget spend. The risk to the client may be smaller in D/B because of the shorter timescale. Also, from the client's perspective, there is only one organization to deal with (usually the main contractor), and there is less chance of 'the buck being passed' when things go wrong. However, many of the apparent advantages of D/B may equally be disadvantages. For example, as Carper (2001) points out, a D/B contractor could take reckless short cuts with materials choices and structural design without consultation, which could result in failures and accidents.

References

Banset, E. A., & Parsons, G. M. (1989). Communications failure in Hyatt Regency disaster. *Journal of Professional Issues in Engineering, 115*(3), 273–288.

Carper, K. L. (2001). Forensic engineering – the perspective from N. America. In: Campbell, P. (ed.), *Learning from Construction Failures*. Caithness: Whittles Publishing.

Conn, R., Jacobitz, T., Olsen, P. & Rains, M. (1982). *The Hyatt Regency walkway collapse*. Retrieved December 8, 2008, from http://www.crewhaltman.edu/Class/ce/HTML/publications/momentold/winter96-97/hyatt.html

Taylor, R. K., & Moncarz, P. D. (2000). Engineering process failure – Hyatt walkway collapse, *Journal of Performance of Constructed Facilities, 14*(2), 46–56.

Case studies in engineering ethics

Marion Butler

Norton & Stamp

First published in 2007
by Norton & Stamp Ltd.
11 Vine Lane, London EC4P 3EJ
© 2007 Marion Butler
Reprinted 2009

All rights reserved. No part of this publication may be reproduced, stored in a retrieval system, or transmitted in any form or by any means, electronic, mechanical, photocopying, recording or otherwise without the prior written permission of the Publishers.

British Library Cataloguing-in-Publication Data
A catalogue record for this book is available from the British Library

Typeset by Ace Graphics, Barnstaple, Devon, UK
Printed and bound by PW Enterprises, Bude, Cornwall, UK

ISBN 0-321-09488-5

83

General note

This lesson focuses on writing references for a bibliography according to the APA (American Psychological Society) system.

Before the lesson, it would be useful to familiarize yourself with this system. See the *Skills bank*, and for more detailed information, websites such as http://owl.english.purdue.edu/owl/resource/560/01.

Lesson aims

- use quotations with appropriate punctuation and abbreviations such as *et al.*
- write a reference list (APA system)

Further practice in:

- the reverse activity to Lesson 10.2, i.e., putting extra information into simple sentences in an appropriate way

Introduction

Introduce the idea of using sources in writing. Look back at the text in Lesson 10.2 and at text B in this lesson on page 83. Ask students to find all the places where a reference to a source is mentioned. Ask whether they are direct or indirect quotations. What are the main differences?

Exercise A

Remind students of the essay plan in Lesson 10.3. If you wish, you can reproduce the following table for them. They should try to get all the information in each numbered point into one sentence.

Para 1	many advantages of D/B, but problems can occur → impact on safety: 1. poor internal communication → problems/decision-making → serious errors → safety issues 2. D/B contractors: cost-cutting on materials → safety issues 3. confusion re. who is in control of project: who takes responsibility for decision-making?
Para 4	positives and negatives: • overall responsibility for project delivery – key to ensuring safety: cannot 'pass the buck' • competent management + communication → key to safety *but*: • cannot eliminate human error • may not satisfy client re. time/money – but if structure is dangerous → bigger problem for client

Do the first sentence with the whole class as an example on the board. Students should feel free to add words as appropriate to make a coherent sentence; they can also paraphrase (e.g., *may not satisfy client* → *the client may not be happy*).

Set the remaining sentences for individual work.

Answers

Possible answers:

1 Although there are many advantages of a D/B approach to project delivery, problems can arise that could have serious impacts on safety.

2 Another drawback is that D/B contractors may be tempted to cut costs on materials to keep within budget, an action which could jeopardize the safety of the whole structure.

3 There can also be confusion over who is in overall charge of the project, and who is responsible for key decision-making, particularly when problems arise.

4 To ensure that safety standards are met, overall responsibility for the delivery of the project should lie with only one of the organizations involved.

5 The client may not be happy with the solution if it results in overspending on the budget or delaying the completion of the project, yet a less well-managed alternative that puts safety at risk could ultimately pose the larger problem.

Exercise B

Tell students that this is a list of references from the text in Lesson 10.2. Note that it is called 'References' because it lists all the references actually given (it is not a list of all the references the author might have consulted but not referred to – this is called a bibliography).

Set for individual work and pairwork checking. Note that these tables are intended to help students identify some key information. For a full set of categories to include in a reference list, see the *Skills bank*. Tell students that when writing a reference list, they will need to pay close attention to the detail of the layout which is in the APA style (American Psychological Association). See the *Skills bank* for a website which (at the time of writing) gives further details. In particular, students should note and will need to practise:

- putting the names of writers and multiple writers in the correct alphabetical order according to family name, with the right spacing and punctuation

- writing all numbers correctly, including dates and page references

- using punctuation including the role and placing of full stops, commas and colons

- laying out the references in the correct style with the correct positions (e.g., of indents and tabs)

- using standard APA style features such as italic and brackets

Answers

Table 1: *Books*

Author(s)	Place of publication	Date of publication	Publisher
Carper, K. L.*	Caithness	2001	Whittles Publishing

*note that Carper is one of the writers in a book edited by Campbell – ensure that students understand all the elements of this source in text C

Table 2: *Journals*

Name of journals	Volume	Pages
Journal of Professional Issues in Engineering	115	273–288
Journal of Performance of Constructed Facilities	14	46–56

Table 3: *Websites*

Retrieval date	URL
December 8,	http://www.rose-2008hulman.edu/Class/ce/HTML/publications/momentold/winter96-97/hyatt.html

Language and subject note

In the case of journals, there is an increasing tendency to refer to the volume number only in reference lists, omitting the issue number. Thus, for example,
Journal of Professional Issues in Engineering, 115(3), 273–288 might become *Journal of Professional Issues in Engineering, 115, 273–288*.

Exercise C

Set for individual work and pairwork checking.

Answers

1

Author(s)	Place of publication	Date of publication	Publisher
Butler, M.	London	2007	Norton & Stamp

2 Butler, M. (2007). *Case studies in engineering ethics*. London: Norton & Stamp.

Exercise D

Explain to students that these symbols and abbreviations are related to referencing sources. Some are used in reference lists and bibliographies; some are used when referring to sources in texts. Students should be able to work out or guess some of them from previous exercises. Two of the abbreviations they may not know are *et al.* and *n.d.*

Set for individual work and pairwork checking. Feed back with the class, offering definition prompts for the difficult ones, e.g.,

- an abbreviation from Latin meaning 'and others', used most often in essays when you want to shorten a list of authors, e.g., multiple authors of an article or book (*et al.*)
- an abbreviation to use if you don't know the date of a reference, such as on a website (*n.d.* = no date)

Answers

Model answers:

&	and
©	copyright
edn.	edition
ed(s).	editor(s)
et al.	and other authors
n.d.	no date (used in a reference list if there is no date – as is often the case with web articles)
p.	page
pp.	pages
vol.	volume

Exercise E

Remind students (if you have not done so already) of the two main ways in which students can use sources (i.e., references to other writers' work) in their writing:

- by giving the exact words used by another writer
- by paraphrasing another writer's ideas, i.e., rewriting the ideas using their own, different words, but retaining the meaning

The first method is referred to as quotation or direct quotation. Short direct quotations should be in quotation marks, and incorporated into the paragraph. Quotations of more than one sentence should be 'display quote' style, i.e., on a new line, and indented.

The second method is referred to as paraphrase, summary or indirect quotation. Note that around 90% of the paraphrase should be new words.

1/2 Set for individual work. Tell students to look for all the direct quotations and to identify the research sources. They should then locate the source in the reference list on page 83 of the Course Book. Writing the page numbers on the reference list may seem a mechanical exercise, but it is useful for students to get into the habit of doing this. It will enable them to find an original source book, refer to the relevant part of the book, and read more about the subject.

Students should have discovered that one of the quotations in the text on page 81 has no page number. Elicit why (*because the source – Conn et al. – relates to a website*).

They should also notice that the reference in text B is an indirect quotation (a paraphrase of the source).

3/4 Students should identify the punctuation and introducing phrases used.

Feed back with the whole class.

Answers

Model answers:

Quote	Source	Punctuation/ formatting before/ within each direct quote	Introducing phrase + reason for choice
'a more fundamental cause was a series of communication failures between the structural engineer and the steel fabricator'	page 273 of Banset, E. A., & Parsons, G. M. (1989). Communications failure in Hyatt Regency disaster. *Journal of Professional Issues in Engineering, 115*(3)	'xxx'	However, much of the data also suggested that … reason: to introduce and support a different opinion about the cause of the accident (by establishing – although tentatively – that there is much support for this view)
'an ill-considered change of an ill-defined structural detail'	page 46 of Taylor, R. K., & Moncarz, P. D. (2000). Engineering process failure – Hyatt walkway collapse. *Journal of Performance of Constructed Facilities, 14*(2)	'xxx'	As Taylor and Moncarz observed … reason: to add support to a previous statement, indicating that the writer agrees with Taylor and Moncarz
'ultimately resulted from poor communication between the designers and the fabricators'	no page number – website source: Conn, R., Jacobitz, T., Olsen, P. & Rains, M. (1982). *The Hyatt Regency walkway collapse.* Retrieved December 8, 2008, from: http://www.rose-hulman.edu/Class/ce/HTML/publications/momentold/winter96-97/hyatt.html	'xxx'	However, in parallel with other studies, Conn et al., 1982, considered that the collapse … reason: to introduce and support a different opinion about the cause of the accident (by establishing that there is other support for this view)
'the results of flawed management and project delivery systems rather than technical considerations'	page 1 of Carper, K. L. (2001). Forensic engineering – the perspective from N. America. In: Campbell, P. (ed.) *Learning from Construction Failures.* Caithness: Whittles Publishing	'xxx'	In agreement, Carper stated that many of these types of failures are … reason: to lend further strong support to the previous supporting evidence, thus adding weight to the writer's own view.

Language and subject note

An ampersand (&) is used with multiple authors, preceded by a comma.

The full stop at the end of the reference is omitted in the case of URLs.

Dates are (for example) April 7, not April 7th.

Closure

Refer students to the *Skills bank* for a summary of writing references. Study how the following are used:

- names (order)
- punctuation (capital letters, full stops, commas, colons)
- layout (indentation, spacing)
- style features (italics, brackets)

For further practice, use Resource 10C from the additional resources section. Ask students to check the references on a library database or on the Internet (discuss which sources are likely to be the most accurate and give them all the information they need – often the best way to check bibliographical details is to use a university library catalogue, as information found on the Internet is frequently inaccurate or incomplete). They should also make any necessary changes to ensure the references fit the APA models used in this unit. If possible, they should use the online website references (see *Skills bank*) to help them. Remind students that they will also need to put the references in the right alphabetical order.

Ask students to do a book search on Amazon (http://www.amazon.co.uk). If they type 'construction project management' in the search box, this will reveal all the books listed in the bibliography. If they click on the book cover or the link below the cover, they will be able to look at the table of contents, copyright page, an excerpt from the book and index sample.

Correct versions, in this order, are:

Beavers, J. E., Moore, J. R., & Shriver, W. R. (2009). Steel erection fatalities in the construction industry. *Journal of Construction Engineering and Management, 135*(3), 227–234.

Gransberg, D. D., & Windell, E. (2008). Communicating design quality requirements for public sector design/build projects. *Journal of Management in Engineering, 24*(2), 105–110.

Harris, F., McCaffer, R., & Edum-Fotwe, F. (2006). *Modern construction management.* Oxford: Blackwell.

Hughes, P. & Ferret, E. (2008). *Introduction to health and safety in construction.* London: Butterworth Heinemann.

Linford, S. (2009). Give the architects respect. *Construction News.* Retrieved April 22, 2009, from: http://www.cnplus.co.uk/give-the-architects-respect/5200721.article

Walker, A. (2007). *Project management in construction.* Chichester: Blackwell.

Extra activities

1 Work through the *Skills bank* and *Vocabulary bank* if you have not already done so, or as revision of previous study.

2 Use the *Activity bank* (Teacher's Book additional resources section, Resource 10A).

  A Set the wordsearch for individual work (including homework) or pairwork.

  Answers

```
M  I  N  I  M  A  L  P  E  S  A  S  T  D  V
S  I  G  N  I  F  I  C  A  N  T  A  A  I  E
P  O  S  C  E  R  T  R  U  S  S  I  T  A  S
E  E  N  T  S  C  H  E  M  A  T  I  C  M  T
C  L  L  R  A  F  E  E  D  E  C  F  E  E  I
I  I  E  E  T  U  M  L  N  I  O  A  T  E  F
F  N  V  I  V  L  C  E  A  S  O  I  T  E  A
I  Q  I  O  O  A  P  T  O  N  S  P  C  R  B
C  U  D  I  B  S  T  C  U  U  G  S  O  L  R
A  I  E  U  V  W  I  M  R  S  E  L  L  S  I
T  R  N  S  E  E  I  I  O  E  A  T  L  T  C
I  Y  C  E  R  L  A  O  R  N  I  L  A  R  A
O  P  E  C  R  L  P  T  U  S  S  S  P  I  T
N  N  S  N  C  N  S  A  R  S  A  I  S  V  E
A  C  C  E  I  I  F  A  I  L  U  R  E  E  S
```

  B Set for individual work (including homework) or pairwork. Accept all reasonable answers. Students should be able to explain the meaning. The phrases are mainly from Lesson 10.1 and Lesson 10.2. You may allow students to refer to the various texts in the unit if they have difficulties.

  Answers

  Possible answers:

building	code, project
continuous	threaded rod
design	specifications, flaw, engineer
financial	pressure, impact
hanger	rod
internal	inquiry, communications
live	load
property	developer, development
roof	truss
structural	engineering, design, failure

3 Ask students to choose one of the other essays in Lesson 10.3 and make a plan. They can also write topic sentences for each paragraph in the essay.

11 WIND TURBINES

This unit looks at the theoretical and practical aspects of wind turbine design and operation. The lecture focuses on several key factors that engineers must take into consideration, particularly the technical problems and solutions with regard to wind energy extraction in real-world conditions. The research task requires students to find out the advantages and disadvantages of both horizontal-axis and vertical-axis wind turbines.

Skills focus

🎧 Listening
- recognizing the speaker's stance
- writing up notes in full

Speaking
- building an argument in a seminar
- agreeing/disagreeing

Vocabulary focus

- words/phrases used to link ideas (*moreover*, *as a result*, etc.)
- stress patterns in noun phrases and compounds
- fixed phrases from academic English
- words/phrases related to wind energy and wind turbines

Key vocabulary

See also the list of fixed phrases from academic English in the *Vocabulary bank* (Course Book page 92).

aerodynamics	efficiency	motive power	theoretical
aileron	electrical grid	optimum	tip speed ratio
alter	engineer (v)	pitch control	torque
apparatus	environmental	power conversion	urban
Betz limit	extract (v)	practical	variable
blade	fibre-optic	quadrillion	VAWT (vertical-axis wind turbine)
control	frequency	radar	
conversion	generator	regulation	wind turbine
cost-effective	govern	rotate	windmill
cylinder	gust	rotor	yaw control
device	HAWT (horizontal-axis wind turbine)	spin	
drag force		stationary	
durable	instrument	structural	
effect (n or v)	mechanism	sustainable energy	

11.1 Vocabulary

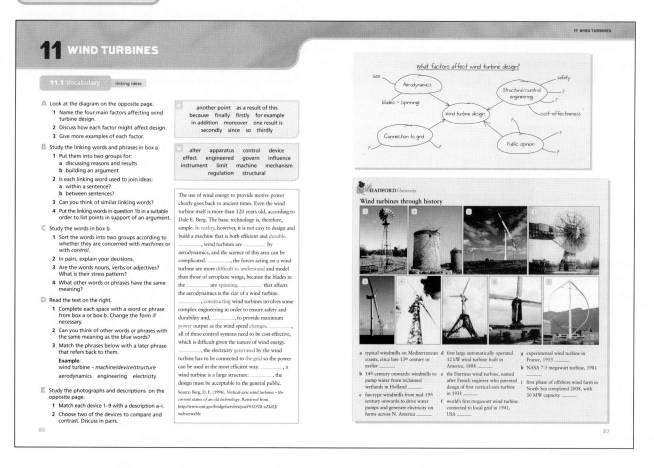

Source: Berg, D. E. (1996). *Vertical-axis wind turbines – the current status of an old technology.* Retrieved from http://www.osti.gov/bridge/servlets/purl/432928-xZkiEJ/webviewable

General note

Read the *Vocabulary bank* at the end of the Course Book unit. Decide when, if at all, to refer your students to it. The best time is probably at the very end of the lesson or the beginning of the next lesson, as a summary/revision.

Lesson aims

- use rhetorical markers: to add points in an argument; to signal cause and effect (between- and within-sentence linking)
- further understand lexical cohesion: the use of superordinates/synonyms to refer back to something already mentioned; building lexical chains

Further practice in:

- synonyms, antonyms and wordsets from the discipline

Introduction

1 Revise some vocabulary from previous units. Give students some key words from the previous unit (in italics below) and ask them to think of terms connected with these words (for example, some key phrases from building engineering):

design: design specification, design flaw, design and build contract (D/B)

project: project management, project delivery, building project

structural: structural design, structural engineering, structural design engineer, structural damage

building: building code, building contractor, building materials

2 Introduce the topic: before asking students to open their books, tell them that this unit will focus on the theoretical and practical aspects of wind turbines. Ask students what they already know about wind power and wind turbines. Elicit a few opinions on whether wind energy can be a viable alternative to traditional energy sources. Accept any reasonable contributions.

Exercise A

Ask students to open their books and look at the diagram on page 87.

1 This question is for orientation purposes and to find out what students already know. Ask one of the students to briefly explain the diagram and invite others to comment. Check understanding and pronunciation of the words in the diagram. You may have to explain the meaning of *connection to grid*. Do not ask them to complete the diagram at this stage. If you wish, you could copy the diagram onto the board or display on an OHT.

2/3 With the whole class, discuss the aerodynamics factor. Elicit why the size of a wind turbine and the blades might affect the aerodynamics. If students have difficulty with this one, explain that they will find out in the course of this unit.

Next look at the structural/control engineering factor. Discuss with the class why safety and cost-effectiveness would have an impact on design. Ask the students to suggest more examples to complete this part of the diagram. Accept any reasonable suggestions, but do not correct at this point.

Set the remaining factors (*public opinion* and *connection to grid*) for pairwork discussion. Ask a few pairs to feed back to the class. Accept any reasonable suggestions.

Answers

Possible answers:

2/3 Answers depend on the students. See diagram below for possible answers. You may wish to add some of these to the diagram, as appropriate, and as students suggest them. It would be a good idea to make a large poster-sized copy of the diagram or put it on an OHT or other visual medium, to which you can add more examples as the unit progresses.

See diagram below.

Exercise B

1 Set for individual work and pairwork checking. Feed back with the whole class, building the table in the Answers section.

2 Explain what is meant by 'within' and 'between' sentences: 'within-sentence' linking words or phrases join clauses in a sentence; 'between-sentence' linking words or phrases connect two sentences. Demonstrate with the following:

Within-sentence linking words:
The cost of producing electricity from wind power has decreased <u>because</u> wind turbine technology has improved recently.

Make sure students can see that within-sentence linking words precede dependent clauses.

Between-sentence linking words:
Wind turbine technology has improved recently. <u>As a result</u>, the cost of producing electricity from wind power has decreased.

Point out that with between-sentence linking words there is usually a comma before the rest of the sentence.

Ask students to say which of the other words in box a are 'between' and which are 'within'.

3 Ask for suggestions for synonyms and add to the table.

4 First make sure that students understand the basic principle of an argument, which is:

Statement

+

one or more support(s) for statement (= more facts, reasons, results, examples, evidence, etc.)

Constructing a complex argument will usually entail a statement plus several supports.

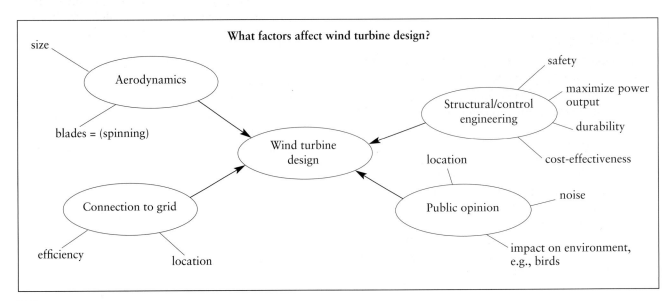

What factors affect wind turbine design?

size — Aerodynamics — Wind turbine design
blades = (spinning)
Connection to grid → Wind turbine design
efficiency   location
safety
maximize power output
Structural/control engineering
durability
location
cost-effectiveness
noise
Public opinion
impact on environment, e.g., birds

With the whole class, elicit suggestions for how to use the linking words/phrases when constructing an argument. Build the table in the Answers section on the board.

Answers

Possible answers:

1/2/3

Linking words/phrases	Use for	Within or between sentence	Other similar words/phrases
Another point ...	building an argument	between	And another thing,
As a result of this,	reasons and results	between	Consequently,
because	reasons and results	within	as
Finally,	building an argument	between	Lastly,
Firstly,	building an argument	between	To begin with,/To start with, For one thing,
Thirdly,	building an argument	between	Next,/Then,
For example,	building an argument	between	For instance,
In addition,	building an argument	between	Also,
Moreover,	building an argument	between	Furthermore,
One result is ...	reasons and results	between	One consequence of this is ... Because of this,
Secondly,	building an argument	between	Next,/Then,
since	reasons and results	within	As
So,	reasons and results	between	Therefore,/Thus,/Hence

4 A typical argument is constructed like this:

Firstly,	making the first major support point
For example,	supporting the point with a specific example
In addition,	adding another related point in support
Secondly,	making the second major support point
Another point is ...	adding another related point in support
Moreover,	adding more information to the point above
Finally,	making the last point

Language note

1 Note that within-sentence linking words may be placed at the beginning of the sentence with a comma after the first clause, as in:
Because wind turbine technology has improved recently, the cost of producing electricity from wind power has decreased.

2 Although the between-sentence linking words are described above as joining two sentences, they can of course link two independent clauses joined by coordinating linking words *and* or *but*, as in:
Wind turbine technology has improved recently and, as a result, the cost of producing electricity from wind power has decreased.

Exercise C

1 Set for individual work. Note that students should try to put each word into one of the two categories, even if it is not immediately clear how it could be relevant. If they are not sure which category to use, they should try to think of a phrase containing the word and imagine how it could be relevant to one of the categories.

2 Ask students to compare their answers and to justify their choices. Feed back with the whole class, discussing the words for which students feel the category is not obvious. If no decision can be reached, say you will come back to the words a little later.

3/4 Set for pairwork. Feed back with the whole class if you wish.

Answers

Model answers:

Word	Suggested categories	Part of speech	Other words/phrases
'alter	control	v (T)	change
appa'ratus	machines	n (C/U)	device
de'vice	machines	n (C)	apparatus
e'ffect	control	n (C); v (T)	result; to cause something to happen
engi'neered	machines	adj	machined
'govern	control	v (T)	control, rule
'influence	control	v (T); n (C/U)	affect
'instrument	machines	n (C)	measuring device
'limit	control	v (T); n (C)	endpoint, maximum value
'mechanism	machines	n (C)	working parts
regu'lation	control	n (C)	rule
'structural	machines	adj	integral

Note: *control* and *machine* have been omitted from the first column, as they are already clearly categorized.

Exercise D

Note: Students may need to use dictionaries in question 2.

Students should first read through the text to get an idea of the topic.

1/2 Set for individual work and pairwork checking. Feed back with the whole class.

Point out that having done these questions, it should now be possible to say whether the words in box b can be put into a 'machines' or a 'control' group. The point here is that the context will make clear what the meaning of a word should be. This is important when it comes to making a guess at the meaning of a word you are not sure of initially.

Tell students that a particular topic will have groups of words which are connected to or associated with it – known as 'lexical chains'. These lexical chains show us the themes that run through the text and which help 'glue' the ideas together to make a cohesive piece of text. It is a good idea, therefore, to learn vocabulary according to topic areas.

3 It is also common to use synonymous words and phrases to refer back to something already mentioned. Ideally, use an OHT or other visual medium of the text (see Resource 11B in the additional resources section), and with a coloured pen draw a line to show how *wind turbine ... machine* is referred to later in the text by *device* and *structure*. Set for individual work and pairwork checking. Feed back with the class (linking the phrases with coloured pens if using Resource 11B).

Answers

Model answers:

1 The use of wind energy to provide motive power clearly goes back to ancient times. Even the wind turbine itself is more than 120 years old, according to Dale E. Berg. The basic technology is, therefore, simple. In reality, however, it is not easy to design and build a machine that is both efficient and durable. Firstly, wind turbines are governed by aerodynamics, and the science of this area can be complicated. For example, the forces acting on a wind turbine are more difficult to understand and model than those of aeroplane wings, because the blades in the device are spinning. Another point that affects the aerodynamics is the *size* of a wind turbine. Secondly, constructing wind turbines involves some complex engineering in order to ensure safety and durability and, in addition, to provide maximum power output as the wind speed changes. Moreover, all of these control systems need to be cost-effective, which is difficult given the nature of wind energy. Thirdly, the electricity generated by the wind turbine has to be connected to the grid so the power can be used in the most efficient way. Finally, a wind turbine is a large structure. As a result of this, the design must be acceptable to the general public.

Source: Berg, D. E. (1996). *Vertical-axis wind turbines – the current status of an old technology*. Retrieved from http://www.osti.gov/bridge/servlets/purl/432928-xZkiEJ/webviewable

2

Word	Synonym
in reality	actually
durable	long-lasting
difficult to understand	complicated, complex
spinning	rotating, turning
constructing	building
power	energy
changes	increases or decreases
generated	produced
the grid	the national power supply system

3

First phrase	Second phrase
aerodynamics	this area
engineering	control systems
electricity	power

Exercise E

1 Set for individual work and pairwork checking. Students may find some of these items difficult to match. Tell them to attempt the most obvious ones first and try to guess others by using clues from the descriptions and photographs. Feed back to the class.

2 Set for pairwork discussion. Tell students to think about factors in addition to physical similarities and differences if they can, such as functions and operating principles. Encourage them to use some of the language in the lesson so far. Feed back to the class.

Answers

Model answers:

1 a = 2
  b = 8
  c = 1
  d = 4
  e = 9
  f = 6
  g = 7
  h = 3
  i = 5

2 Answers will depend on students.

Closure

Ask students to review the lesson and list the factors which affect wind turbine design. Then divide the class into groups and tell the groups to discuss the factors and try to rank them in order of importance. They should give reasons for their ranking.

11.2 Listening

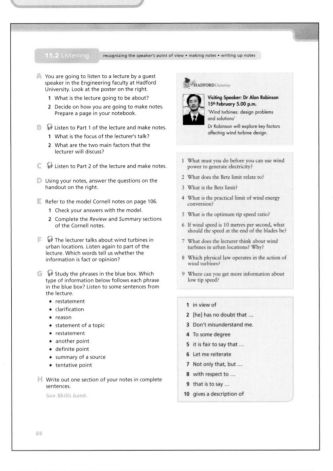

Introduction

1 Review phrases indicating a speaker's view of the truth value of a statement. Write a sentence such as the following on the board (i.e., a 'fact' about which there may be differences of opinion): *Energy produced from wind power is not cost-effective at present.*

Ask students to say whether they think this is true or not. Elicit phrases they can use before the sentence to show how certain they are about their opinion.

Dictate or write on the board the following phrases. Ask students to say what the effect of each phrase is when put before the sentence on the board. In each case, does it make the writer sound confident or tentative?

The research shows that …

A survey found that …

The evidence does not support the idea that …

It appears to be the case that …

The evidence suggests that …

The evidence shows that …

It is clear that …

It is possible that …

2 Revise the Cornell note-taking system. Elicit the R words. Ask students to describe how to divide up the page (refer to Unit 9). Revise the other ways to take notes (see Units 1 and 3).

3 Revise note-taking symbols and abbreviations (see Units 5 and 9, and Unit 9 extra activity 4).

Exercise A

Refer students to the Hadford University lecture announcement. Tell them to look at the title and the summary of the talk.

Set the exercises for pairwork discussion. Feed back with the whole class.

Answers

1 Accept any reasonable suggestions.

2 The lecturer is clearly going to discuss a range of key factors that have to be considered in wind turbine design. This suggests that a spidergram might be a suitable form of notes (as in Unit 1), as well as the Cornell system (which is used here) or the more conventional numbered points system.

General note

Read the *Skills bank – Writing out notes in full* at the end of the Course Book unit. Decide when, if at all, to refer students to it. The best time, as before, is probably at the very end of the lesson or the beginning of the next lesson, as a summary/revision.

Lesson aims

- recognize and understand phrases that identify the speaker's point of view
- use background knowledge in listening comprehension
- convert notes into full sentences and paragraphs

Further practice in:

- making notes (use of heading systems and abbreviations)
- referring to sources
- general academic words and phrases

🎧 Exercise B

Play Part 1 once through *without* allowing students time to focus on the questions.

Put students in pairs to answer the questions by referring to their notes. Feed back with the whole class, building a set of notes on the board if you wish.

Add the examples to your spidergram from Lesson 11.1 if you have not already done so.

Ask students which method they are going to use to make notes, now that they have listened to the introduction. They should make any adjustments necessary to the page they have prepared in their notebooks.

Answers

Model answers:

1 Design and installation of wind turbines.
2 Theory and practical aspects of design.

Transcript 🎧 2.16

Part 1

Good morning everyone, and welcome to today's talk on wind turbines. As you no doubt know, wind turbines are devices that extract energy from the wind, turning it into mechanical energy or electrical energy. In some form or other, wind turbines, or windmills, as they have been known, have existed for hundreds of years, and were used in the distant past, for example, to drain marshlands in areas of Holland. But in view of the world's need for cleaner, renewable sources of electricity, wind turbines have become a feature of modern power generation, and MacKay, in his excellent analysis of sustainable energy options, has no doubt that wind power will form a significant part of the answer to our future energy needs. Today, however, we're going to talk about the factors which must be taken into account by mechanical engineers when designing and installing wind turbines to generate electricity.

Don't misunderstand me. I don't want to imply that only *engineering* factors affect the widespread use of wind turbines. There are many other factors related to public opinion, such as the impact on wildlife and the visual effect on the environment. To some degree, I think engineers must take into account these aspects, but in this lecture, I am only going to consider design. In particular, I'm going to look at the theory behind wind power and then consider some of the practical aspects.

🎧 Exercise C

Play the whole of the rest of lecture through once without stopping. Students should make notes as they listen.

Answers

See *Notes* section of the table in the Answers section for Exercise E.

Transcript 🎧 2.17

Part 2

So, I want to begin by examining the theoretical maximum power extraction from the wind – a key consideration in wind turbine design. First of all, it is fair to say that the higher the wind speed, the more energy can be extracted. However, no matter how high the wind speed is, not all of the wind's energy can be extracted, as I will explain. The problem is … we have to slow the wind down in the turbine in order to extract energy from it. Of course, we do not slow the wind down to zero, because then we could not extract any energy. But there is an optimum point at which the maximum energy can be extracted. It turns out that this theoretical limit is just under 60%. This is called the Lanchester-Betz-Joukowsky limit, but let's just call it the Betz limit for short! (That's spelt B-E-T-Z.) Let me reiterate: it is impossible to build a wind energy extraction device that converts more than 60% of the energy in the wind. Not only that, but real-world conditions limit the power conversion even more. Real wind turbines suffer further losses with respect to real-world conditions, and, therefore, with a *real* turbine, one can only expect to extract perhaps a maximum of 40% of the energy in the wind.

So far, I've been talking about the *theoretical* limit for wind power compared with the *practical* limit for real-world wind turbines. Now let's talk about wind turbine design. Why do most modern wind turbines have three blades and point into the wind? To understand this, we need to talk about an important number called the tip speed ratio, that is to say, the ratio between the speed at the tip, or end, of the wind turbine blades and the oncoming wind speed. Now, it may seem strange, but in modern wind turbines, the tip of the blades is actually rotating faster than the speed of the oncoming wind. The optimum ratio is 6. In other words, if the wind speed is 8 metres per second, the tips of the blades are rotating at … have you worked it out? Yes, 48 metres per second. In case that doesn't mean much to you, that is the same as 172 kilometres per hour. The best way to get this high tip speed is with three blades, pointing into the wind. This gets the maximum lift, which is the same force that enables a plane to take off and fly.

As an aside, some people say that wind turbines can be used in every kind of environment, including urban locations. However, in my view, these turbines are usually very poor. The data shows that, in these locations, the wind is very gusty, or completely blocked by other buildings. This means, unfortunately, that the efficiency will be low, which makes them almost useless.

Why is the efficiency low if the tip speed is low? Well, we know from Newton's second law that forces come in pairs – 'every action has an equal and opposite reaction'. Now, as the air passes the wind turbine blades, it exerts a force on the blades, which results in a torque which turns the blades. However, the opposite is also true – the blades exert an equal and opposite torque on the air. If the blades are rotating slowly, there will be a high reaction torque, which will result in a large swirling cylinder of air behind the turbine, which represents lost energy. Have a look at the book by Dixon, which gives a description of this.

To recap, so far we've looked at the maximum limit for power extraction for any kind of wind power device. We've also discussed briefly why most modern turbines have high tip speed ratios. Now, there are so many things I could talk about – we could go into real detail regarding the aerodynamics of wind turbine blades, but I would rather look briefly at four other issues associated with turbine design, so let's go on to that.

Exercise D

Put students in pairs to answer the questions by referring to their notes. Feed back with the class to see how much they have been able to get from the lecture. If they can't answer something, do not supply the answer at this stage.

Answers

Model answers:

1 have to slow wind down
2 the theoretical limit of efficiency of a wind turbine
3 just under 60%
4 40%
5 6
6 60 metres per second
7 Newton's second law
8 a low tip speed will lead to a high opposite torque → swirling cylinder of air behind the blades = lost energy
9 book by Dixon

Exercise E

1 Set for individual work.
2 Set for individual work and pairwork checking. Feed back with the whole class.

Answers

Possible answers:

See opposite page.

🎧 Exercise F

Discuss the question with the whole class. Ask them if they can remember any phrases which signal whether comments are fact or just opinion.

Play the extract. Ask students to tell you to stop the recording when they hear key phrases. Write the phrases on the board.

Remind students that it is important to recognize when someone is giving only their opinion, which others might well disagree with.

Answers

Model answers:

As an aside, *some people say that* (wind turbines can be used in every kind of environment, including urban locations.)	This phrase can be used to give both a speaker's own opinion as well as an opposing view.
However, *in my view*, these turbines …	This is clearly the lecturer's opinion.
… are usually *very poor*.	This is a continuation of 'in my view'.
The data shows that, (in these locations, the wind is very gusty, or completely blocked by other buildings.)	Sometimes, to put their case strongly, people will present opinions based on research as facts, very strongly stated, with no tentativeness.
This means, *unfortunately*, (that the efficiency will be low, …)	This word shows the lecturer's opinion on the meaning of the data.
… which makes them almost *useless*.	This is a continuation of the lecturer's opinion on the meaning of the data with regard to the efficiency of wind turbines in urban locations.

Transcript 🎧 2.18

As an aside, some people say that wind turbines can be used in every kind of environment, including urban locations. However, in my view, these turbines are usually very poor. The data shows that, in these locations, the wind is very gusty, or completely blocked by other buildings. This means, unfortunately, that the efficiency will be low, which makes them almost useless.

Review	Notes
	Wind turbine design
	1 Max. power extractn. from wind
	a) theoretically:
All energy cannot be extracted from wind because …?	• higher the wind speed = more energy extracted
	• <u>but</u> not all energy can be extracted – have to slow wind down in turb. to extract energy
Betz limit (optimum point) is …?	• optimum point for max. energy extractn. = just < 60% (Betz limit)
Effect of real-world conditions?	b) <u>real-world conditions</u>
	• limit power conversion even more – further losses re. conditions
Optimum energy in real-world conditions is …?	• ∴ real turbs. = c. max. 40% energy from wind
	2 Turbine design
Most modern turbines have …?	a) why most modern wind turbs. = 3 blades + point into wind:
Tip speed ratio is …?	• ∵ tip speed ratio (= ratio betw. speed at tip of turb. blades) + oncoming wind speed
Optimum ratio is …?	• in mod. turbs. – tip of blades rotate faster than speed of oncoming wind – optimum ratio = 6
	• i.e., if wind speed = 8 m/s*, tips of blades rotate at 48 m/s = 172 kph
Why is modern design best way?	• best way to get high t/speed = 3 blades pointing into wind → max. lift = same force to enable plane to take off + fly
	b) why efficiency low if t/speed low:
What creates a torque?	• ∵ as air passes turb. blades → force on blades → a torque which turns blades
	• opposite also true: blades exert equal + opposite torque on air
What happens when tip speed is low?	• if blades rotating slowly = high reaction torque → large cylinder of air behind turb. = lost energy (see Dixon bk.)

Summary

Wind turbines cannot extract all the energy from the wind, as the wind speed has to be slowed down in the turbine to be able to extract the energy. There is a significant difference, though, between the *theoretical* maximum extraction of power from the wind (just under 60% and maximum extraction in *real conditions* (around 40%), because real conditions are not ideal and cause further losses. This is an important consideration for wind turbine design. Most modern wind turbines have three blades and point into the wind because this is the best way to get a high tip speed for maximum lift. If the tip speed is low, the efficiency of the turbine will be low, because slowly rotating blades will create a high reaction torque, resulting in lost energy.

*m/s = one of the standard abbreviations for metres per second

Note

Source references for lecture:

Dixon, S. (2005). *Fluid mechanics and thermodynamics of turbomachinery* (fifth ed.). Amsterdam: Elsevier.

MacKay, D. J. C. (2008). *Sustainable energy – without the hot air.* UIT Cambridge. PDF available free online at www.withouthotair.com.

Manwell, J. F., McGowan, J. G. and Rogers, A. L. (2002). *Wind energy explained: theory, design and application.* Chichester: John Wiley and Sons Ltd.

🎧 Exercise G

Allow students time to read the phrases and the types of information, making sure that they understand any difficult words. Remind students that 'type' of information tells you what the speaker *intends to do* with the words. The words themselves are something different.

Ask students to try to match the phrases and types of information as far as they can. Note that it is not always possible to say what the function of a phrase is outside its context, so they may not be able to match all the phrases and information types before hearing the extracts. Note that some types of information are needed more than once.

When they have done as much as they can, play the extracts one at a time, allowing time for students to identify the type of information which follows. Check answers after each extract, making sure that students understand the information that actually follows the phrase. If possible, students should also give the actual words.

Answers

Model answers:

Fixed phrase	Type of information which follows the phrase
1 in view of	reason
2 [he] has no doubt that …	definite point
3 Don't misunderstand me.	clarification
4 To some degree	tentative point
5 it is fair to say that …	tentative point
6 Let me reiterate	restatement
7 Not only that, but …	another point
8 with respect to …	statement of a topic
9 that is to say	restatement
10 gives a description of	summary of a source

Transcript 🎧 2.19

Extract 1

But in view of the world's need for cleaner, renewable sources of electricity, wind turbines have become a feature of modern power generation …

Extract 2

… and MacKay, in his excellent analysis of sustainable energy options, has no doubt that wind power will form a significant part of the answer to our future energy needs.

Extract 3

Don't misunderstand me. I don't want to imply that only engineering factors affect the widespread use of wind turbines.

Extract 4

There are many other factors related to public opinion, such as the impact on wildlife, and the visual effect on the environment. To some degree, I think engineers must take into account these aspects, but in this lecture, I am only going to consider design.

Extract 5

First of all, it is fair to say that the higher the wind speed, the more energy can be extracted.

Extract 6

But there is an optimum point at which the maximum energy can be extracted. It turns out that this theoretical limit is just under 60% … Let me reiterate: it is impossible to build a wind energy extraction device that converts more than 60% of the energy in the wind.

Extract 7

Not only that, but real-world conditions limit the power conversion even more.

Extract 8

Real wind turbines suffer further losses with respect to real-world conditions, …

Extract 9

To understand this, we need to talk about an important number called the tip speed ratio, that is to say, the ratio between the speed at the tip, or end, of the wind turbine blades and the oncoming wind speed.

Extract 10

If the blades are rotating slowly, there will be a high reaction torque, which will result in a large swirling cylinder of air behind the turbine, which represents lost energy. Have a look at the book by Dixon, which gives a description of this.

Exercise H

Use this section from the Cornell notes to demonstrate what to do:

Notes
Wind turbine design
1 <u>Max. power extractn. from wind</u>
a) theoretically:
• higher the wind speed = more energy extracted
• <u>but</u> not all energy can be extracted – have to slow wind down in turb. to extract energy
• optimum point for max. energy extractn. = just < 60% (Betz limit)

Elicit from students suggestions on how to write up the notes in complete sentences. Write the suggestions on the board.

Ask students to say what they need to add in to the notes to make a good piece of writing, e.g.,

Grammar: relative pronouns, articles and determiners, prepositions, auxiliary verbs, linking words, 'there was/were' clauses (in italics in the model notes below).

Vocabulary: some vocabulary may need to be added, particularly where symbols are used in the notes, or where extra words are needed to make sense of the information or give a good sense of flow in the writing (in bold below).

Note that this of course works the other way: when making notes, these elements can be excluded from the notes.

Possible rewrite of the notes:

Wind turbine design **has to take into consideration** maximum power extraction from *the* wind. Theoretically, *the* higher the wind speed, *the* more energy *can be* extracted. *However*, not all *the* energy *from the* **wind** can be extracted, *as the* wind **first** *has to be* slowed down in *the* turbine **to enable** extraction **to occur**. *The* optimum point *at which* maximum energy *can be* extracted *is* just **under** 60%. *This is* **called** *the* 'Betz limit'.

Set another section for individual writing in class or for homework. Either ask students to refer to their own notes, or to the Cornell notes on page 107 of the Course Book.

Closure

1 Tell students to review and make a list of the main topics and arguments presented in this lesson. Then ask them to try and summarize the viewpoints, using some of the language they have practised.

2 They could also give a two- or three-sentence summary of anything that they themselves have read, e.g., *I read a useful article on X by Y. It said that …*

3 Ask students to do some research and to make a list of useful or interesting books/articles/websites on the topics in this lesson. They should draw up a list, including correct referencing, and share their sources with other students.

11.3 Extending skills

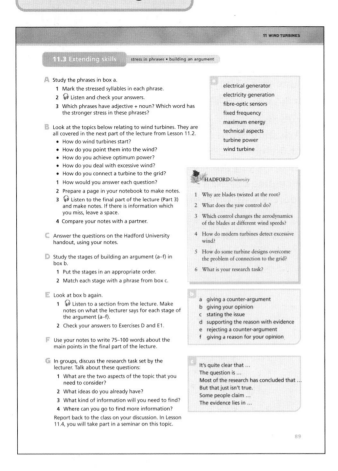

Lesson aims

- recognize stress patterns in noun phrases
- understand how to develop an argument:

  stating the issue

  giving a counter-argument

  rejecting a counter-argument

  giving opinions

  supporting opinions

  understand more general academic words and phrases mainly used in speaking

Further practice in:

- expressing degrees of confidence/tentativeness
- reporting back

Introduction

1 Revise the lecture in Lesson 11.2. Ask students to use the model Cornell notes on page 107. They should cover up the *Notes* section and use the *Review* and *Summary* sections (which they completed in Lesson 11.2) to help recall the contents of the lecture. They could work in pairs to do this.

2 Revise phrases which express degrees of confidence in 'facts'. Dictate these phrases. Do they show that the speaker is certain or tentative?

> *There is no question that* (= certain)
>
> *We have to accept the evidence* (= certain)
>
> *Some people claim that* (= tentative)
>
> *What seems obvious is that* (= certain)
>
> *As everyone is aware* (= certain)
>
> *To some degree* (= tentative)
>
> *This means ultimately that* (= certain)
>
> *It's quite clear that* (= certain)
>
> *We could argue that* (= tentative)

🎧 Exercise A

1/2 Set for individual work and pairwork checking. This is an exercise in perceiving rhythm. At this point there is no need to distinguish between different levels of stress. Students can underline all the stressed syllables. They will also need to count all the syllables.

Feed back with the whole class, checking pronunciation of the phrases and meanings.

3 Discuss this with the class first. Demonstrate with ˌtechnical 'aspects, showing how if you say 'technical ˌaspects, it appears that a contrast is being made with other aspects. Tell students that the usual pattern for the adjective + noun phrase is for a heavier stress to go on the noun. *Wind turbine* is, however, different: it is a compound made from a noun + noun, and the stress is: 'wind ˌturbine – i.e., the heavier stress goes on the first noun. Set students to pick out the other adjective + noun patterns, writing each one on the board. Elicit the stress patterns and give students time to practise the phrases.

Answers

Model answers:

1/2 electrical 'generator (adj / noun)

elec'tricity generation

fibre-optic 'sensors (adj / noun)

fixed 'frequency (adj / noun)

maximum 'energy (adj / noun)

technical 'aspects (adj / noun)

'turbine power

'wind turbine

3 Adjective + noun (second word has stronger stress): electrical generator, fibre-optic sensors, fixed frequency, maximum energy, technical aspects

Transcript 🎧 2.20

electrical 'generator

elec'tricity generation

fibre-optic 'sensors

fixed 'frequency

maximum 'energy

technical 'aspects

'turbine power

'wind turbine

🎧 Exercise B

1 Look at the five topics. Discuss with the class what they know already about the first topic (How do wind turbines start?). Accept any reasonable suggestions but do not correct at this point. Put students in pairs and ask each pair to discuss the other four topics.

2 Set for individual work.

3 Play Part 3 straight through; students make notes.

4 Put students in pairs to compare their notes and fill in any gaps they may have.

Transcript 🎧 2.21

Part 3

OK. So let's look at some of the most important practical points about wind turbine design. First of all, how do we make wind turbines start? When there is no wind, the blades are stationary, of course. In order to ensure that the turbine will start, when the wind starts to blow, there has to be some torque applied to the blades. To achieve this, we have to twist the blades near to the centre (or 'root') of the blade. By twisting the blades, a small amount of torque will be applied when the wind starts to blow, and hopefully this is enough to start the rotor spinning!

A second point we have to think about is how to ensure that the rotor points into the wind. If the rotor doesn't point into the wind, we will not extract the maximum energy from the wind and we might have a problem getting started, so we need a mechanism to make sure this happens. Most large turbines use a small motor to turn the whole machine into the wind. This is called 'yaw control' (that's Y-A-W), because yaw is side-to-side movement.

A third issue is 'pitch control'. Pitch is, of course, up and down movement. Pitch control varies the angle of the blades relative to the plane of rotation. This works in a similar way to the ailerons, or small wing tabs, on an aircraft. By adjusting the pitch, we change the aerodynamics of the blade and this means we can extract optimum power at different wind speeds. Manwell, McCowan and Rogers explain in a lot more detail how pitch control works, and many other aspects of wind turbines.

Fourthly, we have the problem of too much wind. Wind turbines are, obviously, sited in windy locations, but inevitably such locations sometimes experience extremely high winds. Excessive wind can damage a turbine by making the blades rotate too quickly. Modern turbines have wind sensors, including fibre-optic sensors to monitor tiny changes in the shape of the blades when the wind is gusting. They also have a form of radar which can predict the arrival of a gust. When excessive wind is detected or predicted, the blades are turned slightly so they catch less wind and are therefore protected.

One last thing. In order to turn the turbine power into electrical power, we need an electrical generator. The problem is, we can extract more power if we allow the turbine to turn at different speeds (depending on the wind speed), but many generators which are directly connected to the grid need to run at a fixed speed, because the electrical grid is at a fixed frequency. Fortunately, there are some ways to get around this. One approach is to convert the generator output into DC, and then recreate the fixed frequency mains AC using power electronics. This involves extra cost and some power lost in the conversion, but this has to be traded against the extra wind energy that can be extracted by variable speed operation. Another approach is to use a cleverly designed electrical machine called a doubly-fed induction generator (DFIG). But we'll have to talk about that next time!

So, today we have seen some of the technical aspects of designing wind turbines. As I said at the beginning, there are other aspects, including environmental concerns. I suppose for people outside the mechanical engineering field, the question is: *Do the benefits of wind turbines outweigh any problems they may cause?* Some people claim that wind turbines are ugly, kill birds and hardly generate any power. But that just isn't true. It's quite clear that the benefits far outweigh the perceived problems. Most of the research has concluded that, if turbines are sited correctly – out of sight, in areas with sufficient average wind, and away from major bird migration routes – they do not create extra problems. The evidence lies in the increasing use of wind power for electricity generation, from around 28 quadrillion BTUs (British Thermal Units) in the year 2000 to more than 40 quadrillion in 2009.

Now, I'm going to set you a task to do some further research on wind turbines. Perhaps you think that there is only one kind of modern wind turbine, but in fact there are two, although one is much more popular than the other. The well-known type is the horizontal-axis wind turbine or HAWT. The axis is horizontal, which means that the turbine blades look like the hands on a clock. The other type is the vertical-axis wind turbine or VAWT. I'd like you to do some research and find out the advantages and disadvantages of each kind, the HAWT and the VAWT.

Exercise C

Set for individual work and pairwork checking. Feed back with the class on question 6 to make sure that it is clear.

Answers

Model answers:

1 To enable the rotor to start spinning.

2 It ensures that the rotor points into the wind.

3 The pitch control.

4 Through wind sensors that monitor changes in blade shape, and also a type of radar to predict the arrival of excessive wind.

5 They convert output into DC, then back to AC before connection.

6 To research the advantages and disadvantages of the two types of wind turbine (HAWT and VAWT).

Exercise D

1 Set for pairwork discussion. Point out that there is no one 'correct' order; students should try to identify the most logical sequence for the argument. Explain that a 'counter-argument' means an opinion which you do not agree with or think is wrong. 'Issue' means a question about which there is some debate.

2 Set for individual work and pairwork checking.

Do not feed back with the class at this point, but move on to Exercise E where the answers will be given.

🎧 Exercise E

1 Play the extract. Tell students to stop you when they hear each item. Make sure students can say exactly what the words are in each case. Ask them also to paraphrase the words so that it is clear that they understand the meanings.

2 If necessary, play the extract again for students to check that they have the phrases and types of statement correct. Ask how many students had the stages of an argument (Exercise D, question 1) in the same order as the recording/model answers below. Discuss any alternative possibilities (see Language note opposite).

Answers

Model answers for Exercises D and E:

Type of statement	Phrase	Lecturer's words
c stating the issue	The question is …	… the question is: *Do the benefits of wind turbines outweigh any problems they may cause?*
a giving a counter-argument	Some people claim …	Some people claim that wind turbines are ugly, kill birds and hardly generate any power.
e rejecting a counter-argument	But that just isn't true.	But that just isn't true.
b giving your opinion	It's quite clear that …	It's quite clear that the benefits far outweigh the perceived problems.
f giving a reason for your opinion	Most of the research has concluded that …	Most of the research has concluded that, if turbines are sited correctly – out of sight, in areas with sufficient average wind, and away from major bird migration routes – they do not create extra problems.
d supporting the reason with evidence	The evidence lies in …	The evidence lies in the increasing use of wind power for electricity generation, from around 28 quadrillion BTUs (British Thermal Units) in 2000 to more than 40 quadrillion in 2009.

Language note

A common way in which an argument can be built is to give a counter-argument, then reject the counter-argument with reasons and evidence. There are, of course, other ways to build an argument. For example, the counter-arguments may be given after the writer/speaker's own opinion. Or all the arguments against may be given followed by all the arguments for an issue (or vice versa), concluding with the speaker/writer's own opinion.

Transcript 🎧 2.22

So, today we have seen some of the technical aspects of designing wind turbines. As I said at the beginning, there are other aspects, including environmental concerns. I suppose for people outside the mechanical engineering field, the question is: *Do the benefits of wind turbines outweigh any problems they may cause?* Some people claim that wind turbines are ugly, kill birds and hardly generate any power. But that just isn't true. It's quite clear that the benefits far outweigh the perceived problems. Most of the research has concluded that, if turbines are sited correctly – out of sight, in areas with sufficient average wind, and away from major bird migration routes – they do not create extra problems. The evidence lies in the increasing use of wind power for electricity generation, from around 28 quadrillion BTUs (British Thermal Units) in the year 2000 to more than 40 quadrillion in 2009.

Exercise F

Set for individual work – possibly homework – or else a pair/small group writing task. If the latter, tell students to put their writing on an OHT or other visual medium, so that the whole class can look and comment on what has been written. You can correct language errors on the OHT.

Exercise G

Set students to work in groups of three or four. Make sure they understand that they should consider the advantages and disadvantages of *either* a HAWT *or* a VAWT. Ask one person from each group to present the results of the group's discussion.

Tell the class that they should carry out research in their group. You will also need to arrange the date for the feedback and discussion of the information – this is the focus of Exercise G in Lesson 11.4.

Closure

Arguments, counter-arguments and giving opinions:

Ask students to think about the methods seen above to build an argument. As they do this, choose some of the statements below and write them on the board, or display them on an OHT or other visual medium. Ask students to think about whether they agree with the statements. They should prepare a brief summary of their viewpoints on the topics; they should also try to use some of the phrases used in this lesson.

1 Global warming is inevitable and there is nothing anyone can do about it.

2 Renewable energy schemes cause as much damage to the environment as traditional energy production.

3 Future global energy needs can be entirely met by solar, water and wind power.

4 Nuclear energy is the only safe and reliable alternative to fossil fuels.

5 Reducing energy consumption in the home will be the largest contributor to allaying the global energy crisis.

6 Small domestic wind turbines are a waste of money.

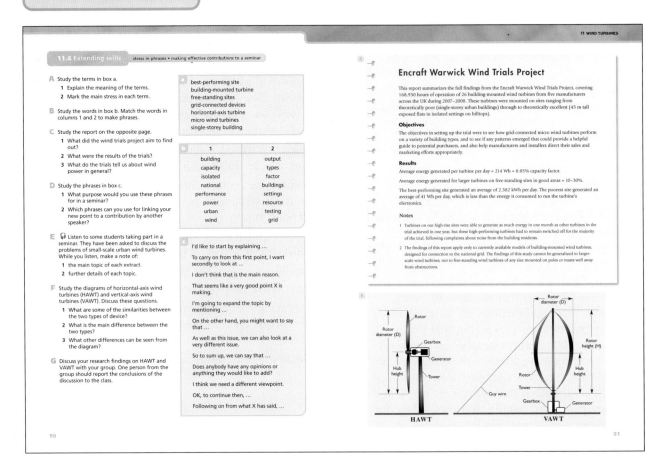

Lesson aims

- recognize stress in compound phrases
- link a contribution to previous contributions when speaking in a seminar
- understand vocabulary in the area of wind turbine research and development

Further practice in:

- taking part in seminars:
  introducing, maintaining and concluding a contribution
- agreeing/disagreeing with other speakers

Introduction

Remind students that they are going to be presenting their research findings on HAWT and VAWT devices later in this lesson. Tell them that they will also be looking at diagrams of both devices in this lesson, and that the vocabulary from this exercise will help with their discussion.

Check that they can remember the main points from the Lesson 11.3 lecture extracts; key phrases from the lecture could be used as prompts, e.g.,

So how serious a problem is it? (evidence of human and business activity)

Business will have to be a part of the solution (i.e., a key role in trying to improve a dangerous situation)

Other threats to the environment (e.g., pollution, waste, emissions)

The big question is … (how are we going to manage these problems?)

But the real question is … (is global warming the result of human activity?)

The following activity is a good way to check that students are familiar with the terminology and vocabulary from Lesson 11.3. Ask students to write down 5–10 words or expressions from the previous lesson relating to how wind turbines work. Then use two or three students as 'secretaries'. Ask the class to dictate the words so that the secretaries can write the vocabulary on the board. Use this as a brainstorming session.

Exercise A

These are more complex noun phrases than in Lesson 11.3, since they are made up of three words.

- In some cases, the pattern is noun + adjective + noun, where the compound is made from the first noun and adjective (and hyphenated in the examples here).

- In other cases, the pattern is adjective + adjective + noun, where the compound is made from the first two adjectives.
- Or the pattern may be adjective + noun + noun, where the compound is formed by the adjective and first noun, but not always. In one of the examples, the compound is formed by the two nouns.

These patterns should become clear once the meaning is understood.

1 Discuss *building-mounted turbine* with the class as an example. Elicit that it is a wind turbine attached to a building. In this case, the hyphenated words will help students to understand the phrase more easily. Set the remaining phrases for individual work and pairwork discussion. The meaning of some of the phrases may be difficult to guess out of context, but if students can identify the two-word compounds within each phrase, it may help with understanding. Feed back with the whole class, writing each phrase on the board and underlining the words which make a compound.

2 Tell students to try to identify where the main stress should come in each phrase. The key to this is finding the two-word compound which is at the base of the three-word phrase. The stress will normally fall in the same place as if this two-word compound was said without the third word, but not always. Demonstrate this with *building-mounted turbine*. The two-word compound here is not *mounted turbine*, but *building-mounted*. This is an noun + adjective, so the rules say that the stress will normally be on the noun (*'building-mounted*). However, when the third word is added (a noun), the main stress of the phrase changes to the third word.

Tell students only to identify the syllable on which the heaviest stress in the phrase falls. (See also *Language note*.)

Answers

Model answers:

The basic compound is underlined in each case.

best-performing 'site	a site, used in a trial, that performs the best
building-mounted 'turbine	a turbine which is attached to a building
free-standing 'sites	independent sites
horizontal-axis 'turbine	a turbine with a horizontal axis, as opposed to a vertical axis
grid-connected de'vices	devices (turbines) that are connected to the national grid
micro 'wind turbines	very small (domestic) turbines
single-storey 'building	a building with only one floor/level

Language note

Stress placement, especially in complex compound noun phrases, is notoriously unstable. Stress may often move, depending on the context: for example, *bad-'tempered* – but *'bad-tempered 'teacher*. In the case of *horizontal-axis 'turbine* above, if this term was being compared specifically with a vertical-axis turbine, then the stress would fall on the first word (hori'zontal-axis turbine). It's also possible that some native speakers may not agree about some of the phrases above. The main point is to try to notice where the main stresses fall.

Exercise B

Set for individual work and pairwork checking. Tell students that although in some cases it will be possible to make a phrase with more than one option, they must use each word once, and they must use all the words.

Feed back with the whole class. Check that the meaning of all other phrases is understood. Check pronunciation.

Answers

Model answers:

building	types
capacity	factor
isolated	settings
national	grid
performance	testing
power	output
urban	buildings
wind	resource

Language note

Although in most noun–noun compounds the main stress comes on the first element, there are some compounds where this is not true. Definitive pronunciation of compounds can be found in a good pronunciation dictionary.

Exercise C

Refer students to the report on page 91 of the Course Book. Before reading, tell students to look at the layout of the report and the headings, and elicit some of the features (e.g., headings, sections). Ask them for an alternative word for *Objectives* (= *Aims*). Set the reading task and questions for individual work and pairwork checking. Feed back with the whole class.

As an extra activity, tell students to find and underline three-word phrases from Exercise A to raise awareness of their use in context.

Answers

1 The performance of grid-connected micro wind turbines on a variety of urban building types.

2 The results showed that the average capacity factor was very low compared with larger turbines in more appropriate locations. The findings also highlighted noise problems for building residents, which were claimed to have affected the trial and the results.

3 As the trial focused only on small devices in urban areas, the results are not significant for wind power in general (the report points out the limitations of the trial).

Exercise D

This is mainly revision. Set for individual work or pairwork discussion. Feed back with the whole class.

Answers

Model answers:

I'd like to start by explaining …
= beginning

To carry on from this first point, I want secondly to look at …
= maintaining/continuing a point

I don't think that is the main reason.
= disagreeing

That seems like a very good point X is making.
= confirming

I'm going to expand the topic by mentioning …
= adding a new point to someone else's previous contribution

On the other hand, you might want to say that …
= offering an alternative point

As well as this issue, we can also look at a very different issue.
= adding a new point to someone else's previous contribution

So to sum up, we can say that …
= summarizing/concluding

Does anybody have any opinions or anything they would like to add?
= concluding

I think we need a different viewpoint.
= disagreeing

OK, to continue then, …
= maintaining/continuing a point

Following on from what X has said, …
= adding a new point to someone else's previous contribution

Exercise E

Before students listen, tell them to look at the exercise and questions. Check that students understand the topic for the seminar discussion. Ask them what they might expect to hear.

Play each extract one at a time and ask students to identify the main topic and some further details. Feed back with the whole class.

Answers

Model answers:

	Main topic	Further details
Extract 1	small domestic wind turbines	two main problems: • wind resource in urban environments – insufficient & unreliable • no suitable manufacturers' performance standard
Extract 2	financial investment in small urban wind turbines	• produce much less energy than large turbines • not a good investment compared with large wind projects
Extract 3	intermittency of wind power	• intermittent power output (wind turbines in general) • swings in demand in household consumption – engineers should be able to solve problem
Extract 4	Longer-term lulls in wind speed nationwide	ways to store energy: • pumped storage • large specialized batteries systems (flow batteries)

Transcript 🎧 2.23

Extract 1

MAJED: Our lecture on wind turbines last week raised a number of interesting issues. In my part of the seminar, I would like to start by discussing very small domestic wind turbines, the type you might attach to the side of your house. The question is: Are they worthwhile? How do they compare to big turbines? I found a recent report which suggests that, unfortunately, they are usually not a good idea compared to big turbines. There seem to be two problems: The first is that in urban environments the wind resource is simply insufficient. The wind speeds are not high enough and the wind is too unsteady. The second problem is that often the performance of these domestic wind turbines does not match expectations, and there is no suitable standard for performance testing to make sure that manufacturers are all talking about the same thing.

Extract 2

EVIE: OK, following on from what Majed has said, I'd like to mention that, from a financial point of view, small wind turbines in urban areas are not a very good investment. If you combined the two factors that Majed talked about, you find from the report that small wind turbines in urban areas produce about 10–30 times less energy than large wind turbines in windy areas. So, if I was an investor who wanted to produce as much renewable energy as possible and make a return, I would rather invest in large wind projects.

Extract 3

JACK: Right. Thank you, Evie. I'm going to expand the topic by mentioning another issue related to wind turbines in general, whether small or large. This is the issue of intermittency. Wind turbines produce power when it's windy, but it's not always windy, so the power output varies. How do we cope with this? Well, electricity companies are already used to coping with massive short-term swings in demand in household consumption – the classic example is when everyone in the country is watching a football match. At half-time, everyone wants a cup of tea and the electricity demand rockets! So, although it will take some thought, engineers are already used to solving this kind of issue.

Extract 4

LEILA: As well as short-term intermittency, we should also look at longer-term lulls. This is when the wind speed over the whole country drops for a period of a few days. In this scenario, if we are heavily depending on wind as an energy source, we need a way to store the energy for days. There are a few options out there, but I want to suggest that

pumped storage is probably a good way of solving this problem, combined with very large specialized battery systems called flow batteries.

Exercise F

Set for individual work and pairwork checking. Tell students to look at the questions and then study the diagrams (B) on page 91 of the Course Book. Check that they understand the vocabulary in the diagrams. Tell them to make brief notes for answers before checking with a partner. Feed back with the whole class.

Answers

Possible answers:

1 Both devices have the same parts, although some are in different locations.

2 The HAWT blades rotate like the hands of a clock (on a horizontal axis), while the VAWT blades rotate like a merry-go-round (on a vertical axis).

3 Some other differences are:
   - location of generator and gearbox
   - need for guy wire in HAWT
   - rotor diameter much larger in HAWT

Exercise G

Remember this comes from Lesson 11.3, Exercise G.

In their groups, students should now present their research findings on the HAWT and the VAWT. Remind them that the task was to find out the advantages and disadvantages of each kind of wind turbine.

Encourage students to use the seminar language practised in this unit and earlier. In addition, students can, of course, make use of the information in the diagrams in Lesson 11.4. They should be discussing, or at least mentioning, some or all of the following:

	HAWT	VAWT
Advantages	• relatively efficient in power production • start themselves • smooth transfer of power from rotor to gearbox • mounted on taller towers so have access to higher wind velocities • small footprint	• generator and gearbox on the ground – can even be some distance away from the turbine = easier to maintain • some designs do not require a yaw control • smaller towers – can be built in places where taller turbines not allowed • may have reduced noise problem
Disadvantages	• difficult to transport for set-up (= size of towers and blades) • require tall cranes for installation = expensive • require a yaw control system • difficult to maintain • often negative public opinion due to height; regarded as ugly intrusions in natural landscapes	• operate near ground = not much wind • produce wavy (sinusoidal) power pulses • don't start themselves • whole machine needs to be taken apart to repair main bearing • 40 per cent less efficient than HAWT – therefore need machine twice as big as HAWT to produce same amount of power • relatively large footprint

As a group, students should try to come to an overall conclusion in weighing up the advantages and disadvantages of both types of turbine. This conclusion should be presented to the rest of the class, together with supporting evidence from students' own research.

Closure

Ask students to imagine that they are 10–15 years in the future. What differences do they think there will be in renewable energy production, particularly in wind power technologies? How will situations have changed? Ask them to think about the following:

- the role of engineers in the future
- the problems of energy storage of wind power due to intermittency
- the efficiency of small domestic wind turbines
- the challenge of overcoming public opinion on the location of wind turbines
- possible alternative wind turbine design

Extra activities

1 Work through the *Vocabulary bank* and *Skills bank* if you have not already done so, or as revision of previous study.

2 Use the *Activity bank* (Teacher's Book additional resources section, Resource 11A).

A Set the crossword for individual work (including homework) or pairwork.

Answers

B Set for individual work (including homework) or pairwork. Check students understand the meanings.

Possible answers

capacity	factor
fixed	frequency
gear	box
guy	wire
household	consumption
national	grid
power	output
public	opinion
pumped	storage
wind	speed

3 Tell students to add other words to each of the words below to make as many two-word phrases as possible. Elicit one or two examples, then set for individual work or pairwork.

- electricity
- wind

Possible phrases:

electricity generator, electricity generation, electricity demand, electricity supply, electricity company

wind power, wind energy, windmill, wind turbine, wind speed, wind resource, wind farm

4 Use an extended role-play activity with role cards to allow students to discuss some of the issues in this unit.

Tell students to work in groups of five where possible. Explain the scenario to them and write key points on the board or display on an OHT. They will be participating in a 'meeting' to discuss the proposed installation of a wind farm in the rural location of Moortop, considered to be an area of natural beauty and conservation. The proposal is to install 20 large wind turbines at upland locations in this area, which is surrounded by small villages. Most of the residents of the villages are against the proposal and have asked for a meeting with the leader of Moortop Council (local government) and the chief engineer of the installation company. (To prepare for this activity, students should do some Internet research for homework on the advantages and disadvantages of wind farms.)

Each student should take one of the following roles. Either write the roles on the board or display them on an OHT:

1 the local council leader
2 the chief engineer of the installation company
3 local resident representative (1)
4 local resident representative (2)
5 local resident representative (3)

Divide the activities into stages as follows:

a Put students into groups of six. If there are fewer students in a group, make sure that the roles of council leader and chief engineer are taken, and reduce the number of residents. If there are more students in a group, increase the number of residents.

b When each student in the group has chosen a role, distribute the relevant role cards. (Copy and cut up sufficient role cards from Resource 11C on pages 283–285 of the Teacher's Book.)

c Tell students to study their role cards and then spend about five minutes thinking of and noting down briefly on their cards any additional ideas they have that could be relevant to their role. Encourage them to 'get into character'. Monitor this activity and deal with any vocabulary problems. You may need to prompt weaker students.

d Before the meeting, put students into new groups, depending on their roles, i.e., council leaders together, engineers together, residents divided into groups according to their role card. Tell groups to discuss their 'character' and share their ideas. They should add further notes to their cards if necessary. Allow about 10–15 minutes for this activity.

e Ask students to return to their original groups and conduct their meeting. Allow about 20–25 minutes for this part, but be prepared to extend the time if the activity is going well. Encourage them to use language practised in seminars for turn-taking, interrupting, adding points, asking for clarification, summing up, etc.

f At the end of the meeting, ask groups to report back to the class on the success of their meeting (e.g., Was it a polite meeting? Did anyone get angry in their role? Did participants listen and respond to each other? Was anyone persuaded against their original viewpoint?).

12 WATER ENGINEERING

This unit provides an opportunity for extending some of the key skills practised in the book. It features two main topics within the theme of water engineering. Lessons 12.1 and 12.2 focus on water distribution and two major desalination technologies: reverse osmosis and thermal desalination. Lessons 12.3 and 12.4 focus on technical report writing in the field of fluid mechanics. The featured experiment – flow rate in pipes – is a classic laboratory experiment in this area of study.

Skills focus

Reading

- understanding how ideas in a text are linked
- note-making from texts
- labelling a diagram

Writing

- writing a comparison summary from notes
- writing a laboratory section from notes

Vocabulary focus

- definitions
- referring back using pronouns and synonyms
- words/phrases to describe mechanical processes in water engineering
- common verb + noun phrases used in laboratory reports

Key vocabulary

acidic	distillation	laboratory	saline
alkaline	evaporation	laminar flow	salinity
apparatus	experiment (n)	membrane	scale (n)
aquifer	facility	minerals	TDS (total dissolved solids)
brackish	feedwater	organic	
brine	filtration	oxide	thermal desalination
capacity	flow rate	ozone	toxic
chlorination	fluctuate	perforation	treatment
cogeneration	fluid mechanics	permeable	turbulent flow
concentrate (n)	foulant	plot (v)	vapour
condense	hydraulics	porous	velocity
corrosive	hydrology	potable	viscosity
desalination	hydropower	ppm (parts per million)	wastewater
desalting	impurity	purify	
disinfection	irrigation	reverse osmosis	

12.1 Vocabulary

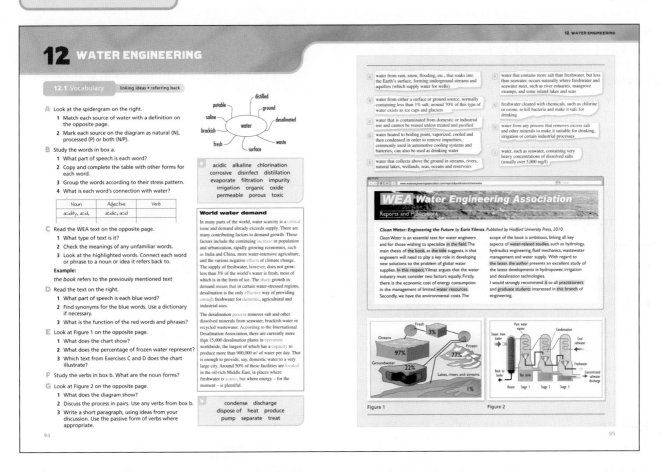

General note

Read the *Vocabulary bank* at the end of the Course Book unit. Decide when, if at all, to refer your students to it. The best time is probably at the very end of the lesson or the beginning of the next lesson, as a summary/revision.

Lesson aims

- further understand lexical cohesion: referring back using synonyms
- interpret charts and diagrams
- explain a process orally and in writing

Further practice in:
- definitions
- word formation
- words and phrases from the discipline

Introduction

1 Revise the following words and phrases from the previous unit. Some of the words will appear in this unit's materials too. Ask students to say which grammar class the words belong to and to provide definitions of them.

apparatus (n, U)

cylinder (n, C)

durable (adj)

efficiency (n, C/U)

environmental (adj)

extract (v)

generator (n, C)

optimum (adj)

rotate (v)

sustainable energy (adj, n, C/U)

effect (n, C)

urban (adj)

2 Introduce the topic of the unit: write the words *water* and *engineering* on the board. Ask students why water is a key field in engineering. Elicit the types of engineering connected with water (e.g., in domestic, industrial and agricultural contexts) and what types of processes are involved. Accept any reasonable suggestions. Do not elaborate, but tell students that this will be the topic of this unit.

Exercise A

Ask students to say briefly what the diagram shows (*different types of water/water resources*), but don't explain any unfamiliar words at this point.

1 Set for pairwork. Feed back with the whole class. Check meanings of other words in the definitions, such as *contaminated*, *aquifer*, *dissolved*, but try not to pre-empt later vocabulary exercises. Make sure students realize that all the words are compound nouns. Elicit which compounds are noun + noun and which are adjective + noun. See also the Language note below.

2 Set for individual work and pairwork checking. Feed back with the whole class. There may be some disagreement about some of the answers. For example, it could be argued that freshwater can also be the result of recycled wastewater and desalination, and therefore processed. However, in most explanations of the distribution of the world's water, freshwater is considered in its natural form.

Answers

1/2 Model answers:
  See table below.

Type	Meaning	Natural (N), Processed (P) or both (N/P)
distilled water (adj + n)	D water heated to boiling point, vaporized, cooled and then condensed in order to remove impurities; commonly used in automotive cooling systems and batteries; can also be used as drinking water	N/P: commercial distillation imitates the natural water cycle, i.e., heat causes the surface of the sea to evaporate and form clouds, which then fall as rain
groundwater (n + n)	A water from rain, snow, flooding, etc., that soaks into the Earth's surface, forming underground streams and aquifers (which supply water for wells)	N
desalinated water (adj + n)	H water from any process that removes excess salt and other minerals to make it suitable for drinking, irrigation or certain industrial processes	N/P: one method of desalination uses the distillation process – see comments above
wastewater/ waste water (n + n) and (adj + n)	C water that is contaminated from domestic or industrial use and cannot be reused unless treated and purified	P
surface water (n + n)	E water that collects above the ground in streams, rivers, natural lakes, wetlands, seas, oceans and reservoirs	N
freshwater/ fresh water (adj + n)	B water from either a surface or ground source, normally containing less than 1% salt; around 70% of this type of water exists as ice caps and glaciers	N
brackish water (adj + n)	F water that contains more salt than freshwater, but less than seawater; occurs naturally where freshwater and seawater meet, such as river estuaries, mangrove swamps, and some inland lakes and seas	N
saline water (adj + n) and (n + n)	I water, such as seawater, containing very heavy concentrations of dissolved salts (usually over 5,000 mg/l)	N/P: the by-product of desalination (brine) has very high salinity
potable water	G freshwater cleaned with chemicals, such as chlorine or ozone, to kill bacteria and make it safe for drinking	P

Language and subject note

Note that some of the compound nouns to describe water types will occur as both 'closed' compounds (where the two words are joined together) or 'open' (where they remain as two separate words, as in *freshwater / fresh water*, and *wastewater / waste water*, even in the same or similar technical contexts. Note, however, that *seawater* and *groundwater* are well-established n + n closed forms in technical contexts.

Open compounds tend to consist of newer word combinations and/or longer adj + n combinations, as in *brackish water*, *potable water*, *saline water* and *desalinated water*.

For more information on compound words, consult a good grammar reference book or explore some of the many grammar websites on the Internet.

Exercise B

Allow time for students to look at all the questions and copy the table into their notebooks.

1 Set for individual work and pairwork checking. Students should try to identify part of speech for each word from the suffix. Do not allow the use of a dictionary for this question. Feed back with the class. Ask students to identify the common suffixes for nouns (~*tion*, ~*sion*, ~*ity*, etc.) and those for adjectives (~*ic*, ~*able*, ~*ous*, ~*ive*, ~*ed*, etc.).

2 Set for pairwork or individual work and pairwork checking. Allow the use of dictionaries, if necessary. Feed back with the class, building up the table on the board.

3 Set for individual work and pairwork checking. Feed back with the class.

4 Set for pairwork. Tell students that some connections may be obvious, but others may seem to have no connection. Ask them to put a question mark by the words they are not sure about. Feed back with the class to share ideas, making a note of all the words students found difficult to connect. Tell them that this question will be revisited at the end of Lesson 12.2 when they should be able to explain more of the connections. Decide how you would like students to do this. For example, some of the words can be grouped according to their meaning (*permeable*, *porous*) and some according to their relationship in a particular process. See the answers section below for one way of organizing the words and explaining the connections, using information from the texts. Allow students to use any form of each word.

Answers

Model answers

1/2

Noun	Adjective	Verb
acidity, acid	**acidic**, acid	
alkali	**alkaline**	
chlorination, chlorine	chlorinated	chlorinate
corrosion	**corrosive**	corrode
disinfection	disinfected	**disinfect**
distillation	distilled	distil
evaporation	evaporated	**evaporate**
filtration, filter	filtered	filter
impurity	impure	
irrigation	irrigated	irrigate
organism	**organic**	
oxide	oxidic	oxidize
permeation	**permeable**	permeate
porousness, pore	porous	
toxicity	**toxic**	

3

Oo	oxide, toxic, porous
Ooo	alkaline
oOo	acidic, corrosive, filtration, organic
ooO	disinfect
Oooo	permeable
oOoo	evaporate, impurity
ooOo	chlorination, distillation, irrigation

4 Possible answers:

When water is distilled, it evaporates.

Distillation removes impurities that exist in water, such as organic matter and toxic materials, such as metal oxides.

Water produced for human consumption is commonly treated with chlorine, which is a form of disinfection.

Desalinated water can be used for irrigation in water-stressed regions.

Desalinated water is acidic and corrosive because its natural minerals have been removed during the desalting process. It needs to be remineralized to restore the acid/alkaline balance.

Membranes used in RO water filtration are permeable, or porous.

Exercise C

1 Set for individual work. For this exercise, tell students to read the text quickly for an overall idea of content and style. This will be sufficient to enable them to answer the question, and is a good skill to develop when close reading is not required. Feed back with the class.

2 Set for pairwork. Tell students to read the text again more closely, and to try to guess the meanings of unfamiliar words from the context, from part of speech, and from affixes, before using a dictionary. For example, a knowledge of the prefixes *hydro~ hydra~* would tell students automatically that hydrology and hydraulics have meanings connected with water.

3 Set for individual work and pairwork checking. Remind students of the idea of textual cohesion, created by referring back to words or ideas already mentioned with words/phrases with a similar meaning, so that the text flows without too much repetition of the same words and phrases. Refer them to Unit 11 *Vocabulary bank*. Feed back with the class.

You can build up the answers to question 3 by copying Resource 12B in the additional resources section onto an OHT or other visual medium.

Answers

Model answers:

1 A book review

3

Word/phrase	Refers back to	Comments
the field	*water engineers* in the same sentence	implied, i.e., field of water engineering
the book	*text* in the previous sentence	synonym: avoids using the same word twice in proximity
the title	*Clean Water: Engineering the Future*	refers back to the *meaning* of the full title in the heading (*as the title suggests ...*)
(In) this respect	Statement in previous sentence: *... engineers will need to play a key role in developing new solutions to the problem of global water supplies.*	a phrase used to refer to something previously said as a way of both linking to it and building on it
water resources	*water supplies*	synonym: avoids using the same phrase twice in proximity
water-related studies	*the field*	another way of referring to water engineering
the latter	*water supply*	the last of several things just mentioned; has to be used in proximity to the word/phrase it refers back to
the author	*Yilmaz, Esrin Yilmaz*	clear reference to Yilmaz in the context
it	*an excellent study, the book, the text*	use of pronoun where the reference should be easily understood in the context (i.e., a book review recommends a book)
practitioners	*water engineers*	refers back to beginning of text
graduate students	*those wishing to specialize*	refers back to beginning of text; implies that they are one and the same
this branch	*water-related studies, the field* (and generally water engineering)	use of synonyms throughout the text in a constant referral

Exercise D

The text in this exercise introduces the main theme of Lesson 12.2 by connecting water demand with desalination. It features a lot of vocabulary related to the topic without being too technical at this point. Students should first read through the text to get an idea of the topic, and then study all the questions before proceeding.

1/2 Set for individual work and pairwork checking. These two exercises revise and extend work on synonyms without supplying alternative choices within the lesson. The focus on part of speech in question 1 makes students think about both the function and meaning of a word in context and helps to reduce reliance on a dictionary. This is an important academic reading skill to develop, and can increase reading speed. Feed back with the class, building up the table on the board.

3 Set for pairwork discussion. Tell students to discuss the general function of the red words and phrases and be able to explain the purpose of each one. Feed back with the class, eliciting alternatives for each word or phrase to check understanding.

Answers

Possible answers:

1/2

Word	Part of speech	Synonym(s)
critical	adj	serious
increase	n	rise , growth, expansion
effects	n (pl.)	consequences, outcomes, results
sharp	adj	rapid
effective	adj	successful, suitable, convenient, practical, economical, efficient (*effective* can mean several things in this context)
enough	adj	sufficient, adequate
domestic	adj	household
process	n	procedure
operation	n	use, service
capacity	n	ability, capability (+ of + ~ing form of verb)
located	adj (not before noun)	to be found, sited
scarce	adj	in short supply, limited

3 The red words and phrases are examples of linking expressions.

Expression	Meaning	Alternatives
such as	to introduce examples	including ('for instance' and 'for example' can also be used, but the grammar of the sentence would need adjusting)
however	to present an opposite/contrasting idea/situation	though, nevertheless
means that	to show an implication or a result/consequence	implies that
According to	to introduce supporting evidence for a statement	Fixed phrase – no suitable alternative at this point in a sentence
but	to show two things or ideas in opposition	though, while, whereas

Exercise E

1 Set for pairwork. Ask pairs to study the diagram carefully and compose a precise description of it in one sentence. Feed back with the class, writing some of the suggested sentences on the board. Invite other pairs to judge and, if necessary, improve on the descriptions. Key words that the sentence should contain are underlined in the answers section below.

2/3 Set for individual work and pairwork checking. The purpose of question 2 is to make sure that students read the diagram correctly. It would be easy to mistake the 77% as a percentage of all water, instead of the percentage of freshwater only. Students should also remember that the text they have just read in Exercise D tells us: *... less than 3% of the world's water is fresh, most of which is in the form of ice.* For question 3, tell students to be prepared to give any reasons to support their answer. Feed back with the class.

Answers

1 The diagram shows the <u>percentage distribution</u> of the various <u>natural types of water</u> found on <u>Earth</u>/in the world.

2 The 77% represents the share of the world's freshwater that is frozen, i.e., 77% of only 3% of total water.

3 The diagram best illustrates the text in Exercise D. The text refers to the world's supply of freshwater in paragraph 1.

Exercise F

Set for individual work and pairwork checking. Tell students that these verbs will be needed for the following exercise. Tell them to use their knowledge of suffixes to guess any of the noun forms for verbs they are not familiar with. If you wish to give them a clue, say that three of the verbs have the same noun form. Do not allow the use of dictionaries for this exercise. Feed back with the class, checking pronunciation and the meanings of any unknown verbs.

Answers

Model answers:

Verb	Noun form
condense	condensation
discharge	discharge
dispose of	disposal of
heat	heat
produce	production
pump	pump
separate	separation
treat	treatment

Exercise G

1 Set for individual work. Allow enough time for students to study the diagram before feedback, as this will help towards question 2. However, only a brief statement is required rather than a full description at this stage. Students will probably realize that the diagram is connected with the subject of the second paragraph of the text in Exercise D.

2 Set for pairwork discussion. Feed back with the class. Invite one pair to share their explanation of the process, with input from others as and when appropriate, so that feedback becomes a collaborative activity. Students are likely to use a mix of active and passive expressions. Write some of the suggestions on the board, checking the grammar at the same time.

3 Set for individual work/homework. Before setting the students to write, explain that when writing about a process or procedure, the passive voice is generally used, but not exclusively. Some explanations will only be possible in the active voice. As an example of this, and as a possible prompt for beginning the paragraph, write the following on the board:

Cool saltwater <u>enters</u> the desalination system and ...

Ask students whether it is possible to change this to the passive, and if not, ask how a different verb could be used for a passive sentence, for example:

Cool saltwater is pumped into the system and ...

The model paragraph in the answers section below is also available in Resource 12C in the additional resources section. For feedback purposes, you may wish to copy the resource onto an OHT or other visual medium for students to compare with their own paragraph. Alternatively, set students to work in pairs to compare and discuss each other's work. Then ask them to write an improved version, combining their ideas.

Answers

Possible answers:

1 The diagram shows an industrial desalination process using steam energy.

2 Answers depend on students.

3 Model answer:

In this process, cool saltwater is heated and distilled in a series of chambers. Firstly, the cool saltwater is pumped into the system along condenser pipes that run through the top of all the chambers. The water gradually warms as it passes through these chambers. It is then heated by steam from a boiler, which turns it into hot brine. The hot brine enters the base of the first chamber where part of it vaporizes, rises, and is then condensed by pipes containing the cool saltwater continuously entering the system. The pure condensate is collected and forms part of the freshwater outflow. Meanwhile, the brine left behind in the first chamber enters the second chamber and the process is repeated again and again, depending on the number of chambers. The collected condensate leaves the system as freshwater, and the remaining brine or concentrated saltwater is discharged from the system.

Closure

Put students into small groups. Each student should describe how something works, while trying not to name the item or process or give away too many clues all at once. They should start with just one sentence, adding extra information until the others guess what it is. Encourage them to choose something they can describe in a technical or semi-technical way. Start the activity with the whole class, using the example below if you wish:

This domestic item is driven by an electric motor attached to an inner steel drum.

It has a set of controls for different programmes.

The drum spins and vibrates.

It uses water to perform its function.

The water can be either hot or cold.

The controls determine speed and temperature.

In some models, the drum is accessed from the front, on others it is accessed from the top.

etc.

Answer: *a washing machine*

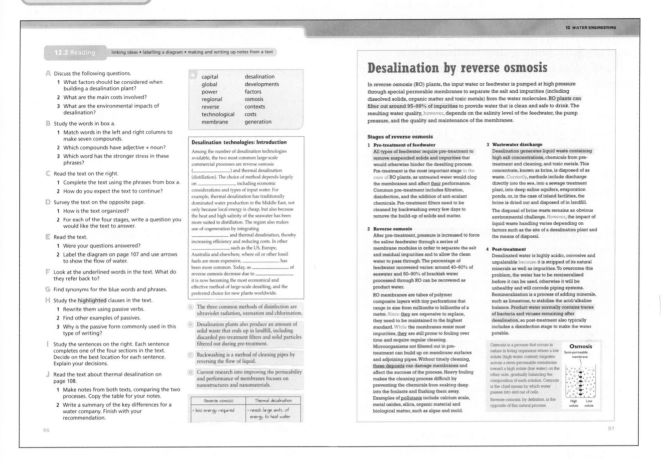

General note

Read the *Vocabulary bank* at the end of the Course Book unit. Decide when, if at all, to refer students to it. The best time is probably at the very end of the lesson or the beginning of the next lesson, as a summary/revision.

Lesson aims

- further understand how ideas in a text are linked: referring back using pronouns and synonyms matching new with given information
- label a diagram from textual information
- understand the use of the passive form in technical writing
- make notes from written sources and write a comparison summary

Further practice in:

- noun + noun and adjective + noun compounds
- predicting content
- words and phrases from the discipline

Introduction

Revise types of water from Lesson 12.1. Elicit a definition of each type, or give a simplified paraphrased definition from the list in Lesson 12.1 and ask students to name the water type.

To prepare students for the lesson's theme, ask them to think about their own country's water resources and water supply systems, for example:

Where does their domestic water come from?

Is domestic supply drinkable, or do people mostly drink bottled water?

What industries in their country use a lot of water?

Does their country have any desalination plants?

In your teaching context, you may find that some classes are familiar with aspects of desalination. If they are, try not to let the discussion pre-empt the content of the lesson too much.

Exercise A

1–3 Set for small group work. Ask students to brainstorm all three questions and incorporate their ideas into a spidergram. Make sure that they understand the questions. If possible, supply each pair or group with a large sheet of paper or an OHT with pens so that they can display their spidergram during class feedback. Alternatively, copy the spidergram outline in Resource 12D in the additional resources section onto an OHT or other visual medium. During class feedback, elicit students' ideas to complete the diagram. Accept any reasonable suggestions. However, as the students may only be able to come up with a few ideas for the spidergram at this point, you may wish to return to the activity at the end of Lesson 12.2 and fill in the gaps.

Answers

Possible answers:

1–3

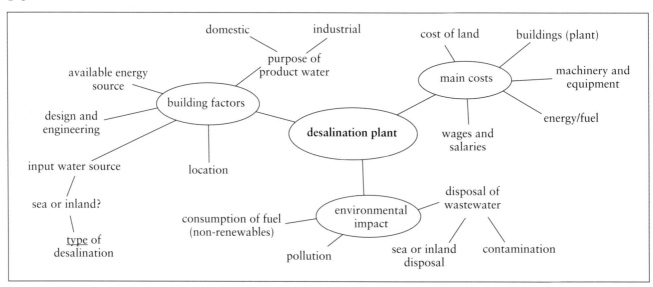

Exercise B

1 Set for individual work and pairwork checking. Allow the use of dictionaries, if necessary. The purpose of this exercise is to prepare students for the texts in Exercises C and D. Most of these compounds are not fixed expressions, and so students may come up with several possibilities for some of the words, such as *technological developments / factors / costs*. However, tell students that each word in each column can be used only once, so this will narrow down other possibilities. If question 1 proves too difficult at this point, an alternative approach is to move directly on to Exercise C, returning to questions 2 and 3 after students have completed the gaps in the text in Exercise C.

2/3 Set for individual work and pairwork checking. Feed back with the class.

Answers

1–3 Model answers:

capital costs	n + n
global contexts	adj + n
power generation	n + n
regional factors	adj + n
reverse osmosis	adj + n
technological developments	adj + n
membrane desalination	n + n

Exercise C

Students should first read through the text to get an idea of the topic.

1 Set for individual work and pairwork checking. Tell students to look at each gap in the context of the sentence and to pay attention to the words that immediately precede it and follow it. If you have moved directly to this exercise from question 1 of Exercise B, remind students that each word from the table can be used only once when making the compound nouns. Once they have completed the gaps, ask them to read the text again to make sure that the phrase they have chosen for each gap makes sense within the context. Feed back with the class.

2 Approach this question with the whole class. Elicit ideas and reasons from individuals, i.e., information in the text that lends support to ideas. Accept any reasonable suggestions, and write them on the board.

Answers

Model answers:

1 **Desalination technologies: Introduction**

Among the number of desalination technologies available, the two most common large-scale commercial processes are reverse osmosis (membrane desalination) and thermal desalination (distillation). The choice of method depends largely on regional factors, including economic considerations and types of input water. For example, thermal desalination has traditionally dominated water production in the Middle East, not only because local energy is cheap, but also because the heat and high salinity of the seawater has been more suited to distillation. The region also makes use of cogeneration by integrating power generation and thermal desalination, thereby increasing efficiency and reducing costs. In other global contexts, such as the US, Europe, Australia and elsewhere, where oil or other fossil fuels are more expensive, reverse osmosis has been more common. Today, as capital costs of reverse osmosis decrease due to technological developments, it is now becoming the most economical and effective method of large scale desalting, and the preferred choice for new plants worldwide.

2 Answers depend on students. Based on the title of the text (Desalination technologies), and the introductory sentence (... the two most common large-scale commercial processes are ...), the text is likely to continue by providing a detailed description of these technologies. It is likely continue with reverse osmosis first, as this is mentioned first in the introductory sentence, and again at the end of the *Introduction*.

Exercise D

Elicit what surveying a text means, as a reminder (skim-reading to get an approximate idea of the text contents by looking at the title, any headings and diagrams, looking at the beginning few lines and the final few lines of the text, and by looking at the first sentence of each paragraph).

1 Set for pairwork discussion after giving students one minute to survey the text, to ensure that they skim-read rather than close read. Feed back with the class. Ask how the organization of this text helps with skim-reading. Check back on the suggestions students gave about text continuation from the previous exercise and ask who predicted correctly.

2 Set for pairwork. Each pair should agree four questions. Feed back with the class. Write some questions on the board.

Answers

Possible answer:

1 The title states clearly what the text will be about. There is an introductory paragraph, followed by four numbered and labelled sections that describe each stage of the process. Two of the sections are further divided into shorter paragraphs. A text box with a small diagram explains some detail of the text.

The organization helps with reading because of the way the text is divided up into shorter sections. This makes finding and retrieving information easier. The titles of the four sections also give a clear indication of their content.

2 Answers depend on students.

Exercise E

1 Set for individual work followed by pairwork discussion. Feed back with the class. Ask whether the questions you have put on the board have been answered in the text.

2 Set for individual work and pairwork checking. Make sure that students understand the task. Tell them to first study the diagram on page 107 carefully to determine the type of information they are looking for.

They will need to read the text again, but ask them which type of reading skill they should use to be able to complete the labelling and indicate the flow of water (scanning for specific information). Feed back with the class. Copy the fully-labelled diagram in Resource 12E in the additional resources section onto an OHT or other visual medium so that students can check their answers. The labelled diagram is also provided in the answers section on the next page.

Answers

2 Model answer:

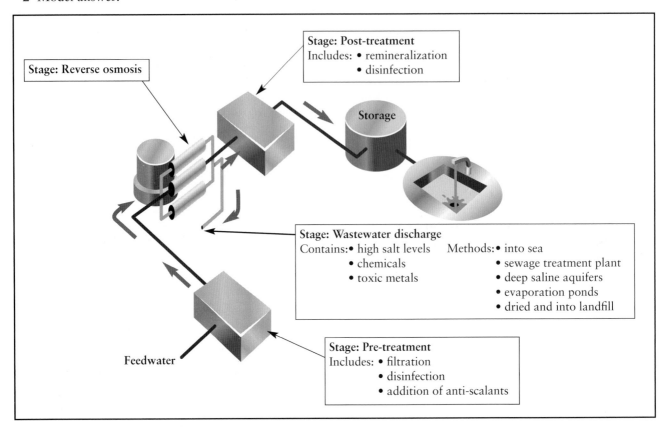

Language and methodology note

When note-making in technical subjects, it is always a good idea to draw quick diagrams and mind maps where possible and to add notes to any diagrams you are given in handouts, etc. It is easier for many people to learn from a diagram, rather than from a page full of notes. It is also easier to recall information.

Exercise F

Set for individual work and pairwork checking. Tell students to number the text paragraphs 1–7 to make it easier to provide feedback. Feed back with the class.

Answers

Model answers:

Word	Paragraph	Refers to
their	2	membranes
they	4	RO membranes
they	4	membranes
these deposits	4	microorganisms not filtered out in pre-treatment
pollutants	4	these deposits, microorganisms not filtered out in pre-treatment

Exercise G

Refer students to the blue words in the text. Elicit that they are all linking words and phrases either within sentences or between sentences. Remind students that some of these words and expressions were dealt with in Units 7 and 11. Feed back with the class, building up the table below on the board.

Answers

Model answers:

Linking word/ phrase	Possible synonym in context
however	though
in the case of	in, with regard to, as regards, as far as [RO plants] are concerned
Since	Because, As
While	Although, Even though
Currently	At the present time (warn students about using the word 'presently' as this tends to mean 'soon')
However	Nevertheless
because	as, since, due to/owing to the fact that …

Exercise H

1 Set for individual work and pairwork discussion. Tell students to think about the choice of preposition after the passive verb in each case. Feed back with the class, building up the passive clauses on the board. Ask students whether they think the passive clauses are an improvement on the original active clauses and why/why not. (Some clauses may appear awkward in the passive voice; others may alter the main focus, by making the subject the object of the verb).

2 Set for individual work and pairwork checking. Tell students to underline examples in the text and to pay particular attention to any examples of passives in reduced clauses. See the Language note at the top of the next page. Tell students to also circle any prepositions following the verbs that indicate an agent or other action, but warn them to be aware of any phrasal verbs. Feed back with the class.

3 Elicit ideas from the whole class. If they find it difficult to explain, use one of the passive examples in the table in the answer key to question 2 below to show why the passive is used. For example:

> ... the brine _is dried out_ and _disposed of_ in _landfill_.

If this example was written as an active sentence, there would have to be a subject: someone who dries out the brine and disposes of it. However, in this case, as in all the other examples, we are not interested in who performs the action, but rather what happens to the brine. The use of the passive voice therefore emphasizes the process rather than the agent (which in most cases is either irrelevant, obvious or implied).

2

Paragraph	Examples of passives
1	... the input water or feedwater <u>is pumped</u> at high pressure through special permeable membranes ...
2	Pre-treatment filters <u>need to be cleaned</u> by backwashing every few days to remove the build-up of solids and matter.
3	After pre-treatment, pressure <u>is increased</u> ...
3	The percentage of feedwater <u>recovered</u> varies: around 40–60% of seawater and 50–90% of brackish water <u>processed</u> through RO <u>can be recovered</u> as product water. (note reduced relative clauses)
4	... they <u>need to be maintained</u> to the highest standard.
4	Microorganisms <u>not filtered out</u> in pre-treatment can build up on membrane surfaces ...
5	This concentrate, known as brine, <u>is disposed of</u> as waste. (note phrasal verb)
5	... in the case of inland facilities, the brine <u>is dried out</u> and <u>disposed of</u> in landfill. (note phrasal verbs)
7	Desalinated water is highly acidic, corrosive and unpalatable because it <u>is stripped</u> of its natural minerals ... (note phrasal verb)
7	To overcome this problem, the water <u>has to be remineralized</u> before it can be used ...

3 In most scientific and technical writing, the passive voice is used to emphasize the process rather than the agent (the person or thing performing the action). See also the explanation in the notes to this question above.

Answers

Model answers:

1

Clause from the text	Passive clause
RO plants can filter out around 95–99% of impurities ...	Around 95–99% of impurities <u>can be filtered out</u> by RO plants ...
All types of feedwater require pre-treatment to remove suspended solids and impurities ...	Pre-treatment <u>is required</u> for all types of feedwater to remove suspended solids and impurities ...
... these deposits can damage membranes ...	... membranes <u>can be damaged</u> by these deposits ... NB: changing this to a passive clause would also require modification of the rest of the sentence: ... <u>_and this would affect the success of the process_</u>
Desalination generates liquid waste containing high salt concentrations, ...	Liquid waste <u>generated</u> by desalination contains high salt concentrations ... OR Liquid waste, which <u>is generated</u> by desalination, contains high salt concentrations ...
Product water normally contains traces of bacteria and viruses remaining after desalination, ...	Traces of bacteria and viruses remaining after desalination <u>are normally contained</u> in product water, ...

Language note

A *reduced* clause is where the relative pronoun (*which/that*) can be omitted, and where the verb is reduced to the past participle. An example sentence from the text, also in the answers section on the previous page, would be written the following way if the relative pronouns were included:

*The percentage of feedwater **which is** recovered varies: around 40–60% of seawater and 50–90% of brackish water **which is** processed through RO can be recovered as product water.*

Not all relative clauses can be reduced. See a good grammar reference book for a full explanation.

Exercise I

Set for individual work and pairwork checking. This exercise provides further practice in linking ideas in a text by focusing on the logical flow of information in a paragraph. Ask students to study the four sentences first and try to predict which section the information belongs in before checking with the text. Feed back with the class.

Answers

Model answers:

Sentence	Location in text	Reason
A	at the end of section 4: Post-treatment	because the final sentence in this section refers to a disinfection stage for product water
B	At the end of section 3: Wastewater discharge	the paragraph in the text talks about the challenges of liquid waste disposal, and sentence B implies that that there are also challenges with solid waste
C	at the end of section 1: Pre-treatment	because the final sentence in this section mentions backwashing, and sentence C provides a definition of backwashing
D	at the end of section 2: Reverse osmosis	because this paragraph describes the problem of fouling of reverse osmosis membranes; sentence D indicates that there will be solutions to this problem in the future

Exercise J

Tell students to read both questions carefully. Before they start the exercise, write the following sentences on the board/OHT. Ask them to suggest possibilities for the missing word or words in each sentence and say what type of words they are.

1 *Reverse osmosis plants use membrane filtration, _____ thermal desalination plants use the distillation method.*

(*whereas* or *whilst* = showing contrast)

2 *_____ reverse osmosis and thermal desalination produce high-quality water.*

(*Both* = comparing similar features/things)

3 *Thermal desalination uses _____ energy _____ reverse osmosis.*

(*More ... than* = comparing using the comparative form + *than*)

Ask students to work in pairs to make a list of linking expressions commonly used when comparing or contrasting two or more things. Elicit their ideas, building up the table below on the board.

Compare expression	Contrast expressions
similarly	whereas
similar to	whilst
compared (with/to)	while
also	unlike
the same as	in contrast (to/with)
likewise	on the other hand
like	

Others ways to compare/contrast
both
more than/less than
smaller than/greater than
as ... as
not as ... as

Language note

Make sure students are aware that the following expressions, commonly found in such compare/contrast lists, are mainly used to show concession (i.e., used to concede/accept a point which simultaneously contrasts with the main point in a sentence or paragraph):

although, though, even though, however, nevertheless, yet, still, at the same time, on the other hand

For example:

Thermal desalination methods can produce very large quantities of clean water. <u>However</u>, these methods are costly because of the amount of energy required to heat the input water.

1 Set for individual work (possibly for homework) and pairwork discussion of notes. Before students read the text on page 108, refer them to the table containing the given notes. Elicit a logical way to carry on making notes from both texts (they should find points of comparison from both texts and record them side by side in the columns – this makes it easier to write up the notes).

Remind students to use symbols and abbreviations, and to survey the text before closer reading. Tell them that they should also use information from the short text in Exercise C, and from the sentences in Exercise I.

Feed back with the class and ask for some examples of key points from both texts for comparison/contrast. You may wish to display all or part of the model notes in the answers section below (available in Resource 12F).

2 Set for individual work. Alternatively, set for pair or small group work as a collaborative writing activity. Students could write the summary on an OHT or other visual medium, which you can display and give feedback on with the whole class.

To expand on the question to make it more authentic, write the following scenario on the board/OHT, or invent an alternative scenario for your class. Change the wording where appropriate for a collaborative writing activity:

> Imagine that the water-treatment company you work for is thinking about building a

desalination plant in Southern Europe in a coastal location. As one of the engineers, you have been asked to present your views. Write a summary of around 250 words, comparing the two technologies and finishing with your recommendations.

Tell students that they will need to think about which points to select from their notes for the summary, and in what order to present them. This decision will depend on which factors they want to highlight. For example, they might want to focus more on costs than environmental factors or vice versa, or have a balance of factors. Or they might decide that the most important factor is the technology. Encourage students to think in the role of one of the engineers.

The summary in the answers section on the next page can be used as a model to display and/or as an extra activity in identifying key comparison/contrast and concession words and phrases.

Answers

Model answers:

1 See table below.

Reverse osmosis	Thermal desalination
• less energy required	• needs large amts. of energy to heat water • can produce v. large amounts freshwater, but expensive • but – most desalination plants operating in, e.g., M.E. – cogeneration (produce water + energy) → reduces costs
• less initial capital expend. = c. half thermal desal. costs	• initial capital costs high = c. 2 x RO systems
• feedwater pre-treatment most imp. stage (filtration, disinfection & anti-scalant chemicals + backwashing of filters): untreated water → membrane fouling → affect performance = expensive	• feedwater pre-treatment = limited (normally only anti-scalants): no membranes to foul/damage; no backwashing of filters
• waste: liquid waste = high salt concentrations + chems. from pre-treatment & cleaning + toxic metals → discharge into sea, sewage treatment plant, saline aquifers, evap. ponds, or brine dried out → landfill (inland facilities) • + solid waste → landfill, incl. discarded pre-treatment filters + solid particles from pre-treatment • recovery rate = c. 40–60% seawater & 50–90% brackish water	• waste: limited chemicals in feedwater = reduced environ. effects of hot brine concentrate into sea • recovery rate = c. 30–50% of source water → v. large quants. brine waste
• expensive to replace RO membranes – high maintenance • but capital costs decrease due to technological developments – becoming most economical + effective method of large-scale desalting + choice for new plants worldwide • current research into improving permeability + performance of membranes = nanostructures & nanomaterials	• since 1950s: experience in technology, design, construction = operational problems, e.g., scaling, fouling, corrosion, already solved • simple, robust, reliable tech. – small number of connection pipes; no moving parts except conventional boilers → reduces leakage + maintenance • highly automated: needs limited number of staff to operate, except during inspections, maintenance, cleaning of pipes/pumps

• post-treatment: water acidic, corrosive & unpalatable ∵ stripped of nat. minls. as well as impurities
  ○ water remineralized before use
  ○ disinfection stage to make water potable
• RO filters c. 95–99% impurities (prod. water from 10–500 ppm/TDS)
	• post-treatment: product water for domestic use = processes similar to RO process for health standards for drinking
	• pure distilled water used mostly in industrial processes, e.g., power plant boilers
	• high-quality water with a range of 1.0–50 ppm/TDS

2 Model summary:

The following summary presents key differences between thermal and RO desalination, with a focus on economic considerations.

Firstly, the initial capital cost of building a distillation plant is about twice as much as that for RO plants. Energy costs are also much higher, because feedwater has to be heated.

Although efficiency savings can be made by investing in a cogeneration plant, conventional energy costs can still be very prohibitive.

On the other hand, the current cost of pre-treatment of RO feedwater is much higher because the expensive membranes have to be carefully maintained. In contrast, feedwater in thermal plants requires limited pre-treatment because there are no membranes to foul. However, recovery rates tend to be higher with RO, even though seawater has traditionally been more suited to thermal desalting.

Both processes produce high-quality clean water, requiring similar treatment for domestic use and drinking. Although RO product water has a higher range of ppm/TDS, the process does filter out almost all harmful impurities.

The disposal of liquid waste from any desalination process is an environmental challenge. Whilst the brine from RO plants contains more chemicals and toxic metals from pre-treatment, greater quantities of hot brine concentrate from thermal plants pose equally serious problems for ecosystems.

Even though thermal desalination is a more robust and mature technology with fewer operating and maintenance problems, my/our view is that reverse osmosis would be the better choice for our company. Current research into improving RO membranes, together with other technological developments and lower energy costs, means that RO now tends to be the popular choice for new plants, even in the Middle East.

(271 words)

Closure

1 As extra practice in using linking words and expressions to show comparison and concession, copy the gapped sentences below onto an OHT or other visual medium for whole class work.

The sentences are adapted from the information in the texts in the unit. Ask for suggestions to complete the sentences. There may be more than one answer in some cases. You could also ask students to rewrite the sentences using a different expression, paying attention to punctuation and any other changes they would need to make.

a) RO membranes resist most impurities, _____ they are still prone to fouling and require regular cleaning.

b) _____ RO, feedwater in thermal processes requires limited pre-treatment because there are no membranes to foul or damage.

c) _____ initial capital costs of thermal desalination are high, it is capable of producing very large quantities of potable water.

d) Thermal desalination produces _____ brine waste _____ reverse osmosis.

e) Recovery rates in thermal desalination are _____ high _____ those in reverse osmosis plants.

Possible answers:

a) yet, but (without preceding comma), though, although, nevertheless (preceded by semi-colon), at the same time (preceded by semi-colon) = concession

b) Unlike, In contrast to = showing contrast

c) Although, Even though, Though = concession

d) more ... than = comparison

e) not as ... as = comparison

2 Put students into small groups. Ask them to choose one of the following countries or a country of their choice to research with regard to desalination facilities.

China, United Arab Emirates, Spain, the US, Brazil, the UK

Ask them to prepare a short presentation (about five minutes) using an OHT or other visual medium to present key points. They should address all the questions below:

How many desalination plants are there?

When was the first plant built?

What desalination methods are used? Do any plants use renewable energies?

How typical is cogeneration in the country?

Where does the feedwater come from?

What is the product water used for?

What are the country's future plans?

12.3 Extending skills

12.3 Extending skills — structure of laboratory reports • understanding technical terms

A Look at the diagram on the right.

1 What does the diagram show?
2 What other factors can you add?
3 Why is it important to know how much fluid can flow through a pipe?
4 How can flow rates be calculated?

fluid flow rate through pipes

pressure — viscosity — ? — ?

Introduction	___
Theory	___
Experimental Procedure	1
Results	___
Discussion	___
Conclusions	___
References	___

B Study the section headings for a laboratory report on the right. Which question(s) below does each section answer? Write the number of each question by the correct heading.

1 How was the experiment done?
2 What was found?
3 What do we definitely know from the findings?
4 What apparatus was used?
5 What is the significance of the results?
6 Where are sources of information recorded?
7 Why was the experiment done?
8 What theories are the experiment based on?

C Read the Hadford University handout.

1 Work in groups of three. Each person should choose one of the terms to research, using notes provided by the teacher.
2 Explain your term to your group.

HADFORD University

Fluid Mechanics Course

Course tutor: Dr Ian Jones

In our lab session next week, we'll be conducting an experiment to demonstrate how fluids flow through pipes. Before the session, you'll need to find out the meaning of the following terms:
• Laminar flow
• Turbulent flow
• Reynolds number
Also, please read the guidelines on the module homepage for writing a lab report.

12.4 Extending skills — structure and content of laboratory reports • linking ideas

A Read text A on the opposite page.

1 Which section of a lab report is this?
2 What are its two main functions?

B Look at the verbs in column 1 in the blue box. Which nouns from column 2 can each verb go with?

C Read text B from the same report.

1 Put the verbs in brackets in the correct tense.
2 Which section of the report does text B belong to?

D Study the six parts from the same report on the opposite page.

1 Which section does each part belong to?
2 Find synonyms for the blue words.

E Look at a student's lab notes on the right.

1 Which report section are the notes for?
2 Write a paragraph using the notes.

1	2
measure take give collect show compare plot discuss	readings results data agreement temperature

Notes
Experiment + good agreement to theory (predictions) of lam. + turb. flow:
• critical Re. no. accurately predicted
• gradients of diff. flows (lam. + turb.) + good agreement to predictions
• demonstrated: pressure drop in straight pipe depends on: λ fluid vel. λ pipe length + diameter λ pipe friction factor
• demonstrated: pipes of diff. diameters, lengths + with diff. fluids show same lam., transition + turb. flow regions when compared

98

General note

Read the *Vocabulary bank – Understanding technical terms* and the *Skills bank* at the end of the Course Book unit. Decide when, if at all, to refer your students to it. The best time is probably at the very end of the lesson or the beginning of the next lesson, as a summary/revision.

Lesson aims

● understand the structure of a laboratory report
● understand the purpose of each laboratory report section
● understand and explain key terms in fluid mechanics

Introduction

In preparation for looking at the structure of a laboratory report, revise the sections for an essay: introduction, body, conclusion. Ask students what should go in each section. Elicit ideas for introductions and conclusions. Do not correct at this point.

Language and subject note

The theme of Lessons 12.3 and 12.4 connects with the subject of desalination by focusing on a central topic in the field of fluid mechanics: flow in pipes. The lessons also introduce aspects of writing laboratory reports, but in a simplified way. Laboratory reports are best taught in the context of practical laboratory sessions. However, it is hoped that this short introduction to the genre will be helpful in familiarizing students with an important aspect of engineering practice.

Exercise A

1/2 Set for pairwork discussion. Allow the use of dictionaries to check the meaning of *viscosity*. Feed back with the class and write some suggestions on the board. Ask students to give examples of fluids with a low viscosity and those with a high viscosity.

3/4 Set for pairwork discussion. Question 4 is designed to prompt students to think about testing, experiments, established mathematical models and calculations, etc., as a lead into the topic of laboratory experiments. It may help them to look back at the ideas they had in question 2. Feed back with the class.

Tell students that the rest of the lesson and the following lesson will focus on laboratory reports. Tell them that the focus will be on the structure and style of lab reports, and that understanding all the details of the experiment is not expected.

Answers

Possible answers:

1 The diagram shows the factors that affect the flow rate of fluid in a pipe. Pressure and the viscosity of the fluid are two of these factors.

Examples of fluids with a low viscosity are water, blood, milk, gases and chemicals (such as ether, carbon, chloroform, benzene).

Examples of fluids with a high or higher viscosity are most oils including castor oil and olive oil, pitch, tar, lava, molten glass, sulfuric acid and liquid food substances such as honey.

2 Accept any reasonable suggestions. Other factors (some interrelated) include:

● the size of the pipe (length and diameter)
● the internal roughness of the pipe
● the speed of flow (velocity)
● rises and falls within the piping system

- bends in the pipe layout
- types of valves and other fittings
- changes in direction of flow
- the position of the supply container/tank in relation to the pump

3 It is important because pipes transport vital fluids (liquids and gas) to and from domestic and industrial facilities. If the flow rate is too low or too high, this will cause distribution problems. In some industrial operations, inaccurate flow calculations can cause serious or disastrous results.

Ask students to think of some examples of industrial applications where the flow rate of fluids is key to operations. Some examples are oil pipelines, gas pipelines, wastewater treatment facilities, chemical plants, irrigation and food processing.

4 By performing experiments to test existing theories and calculations of flow rates.

Exercise B

Set for individual work and pairwork checking. Feed back with the class. Explain that there are several variations of lab report structures, but whatever the format, the aim is the same – to record results of an experiment and discuss their significance. (Some of these variations are addressed in Closure activity 2 at the end of the lesson).

Answers

Model answers:

Introduction	7
Theory	8
Experimental Procedure	1, 4
Results	2
Discussion	5
Conclusions	3
References	6

Exercise C

1/2 Set for individual work and small group discussion. Allow time for students to read the handout. Copy and cut up the notes in Resource 12G in the additional resources section, sufficient for all the groups.

If there are more than three students in a group, give two students the notes on the Reynolds number, as this is the most difficult concept. If students work in pairs, give one student the notes for both laminar and turbulent flow, as these two concepts are interrelated. It is best if students begin their group work with the explanations of laminar and turbulent flow rather than the Reynolds

number, as this equation is complex and depends on an understanding of the previous two terms.

Allocate a set time for students to study the notes and any diagrams. They should make their own notes from the information provided and then take turns to explain their concept to the group. Encourage those with diagrams in their notes to draw a quick sketch for other group members during their turn, and encourage others to seek clarification where necessary. Monitor the groups to make sure that students are not just reading from the notes provided. Check pronunciation of key terms at the same time.

Feed back with the whole class. Check understanding by asking a few key questions about each term and invite students to ask questions if they need further clarification.

Closure

1 Refer students to the *Skills bank* to consolidate their understanding of the sections of a laboratory report and their contents.

2 Put the following words on the board.

Abstract

Materials

Methods

Findings

Appendix/Appendices

Tell students that these are different headings in alternative laboratory report structures. Ask them to find out for homework what these sections do, and which ones are extra to the model used in this unit.

12.4 Extending skills

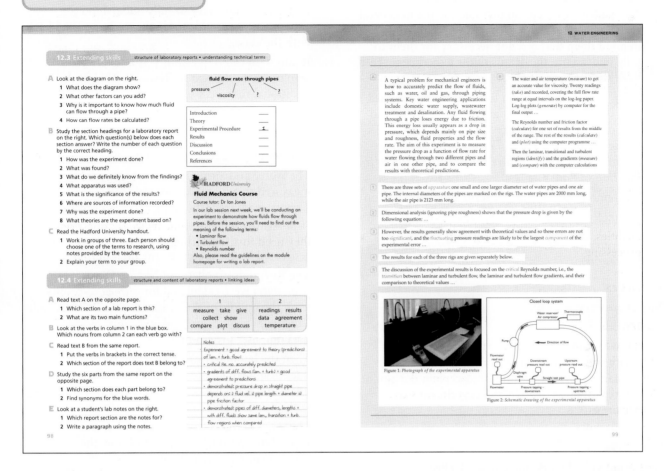

Lesson aims

- identify parts of a laboratory report
- use the correct tense in laboratory report sections
- write a section of a laboratory report from notes: *Conclusions*

Further practice in:

- synonyms
- passives
- verb and noun collocations from the discipline

Introduction

Write the sections of a laboratory report on the board in the incorrect order. With course books closed, ask students to say what the correct order should be. Check stress and pronunciation. Test their understanding of the sections by asking a selection of paraphrased questions from Exercise B in Lesson 12.3:

What <u>equipment</u> was used? (Experimental Procedure)

What do the results <u>imply</u>? (Discussion)

What was the <u>reason</u> for the experiment? (Introduction)

What <u>procedure</u> was followed? (Experimental Procedure)

What was the <u>outcome</u> of the experiment? (Results)

What do we <u>know for sure</u> as a result of the experiment? (Conclusions)

If you gave students Closure activity 2 from Lesson 12.3, ask them what they found out about the section headings below:

Abstract (= extra to unit model; a clear and concise summary of around 100–200 words at the beginning of the report which summarizes the four key aspects: the aim of the experiment, key results, significance of results and main conclusions. The abstract should help readers to decide whether they need to read the whole report.

Materials (= an alternative report format often has two sections in place of *Experimental Procedure*; namely, *Materials* and *Methods*)

Methods (= see above)

Findings (= another name for *Results*)

Appendix/Appendices (= extra to unit model; would include raw data, calculations, graphs, tables, etc.; materials that are included in *Experimental Procedure* in unit model)

Exercise A

1/2 Set for individual work and pairwork checking. Tell students to focus on the functional and general academic language more than the actual content. Remind them that it is not necessary for them to fully understand the details of the experiment. Feed back with the whole class.

Bring the class's attention to the tense that is used here (present simple), but explain that the second part of the *Introduction* could also have been written in the past tense: *The aim of this experiment <u>was</u> to measure the pressure drop as a function of flow rate ...*

To connect this exercise with the following one on verb and noun collocations, ask the class to say briefly what two specific things will be done in the experiment (*measure the pressure drop, compare the results*).

Answers

Model answers:

1 *Introduction*
2 Its two main functions are a) to provide background information to the experiment, including known facts and b) to explain the aim of the experiment (i.e., why the experiment was performed).

Exercise B

Set for individual work and pairwork checking. Explain that these are common verb and noun combinations used when reporting on lab experiments. Make sure students understand that some of the verbs collocate or go with more than one noun. Feed back with the class, building up the table on the board.

Answers

Model answers:

measure	temperature
take	readings, temperature
give	results
collect	data
show	readings, results, agreement
compare	readings, results, data, temperature
plot	readings, results
discuss	results, data

Exercise C

1/2 Set for individual work and pairwork checking. Tell students to read through the text first for overall understanding. Explain that this text shows only selected extracts from a report section (indicated by the row of three periods or full stops at the end of each paragraph), and remind students that they do not have to fully understand the experiment to be able to do the exercise. Feed back with the class.

If you wish to do question 1 as a whole class activity, copy the text in Resource 12H in the additional resources section onto an OHT or other visual medium.

Answers

Model answers:

1 The water and air temperature (*measure*) <u>were measured</u> to get an accurate value for viscosity. Twenty readings (*take*) <u>were taken</u> and recorded, covering the full flow rate range at equal intervals on the log-log paper. Log-log plots (*generate*) <u>were generated</u> by computer for the final output ...

   The Reynolds number and friction factor (*calculate*) <u>were calculated</u> for one set of results from the middle of the range. The rest of the results (*calculate*) <u>were calculated</u> and (*plot*) <u>plotted</u> using the computer programme ...

   Then the laminar, transitional and turbulent regions (*identify*) <u>were identified</u> and the gradients (*measure*) <u>were measured</u> and (*compare*) <u>compared</u> with the computer calculations ...

2 These are extracts from the *Experimental Procedure* section: an account of how the experiment was carried out.

Language note

The impersonal use of the passive for laboratory reports is not absolutely required. It is often possible to find students' work which contains the use of the first person singular or the third person singular if the report is the result of group work. However, in formal writing – especially for publication in the field – the passive is typically used. In higher education, students should always follow instructions from their subject lecturers.

Exercise D

1 Set for individual work and pairwork discussion. Tell students to read through all six parts first for overall understanding before discussing in pairs. Feed back with the class.

2 Set for individual work and pairwork checking. Remind students that synonyms are not always precise and so they need to be careful that the words they choose are appropriate in the context. The meanings of words such as significant and critical, for example, are very context-dependent. Feed back with the class.

Answers

Model answers:

1

1	Experimental Procedure
2	Theory
3	Discussion
4	Results
5	Discussion
6	Experimental Procedure

2

Word in context	Possible synonyms
apparatus	equipment
significant	important
fluctuating	variable, changing, irregular (though *fluctuating* is the best word in this context)
component	element (could also be replaced by *reason for* in this context)
critical	vital, essential, crucial
transition	change, shift (though *transition* is the best word in this context, as it indicates that a change takes place gradually)

Exercise E

1 Set for individual work and pairwork checking. Feed back with the class. Elicit the meanings of the symbols and abbreviations, most of which students have already encountered in previous units.

2 Set for individual work and pairwork checking/review. Alternatively, this task could be done as homework. Tell students to include the section heading when they write the paragraph. As a reminder about things to consider when writing up from notes, elicit aspects of grammar that are commonly omitted in notes, such as prepositions, linking words, articles, punctuation, pronouns and the full form of verbs. Feed back with the class. Copy the model paragraph in the answers section, available in Resource 12I, onto an OHT for comparison with students' own work. Underline or highlight salient aspects of the paragraph that show how the notes have been reconstructed into sentences. Invite feedback from students on how the model compares with their own paragraph.

Answers

Model answers:

1 The *Conclusions* section.

2 Possible answer:

Conclusions

The experiment showed good agreement to the theoretical predictions of laminar and turbulent flow. The critical Reynolds number was accurately predicted and the gradients of the different flows, laminar and turbulent, also showed good agreement to predictions. It was demonstrated that pressure drop in a straight pipe is dependent on three factors: the fluid velocity, the pipe length and diameter, and the friction factor of the pipe. The experiment also demonstrated that pipes of different fluids show the same laminar, transition and turbulent regions when they are directly compared.

Closure

1 Write the following five strings of words on the board or on an OHT. With books closed, elicit suggestions from students on how to build a complete sentence for each string. Tell them to think about the meaning of the combination of words in the order they are given, and about extra words needed, such as determiners, prepositions, and verbs or correct verb endings. Do the first one with the whole class as an example.

1 *typical problem / mechanical engineers / accurately / predict / flow of fluids*

2 *results / agreement / theoretical values*

3 *aim / experiment / measure / pressure drop*

4 *Reynolds number / important / determine / transition point / laminar / turbulent flow*

5 *It / demonstrate / pressure drop / straight pipe / dependent / three factors*

Suggested sentences:

1 *A typical problem **for** mechanical engineers **is how to** accurately predict **the** flow of fluids.*

2 ***The** results **showed** agreement **with** theoretical values.*

3 ***The** aim **of the** experiment **is/was to** measure the pressure drop.*

4 ***The** Reynolds number **is** important **in** determining **the** transition point **from** laminar **to** turbulent flow.*

5 *It **was** demonstrated **that** pressure drop **in a** straight pipe **is** dependent **on** three factors.*

2 Set students to research more about laboratory reports on the Internet. Things to notice in sample reports they find are variations on structure, use of tense in different sections, common verbs used in reporting on experiments and fixed phrases in the discipline. The following websites are particularly useful (URLs correct at the time of writing):

http://www.writing.engr.psu.edu/workbooks/laboratory.html (on the structure of lab reports)

http://www.writing.engr.psu.edu/workbooks/labreport2.html (a sample authentic report)

http://www.ncsu.edu/labwrite/index_labwrite.htm (guide to writing lab reports)

http://www.egr.msu.edu/cee/techcom/ce321/sample_rpts.pdf (sample lab report on fluid discharge from a pipe)

Extra activities

1 Work through the *Vocabulary bank* and *Skills bank* if you have not already done so, or as revision of previous study.

2 Use the *Activity bank* (Teacher's Book additional resources section, Resource 12A).

A Set the wordsearch for individual work (including homework) or pairwork.

Answers

B Do the quiz as a whole class, or in teams, or set for homework.

Answers

1 a brackish
  b distilled
  c surface

2 a membrane
  b feedwater
  c brine
  d filter
  e alkaline

3 **capital** costs
   fluid mechanics
   desalination/distillation plant
   laminar/turbulent flow
   energy/oil consumption
   fossil fuel
   experimental procedure
   dissolved minerals
   Reynolds number

   (accept any other words that form acceptable alternative phrases within the discipline)

Activity bank

A Solve the crossword.

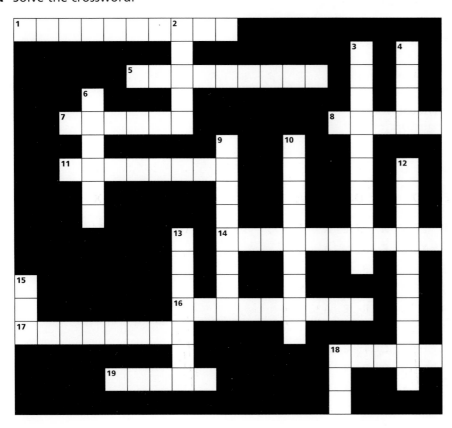

Down

2 A … is one stage of a process.
3 To make stronger.
4 A … of paint is one layer.
6 To make looser.
9 … is the relationship between forces and motion.
10 The bottom layer of paint.
12 Above the speed of sound.
13 Metal … is the gradual weakening of metal under repeated stress loading.
15 The part of a crane which extends.
18 You must … an oil well to stop the oil escaping.

Across

1 Always use an … screwdriver when you are working on a circuit.
5 We should … this job. I'm sure we could get a machine to do it.
7 To join two sections together.
8 The … are the cutting part of a saw.
11 Most cars are built on an … line.
14 A … is a device for measuring tiny lengths.
16 Plastic is a good … .
17 The … is the way a machine is attached.
18 … engineering is about building houses and bridges.
19 To make wider.

B Play noughts and crosses. Use the words in context or explain what they mean.

miscalculate	millilitre	overengineer	Willis Carrier	RDD	Thomas Newcomen
prevention	pressurize	classify	SSBB	Venturi effect	Charles Babbage
accuracy	petrology	replacement	The Comet	James Watt	Industrial Revolution

Activity bank

A Find 20 words from this unit in the wordsearch.

- Copy the words into your notebook.
- Check the definition of any words you can't remember.

V	M	N	G	L	X	S	H	F	A	P	P	A	R	A	T	U	S
O	A	R	V	M	C	E	E	N	E	R	G	Y	C	H	A	N	I
C	A	L	L	A	E	O	N	G	I	S	N	E	E	R	S	N	G
S	T	U	V	D	P	I	N	E	P	S	H	N	D	Z	J	D	Y
E	K	M	X	E	F	O	N	D	R	W	Y	A	D	C	I	L	X
F	L	V	L	N	W	T	U	K	E	F	Q	X	F	U	Q	S	M
F	R	I	C	T	I	O	N	R	S	N	D	P	L	T	C	N	E
I	N	T	E	X	J	I	L	E	S	R	S	F	B	I	O	M	C
C	L	P	L	X	X	L	D	K	U	M	F	E	N	I	M	A	H
I	H	J	K	Y	T	H	R	M	R	G	N	A	T	K	P	C	A
E	D	G	G	N	G	Y	A	K	E	D	H	A	P	F	R	H	N
N	T	N	E	M	E	G	D	M	Z	C	R	T	F	P	E	I	I
C	C	T	V	T	Q	Y	I	L	E	E	H	D	V	N	D	N	Z
Y	A	D	G	Q	K	Y	A	M	P	W	Q	A	A	K	Q	E	A
P	Z	A	N	H	L	Z	T	O	H	H	R	R	N	B	K	R	T
H	W	H	N	C	L	G	O	D	T	R	C	Q	R	I	R	Y	I
D	E	V	I	C	E	V	R	Y	L	M	J	J	Q	R	S	P	O
R	E	F	R	I	G	E	R	A	T	I	O	N	R	X	T	M	N

B Do the quiz.

1 Who invented refrigeration?
2 When, approximately, did he invent it?
3 What kind of system did he use?
4 Who developed refrigeration?
5 Who invented air conditioning?
6 When, approximately, did he invent it?
7 What did Denis Papin invent for the steam boiler?
8 Why are steam boilers dangerous?
9 What do we call the period of fast progress in mechanization in the 18th and 19th centuries?
10 Who invented the first practical steam engine?
11 Who made the steam engine more efficient in 1769?
12 What is atmospheric pressure?
13 What led to the Boiler Safety Code?
14 Name four areas of mechanical engineering which have codes of standards.

Before engineers learnt how to cool air, life was very different.	Food had to be bought the same day it was used. Most foodstuffs could not be transported long distances, so people had to live close to the source of food. Most foodstuffs could not be stored, so surplus food could not be kept. A lot of food went bad and had to be thrown away, or gave people food poisoning. In addition, in many countries, it was impossible to work during the heat of the day and many areas were uninhabitable during the summer months. Some ancient peoples designed cooling methods for food and spaces. Some people kept fresh food under running water. The Indians had wet mats hanging at windows. The Arabs had cooling towers which sucked hot air out of the rooms at their base. However, these early cooling systems were limited in their extent and efficiency.
The inventor of refrigeration was Jacob Perkins.	He was an American, but he lived most of his life in Britain. Perkins was a true mechanical engineer. He invented a machine for cutting and heading nails and he was the first person to use steel to make plates for engraving bank notes. He invented machines for measuring the depth of water and the speed of a ship. He improved gun manufacture. In 1830, he invented a radiator which attached to a steam engine, an early form of central heating. But perhaps his greatest invention was the first refrigerator.
In 1834, Perkins obtained a patent for a vapour compression system of cooling.	In his patent application, he described how the device worked by 'constantly condensing volatile fluids and bringing them again and again into operation without waste.' The recycling of fluids was an important feature of the process as, later, it enabled refrigeration engineers to use hazardous fluids and gases, such as CFCs.
Perkins often does not get the credit for his important invention, because he did not develop it.	This was done by a Scottish printer, James Harrison. He showed his design at the International Exhibition of 1862 in London. Like all good engineers, Harrison was responding to a problem. He realized that there was a surplus of meat in Australia, a British colony at the time, while at the same time there was starvation in Britain. In 1873, he made his first attempt to bring frozen meat from Australia to Britain, but it was a disaster. However, his idea sparked the development of the worldwide 'cold chain' which we have today.
The work of Perkins and Harrison did not directly lead to the cooling of rooms.	That honour belongs to an American called Willis Carrier. However, Carrier did not start with space cooling. He worked, instead, on devices for cooling machines. When machines work, surfaces rub against each other and this contact causes friction, which in turn produces heat. Hot machines are dangerous and inefficient. If a machine overheats, it can break down or even explode.
After cooling machines, Carrier moved on to rooms.	In 1907, he founded the Carrier Air Conditioning Company, using a term that was only two years old. He designed an apparatus to cool air using water sprays. He controlled the dew point of the air, which is the point at which water vapour condenses out of the gas. This way he conditioned the air, making it cooler and less humid.
In 1922, Carrier built his first true air-conditioning machine.	The new invention spread quickly through the United States and then the world. Carrier is often called 'the father of air conditioning', not just for his inventions, but also for his 'psychrometric chart' which is still in use today. This chart defines the relationship between air, water and energy.
Mechanisms for cooling air have had a profound effect on human life all over the world.	With cooled air, we can chill or freeze food to store it or to transport it long distances. We can keep medical supplies in good condition. We can cool machines to keep them running efficiently. Finally, we can cool factories, offices, homes and cars to make them habitable even in the highest ambient temperatures.

Before engineers learnt how to cool air, life was very different.

The inventor of refrigeration was Jacob Perkins.

In 1834, Perkins obtained a patent for a vapour compression system of cooling.

Perkins often does not get the credit for his important invention, because he did not develop it.

The work of Perkins and Harrison did not directly lead to the cooling of rooms.

After cooling machines, Carrier moved on to rooms.

In 1922, Carrier built his first true air-conditioning machine.

Mechanisms for cooling air have had a profound effect on human life all over the world.

Before engineers learnt how to cool air, life was very different.

The inventor of refrigeration was Jacob Perkins.

In 1834, Perkins obtained a patent for a vapour compression system of cooling.

Perkins often does not get the credit for his important invention, because he did not develop it.

The work of Perkins and Harrison did not directly lead to the cooling of rooms.

After cooling machines, Carrier moved on to rooms.

In 1922, Carrier built his first true air-conditioning machine.

Mechanisms for cooling air have had a profound effect on human life all over the world.

What is the first concern of any engineer?	At one time, perhaps, the answer to this question was: to solve a problem or to improve an existing machine, or even to make more money. Nowadays, however, the answer is simple. The first concern is safety. This concern has led to the introduction of worldwide codes and standards for the manufacture and maintenance of machines.
Machinery of all kinds has certainly made the world a more dangerous place.	Hundreds of people are at risk from the crash of a jumbo jet, or the explosion of a power station. At one time, of course, engineers did not know how to make a machine safe. But as they began to understand the science behind the behaviour of metals and other materials, engineers started to construct codes of manufacturing and standards to which machines must be built.
The steam engine was one of the first machines which aroused interest in safety standards.	The danger of steam under pressure was recognized very early in the history of the machine. Denis Papin, a French mathematician, designed the first safety valve for boilers in 1679. But safety valves sometimes failed and explosions were quite common.
The steam engine works on a very simple scientific principle.	When you heat water in a vessel, the molecules expand, until, at a certain temperature, the liquid turns into a gas. This gas needs a greater space than the same volume of liquid. If the vessel is sealed, the gas cannot occupy a greater volume, so the pressure increases.
At first, engineers tried to avoid the problem by only working with low-pressure steam.	The first practical low-pressure engine was built by Thomas Newcomen, an English inventor, in 1712. It was used to pump water out of a coal mine. The invention helped to spark the Industrial Revolution, the time of fast progress in mechanization of agriculture and the textile industry.
James Watt improved the efficiency of the engine.	His first patent, in 1769, included oil lubrication, and insulation of the cylinder to maintain the high temperature needed for efficient operation. Further improvements were made in the 1830s by a man called Jacob Perkins. His boiler could produce 1,400 pounds per square inch (psi). The normal pressure of the air around us, atmospheric pressure, is 14.7 psi.
However, as the boilers used higher temperatures and developed higher pressures, the dangers rose.	In 1854, an explosion in England killed ten people. On 30th July, 1870, the boiler of the Staten Island ferry in New York City exploded, killing 62 people. It was time for mechanical engineers to act.
In 1882, a new law on boiler safety was passed in the UK.	As a result, the number of deaths from boiler accidents fell from 35 in 1883 to 14 in 1905. However, there was no similar legislation in the United States and 383 people died in the same period. Finally, in 1914, the American Society of Mechanical Engineers (ASME) produced the Boiler Safety Code.
The boiler code was only the start.	Over the next 80 years, the ASME produced codes in all areas of mechanical engineering, including safety standards for cranes, industrial ladders, elevators, machinery shafts, liquid fuels and incinerators for hazardous medical waste.
Codes and standards in engineering are often unknown to the general public.	However, they are fundamental to the safety of manufactured products and they have led to a safer world.

What is the first concern of any engineer?

Machinery of all kinds has certainly made the world a more dangerous place.

The steam engine was one of the first machines which aroused interest in safety standards.

The steam engine works on a very simple scientific principle.

At first, engineers tried to avoid the problem by only working with low-pressure steam.

James Watt improved the efficiency of the engine.

However, as the boilers used higher temperatures and developed higher pressures, the dangers rose.

In 1882, a new law on boiler safety was passed in the UK.

The boiler code was only the start.

Codes and standards in engineering are often unknown to the general public.

What is the first concern of any engineer?

Machinery of all kinds has certainly made the world a more dangerous place.

The steam engine was one of the first machines which aroused interest in safety standards.

The steam engine works on a very simple scientific principle.

At first, engineers tried to avoid the problem by only working with low-pressure steam.

James Watt improved the efficiency of the engine.

However, as the boilers used higher temperatures and developed higher pressures, the dangers rose.

In 1882, a new law on boiler safety was passed in the UK.

The boiler code was only the start.

Codes and standards in engineering are often unknown to the general public.

Activity bank

A Solve the crossword.

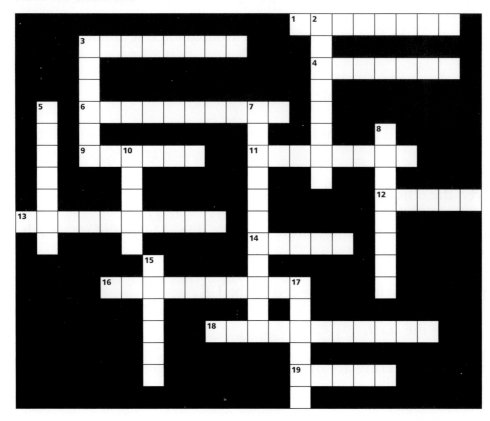

Down

2 … forces are matched by internal forces.

3 Newton's Third Law of Motion describes the … acting on any item.

5 If something is …, it is easy to stretch it.

7 Machines vibrate when the components are not in …

8 … lines never meet.

10 We cannot bend material easily if it is …

15 A screwdriver uses … to put in or take out a screw.

17 The effect of a force on a component is called the …

Across

1 The side of the car was … by the accident.

3 A … material can expand and contract without damage.

4 The cable of a crane uses … to lift a block.

6 Parking spaces are often shaded by a … roof.

9 The deformation caused by stress is called the …

11 Forces which act along the same axis are …

12 An … is a mixture of metals.

13 Rubber has a lot of …

14 Industrial buildings often use large steel …

16 Engineers are very interested in the … of a material.

18 A table vice holds work by …

19 A pair of wire cutters use … to cut the wire.

B Play bingo.

- Think of words for each of the categories and write them on card 1. Think of a word from another category for the last square ('another word').

- Each student says one of their words. Cross the squares on card 2 when you hear a word from that category.

1

material	quality of material	effect of force
_____	_____	_____
structure	verb	another word
_____	_____	_____

2

material	quality of material	effect of force
structure	verb	another word

Activity bank

A Find 20 verbs from the first four units in the wordsearch.
- Copy the verbs into your notebook.
- Write the noun for each verb.

```
M  C  O  N  D  E  N  S  E  I  G  R  P  K  H  H
M  X  O  P  E  R  A  T  E  M  N  J  N  E  P  E
H  W  N  T  N  J  A  M  P  Z  T  S  Z  K  T  L
I  R  R  J  M  L  P  Y  I  Y  Y  I  T  A  H  E
L  N  P  E  U  T  F  R  F  N  R  P  R  A  T  H
N  Z  T  S  F  I  R  I  E  E  N  O  C  J  L  M
T  P  N  E  C  R  S  E  T  S  P  O  R  H  R  L
P  I  M  E  R  S  I  U  C  A  S  G  V  O  B  Q
X  K  P  Y  A  A  P  G  V  T  E  U  F  A  W  Z
R  S  L  L  Q  M  C  E  E  T  I  E  R  K  T  F
E  K  C  W  O  R  T  T  X  R  D  F  T  I  Y  E
P  M  E  C  H  A  N  I  Z  E  A  T  Y  W  Z  K
L  L  U  B  R  I  C  A  T  E  B  T  T  K  H  E
A  Z  N  X  X  C  A  P  P  L  Y  T  E  B  R  K
C  L  I  N  T  E  G  R  A  T  E  R  M  C  C  F
E  L  W  Y  X  G  R  G  M  O  D  I  F  Y  C  K
```

B Play noughts and crosses. You must say the abbreviation or acronym and give the original words to place your symbol in a square.

USB	CAD	HTTP
PIN	DVD	LCD
ROM	PC	HTML

CAM	ISP	CIM
WWW	PPT	CAT
CPU	CAL	PDF

Microprocessors have been part of the manufacturing process since the 1960s.

By the end of the 20th century, a totally new and more efficient approach had become possible.

Many companies, therefore, are unable to use CIM.

CIM is very different from CAM.

CIM is clearly the future.

Microprocessors have been part of the manufacturing process since the 1960s.

By the end of the 20th century, a totally new and more efficient approach had become possible.

Many companies, therefore, are unable to use CIM.

CIM is very different from CAM.

CIM is clearly the future.

CAD	CAL
CAM	DVD
HTML	HTTP
ISP	LCD
PIN	ROM
URL	USB
WAN	WWW

Activity bank

A Solve the synonyms crossword. Find words with the same meaning as the clues.

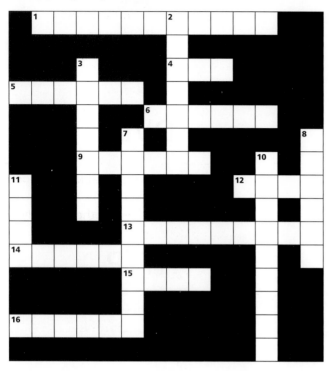

Across
1 produce (v)
4 innovative
5 fluid
6 increase (n)
9 is the same as
12 rigid
13 costly
14 μm
15 nano
16 change (v)

Down
2 regulate
3 topic
7 at the moment
8 device
10 fundamentally
11 particle

B Play opposites bingo.
- Choose six words from the box and write one word in each square of your bingo card.
- Your teacher will call out some words. If you have the **opposite** word on your card, cross it out.
- The first person to cross out all the words on their card is the winner.

dangerous   complex   expensive   fall
flexible   futuristic   less   liquid   micro
passive   productive   relevant   sharply
slightly   transparent

Product	Features and language	Evaluation prompts (suggestions only)
1 wiperless car windshield	<ul><li>no windscreen wipers</li><li>transparent nanomaterial constructed in layers</li><li>properties that repel water and dirt</li><li>can screen out harmful rays</li><li>powered by one of the layers that conducts electricity</li></ul>	<ul><li>quite costly to produce? (only prototype manufactured)</li><li>sophisticated process</li><li>safer?</li><li>stronger, lighter, more durable (longer-lasting)</li><li>would it make a difference to driving in bad weather?</li><li>no need to replace wipers</li></ul>
2 mobile phones made with flexible materials	<ul><li>flexible</li><li>bendable, stretchable</li><li>transparent electronics</li><li>can change shape and size</li><li>self-cleaning surfaces</li><li>nanosensors – to monitor health (e.g., blood sugar) and air pollution</li></ul>	<ul><li>futuristic (not available for a good few years)</li><li>how expensive will they initially be?</li><li>sophisticated</li><li>how practical?</li><li>how appealing?</li><li>just a fashion fad?</li></ul>
3 disinfection light	<ul><li>hand-held device; portable; battery-operated</li><li>nano-UV scanner</li><li>compact, collapsible</li><li>for personal use (e.g., toothbrushes, spectacles, mobile phones, kitchen equipment and utensils)</li><li>for office items (e.g., computer keyboards, phones)</li><li>for travellers (airlines, hire cars, restaurants)</li></ul>	<ul><li>commercially available</li><li>quite expensive</li><li>useful</li><li>efficient</li><li>just the latest fad?</li><li>how important is it to disinfect everything we use?</li></ul>
4 sunscreen	<ul><li>use of nanoparticles (zinc oxide or titanium oxide)</li><li>common in many cosmetics</li><li>nanoparticles can make it transparent</li></ul>	<ul><li>could be risky</li><li>could endanger skin cells</li><li>not enough information available regarding risks of nanoparticles</li></ul>
5 wrinkle-resistant, stain-repellent clothes	<ul><li>cotton fibres treated at molecular level</li><li>can be washed less frequently</li><li>size and colour also locked in through chemical treatment</li><li>not permanent (30–50 washes)</li></ul>	<ul><li>appeal of easy-to-care-for clothes? – saves time/money</li><li>more expensive than ordinary clothing but process not permanent</li><li>wrinkle resistant does not mean wrinkle-free</li></ul>
6 colour-changing car	<ul><li>colour-changing paints</li><li>special polymer contains paramagnetic nanoparticles</li><li>electric current through paint changes ability to reflect light</li></ul>	<ul><li>what are the benefits?</li><li>useful or just a lifestyle product?</li><li>drawbacks (e.g., getaway cars!)</li></ul>

Verbs	Nouns	Adverbs	Adjectives
rise		gradually	
increase		sharply	
grow		slightly	
improve		markedly	
fall		significantly	
decrease		rapidly	
drop		steeply	
decline		steadily	

English for Mechanical Engineering – Copyright © Garnet Publishing Ltd 2010

Poor contributions	Student A	Student B	Student C
disagrees rudely			
doesn't explain how the point is relevant			
doesn't understand an idiom			
dominates the discussion			
gets angry when someone disagrees with them			
interrupts			
is negative			
mumbles or whispers			
says something irrelevant			
shouts			
sits quietly and says nothing			
starts a side conversation			
other:			

Good contributions	Student A	Student B	Student C
allows others to speak			
asks for clarification			
asks politely for information			
brings in another speaker			
builds on points made by other speakers			
contributes to the discussion			
explains the point clearly			
gives specific examples to help explain a point			
is constructive			
links correctly with previous speakers			
listens carefully to what others say			
makes clear how the point is relevant			
paraphrases to check understanding			
says when they agree with someone			
speaks clearly			
tries to use correct language			
other:			

Activity bank

A Find 20 verbs from this unit in the wordsearch.

- Copy the words into your notebook.
- Write the noun for each verb.

R	U	G	M	F	Y	R	K	Q	F	L	Q	G	I	Y
E	V	F	M	D	U	A	R	U	P	L	Y	Q	L	E
D	K	O	A	Y	E	N	P	F	I	S	I	P	I	L
U	B	R	A	P	G	G	C	A	J	N	P	M	H	U
C	S	C	V	I	I	E	F	T	I	A	R	T	N	B
E	S	E	I	N	N	X	N	A	I	O	E	U	O	R
E	P	S	M	I	H	Y	T	E	F	O	F	R	A	I
G	E	Z	M	T	M	N	E	R	R	Q	N	E	F	C
X	C	V	A	I	I	A	E	R	O	A	W	Q	U	A
M	I	C	L	A	Y	P	C	J	O	P	T	H	B	T
O	F	X	M	T	O	E	K	H	L	D	P	E	V	E
V	Y	X	F	E	K	W	U	Z	I	H	E	O	I	J
E	O	Q	B	A	G	V	Y	K	X	N	W	H	S	N
U	R	S	R	H	B	C	K	O	V	U	E	J	R	E
G	Z	B	O	R	E	S	I	S	T	A	O	I	L	I

B Think of a word or words that can go in front of each of the words below to make a phrase from mechanical engineering. Explain the meaning.

Example: *friction = static friction, the force which makes an object difficult to move*

bearing	heat	specification
contact	inefficiency	speed
effect	lubrication	strength
failure	oils	surface
force	pads	system
friction	properties	value
functioning	object	wear

1 Static friction _____ as the applied force increases.

2 At the point of motion, friction force has a _____ value.

3 Kinetic friction is _____ as the applied force increases.

4 The maximum static friction is _____ than kinetic friction.

5 Friction force _____ after the point of motion because it is easier to maintain motion than to initiate it.

6 The _____ axis shows applied force.

1 Static friction increases as the applied force increases.

2 At the point of motion, friction force has a maximum value.

3 Kinetic friction is constant as the applied force increases.

4 The maximum static friction is higher than kinetic friction.

5 Friction force decreases after the point of motion because it is easier to maintain motion than to initiate it.

6 The horizontal axis shows applied force.

a In spite of an increase in the force acting on the object, the value for kinetic friction remains the same.

b The value for applied force is given from left to right along the horizontal axis.

c During application of an external force, there is a rise in static friction.

d The highest value of friction force is not reached until movement begins.

e The value for kinetic friction is not as high as the peak value for static friction.

f Friction force drops once movement is achieved, since starting movement is harder than continuing it.

Original sentence	Student A	Student B
In order to reduce friction, the surfaces that are in contact need to be made smoother.	For reduced friction, surfaces in contact have to be as smooth as possible.	For low levels of friction, designers need to take maximum care that components in contact are not rough.
	not satisfactory: not enough changes; this is patch-writing	*acceptable paraphrase:* *positive changed to negative ('smoother' → 'not rough'); passive changed to active ('surfaces need to be made smoother' → 'designers need to take care that ...'); all words changed except 'friction' and 'in contact', which is acceptable.*
In addition to machining (or polishing), this can be done in two ways.	As well as by polishing, this is done in one of two ways.	There are three main ways of achieving this: a) surfaces can be polished
	not satisfactory: passive repeated; information omitted; words not changed	*acceptable paraphrase:* *1. converting items to a list* *2. to passive → 'can be polished'*

Original sentence	Student A	Student B
Firstly, a lubricant can be added to reduce the coefficient of friction and so minimize wear and heat. There are many types of lubricants: thick or thin oil; powders, like talc; solids, such as graphite, and even acoustic lubrication, i.e., sound.	First, by using a lubricant, e.g., oil, talc, graphite, sound.	b) the system may include the addition of one of a variety of liquids and solids, or even sound, in order to lower friction forces and generate less wear and heat.
	not satisfactory: some words changed, but too short	*acceptable paraphrase: clause changed to phrase ('can be added' → 'the addition of'); reordering of information; all words changed except key terms – friction, wear, heat, sound, which is acceptable.*
Secondly, the components can be designed so that the friction is minimal.	Second, by designing the components so that friction is as low as possible.	c) the design of the parts may be aimed towards the lowest possible resistance to movement.
	not satisfactory: grammar changed, but still too close to original text	*acceptable paraphrase: clause changed to phrase ('components can be designed' → 'the design of the parts'); conjunction changed to prepositional phrase ('so that' → 'aimed towards'); all words changed.*

In many mechanical design specifications, engineers must bear in mind several principles of friction.

If friction is not taken into account by engineers beginning work on a design, the results are both costly and damaging.

In order to reduce friction, the surfaces that are in contact need to be made smoother.

Many examples of components that are affected by friction can be found inside an internal combustion engine.

The lubrication system also provides oil to the moving parts of the engine.

Not all friction is harmful to the performance of a car, however.

In many mechanical design specifications, engineers must bear in mind several principles of friction.

If friction is not taken into account by engineers beginning work on a design, the results are both costly and damaging.

In order to reduce friction, the surfaces that are in contact need to be made smoother.

Many examples of components that are affected by friction can be found inside an internal combustion engine.

The lubrication system also provides oil to the moving parts of the engine.

Not all friction is harmful to the performance of a car, however.

	Main subject	**Main verb**	**Main object/ complement**	**Other verbs + their subjects + objects/ complements**	**Adverbial phrases**
A	this sliding	would (quickly) cause	overheating	and the engine would seize	without lubrication
B	Oil	is passed	(through) a filter	in which all dust and dirt which might cause friction is removed	
C	Corrosive wear	damages	the cylinder head itself	which is a common cause of car engine inefficiency	often
D	designers	reduce	friction	In addition to polishing key components, …	in two ways
E	the lubrication system	pumps	it	Having cleaned the oil, …	to the relevant parts of the engine

A		B	
A	acoustic	B	lubrication
A	ball	B	bearing
A	brake	B	pads
A	constant	B	speed
A	contact	B	surface
A	corollary	B	heat
A	correct	B	functioning
A	design	B	specification
A	detrimental	B	effect
A	engine	B	inefficiency
A	engineering	B	system
A	erosive/abrasive/adhesive	B	wear
A	friction/normal/applied	B	force
A	horizontal/vertical	B	axis
A	machine	B	failure
A	material	B	properties
A	mineral	B	oils
A	scalar/peak	B	value
A	shear	B	strength
A	static/kinetic	B	friction
A	stationary	B	object

Activity bank

A Solve the crossword.

Across

1 If a system works well every time it is used, it has good … .

5 Look … … … way.

7 Gantt charts show what … are happening at any one time.

8 One problem with fuel cells is short … : the cars are not able to travel very far.

10 An engine which combines an ICE with an electric motor is called a … .

12 The … of the matter is that inefficiency affects profitability.

13 Let me … it another way.

14 I'd like to make two … .

15 The most important area for new technologies is research and …

Down

2 The value … is the ratio *Work done : Energy required to do the work*.

3 A … is usually used as the direct power source for electrical systems.

4 A … braking system recycles kinetic energy from the brakes.

6 Researchers test the battery's … under different operating conditions.

9 By making a … , you can test and change the final production version.

10 A simple and common gas, … , is already being used in cars.

11 Internal combustion engines often have a large … to overcome drag.

	Fixed phrase	Followed by ...	Actual information (suggested answers)
1	An important concept (is) ...	a new idea or topic that the lecturer wants to discuss	
2	What do I mean by ... ?	an explanation of a word or phrase	
3	Looking at it another way, ...	a different way to think about the topic	
4	Say ...	an imaginary example	
5	In efficiency terms, ...	a general idea put into an engineering context	
6	As you can see, ...	a comment about a diagram or picture	
7	In this way ...	a concluding comment giving a result of something	
8	The point is ...	a key statement or idea	

Fuel sources

1 Flexibility

- Flexibility is important. Can the technology be applied to different types of vehicle, e.g., for family use, sport, transport?

- New developments: if a fuel source can be upgraded without the need for extensive reworking of the car, as new cells become available, costs can be kept down.

- It may be possible to produce alternative fuel source using a range of materials. However, this may restrict potential applications/lifespan.

Fuel sources

2 Manufacturing

- Costs: industry will not consider manufacturing new technology until it is clear that this will be profitable.

- Tools: can existing machinery be adapted for production? What will be the cost and timeframe for developing any new machinery?

- Can the existing labour force carry out production without the need for extensive retraining?

- The manufacturing process may be subject to special (potentially costly) regulation, e.g., because it is dangerous to workers or environmentally unfriendly.

Fuel sources

3 Power and efficiency

- In engineering terms: what is the rate of conversion of energy to electricity? Are there any limits on the maximum efficiency?

- For marketing: technical data for the fuel source is important; the marketing people will use it to sell the cars.

- Driving conditions: for the international market, the power source must maintain efficiency under a variety of operating conditions – especially climate and the demands of cruising/stop-start driving.

Fuel sources

4 User concerns

- Any inconvenience or potential risk to the buyer will be very unpopular:

  ○ Will any new training or licence be required to drive the new vehicle?

  ○ Is the vehicle clean, comfortable and quiet?

  ○ Is the power source safe, especially if damaged in an accident?

  ○ Is maintenance quick and reasonably cheap – and are workshops easy to find?

- Environmental profile: the new technology will be more attractive if it is 'clean' in terms of its production, use and eventual disposal.

Activity bank

A Find 15 words from this unit in the wordsearch. All the words are uncountable nouns in the texts in this unit.

- Copy the words into your notebook.
- Check the definition of any words you can't remember.

E	S	U	S	T	A	I	N	A	B	I	L	I	T	Y
C	N	R	G	R	O	W	T	H	M	W	L	E	A	S
A	O	E	R	G	S	T	R	R	I	C	U	N	A	G
S	U	N	R	R	E	C	Y	C	L	I	N	G	N	N
A	C	A	S	G	O	A	T	N	U	C	O	I	P	M
N	O	O	T	U	Y	U	T	I	E	A	R	N	R	A
I	S	P	M	T	M	A	L	R	G	U	H	E	O	I
T	S	E	E	B	T	P	E	S	T	A	C	E	D	N
A	G	A	P	U	U	H	T	C	S	T	R	R	U	T
T	U	I	T	N	P	S	A	I	H	I	E	I	C	E
I	G	L	A	S	S	F	T	N	O	T	N	N	T	N
O	R	T	O	T	U	A	N	I	S	N	I	G	I	A
N	T	M	E	N	P	C	M	A	O	T	U	L	O	N
P	T	O	A	I	E	N	W	N	S	N	M	I	N	C
A	C	M	P	O	L	L	U	T	I	O	N	R	T	E

B Rearrange the letters in the words to form a correctly spelt word from this unit.

Jumbled word	Correct spelling
corueser	
wothrg	
tamicle	
clerecy	
moscuptinon	
sycometes	
wablereen	
teenager	
untilloop	
metpoldeven	

Activity bank

A Solve the crossword.

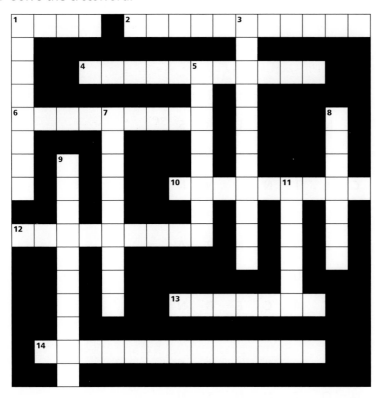

Down

1 Catastrophe.

3 A routine of keeping something (e.g., buildings and machinery) in good working condition.

5 Of a good enough quality for a particular purpose.

7 Not permanent.

8 An official investigation is an …

9 The process of finding out the condition of something by close examination.

11 Risk (n).

Across

1 All managers have a … under the law to protect their employees' health and safety.

2 Ignitable.

4 Rules and …

6 Material.

10 Dangerous to people's health and safety.

12 To guide and oversee those working on a task who may lack the full skills for the task.

13 Plant (n).

14 Refusal or failure to abide by rules or guidelines.

B Are the nouns countable or uncountable? Use a dictionary to check.

Noun	Countable or uncountable?	Notes
accident		
clothing		
emergency		
equipment		
gas		
machinery		
maintenance		
negligence		
oil		
pressure		

Review reduce + recite + review	**Notes** record
Here you write only important words and questions; this column is completed *after* the lecture. Later this column becomes your study or revision notes. You can use it by covering the right-hand column and using the cue words and questions here to remember the contents on the right.	This column contains your notes. You should underline headings and indent main ideas. After the lecture or reading you need to identify the key points and write them in the review column as questions or cue words.

Summary
reduce + recite + review
After the class you can use this space to summarize the main points of the notes on this page.

Review	Notes
Purpose of H&S at work is …?	<u>Principles of H&S in w/place</u>: managers' <u>legal</u> duty – to protect employees, H&S (risks) + good for business; employees also have a duty of 'reasonable care' towards themselves and others.
7 main duties are …?	<u>7 main duties for managers re. safety</u>: 1. risk assessmt.: identify safety implications before *procedures* set up 2. design for safety (machinery, structures, etc.): e.g., machine stops if *control box opened* 3. maintenance of plant & machinery
3 rules for matls. & substances are …?	4. matls. & substances: store, move, use safely (∵ dangerous gases ➔ possible *leaks*)
3 types of assistance when problems occur are …?	5. immediate assistance when probs. occur: • hazards & emergency *buttons* ➔ indicated at point of risk • know who *first aid* officers are • emerg. procedures – established + *practised*
Consequences of serious incidents are …?	6. report & investigate all incidents promptly: • minor incidents ➔ avoid serious incident in future • serious incidents (i.e., loss of life) ➔ *government safety* officers involved ➔ may be legal enquiry + *changes to law*
Possibly most important duty is …?	7. trng. + *supervision* (most imp.?) ➔ for both normal + unusual situations

Summary

There are seven key health and safety principles in engineering workplace contexts that cover risk assessment, safety and maintenance of plant and machinery, hazardous materials, accidents and emergency procedures, and training and supervision. These are all legal requirements and the responsibility of management. However, employees also have a duty of 'reasonable care'.

1 The Great Sheffield Flood (England, 1864)

Background

- Sheffield (mid-1800s) = one of great centres of Industrial Revolution + growing

- many moved to Sheff. to work at new, huge steelworks

- urgent need for better water supply to town; pressure on *Sheff. Waterworks Co.* ➔ plan to build 4 large reservoirs north of Sheff.

- first = *Dale Dyke Dam* on industrial River Loxley: building began 1st Jan., 1859

- embankment = earth construction (500 ft wide x 100 ft high), forming reservoir 1 mile long x ¼ mile wide

- end Feb. 1864 – dam ready + embank. almost finished

Incident

- 11 Mar., c. 5.30 p.m.: worker saw narrow crack along embank.

- chief engr. + contractor inspected embank. – crack thought not serious, but engr. decided to lower water in reservoir until investigation (weather v. stormy)

- ➔ gunpowder to blow hole in side of by-wash ➔ quickly drain off large amount of water

- by 11.30 p.m., several attempts with gunpowder, but rain + spray prevented ignition; water being blown over top of dam

- ➔ large section of dam collapsed ➔ released mountain of water

- c. 3 million m² water swept down R. Loxley valley ➔ continued south to Sheff. city centre + Rotherham

- subsided after c. 30 mins ➔ trail of destruction > 8 miles long

- 240 reported deaths – bodies found all along flood path

- flood also destroyed mills, warehouses, shops, 100s of houses + 20 bridges

Inquiry: cause, responsibility and legal action

- within days of flood, 2 gov. inspectors sent to investigate cause of failure

- their report: dam's break-up = result of bad design + workmanship; poss. fractured outlet pipe in trenches under embank. ➔ leakage + erosion of embank.

- difficult to prove ∴ pipes buried under tons of earth

- chief engr. of Water Co., designer + consulting engr. denied allegations + claimed disaster most prob. caused by landslip

- jury accepted gov. inspectors' findings, i.e., design + work faulty

- but no prosecutions – court: nothing to gain by blaming Water Co. – aim of inquest to obtain facts + decide measures for future

- following mnths.: Sheff. Corporation + Water Co. separately brought in top engrs. to find cause

- those brought in by Sheff. Corp. agreed with 2 gov. inspectors

- those brought in by Water Co. disagreed: both design + workmanship satisfactory; + excavated, examined + tested outlet pipes = sound + watertight; also supported theory of landslip ➔ unavoidable accident

- no one sure why dam failed: over years – experts given many explanations of poss. cause of embank. collapse

- compensation for damages = one of largest insurance claims of Victorian period = > £270,000 for damage to property, injury + loss of life

Sources:

http://mick-armitage.staff.shef.ac.uk/sheffield/flood.html

http://www2.shu.ac.uk/sfca/aboutFlood.cfm

http://en.wikipedia.org/wiki/Great_Sheffield_Flood

2 Buncefield Chemical Explosion (UK, 2005)

Background

- Buncefield Oil Storage Depot = large tank farm 3 miles from Hemel Hempstead – 5th largest of > 100 oil storage depots in UK

- owned by French company, *TOTAL UK Limited* (60%) and *Texaco* 40%.

- key depot for storing + distributing fuels to London + S. E. England, incl. Heathrow Airport

- built 1968, when few bldgs. in surrounding area

- controls in tanks + pipework to prevent overfilling (e.g., alarms) – activated if fuel gets to certain level

- tanks built inside walled enclosures ('bunds') – prevent spills spreading

Incident

- 10 Dec., 7 p.m.: tank to n.west of depot being filled with unleaded petrol

- midnight: terminal closed + check made of contents of tanks → everything normal

- from c. 3 a.m., level gauge for Tank 912 showed unchanging level reading

- tank overflowed at 5.30 a.m.; c. 300 tonnes petrol spilled down side of tank onto ground

- safety systs. to shut off petrol supply to tank failed

- duty supervisor, warned by tanker driver of strong smell, shut off wrong pipeline

- c. 10% turned to vapour cloud (petrol + cold air) → flammable → flowed over bund wall + first explosion at 6 a.m.

- → large fire (23 tanks): burned for 5 days, destroyed most of depot; > 40 people injured

- heavy smoke pollution over S. Engl. + beyond; widespread damage to commercial bldgs + homes in area

- c. 2000 residents/others evacuated; parts of M1 motorway closed

- 1000 firefighters from across UK + national police forces; > 30 hrs. to put out main fire

- biggest explosion in UK since Flixborough (1974)

Cause

- investigation team from HSE + Env. Agency to identify cause of incident → no. of poss. causes (as above), but with time constraints could not test them fully

- ∴ magnitude of explosion still only partly explained

- other experts blamed "weekend effect" in industry, where w/end maintenance → unsafe conditions

Responsibility and legal action

- main trial to establish respons. for damage: High Court, Oct. 2008

- *TOTAL UK* claimed duty supervisor respons. for explosion, but company wouldn't admit liability, i.e., could not have foreseen extent of destruction

- March 2009: High Court found *TOTAL UK* liable (negligence) – that *TOTAL* in charge of tank filling ops.

- + that *TOTAL's* h. office contributed to explosion – did not establish proper syst. for preventing overfilling of tanks – no written procedures in control rm. after near-accident, 2003

Sources:

http://www.buncefieldinvestigation.gov.uk/index.htm

http://en.wikipedia.org/wiki/2005_Hertfordshire_Oil_Storage_Terminal_fire

3 The Windscale Fire (UK, 1957)

Background

- 1946 (after WW2 + in Cold War era), US gov. closed nucl. weapons prog. to other countries
- British gov. began urgent prog. to produce plutonium + build own atomic bomb
- built '*Windscale*' on n.w. coast of England (plant now called Sellafield)
- site chosen due to available water for cooling, existing bldgs. + remoteness in case of accidents
- 2 reactors built (Pile 1 & Pile 2) – graphite-moderated + air-cooled: air filtered to remove stray radioactive matls. + released thro. large chimneys
- reactors had horiz. channels → cans of unenriched uranium were passed to expose them to radiation → production of plutonium (produced plut. for military use from Oct. 1950)
- filters added later – in galleries at top of 400 ft chimneys – thought to be unnecess. by engrs. (waste of time & money) but prob. prevented accident being catastrophe
- Windscale unique in UK, but q. crude technology: little known about reactor design – dangerous features – key to disaster

Incident

- 10 Oct., 1957: fire broke out at Pile 1 during routine maintenance procedure (a 'Wigner release' – procedure also known as 'annealing')
- annealing started 7 Oct. → cooling device switched off to let graphite heat up in controlled situation to release Wigner energy built up when irradiated
- during annealing → control rods lowered back into core to shut down reactor → operators saw Wigner release not spreading through core, but diminishing prematurely
- withdrew control rods to apply 2nd nucl. heating + complete annealing; operators unaware some areas much hotter than others + temp. rising (temp. sensors showed falling temp.)
- graphite core caught fire → large amnts. of radioactive matl. into surrounding area
- operators unsure what to do re. fire → used sticks to push fuel cans out of reactor to help cool it; also flushed reactor with CO_2, but ineffective at high temp.
- finally, fire put out with water (successful but risky → cloud of radioactive steam drifted across Engl. + over to Europe)

Causes and Responsibility

- Board of Inquiry reported Oct., 1957, 16 days after fire: blamed accident on comb. of operator error, poor management + faulty equipt:

- that primary cause: 2nd nucl. heating, 8 Oct., applied too soon + too quickly
- steps to deal with accident: efficient + responsible
- measures to deal with consequences adequate + no immediate damage to public health or workers; unlikely any harmful effects would develop
- but recommendations re. technical + organizational failings:
  - more detailed technical assessmt. needed
  - organizational changes needed
  - clearer responsibilities for health & safety
  - better definition of radiation dose limits
- considered world's worst reactor accident until Three Mile Island (1979) and Chernobyl (1986)

Aftermath

- concern re. release of radioactive matl. into nearby area: radioactive isotope iodine-131 (can cause thyroid cancer)
- no evacuation from surrounding area, but concern re. contamination → milk from c. $500km^2$ destroyed (dumped in local rivers) for a month
- Pile 1 unsalvageable: some fuel rods removed + reactor buried in concrete. Approx. 6700 fire-damaged fuel elements + 1700 fire-damaged isotope canisters remain in pile
- Pile 2: undamaged by fire, but too unsafe for continued use – shut down shortly after
- no air-cooled reactors built since
- Pile 1 core still contains c. 15 tons of highly radioactive uranium; damaged reactor core still heated by continuing nucl. reactions
- process of decommissioning of Windscale reactors since 1980s
- 1990s: UKAEA began plans to decommission (disassemble + clean up) both piles; plans to safely remove fire-damaged core – still radioactive + could burst into flames
- 2005: UKAEA plans to accelerate decommissioning by 35 yrs. (from 2050–2015)
- Windscale site still in use; several mod. nucl. reactors built → renamed Sellafield to avoid bad associations

Sources:

http://en.wikipedia.org/wiki/Windscale_fire

http://news.bbc.co.uk/onthisday/hi/dates/stories/november/8/newsid_3181000/3181342.stm

http://www.chemistrydaily.com/chemistry/Windscale_fire

http://www.damninteresting.com/the-windscale-disaster

http://www.lakestay.co.uk/1957.htm

4 The Chernobyl Nuclear Disaster (Ukraine, 1986)

Background

- Chernobyl Plant in Ukraine (then in Soviet Union) = one of largest in USSR

- construction began 1970s; reactor No. 4 finished 1983

- each reactor = electr.-generating capacity 1,000 m/watts = c. 10% of Ukraine's electr.

- more reactors under construction at time of accident

Incident

- 26 April, 1986, 1.23 a.m. – reactor No. 4 exploded

- operating at low capacity (6/7%) during planned shutdown (test)

- after power surge ➜ 2 explosions destroyed reactor core + tore hole in roof of reactor bldg.

- resulting fire ➜ column of highly radioactive fallout into atmosphere & over wide area

- 2 died in 1st expl., but most deaths from accident from radiation

- clean-up crews – c. 2 wks. to control fires + stabilize plant

- x 400 more fallout released than by atomic bomb in Hiroshima

- fallout over large parts of west. Sov. Union, most of E. Europe + Scandinavia; light nuclear rain as far as Ireland

- large areas in Ukraine, Belarus + Russia ➜ bad contamination ➜ evacuation + resettlement of > 200,000 people

- official data: c. 60% radioactive fallout in Belarus

Causes & Responsibility

- key safety systs. off (e.g., Emerg. Core Cooling Syst.) at time of accident

- as reactor heated up ➜ reactor vessel broke up + further insertion of control rods imposs. – deformed by heat

- reactor's design = unstable at low power + operators careless re. safety during test

- reactor = no secure containment (reduce costs + due to large size) ➜ radioactive contaminants into atmosphere after expl.

- + reactor running for over a yr. + storing fission by-products ➜ pushed reactor towards disaster

- one explanation: power plant ops. violated design specs. + safety measures – lack of knowledge of reactor physics & engineering + lack of exp. & trng.

- + lack of communication betw. safety officers + ops. i/c of experiment that night

- another factor = ops not informed re. problems with reactor (designers knew reactor dangerous in some conditions)

- many or all above factors prob. contributed to disaster

- considered worst nuclear power plant disaster in history

Aftermath

- worries re. safety of Sov. nucl. industry + nucl. power in general ➜ slowed growth for no. of yrs.

- forced Sov. gov. to become less secretive

- Russia, Ukraine & Belarus: probl. with ongoing decontamination + healthcare costs of accident

- diff. to calculate no. of deaths caused by Chernobyl – over time – diff. to determine whether deaths caused by radiation

- 2005 report by Chernobyl Forum, led by Int. Atomic Energy Agency (IAEA) and World Health Org. (WHO): 56 direct deaths (47 accident wrkrs. + 9 children with cancer) + c. 4,000 extra cancer deaths among c. 600,000 highly exposed pop.

- Chernobyl Exclusion Zone + certain areas still off limits, but most of affected areas now thought safe for settlement + industry

Sources:

http://en.wikipedia.org/wiki/Chernobyl_disaster

http://www.world-nuclear.org/info/chernobyl/inf07.html

http://news.bbc.co.uk/1/shared/spl/hi/guides/456900/456957/html/nn1page1.stm

5 The St. Francis Dam Disaster (Los Angeles, California, 1928)

Background

- completed May 1926, 40 miles n.w. of L.A. to provide emergency water in case of damage to L.A. aqueduct (e.g., earthquakes/sabotage)
- concrete dam 185 ft high, built on large ancient landslide – one side anchored in unstable rock; other side in rock composed of gravel + pebbles
- inbetw. anchorage points, dam sat on dense powdered rock (semi-soluble in water)
- dam relied on pure weight to resist elements + pressure of dam water
- held c. 13 bn. galls. water – enough to supply L.A. for a yr.; also provided electr. to sev. counties
- construction supervised by William Mulholland = chief engr. + manager of L.A. Bureau of Water Works + Supply

Incident

- Mar. 12, 1928 (midnight) – dam wall collapsed → wall of water 135 ft high flooded down canyon
- dam broke into sev. large pieces carried downstream; centre section (nicknamed "The Tombstone") still standing
- thick river of mud/water/debris travelling 5 mph → destroyed everything in 50-mile path to Pacific Ocean
- > 450 people killed; > 1,000 homes + 10 bridges destroyed; power outage over wide area
- exact death toll imposs: many bodies washed out to sea + many transient farm wrkrs. + immigrants never counted in official stats.
- one of worst American civil eng. failures of 20th C & 2nd biggest loss of life in Calif. history (after 1906 San Francisco Earthquake + fire)

Lead-up to Incident

- through 1926/27, cracks seen in dam + abutments; leaked muddy water as reservoir filled
- inspected by Mulholland: thought cracks + leaks normal for size of dam + declared it safe
- Mar. 7, 1928: reservoir filled to capacity for first time
- new cracks + leaks spotted up to morning Mar. 12 → Mulholland again inspected + dismissed them as normal + safe
- < 12 hrs later, dam failed + collapsed

Inquiry

- investigation concluded: disaster caused chiefly by unsuitability of rock for supporting dam + reservoir (but not poss. for geologists of 1920s to detect)
- 2 of world's top geologists at time found no fault with rock at dam site
- → jury decided respons. lay with designer/engr. Mulholland + gov. orgs. which oversaw dam's construction
- Mulholland cleared of blame for failure: no one could have known of instability of rock formations
- but inquiry said such constructions should never be left to judgement of one man
- ruined Mulholland's reputation + career → after inquest, retired from LADWP

Sources:

http://en.wikipedia.org/wiki/St._Francis_Dam
http://www.sespe.com/damdisaster/
http://genealogytrails.com/cal/la/disasterstfrancis.html
http://www.britannica.com/EBchecked/topic/1472884/St-Francis-Dam-disaster

Activity bank

A Find 20 words from this unit in the wordsearch.

- Copy the words into your notebook.
- Check the definition of any words you can't remember.

M	I	N	I	M	A	L	P	E	S	A	S	T	D	V
S	I	G	N	I	F	I	C	A	N	T	A	A	I	E
P	O	S	C	E	R	T	R	U	S	S	I	T	A	S
E	E	N	T	S	C	H	E	M	A	T	I	C	M	T
C	L	L	L	R	A	F	E	E	D	E	C	F	E	I
I	I	E	E	T	U	M	L	N	I	O	A	T	T	F
F	N	V	I	V	L	C	E	A	S	O	I	T	E	A
I	Q	I	O	O	A	P	T	O	N	S	P	C	R	B
C	U	D	I	B	S	T	C	U	U	G	S	O	L	R
A	I	E	I	U	V	W	I	M	R	S	E	L	S	I
T	R	N	S	E	E	I	I	O	E	A	T	L	T	C
I	Y	C	E	R	L	A	O	R	N	I	L	A	R	A
O	P	E	C	R	L	P	T	U	S	S	S	P	I	T
N	N	S	N	C	N	S	A	R	S	A	I	S	V	E
A	C	C	E	I	I	F	A	I	L	U	R	E	E	S

B Think of a word or words that can go after each of the words or phrases below to make a phrase from this unit. Explain the meaning.

Example: *property = property developer, property development*

building   _____

continuous   _____

design   _____

financial   _____

hanger   _____

internal   _____

live   _____

property   _____

roof   _____

structural   _____

Introduction	Examples of ideas
introduce the topic area + define any key terms give the outline of the essay	

Body		Examples of ideas
Body	**Para 1:** situation/problems (general)	
	Para 2: problems (specific examples)	
	Para 3: solutions	
	Para 4: evaluations of solutions	
Conclusion		

Walker, A. 2007. *Project Management in Construction*. Chichester, Blackwell.

Harris, F., McCaffer, R., Edum-Fotwe, F. (2006) *Modern Construction Management*. Oxford (Blackwell).

P Hughes & E Ferret (2008) *Introduction to Health and Safety in Construction*. London: Butterworth Heinemann.

Gransberg, D. D. & Windell, E. (2008) Communicating Design Quality Requirements for Public Sector Design/Build Projects. *Journal of Management in Engineering,* Volume 24 (2), Pages 105–110.

Beavers, J. E., Moore, J. R. & Shriver, W. R. 2009 *Steel Erection Fatalities in the Construction Industry.* Journal of Construction Engineering and Management, 135(3), 227–234.

Simon Linford, (2009). Give the architects respect. *Construction News*, [online] available from: *http://www.cnplus.co.uk/give-the-architects-respect/5200721.article* [Accessed: 22nd April 2009].

Walker, A. 2007. *Project Management in Construction*. Chichester, Blackwell.

Harris, F., McCaffer, R., Edum-Fotwe, F. (2006) *Modern Construction Management*. Oxford (Blackwell).

P Hughes & E Ferret (2008) *Introduction to Health and Safety in Construction*. London: Butterworth Heinemann.

Gransberg, D. D. & Windell, E. (2008) Communicating Design Quality Requirements for Public Sector Design/Build Projects. *Journal of Management in Engineering,* Volume 24 (2), Pages 105–110.

Beavers, J. E., Moore, J. R. & Shriver, W. R. 2009 *Steel Erection Fatalities in the Construction Industry.* Journal of Construction Engineering and Management, 135(3), 227–234.

Simon Linford, (2009). Give the architects respect. *Construction News*, [online] available from: *http://www.cnplus.co.uk/give-the-architects-respect/5200721.article* [Accessed: 22nd April 2009].

Activity bank

A Solve the crossword.

Down

1 Most modern wind turbines have three … .
2 The national power supply system.
3 The … control is a motor that turns the turbine rotor into the wind.
5 Newton's second law: every action has an equal and opposite … .
6 Long-lasting.
8 Small domestic turbines are also called … wind turbines.
9 Horizontal-axis turbine as opposed to …-axis.
11 Tip speed.

Across

4 Wind turbines are governed by … .
7 Device.
10 In the past, wind turbines were known as wind … .
12 Spin.
13 The … limit is the theoretical limit for maximum energy extraction.
14 … control varies the angle of the turbine blades.
15 Cost-effective.

B Match a word in the first column with a word in the second column to make a two-word phrase. Make sure you know what they mean.

capacity	box
fixed	consumption
gear	factor
guy	opinion
household	frequency
national	output
power	speed
public	storage
pumped	wire
wind	grid

The use of wind energy to provide motive power clearly goes back to ancient times. Even the wind turbine itself is more than 120 years old, according to Dale E. Berg. The basic technology is, therefore, simple. In reality, however, it is not easy to design and build a machine that is both efficient and durable. Firstly, wind turbines are governed by aerodynamics, and the science of this area can be complicated. For example, the forces acting on a wind turbine are more difficult to understand and model than those of aeroplane wings, because the blades in the device are spinning. Another point that affects the aerodynamics is the *size* of a wind turbine. Secondly, constructing wind turbines involves some complex engineering in order to ensure safety and durability and, in addition, to provide maximum power output as the wind speed changes. Moreover, all of these control systems need to be cost-effective, which is difficult given the nature of wind energy. Thirdly, the electricity generated by the wind turbine has to be connected to the grid so the power can be used in the most efficient way. Finally, a wind turbine is a large structure. As a result of this, the design must be acceptable to the general public.

Source: Berg, D. E. (1996). *Vertical-axis wind turbines – the current status of an old technology.* Retrieved from http://www.osti.gov/bridge/servlets/purl/432928-xZkiEJ/webviewable

Role card: Council leader

- You are the leader of Moortop Council. Your name is John White.
- You are attending the meeting at the request of local residents' representatives.
- You must appear to be unbiased and listen to all points of view. However, you are in favour of the wind farm for the following reasons:
  - The construction, installation and maintenance work will bring many new jobs to a region with a high unemployment rate. In fact, your son-in-law was recently made redundant from a local construction company, and he is now looking for work.
  - Your support for 'green' energy is in line with council policy and that of your political party. You want to be seen to be supporting this policy.
  - Any other reasons?
- Your job is to try to persuade local residents that there are many advantages to the installation.
- You will 'chair' the meeting, so introduce yourself at the beginning and state what the meeting is for. Welcome the participants and ask who would like to speak first.

Your notes:

Role card: Chief engineer

- You are the chief engineer of the installation company (GreenPower Projects Ltd). Your name is Michael Towers.
- You are obviously in favour of the wind farm, but you are aware that there is a lot of opposition to the proposal.
- You are not really looking forward to the meeting, but you need to try to assure all participants that your company cares for the environment and will try to minimize any disturbance during construction work.
- You must listen to all points of view and be prepared to answer questions honestly.
- However, you are quite worried about environmental questions, so you need to try to *predict the issues that are likely to be raised and prepare your answers*. You need to persuade the meeting that renewable energies are for the benefit of all, and kinder to the environment (e.g., wind farms are supported by Greenpeace).

Your notes:

Role card: Local resident representative (1)

- You represent the village of Thornton. You are also the chairperson of the local conservation society and a member of the tourism board. Choose a name for yourself.

- You and most of the people of Thornton are against the installation for environmental reasons, such as:

  ○ danger to the high concentrations of migrant birds

  ○ destruction of conservation sites and damage to ecosystems by the building of access roads, sub-stations and support buildings, together with heavy construction traffic and consequent air pollution

  ○ any other reasons? (e.g., landscape, tourism, archaeological sites, etc.)

- Make sure that you express your concerns clearly and be prepared to ask for clarification if you are not satisfied with the answers.

- Also be prepared to respect and respond to the opinions of others, even though their opinions may annoy you.

Your notes:

Role card: Local resident representative (2)

- You are a local farmer representing the village of Greenwood, the village that will be closest to the proposed wind farm. Choose a name for yourself.

- You and most of the people of Greenwood are against the installation for a variety of reasons, including safety and disturbance, such as:

  ○ noise pollution: you've heard that the minimum distance of a wind farm from housing is one mile because of low frequency noise, yet several of the turbines will be within half a mile of the village

  ○ disturbance from heavy traffic and construction (noise, pollution, congestion, etc.)

  ○ safety factor on local roads – turbines are a distraction to drivers due to blade flickering; also the problem of ice build-up on the blades is a safety issue

  ○ any other reasons? (e.g., affect on farm animals, grazing, access to countryside)

- Make sure that you express your concerns clearly and be prepared to ask for clarification if you are not satisfied with the answers.

- Also be prepared to respect and respond to the opinions of others, even though their opinions may annoy you.

Your notes:

Role card: Local resident representative (3)

- You represent the village of Springfield, a newer 'dormitory' village, where many, like you, commute to the nearest cities for work. You own a catering business. Choose a name for yourself.

- Springfield residents tend not be as attached to the countryside as the longer-term residents in the other villages, and may not be aware of many of their concerns.

- Most Springfield residents are open-minded about the wind farm project and in favour of green energy. Some feel that the other villages are being obstructive and selfish.

- The prospect of business opportunities is also attractive – you are wondering if there will be catering opportunities for you, with the increase in workers on the site.

- However, Springfield residents do have some concerns, such as:
  - house prices: they have heard that houses close to wind farms in other parts of the country dropped in value by as much as 30%
  - road congestion, which would increase travel time to work
  - TV, radio and mobile phone interference
  - any other reasons?

- Make sure that you express your concerns clearly and be prepared to ask for clarification if you are not satisfied with the answers.

- Also be prepared to respect and respond to the opinions of others, even though their opinions may annoy you.

Your notes:

Activity bank

A Find 20 words from this unit in the wordsearch.

- Copy the words into your notebook.
- Check the definition of any words you can't remember.

E	H	T	S	Y	H	Y	D	R	A	U	L	I	C	S
X	F	R	E	S	U	L	T	S	T	O	X	I	C	I
P	T	L	Q	T	F	I	L	T	R	A	T	I	O	N
E	L	U	U	D	I	S	H	H	Z	N	N	L	E	N
R	A	P	R	C	K	J	L	L	X	O	E	A	N	A
I	M	A	X	B	T	O	W	F	I	L	G	B	Q	P
M	I	S	B	P	U	U	S	T	B	D	V	O	M	P
E	N	R	A	I	K	L	A	A	E	I	I	R	E	A
N	A	K	D	L	R	N	E	T	Z	S	S	A	M	R
T	R	W	X	U	I	M	C	N	E	I	C	T	B	A
Y	Z	Y	O	L	R	N	O	D	T	N	O	O	R	T
F	V	P	A	E	O	X	I	D	E	F	S	R	A	U
W	A	S	P	G	B	B	E	T	A	E	I	Y	N	S
V	E	B	R	I	N	E	U	J	Y	C	T	B	E	F
D	O	S	M	O	S	I	S	W	I	T	Y	H	X	K

B Do the quiz.

1 What is the word for:

   a water that is saltier than freshwater, but not as salty as seawater

   b water that is boiled, vaporized and then condensed

   c water that collects in rivers, seas, lakes, oceans and reservoirs

2 Rearrange the letters in the words below to form words associated with reverse osmosis:

   a bamrneme   **c** rebin   **e** keanilla

   b wedtreefa   **d** trifle

3 Think of a word that can go in front of each of the words below to make a phrase from the unit.

   _____ costs   _____ mechanics   _____ plant

   _____ flow   _____ consumption   _____ fuel

   _____ procedure   _____ minerals   _____ number

Clean Water: Engineering the Future by **Esrin Yilmaz.**

Published by Hadford University Press, 2010.

Clean Water is an essential text for water engineers and for those wishing to specialize in the field. The main thesis of the book, as the title suggests, is that engineers will need to play a key role in developing new solutions to the problem of global water supplies. In this respect, Yilmaz argues that the water industry must consider two factors equally. Firstly, there is the economic cost of energy consumption in the management of limited water resources. Secondly, we have the environmental costs. The scope of the book is ambitious, linking all key aspects of water-related studies, such as hydrology, hydraulics engineering, fluid mechanics, wastewater management and water supply. With regard to the latter, the author presents an excellent study of the latest developments in hydropower, irrigation and desalination technologies. I would strongly recommend it to all practitioners and graduate students interested in this branch of engineering.

In this process, cool saltwater is heated and distilled in a series of chambers.

Firstly, the cool saltwater is pumped into the system along condenser pipes that run through the top of all the chambers. The water gradually warms as it passes through these chambers. It is then heated by steam from a boiler, which turns it into hot brine. The hot brine enters the base of the first chamber where part of it vaporizes, rises, and is then condensed by pipes containing the cool saltwater continuously entering the system. The pure condensate is collected and forms part of the freshwater outflow. Meanwhile, the brine left behind in the first chamber enters the second chamber and the process is repeated again and again, depending on the number of chambers. The collected condensate leaves the system as freshwater, and the remaining brine or concentrated saltwater is discharged from the system.

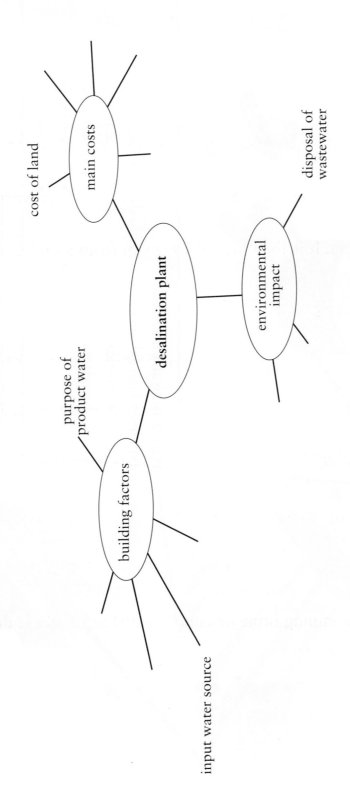

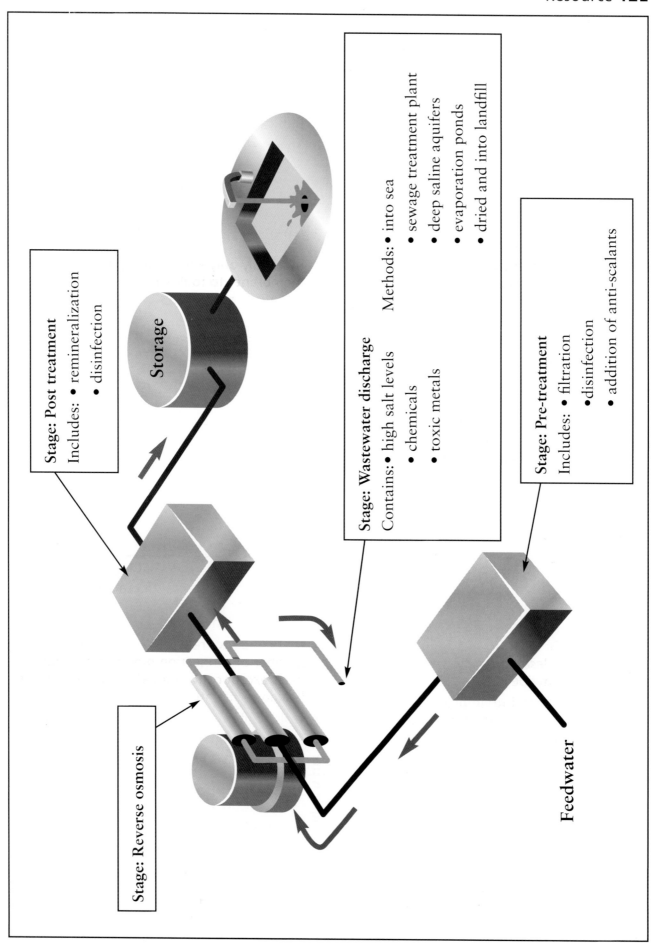

Stage: Post treatment
Includes: • remineralization
• disinfection

Storage

Stage: Wastewater discharge
Contains: • high salt levels
• chemicals
• toxic metals

Methods: • into sea
• sewage treatment plant
• deep saline aquifers
• evaporation ponds
• dried and into landfill

Stage: Pre-treatment
Includes: • filtration
• disinfection
• addition of anti-scalants

Stage: Reverse osmosis

Feedwater

Reverse osmosis	Thermal desalination
• less energy required	• needs large amts. of energy to heat water • can produce v. large amounts freshwater, but expensive • but – most desalination plants operating in, e.g., M.E. – cogeneration (produce water + energy) → reduces costs
• less initial capital expend. = c. half thermal desal. costs	• initial capital costs high = c. 2 x RO systems
• feedwater pre-treatment most imp. stage (filtration, disinfection & anti-scalant chemicals + backwashing of filters): untreated water → membrane fouling → affect performance = expensive	• feedwater pre-treatment = limited (normally only anti-scalants): no membranes to foul/damage; no backwashing of filters
• waste: liquid waste = high salt concentrations + chems. from pre-treatment & cleaning + toxic metals → discharge into sea, sewage treatment plant, saline aquifers, evap. ponds, or brine dried out → landfill (inland facilities) • + solid waste → landfill, incl. discarded pre-treatment filters + solid particles from pre-treatment • recovery rate = c. 40–60% seawater & 50–90% brackish water	• waste: limited chemicals in feedwater = reduced environ. effects of hot brine concentrate into sea • recovery rate = c. 30–50% of source water → v. large quants. brine waste
• expensive to replace RO membranes – high maintenance • but capital costs decrease due to technological developments – becoming most economical + effective method of large-scale desalting + choice for new plants worldwide • current research into improving permeability + performance of membranes = nanostructures & nanomaterials	• since 1950s: experience in technology, design, construction = operational problems, e.g., scaling, fouling, corrosion, already solved • simple, robust, reliable tech. – small number of connection pipes; no moving parts except conventional boilers → reduces leakage + maintenance • highly automated: needs limited number of staff to operate, except during inspections, maintenance, cleaning of pipes/pumps

• post-treatment: water acidic, corrosive & unpalatable → stripped of nat. minls. as well as impurities →
  • water remineralized before use
  • disinfection stage to make water potable
• RO filters c. 95–99% impurities (prod. water from 10–500 ppm/TDS)
	• post-treatment: product water for domestic use = processes similar to RO process for health standards for drinking
	• pure distilled water used mostly in industrial processes, e.g., power plant boilers
	• high-quality water with a range of 1.0–50 ppm/TDS

Laminar Flow

When a fluid flows smoothly and steadily or in regular paths, this is called laminar flow. It is sometimes known as streamline flow. The flow occurs in smooth continuous parallel layers, or streamlines, with no disruption or mixing between the layers or paths, as in the diagram. The velocity, pressure and other flow properties in the fluid remain constant.

Laminar flow generally happens with low flow rates in small pipes. If you open a water tap just a little, you will see that the flow is smooth and regular. Laminar flow is also common when the fluid is moving slowly and its viscosity is high. Examples are lubricating oils, the flow of oil through a thin pipe, and blood flow through small blood vessels. Laminar flow analysis, with regard to the theory of lubricating fluids in bearings, is a highly developed area of fluid mechanics.

Turbulent Flow

Turbulent fluid flow is unsteady and unpredictable with a great deal of disturbance, fluctuation and mixing, as shown in the diagram. In piping systems, it generally happens at high flow rates with larger pipes, and causes significant pressure loss. Turbulent flow is much more usual than its opposite, laminar flow, in both industrial contexts and in the natural world.

In turbulent flow, the velocity of the fluid continuously undergoes changes in extent and direction. Wind and rivers are generally turbulent, even when the currents are mild and even when the main part of the water is still moving in a particular direction.

Most kinds of fluid flow are turbulent, except in cases of high viscosity fluids flowing slowly through small channels. Common examples of turbulent flow are atmosphere and ocean currents, flow through pumps, turbines and many industrial machines, the flow of air around aircraft-wing tips, the effect of obstacles in water, such as the wake left by a boat as it moves and underwater bridge supports in fast-flowing rivers. Blood flow in main arteries is also classed as turbulent, unlike blood flow in smaller blood vessels.

Reynolds Number

In fluid mechanics, the Reynolds number is an important equation used to determine how fluids flow. Specifically, it is used to verify the point of transition from laminar flow (a smooth, regular flow) to turbulent flow (a rough, chaotic flow).

The Reynolds number is named after Osbourne Reynolds, who demonstrated this aspect of fluid flow in the 1880s, using an experiment that is still used in fluid mechanics today.

The Reynolds number (abbreviated to N_{Re} or Re) is a dimensionless number, which means it has no physical measurement. It is expressed in the equation below,

$$Re = \frac{\rho V D}{\mu}$$

where D = the diameter of a tube or pipe, V = velocity or the average speed of flow, ρ = the density of the fluid, all divided by μ = viscosity).

Reynolds demonstrated that the change from laminar to turbulent flow in a pipe occurs when the value of the Re number is greater than 2,100. So, in pipes, laminar flow occurs at *low* Reynolds numbers, indicated by smooth, constant fluid motion, while turbulent flow occurs at a *high* Reynolds number, shown by disturbed and erratic flow.

The water and air temperature (*measure*) to get an accurate value for viscosity.

Twenty readings (*take*) and recorded, covering the full flow rate range at equal

intervals on the log-log paper. Log-log plots (*generate*) by computer for the final

output ...

The Reynolds number and friction factor (*calculate*) for one set of results from the

middle of the range. The rest of the results (*calculate*) and (*plot*) using the

computer programme ...

Then the laminar, transitional and turbulent regions (*identify*) and the gradients

(*measure*) and (*compare*) with the computer calculations ...

Conclusions

The experiment showed good agreement to the theoretical predictions of laminar and turbulent flow. The critical Reynolds number was accurately predicted and the gradients of the different flows, laminar and turbulent, also showed good agreement to predictions. It was demonstrated that pressure drop in a straight pipe is dependent on three factors: the fluid velocity, the pipe length and diameter, and the friction factor of the pipe. The experiment also demonstrated the power of the theory, in that pipes of different fluids show the same laminar, transition and turbulent regions when they are directly compared.